"*The Scholar's Survival Manual* is packed full of useful advice that applies to every stage in the academic life cycle. From applying to graduate school and writing dissertations to seeking jobs and coming up for tenure, then mentoring others, here are the tricks of the trade. All scholars can benefit from the chapters on writing and on academic ethos. The perfect gift for those who wonder how the academy works."

ESTELLE B. FREEDMAN, STANFORD UNIVERSITY, AUTHOR OF
NO TURNING BACK and *REDEFINING RAPE*

"Based on forty years of teaching, fifteen of sitting on university tenure and promotion committees, and blogging on these issues for more than fifteen years, Krieger's insights are smart, friendly, and presented in the most disarming manner. They are for PhD students and junior faculty in all fields, from applied sciences and mathematics to the humanities."

MOSHE SLUHOVSKY, PROFESSOR OF HISTORY,
HEBREW UNIVERSITY OF JERUSALEM

"Original and insightful ... Krieger provides a very demystifying account of how the university professoriat works and practical advice on how academics can successfully navigate through their university tenure and promotion process."

JOHN GABER, UNIVERSITY OF ARKANSAS

"Martin Krieger has a reputation for straight talk, practical advice, iconoclasm, and more; every academic writer should be curious about this provocative book."

JOHN FORESTER, PROFESSOR OF CITY AND
REGIONAL PLANNING, CORNELL UNIVERSITY

The Scholar's Survival Manual

A ROAD MAP FOR STUDENTS,
FACULTY, AND ADMINISTRATORS

MARTIN H. KRIEGER

INDIANA UNIVERSITY PRESS   *Bloomington & Indianapolis*

This book is a publication of

INDIANA UNIVERSITY PRESS
Office of Scholarly Publishing
Herman B Wells Library 350
1320 East 10th Street
Bloomington, Indiana 47405 USA

iupress.indiana.edu

Telephone orders 800-842-6796
Fax orders 812-855-7931

© 2013 by Martin H. Krieger

∞ The paper used in this publication
meets the minimum requirements of
the American National Standard for
Information Sciences – Permanence of
Paper for Printed Library Materials,
ANSI Z39.48–1992.

*Manufactured in the
United States of America*

*Library of Congress
Cataloging-in-Publication Data*

Krieger, Martin H.
   The scholar's survival manual : a
road map for students, faculty, and
administrators / Martin H. Krieger.
   pages cm
   Includes index.
   ISBN 978-0-253-01055-1 (cloth :
alk. paper) – ISBN 978-0-253-01063-6
(pbk. : alk. paper) – ISBN 978-0-
253-01071-1 (electronic book) 1.
Universities and colleges – Graduate
work. 2. Graduate students. I. Title.
   LB2371.K75 2013
   378.1'55 – dc23
                              2013013811

1 2 3 4 5   18 17 16 15 14 13

For

MARTY LEVINE

Quick Guide to Contents

Arabic numerals refer to essay numbers. Roman numerals refer to pages.

Contents

3 GETTING DONE (#96–112) 85

A. FUNDAMENTALS
96 Moses and the Promised Land 97 Brilliant Ideas Are Already in What You Have Drafted 98 Working Hard 99 Catching Up and Getting Down to Writing 100 Taking Notes: Reading Is an Active Process

B. FINISHING
101 Finishing a Project 102 Getting Done 103 "My Professors Keep Asking for Revisions of My Dissertation Draft" 104 Have You Spent Too Long a Time in Graduate School? 105 It Takes Twice As Long As You Planned 106 Focusing on Getting Done 107 Do It Now: Displacement 108 Projects: Doing Better without More Work; Exemplary Faculty 109 Scut Work and Publicizing Your Research 110 Moving to Associate Professorship

C. REFERENCE LETTERS
111 Asking for Reference Letters 112 Writing Academic Reference Letters

4 GETTING THE FIRST JOB (#113–150) 104

A. FUNDAMENTALS
113 Now That You Have Your Doctorate 114 What Do I Do with My Degree? 115 Visibility in Graduate School 116 Job Talks 117 Giving a Talk at a Conference (Or a Job Talk) 118 Speaking, Moderating, Commenting 119 Job Talk Advice 120 The Content of Your Talk 121 Job Search 122 Job Hunting 123 Getting That Job Interview 124 Looking for a Job 125 The Academic Labor Market 126 Finding a Job in a Particular Locale 127 A Market? 128 Being on the Job Market 129 Being in the Job Market, Always 130 Job Search Advice 131 Seeking a Job at a Meeting 132 Application Letter for a Job

B. JOB TALKS AND SEMINAR PRESENTATIONS
133 Compelling Presentations 134 What Makes a Terrific Job Talk? 135 Giving Your Best Talks and Oral Presentations 136 Brief Presentation at a Scholarly Meeting 137 Ways of Surviving a Job Interview 138 Preparing for the Job Search 139 Job Interviews 140 Interviewing for a Job, or in Fieldwork

C. NO OFFERS?
141 You Did Not Get a Job Offer . . . 142 No Job This Year? 143 The Day Job

D. YOU HAVE AN OFFER
144 The Job Market: Counteroffers and Market Signaling 145 Bargaining for Jobs and Fellowships 146 Jobs: Negotiating for a Position

10   SCHOLARLY & ACADEMIC ETHOS (#308–391)   *310*

A. FUNDAMENTALS

B. EXCELLENCE

C. ON TIME

D. OVERLOADED?

Preface

YOU KNOW EVERYTHING IN THIS BOOK. MY JOB IS TO REMIND YOU OF what you already know, make you more likely to *do the right thing the first time.* Here is occasional advice about how to survive and thrive, to do your personal best, and to recover from mistakes – from graduate school through an academic career in the professoriate and university administration. It is also meant for department chairs, deans, tenure and promotion and appointment committees, and the provost.[1] The Scholar's Survival Manual *is meant for grazing, not reading all the way through.* The book is designed to be opened anywhere, or perhaps you will find a topic in the quick guide or the table of contents and read just that section. For *undergraduates,* whatever their future ambitions, there is much that is useful in this manual. See chapter 1, chapter 2 A–C, chapter 3, chapter 4 A and B, chapter 10 A–C, and chapter 11 C.

Do not start from the beginning! Open up the book anywhere and start reading, and then open up at another page and start reading, and continue. . . . There is a good deal of repetition in adjacent essays, so *graze and skip and move around.* That repetition provides a variety of contexts in which to provide counsel, the idea being that one context might work for you better than another.

What matters in the end is *your contribution to scholarship or the arts.* There is a temptation to count the number of articles or books, etc., now made more complicated by many multiply authored contributions. Perhaps too often, I go back and forth on how to count. I do know that collaboration and discussion often facilitate progress on a problem. But in the end, *what is your contribution?*

I should note immediately that I have not always or often enough followed my own advice, and in fact have made every error in the book, and then some.[2] I have paid, and I have recouped. Also, hindsight and advice are both cheap, and so I am not claiming to be wiser than you (you do know everything in this book!), so much as claiming to have learned some lessons from experience and observation. I don't pretend that it is easy to take advice, and perhaps you will find helpful the many self-help books you will find on the racks in your local FedEx Office. They have not worked for me. In any case, *I have pushed for your strongest performance. I sometimes sound harsh and I am hectoring – and that is off-putting. Please think of me as your tough but supportive coach.* I am in effect a Dutch uncle (which, by the way, rhymes with carbuncle), rarely avuncular. We are in a competitive enterprise, and we'll be asked again and again, why not do better? Why not the best?

I do not mean to bully or hound the reader. I do tend to be quite assertive about the Rules of the Academic Game. My view is that *the world is quite unforgiving,* and if you walk in front of an oncoming truck you are likely to be crushed. I am not an advocate of those Rules so much as aware of their consequences. There is much to be said for being less direct and less critical, and for avoiding argument, and being more sympathetic and understanding, more forgiving of human foibles. My sense of urgency, and my feeling that you will get a lot out of following the counsel presented here lead to the book's poignant tone.

These essays are not *romans à clef,* lightly disguised stories about you or someone you know. They are about many of us. These stories are *prêt à porter,* ready to wear, if they fit you – and they fit lots of people.

THE TAKEAWAY

For academic scholars, the takeaway is straightforward: *Do what you are supposed to do:* publish appropriately and make sure you and your work are visible, procure grants as needed, teach decently. The best predictor of your future performance is your performance in the previous five or six years (for assistant professors, their probationary period). If you want to deviate from the conventional path, you will need others to back you up, although that will not make the deviation much less risky. Also, we need to figure out how you are to find out what you are supposed to do! If all else fails and you must leave your university, living well is the best revenge. Maybe you become a screenwriter; maybe you thrive in a very different institution.

For administrators, assume that promotion dossiers will be examined closely by a committee, so appoint your own devil's advocate to find problems in dossiers and then deal with those problems directly. The dossier should not be a whitewash, and it is crucial that it be balanced and informative about weaknesses as well as strengths. *Transparent.* For university tenure committees, an honest assessment of the dossier will serve your provost and university; think in terms of the longer-term future of the candidate and the department. For provosts, your major asset is your currently tenured faculty, and so you must proactively mentor them and raise their own expectations for themselves.

I do not believe such advice is nicely reduced to a list, largely because context matters enormously, and because advice is notoriously hard to take (*resistance* is the psychoanalytic term) – even if you know what to do and are advising yourself. Too many students and professors walk in front of oncoming trucks, ignoring their own knowledge even when it would prevent their becoming roadkill. On the other hand, there is little reason for fatalism, figuring that whatever you do, you will not get tenure or be successful. And surely in this academic bureaucracy there is politics, and the merit system is flawed.

As with many of life's achievements, there seems to be no set of explicit criteria that, were you to fulfill them, would allow you to earn your reward. But you can do your best, avoid gross pathology, and then discover the opportunities the world presents to you.

Ideally, perhaps, I would be talking to you, modifying my tone and advice to suit the moment. And I might follow the more traditional methods suggested by these two stories offered to me by an early reader of the manuscript (Eric Clay).

One would be a tale about a rabbi who is asked by a family to help tame their unruly and perhaps emotionally disturbed son. The son has taken to stripping naked and hiding under the dining room table. The family is unable to dislodge or clothe him. After many unsuccessful attempts, the rabbi takes his clothes off and sits under the table with the boy. After doing this enough that the boy trusts the rabbi, the rabbi suggests that they might be able to sit together with their underwear on. Over time, pieces of clothing are added, and the boy and rabbi move out from under the table.

The other story is from Islam, and it instructs people regarding how to deal with potentially explosive conflicts. The Prophet taught that if two people were discussing a matter and they became agitated to the point of losing their tempers, they should find a less hostile posture from which to communicate. If they were standing, they should turn away from each other or sit down. If sitting down did not work, either facing or not facing each other, they should then sit on the bare floor. If sitting on the bare floor, either facing or not facing each other, did not work, they should lie down on the floor. If they could not effectively communicate at that point, they should agree to put the matter off to another time.

But I am not in the room with you. On the one hand, you have this book, and its text and tone are fixed. On the other hand, you can stop reading and dig in someplace else, and see if what you read there is more comfortable as it pushes you in directions you are anxious about but need to travel. What we learn from Augustine's *Confessions* is that advice needs to come at the right time with the right flavor to penetrate a bubble of excuses and justifications, if we are to hear it. Nothing prepared me for the facts of academic life, even when I received good advice. I do not want others to go through what I went through, even though I could never have done the work I do without that history of mistakes.

Here is Steve Jobs of Apple, toward the end of his life, talking about an *au revoir* conversation with Larry Page of Google:

> We talked a lot about focus. And choosing people. How to know who to trust, and how to build a team of lieutenants he can count on. I described the blocking and tackling he would have to do to keep the company from getting flabby or being larded with B players. The main thing I stressed was focus. Figure out what Google wants to be when it grows up. It's now all over the map. What are the five products you want to focus on? Get rid of the rest, because they're dragging you down. They're turning you into Microsoft. They're causing you to turn out products that are adequate but not great. (W. Isaacson, *Steve Jobs*, 2011, p. 552)

Whatever you may think of Jobs or Page or Gates, there is good advice here.

SOME ADDITIONAL POINTS

1. I have not told you how to focus, just how to do better. I do not know, except that one has to shed distracting tasks and projects.

2. I have not dealt directly with psychological issues. Nor sociological issues about the organization of higher education and the work of professors, central to the research literature. Nor corruption or unfairness. I do not believe it is helpful for a faculty member coming up for promotion and tenure to think of tenure as a right or as something that is earned. I leave these larger issues to lawyers and theorists.

There are many fields in which eminence in performance or writing, or in making works of fine art or music, or in doing clinical work (as in medicine) rather than publication are signs of productivity, and critical reviews play a large role. I realize that I have not said much about these fields, but I think my guidance applies to them nonetheless. Mathematics, theoretical science, and computer science are in many ways performing arts, albeit publication is almost always the mode of dissemination.

Different fields and disciplines have different demands. I have tried to take these into account, especially the differences between book and article fields (although that distinction is surely changing), and between performance and writing and art and the more conventional scholarly fields.

3. I have tried hard to make it possible for you to hear the advice I am providing. Surely, the book is monitory and often sharp or harsh or scary, for I want to help you avoid being hit by a truck. It's not about guilt, but about those oncoming trucks.

4. I work in a large research university, with a large faculty, but many readers will teach at comprehensive universities and at colleges, where the demands for research production are tempered. If the faculty is much smaller, there is room for even more careful consideration. Moreover, many colleges and universities are primarily teaching institutions, with heavy faculty course loads and perhaps close attention to students (al-

though that commitment may also be found in research universities). Much of what I say here may not be applicable. Also, there has developed a large literature on "the scholarship of teaching" or "the scholarship of community engagement," but here I assume that research is the major contribution expected of most faculty.

And despite the wishes of provosts, very few institutions can have one of the top five or top ten scholars in each field, and very few faculty can consistently publish in the strongest journals or with the strongest presses, or receive large NIH or NSF grants: there's not enough room or money at the top. *So when I speak of strong or strongest work, please keep in mind the standards of your particular institution.*

5. Since about 1997 I have put out a blog, *This Week's Finds in Planning* (http://blogs.usc.edu/sppd/krieger), the source for this book. Some of the advice is instrumental and about matters of expediency; some demands our highest aspirations. This is not a conflict, since when one is stuck, expedience is the order of the day, while when one is actually working one might aim for one's personal best.

6. People who have read drafts of this book have mentioned more than once that I have not addressed academic pathologies, especially arbitrary decisions or ones informed by avarice or meanness, or gender and race discrimination and preferences. There is surely room for an academic pathology book. Here, however, my purpose is to help people push their way forward. It should also be clear that my advice has those pathologies in mind.

7. At least for me, teaching and research contribute to each other. I am driven more by norms I have internalized from my teachers than by occasional incentives. I have discovered that whining and complaining and worrying are too costly, and taking charge of your problems is what you must do. And from my teachers, I have come to prefer what some call "Chicago style" seminars, where the speaker is subject to vigorous questioning all the time. I gather this style characterizes Russian mathematics and physics seminars, too. A seminar comment might begin with "That's all wrong . . . ," and the tone might be assertive, conceited, and rude, even if no animus is intended. I suspect that the motivation is a combination of deep curiosity and the fact that the consumers of our research are our competitors as well.

YOUR AUTHOR

It may be useful to say a bit about my own career and background. I have been a university teacher for more than 40 years, working at five universities, with several year-long fellowships, two at residential research centers. This is my ninth book. Though I was trained as a natural scientist, almost all of my teaching has been in city planning and public policy, with shorter periods in science, technology, and society and in business administration. I have been on many sides of the disciplinary street. As for my work over the years:

1. I try lots of topics, and only some prove fruitful for me. Hence, the topics that characterize my work may be diverse, but, as in species evolution, there is continuity with the past even though much of the intermediate material is no longer much available. What is apparently incommensurable and diverse and discrete is actually historically linked. Topics may come up by chance, but they are not likely to be pursued unless they fit into a larger agenda.

2. Whatever the topic, I explore the research literature, finding the authoritative works, often going backward in time, and ground myself in what is known or understood. I rarely if ever master the subtleties of many of the subfields and subjects. I do want to avoid making egregious mistakes, and to be sure that I am decently grounded in scholarship. Has this topic been so well explored that there is little I can contribute?

3. I was trained in physics, but also had an undergraduate education that emphasized the Great Books, and thinkers about politics and society. It took me many years of subsequent reading and thinking to have any decent critical sense of the Great Books and thinkers, but the origin is in my first two years of college as well as in high school.

4. Over the now many years, I have developed an informed sensibility, reading bits and pieces of scholarship. More to the point, there is lots I have no real feeling for, but others ignore those blind spots because they see only what I do know. In any case, I seem to have no reluctance to try to figure out foreign material. I assume all is understandable: there is a story here; it's like something else I do know. And if I really do not know anything, or have no feeling for the problem, I find people (or sources, maybe even *Wikipedia*) who can help me. Or I make an informed guess,

and have others correct me, or I read further and get corrected by what
I read.

5. In any case, the topics that capture my attention for more than
an instant are almost always informed by past experience and scholarly
knowledge. When I was starting out, I surely went down less fruitful
paths. But, in the end, even the diversions prove useful, often years later.
(I *make* them useful.) What I recall is that by the time of college I had
some sort of taste that was reliable enough for me. I was an outsider, my
nose pressed against the glass, and I wanted in.

6. More generally, I find topics because my eyes and ears and mind
are open enough. Things come along, and as mentioned earlier many
topics do not pan out. I am always in business.

I was born at the Israel-Zion hospital in Brooklyn toward the end of
World War II. We lived in Bensonhurst and later in East New York, at
the ends of the Sea Beach and New Lots lines, respectively. I come from
a working-class Orthodox Jewish family. I went to New York City public
schools, and was an undergraduate and graduate student at Columbia
University, majoring in physics and doing a dissertation in experimental
elementary particle physics (1969). I am a late bloomer, my early flow-
ering almost frozen on the vine despite having published a home run
article when I was 29. I received tenure when I was about 45, and all but
one of my books have appeared since then.

For much of my time at my current institution, I have served on its
promotion and tenure committee and have read perhaps 750+ dossiers.
What I write here is drawn from that experience, the scholarly literature,
and anecdotal evidence from other institutions. In effect I am an amateur
ethnographer. In reading a dossier I try to figure out what is really going
on: I assume that I can understand anything, at some limited level to be
sure. Namely, it must be *like* something I know already.

1. *There must be a story here. What are you up to?* What is the punch
line? What is the claim?

    a. How does X work, where X is an argument
      or an object or a process?

    b. What is the method of inquiry? How do
      you go from the materials you work with
      (and what are they?) to your claims?

2. Are the evidence and theory potentially adequate to the claim?

3. Is the argument I am reading or hearing experiential? That is, the punch line is less important than following the argument through. This is true of a mathematical proof, poetry, or a novel.

4. What is at stake here? Identify the field of argument in this discipline or arena.

5. Nothing is new; all is a repetition and variation. Analogy is destiny.

6. Am I being snookered? What is hidden, left out, inconsistent? Does it make sense as a whole? Are the special arguments really special? Are the outliers ignorable; should they be trimmed off; are they part of the story?

7. How does the work deal with arguments within the field, and with matters of truth or reliability or credibility? I do not concern myself much with whether the claim is empirically true or supported by the evidence or whether the argument has flaws. (I assume that I can be effectively deceived on matters at this level of detail. Stuff is outside my ken. Arguments must have apparently fatal flaws.) I leave this to the experts on the archives, the statistics, or the internal issues within the field.

8. Would you buy a used car from this scholar or dean? In the end, are you being given a fair representation of the facts and judgments and arguments so that you could make your own decision? Can I supply (perhaps from other sources) what is missing, and so make a judgment?

9. When I ask a question, I am trying to find out what is really going on. Am I on track?

I always say we are paid to teach, to go to meetings, and to attend ceremonies. Fischer Black, a distinguished economist, believed that professors "should be paid for their teaching only, since the ones who are not interested in research will stop producing it, and the ones who are interested in research will do it anyway" (P. Mehrling, from P. Mehrling, Fischer Black and the Revolutionary Idea of Finance (2005), pp. 300–301).

---

1. Departments are headed by chairs; departments are grouped into colleges or schools, each headed by a dean; deans report to the chief academic officer, often called the provost, usually second in command to the head of the institution, the president.

2. So, if you find errors or advice that you disagree with or which could be better stated, please write me at *krieger@usc.edu*. See *http://scholarssurvival.blogspot.com* for a continuation of my blog.

Acknowledgments

SINCE I WAS WRITING A BLOG, I WAS LESS CAREFUL THAN I
might have been about exact sources. And the sources of some colleagues' contributions have been lost. If you have any corrections or
emendations, I would be grateful for them.

Susan Krieger taught me how to write. More than 30 years ago, Larry
Susskind at MIT asked me to coach students on how to structure their
work and how to get done. Professor Marty Levine at the University of
Southern California has encouraged me to make my blog into a book. I
am grateful to Marty and to my provosts Lloyd Armstrong, Max Nikias,
and Beth Garrett for the chance to serve my university. I have included
comments I have received from students and colleagues, and their criticism along the way made me a better blogger. The Press's reader, John
Gaber, provided detailed advice that made this a much better book.
Other readers of the draft included Gerald Caiden, Eric Clay, Robert
Florkowski, Sandi Rosenbloom, Simone Schenkel, and David Sloane. I
am grateful for their suggestions, whether or not I took them in just the
way they wished. My students' and colleagues' problems and questions
led me to write it all down. Professor Gian-Carlo Rota was a wonderful
friend and monitor. Soon after my PhD, Professor Melvin Webber took a
bet on me, and for that I remain grateful, and later in my career Professor
Alan Kreditor continued the bet.

My son, David, watched me get my second or third education, and
was kind enough to just go along for the ride.

A Way into This Guide

THE ADVICE AND COUNSEL I OFFER IS CONTEXTUAL, ARISING in particular situations, with some sensitivity to your nature (although that is quite difficult to achieve for an unknown reader, and that advice is not too forgiving). In the academic life, there are a small number of questions that recur again and again, and so there are parts of the book that are most relevant – yet the main notions are present in every part.

How do I get into the business? It may be a matter of attending graduate school, choosing your research project and doing it well, showing off your work to others, making sure you get done by actually writing it all up, and eventually obtaining your first job. Chapter 1.

How do I manage traps and temptations? Some of these are matters of bureaucratic or departmental politics; some are just ways of losing your way and *not* Getting Done. You want to get done so that you can actually do more work, and also let go of a line of work that no longer provides you with real challenges. How do you get back to work after you are stuck? How do you start on a project, or at least get into it so that eventually you realize you have started and made some improvements? Chapters 1, 10.

How do I write and publish for a scholarly audience? Your readers are sophisticated, and they need to know the nature of your contribution and that you are authoritative. You publish so that your work is seen more widely by authoritative others whom you may not know, including future scholars. Chapters 2, 6.

How do I do my best work without being paralyzed by perfectionism? The notion of "good enough," as used by D. W. Winnicott in his description of the "good enough mother," is a counsel to be responsive to the current situation. The notion of "personal best" forces us to push ourselves without killing ourselves. Chapter 3.

How do I get a job, and how do I get tenure? From your CV to your job talk to your meeting potential future colleagues, be a focused contributor to the academic and research enterprise. Learn how to say *no*, so that you do what you have to do. Never delude yourself about what you have done or what is required; your colleagues and deans usually mean what they say despite occasional exceptions. Chapters 4, 5, 7, 8.

How do I make an enduring contribution to the research enterprise? How do you have impact rather than being lost in the noise? Get the support you need to do your projects. Be smart about publication venues, making sure people know of your work, and making sure they can see your work as a whole. Chapters 2, 9, 10.

How do I make for a stronger university? Mentoring, dementoring, and tormentoring. Select your colleagues, achieve tenure, earn awards, and encourage the next generation. Chapters 8, 11.

Glossary

Assistant professor: The sequence is assistant, associate, and (full) professor. Tenure is often granted with promotion to associate professor, after a probationary period of about 5–6 years. In some universities and schools the period may be 7–9 years, or tenure may be granted only with promotion to full professor. In other universities, there are steps within each rank, including super-steps for professors of the greatest distinction. Ideally, one is an associate professor for about 6 years before promotion to full.

cv, Résumé: A Curriculum Vitae (cv) typically includes name, address, contact information, education and degrees, awards and honorifics and presidencies of scholarly organizations, previous positions, books, articles (probably in reverse chronological order), memberships, presentations at meetings and universities, and grants and contracts. It may also list doctoral dissertations supervised. A cv might well be 10–50 pages long. A résumé is usually a one-page summary, for positions that are not scholarly, but for some systems it can be much longer. In any case, it lists your positions and your responsibilities, usually in reverse chronological order.

College or *School:* A college or a school consists of departments, each headed by a chair, the college or school being headed by a dean or president.

Dossier: The collection of documents justifying a promotion and tenure decision: a letter from the dean, a memo or letter from the school's promotion and tenure committee, a letter from the department chair, plus other committee reports; a cv, a personal statement describing research contributions and future trajectory (a prospective chair of a department might discuss their plans) and the candidate's philosophy of teaching, information about teaching performance, quantitative comparisons with other scholars (citations, publications, venues), a list of letter-writers, the reference letters, and some sample publications.

Fellowship, Grant, Contract: A fellowship pays some fraction of the salary, allowing a scholar to pursue a project. Grants may well pay for part of salary, for research students, for equipment, or for laboratory or research personnel. Contracts are much like grants, but often the deliverables are specified in advance.

NSF, NIH, NEH, NEA: National Science Foundation, National Institutes of Health, National Endowment for the Humanities, National Endowment for the Arts.

Overhead: In a grant, above and beyond direct expenses, overhead pays for administration and plant provided by the recipient organization. It is typically a percentage of the itemized costs of the grant.

PI: Principal Investigator, the main person on a large grant, with whom the granting agency corresponds. There may be a co-PI. PIs take credit for the amount of money they raise.

Postdoc: A postdoctoral position, usually lasting from one to four years, allows a scientist time to develop their skills under the supervision of a professor at an institution different from where they received their PhD. They might teach a course or two, giving them valuable teaching experience. It is preliminary to an assistant professorship or a career outside the university. Similar positions have developed in the humanities and other fields.

Provost: Chief academic officer of a university. The provost reports to the president, and the deans report to the provost.

Research university: Most institutions of higher education are focused on teaching and service. A fraction have a research mission, usually supported by contracts and grants and fellowships, federal and state allocations, and indirectly by grants and loans to students, as well as by research funds provided in the university endowment. Professors in research universities are expected to do publishable research or other demonstrations of their scholarly and professional commitments (performances in the arts, clinical investigations in medicine). Professors in teaching-oriented colleges and universities may well do fine research as well.

Scholar: I will use "scholar" to refer to conventional scholars, scientists, engineers, physicians, researchers, and practitioners in the professional schools, as well as those whose focus is the performing arts, visual arts, etc., insofar as they are professors in the university. Often their production is not conventional articles or books, but works of art, or service in government, or patients' well-being.

Story: I have used the term in two incompatible ways. I sometimes refer to a story you tell yourself that justifies or excuses your actions. I also speak of telling a story when I am referring to an attempt to give a coherent account of your work as a whole.

Strong: My term to designate institutions, work, and people that are excellent performers and that tend to dominate most of their competition.

The Scholar's Survival Manual

Do Not Start from the Beginning!

Graze. Skip. And Sample.

If It Feels Repetitious, Move On.

ONE

Graduate School (#1–54)

A. FUNDAMENTALS

1 *"I Can Do That!"*

Hans Bethe (1906–2005) was a Nobel Prize–winning physicist known for his capacity to solve problems, moving through them much as would an armored tank. He was conservative and cautious in choosing problems and areas in which to work. He recognized his strengths and his limitations. And he believed that the empirical data and the theory must be ready, so that he might be able to make a contribution. And then he would say to himself, "I can do that!" and go about doing his work. (S. S. Schweber, *Nuclear Forces: The Making of the Physicist Hans Bethe*, 2012)

Few of us have talents in our fields comparable to Bethe's (as did few physicists). But his philosophy might well apply to many of us as we choose areas to work within. There are other models of productive scholars, and our task is to find one that works for us.

2 *What Is Graduate Education for?*

Graduate education at a university is only partly about taking courses, mastering their contents, and doing projects and passing exams. What's important, what is unique and distinctive, *what you are paying for in the end, is the fact that the university is now based on research, done by its faculty or by scholars and scientists elsewhere. This means that your teachers are at the forefront of investigations of how the world works, of ideas about litera-*

ture, art, and society, and of the practice of the professions. Watching your professors in action, interacting with them, asking them your particular questions, working with them on their projects, having them supervise your research and mentor you – this is what makes the real difference. Moreover, the university offers a very wide range of seminars and lectures concerned with your fields of interest. Depending on the stage of your career and whether you are doing a professional masters or a doctoral degree, you might expect yourself to attend anywhere from one to three seminars each week. The questions from the audience are crucial, and you will be able to ask questions if you listen and prepare.

Moreover, there are journals to read, books you want to look at, other courses you might sit in on. Graduate education is a full-time activity, if you want to benefit from it in the deepest sense. Many students have other obligations: full- and part-time jobs, bringing up a family. Still, pack it in, and build up your intellectual assets so they serve you for the rest of your career.

3   Getting into Graduate School

Of course, it is vital that you have good grades if you want to go on to graduate school or to get certain sorts of jobs. (Other jobs may depend on qualities that are poorly measured by grades.) But I suspect that the tiebreakers are not small GPA differences but other assessments:

1. The letters written about you by your teachers or bosses can make all the difference. How do they see you working? What kinds of promise do they discern in you? Do you evidence integrity, reliability, and self-discipline? Do some of them know you and your work?

2. Can you give evidence of quality work in a portfolio or a website? Do you have a spectacular piece of work that you might excerpt, for those places that do not want to see a portfolio? (If you go for an interview, bring along the portfolio. They cannot resist giving it a look.)

When you write your personal essay, do you sound like you know what you are doing? Is it well enough written that people do not have to worry about grammar, diction, or meaning?

Have you experience that transcends your grades or your school performance? You may have been an indifferent student, but then developed a strong record in your first jobs. You may show leadership or discipline in athletics. People do notice.

3. The United States is a particularly diverse place. YES, it is nicest to attend an elite institution, get the best grades, get hired by the most prominent firm, and move up the ladder – all the evidence suggests it helps. But it would seem that that rarely describes what happens. Rather, there are many starting places; there are many opportunities to evidence strength in your work and many paths along the way, surprising paths with interesting outcomes. Matching your strengths and the path you choose is what is crucial.

There's evidence that those who have lots get even more. But especially for graduate school, the spectrum of quality is too broad for there to be a simple peak pointing to a small number of institutions or departments, unless you have very narrow interests. What matters in the end is what you do with your capabilities and talents and energies. Match your interests and style and ambitions with an institution where you might excel and where you might have colleagues whom you can learn from.

People show strength, commitment, and focus in some areas. And that focused energy is what serves them in the longer run.

4 *Matching and Searching*

There are two problems for prospective students: finding a program that fits them (their needs, their location, their interests), what I shall call matching; and finding the best program with or without matching considerations, what I shall call ranking. The matching/ranking issue is resolved for thousands of medical students each year by a computer algorithm that can be shown to be optimal under reasonable but not totally realistic conditions (A. Roth and M. Sotomayor, *Two-Sided Matching*, 1992). For most students, matching should dominate ranking considerations.

5 *Taking Advice*

Here is Peter Debye, professor of physics at the ETH in Zurich, giving advice to Erwin Schroedinger, professor of theoretical physics at the University of Zurich, fall 1925:

> Schroedinger, you are not working now on very important problems anyway. Why don't you tell us sometime [in our joint seminar] about that thesis of de Broglie [associating a wave with the electron orbiting a nucleus], which seems to have attracted some attention. (Schweber, *Nuclear Forces*, pp. 411–412, quoting from F. Bloch, *Physics Today*, 1976)

After Schroedinger gave the seminar, Debye told him that "this way of thinking was rather childish." As a student of Sommerfeld, Debye believed that you needed a wave equation to deal with waves, not just pictures à la de Broglie.

At a subsequent seminar, Schroedinger said, "My colleague Debye suggested that one should have a wave equation: well, I have found one."

Could your advisor say to you, "you are not working now on very important problems anyway"? Of course, Schroedinger was no longer a student, but still . . .

One recurrent theme in my conversations with colleagues is that students resist taking our advice. We tell them to do X by a certain date, and they believe such is optional.

The major cost of resistance is that your advisor gives up on you. As you can imagine, this is not a good thing (in general). We want you to be very successful, and if your own path turns out to be right, and our advice is wrong, many of us are generous enough to delight in your success and our humiliation. However, this scenario is rarer than comedies allow you to believe.

If you decide not to follow your advisor's counsel, and you are explicit to your advisor about why, you may convince your advisor that you are right, or that at least you know that you are not taking the advice. But "resistance" describes ways that we do not consciously face what we are doing.

I have a catalog of good advice I have not taken – for which I have paid substantially. I consider myself a fluke, a survivor, someone who has paid handsomely for going my own way. I was under no heroic/comedic illusion. I always thought I had a very good sense about what I was doing. I did. But the advice was mostly about how not to fall into crevasses – and I have fallen.

6   Students

There have always been grinds and nerds and intellectuals and artists, but much of the university student body lives not through the classroom and library and laboratory, but through undergraduate life, now enhanced by fitness centers and therapy. And graduate students in the professional schools are often not so different from the undergraduates, albeit they ought to be more focused on their schoolwork and often are. Whatever aura professors used to have has somewhat diminished.

In the end, discipline and character are what count, although there's no substitute for brains.

7   Advice to New Doctoral Students

1. You are being trained to do research and participate in a community of scholars. Find a faculty member with whom you can work, at first on their ongoing projects, and link up early. You want someone who "owns" you, who feels responsible for you.

2. Attend public lectures and research seminars, often. People will notice that you are there. When you have questions, ask them.

3. Start looking at the top five journals in your area of concern or your field. If you have time, look at the last five years of issues.

4. Find peers, in your own department or in allied departments.

5. Start thinking about your future career. Go to meetings in your field, and eventually present at those meetings. It's fine to talk to anyone whose work interests you. Even the most prominent people rarely feel they are being attended to enough – they hunger for attention.

6. Start reading in your field, above and beyond your courses.

7. Look respectable. No flip-flops, no too-casual clothes. You really do not want to look like an undergraduate.

8. Prepare for your classes, so that you are able to contribute, to ask questions. If you are shy, you will have to learn to speak up.

9. If you have made a mistake in coming to this university, speak to your advisor early on, and see if something can be done. If nothing can be done, go to another university.

10. Intellectual and cultural life at a research university is usually rich, and you might as well enjoy it – seminars in other departments, visiting big shots.

8   Why Get a PhD? Why Be a Professor? And Where?

1. The only good reason to get a PhD is that you want to pursue a research and teaching career. Almost surely in academia, sometimes in an appropriate consulting/research institution, or in industry or government.

2. There are two good reasons to become a professor: you want to do research; you want to teach. If you want to teach, mainly, be sure to find a position at an institution where teaching is a primary value – an undergraduate college or a comprehensive university that is not trying too hard to become a research university. If you do not want to teach, do not go to a university or a college – consulting/research will work better for you.

3. If you do not want to teach, and do not want to do research, why are you doing a PhD? If it is to challenge yourself intellectually, that is fine. If you want to write books, and have a good day job, that is fine, too. Otherwise, perhaps you ought to go to medical school or law school?

9   For New Graduate Students

1. You can get a terrific education at the university. You need to do some course planning, sketching out what you might take each semester while you are here. You'll surely revise your plan, but at least you will be able to make sure you get the depth and focus you want, in the areas you want (rather than taking courses because they are offered conveniently and are still open).

Look beyond your degree faculty. The divisions we make by field among the faculty are to some extent arbitrary. There may be courses elsewhere that do just what you want – even if they are not "in" your degree program.

You may want to get involved with research projects of the faculty, even if they are not advertising for paid assistants. As a faculty, we have a deep research portfolio, with lots of external grants, and your interests and ours are likely to overlap.

2. Your main task is to learn to "think like a professional" in your field. It also means that you want to learn to write professionally, and in many fields to use the richer data sets we now have available, to be able to give oral presentations of your work, and to work in teams. You want to be able to serve your audience by writing an executive summary or introductory paragraph that gives away the whole story, and organizing the material in well-defined sections (each of which begins with a good one-paragraph summary and has a transparent heading). Simple and straightforward, clear and pointed, carefully argued but not obscure – these all matter.

3. One of my colleagues points out that you are a professional *now*. Act like one. Deliver on time. Do a more than good enough job. Act graciously in class and in public settings. The habits that might have worked for you as an undergraduate may not work at all in professional settings, and now is the time to become the person you want to be.

10   *Excellent Work*

You go to the heart surgeon, and you hope that she has been well trained so that when you put your heart in her hands she will not mess up. You hope her reputation has been honestly earned.

There is surely a role for mercy and understanding in a university. But grades indicate quality of work, and that work should be commensurate with the grade. I might write a supportive letter for someone who has received a C in my class, for there are many reasons for someone to be commended besides their grade. For your grade, what matters is consistent work, doing the homework, multiple drafts or revisions, and professionalism.

In any particular area, some people are more talented than most others. They not only do well with less effort, but they may well do better than those who exert a great deal of effort. Hence, when I am asked what makes a paper excellent, I may well be thinking how much better the paper was in its final version than when it was first drafted (it went from C– to B+, say). Excellent work stands out; you want to show it to colleagues. And some project topics do not allow you to excel.

11 *Thinking Analytically while Reading a Paper or Listening to a Talk*

Say that the first page or the first five minutes fail to clue you in to what is going on, what will be the results, and why they are interesting. Ask yourself the following questions:

- What is going on here? What is the story?
- What is strong about this work?
- Does it make sense? Is it surprising? Is it interesting?
- What did they do to find out?
- Would you buy a used car from this person?
- Would you buy this used car?
- Are they using models that have systematic lacunae or errors? Does that matter here?
- Are the fixed boundaries of the discipline blinding them to interesting analogies from other fields?
- What's at stake here? What would happen if the work were good and valid?
- Is the work credible on its face?
- In quantitative work do they give error bars that are reasonable? Did they include systematic errors?
- Are there alternative explanations that would seem to be easier to countenance, or are there manifest counterexamples – and have they presented them and argued them away reasonably?
- Are the arguments robust, or will they fall apart readily?
- Can you extend the proposed explanation or mechanism to other cases you know well?

· Analogy is a powerful tool for understanding. Is the
  story analogous to one you know already?
· Is the claim here distinctive, or has it been studied before?
· Are any of the above questions and problems indicative of a
  flaw or are they indicative of systematic misrepresentation?
More generally:
· Are the abstract, conclusion, or introduction
  informative? Was there a good preview?
· Did they hold back the main point until three-
  quarters of the way through the presentation?
· Is the presentation nicely divided into sections,
  deliberately labeled by subheads?

My experience is that error bars are often missing, stories are absent, numbers are hyperbolically exaggerated, and effects are claimed at incredible levels of accuracy.

12   Excuses

I wrote to one student: You are very good at saying to me that you get my point, and then delivering something that is just barely good enough. Sort of how to cool out the professor. This may work in your professional environment, but it does not work well for me. I understand how you have to balance a variety of demands. Just so you know that your charm and intelligence and experience only go so far. Delivering well-thought-out work, on time, in depth, is what you want to aim for. I appreciate your having personal demands put on you, and perhaps this is your year from hell.

You see, the problem is that some students actually do deliver, on time, with good work. Perhaps it is one student in a class of thirty, maybe two in a class of eight. You actually do live in a competitive environment with some quite ambitious, very practical people. Again, I understand there are real reasons why one cannot deliver. But do not delude yourself – in the end you pay.

13 *Getting Your Doctoral Degree in the Fabled Four Years*

Proviso – if you are starting in a new field of study, or if the doctoral research period may involve lab or fieldwork of two or three years, the following does not quite apply.

1. In your first two years you should take all your coursework and at the end take your qualifying exams. No later than the beginning of your second year, get linked up with a faculty advisor and start thinking about your research.

2. In year three do the fieldwork, data gathering, learning the advanced theory, archival work, experimental laboratory work (this may well require several years, so four years is unrealistic), proving.

3. In year four you write and look for a job. (The latter may fall in year five, since if you are looking for a job, you usually have to have something of your dissertation to show by the fall, and that is hard to do for fall of year four.)

What slows things down:

4. Not finishing your courses in two years. If you need to borrow money to pay for course units, that makes sense if you can get a job a year earlier.

5. Delaying qualifying exams and thesis proposal into third year. You should be thinking in terms of a thesis project as soon as you start working with your advisor in year two. You should begin reading for your qualifying in your first year.

6. Fieldwork and gathering and analyzing data are often grueling enterprises.

7. Writing blocks are OK, but only if you have a writing block about checks and e-mail. Otherwise, you've made this into a much bigger project than it is. The idea is to get out, get a job, and then do a better job on your research, publish it in your first three years, and begin another project.

This is a very tight schedule. The cost of delay is at least $75,000 for every year you delay. If you have family responsibilities, illness, or tragedy, it will not go so rapidly. If you have a job outside of a research assistantship, again it may not go so rapidly. But, keep in mind that every extra year of graduate school probably costs $100,000, once we include tuition, in university costs and forgone earnings (discounting earnings increments the rest of your life). Besides, if you get into the right disciplined relationship to your work, you will advance more rapidly in your new job and do even better.

14   The Limits of What You Learned in College or High School

National primary and secondary educational systems tend to aim for rote learning and national patriotism rather than scholarly depth and complexity. You learn a rather more objective way of thinking in university, if you are fortunate. The characteristic feature of scholarship is providing a wide range of evidence for your argument, and a realization that your argument has a counter that can also muster a wide range of evidence. Often, there is more than one counterargument. Some positions do not hold up well under such an assault; others are credible and worthy of further elaboration.

15   Graduate Student Ambitions

"Like many second-rate graduate students, I pursued ideas from my thesis topic for over fifteen years before disengaging from it. I was making progress without getting to useful results too quickly. Getting results too quickly would mean that the problems I was working on were not difficult enough to be as challenging as I wanted them to be." – Ken Wilson, 1982 Nobel Laureate in Physics

16   Advice to an Ambivalent but Strong Doctoral Student in a Practical Field

In fields such as urban planning, public administration, and social work, students enter a doctoral program with both a keen interest in research and often a strong commitment to making the world better. They may feel ambivalent about an academic career, since they do not readily see role models among their professors for a mixed role of research and practice. They might enter a professional doctoral program, where the thesis might be an advance in practice, an invention, rather than a conventional PhD.

Students are sometimes told that a solution to a problem will happen, often by chance, with someone in practice or in politics having picked up on your research and seen its usefulness. It is true that your professors are expert in finding out what does not work and why, rather than in inventing and discovering what might work at all. (But this is not true in engineering, and in fact it is not true in the fields that concern you.) In effect, you are much like the priest who might want to serve the poor, but first must master theology from a professor. (In contrast, I am thinking of the work of Albert Hirschman and his student Judith Tendler, where one focuses on finding those situations where there is hope and things actually work despite proofs that they cannot.)

You are compelled to serve and make for a better society, to be honorable and to sacrifice self if necessary to improve things for others, as one student said to me. He draws his energy from such a commitment and he feels blessed to have a role in society that allows him to be effective.

I believe that those commitments to service will not desert you, and they will force you to be the academic you wish to be. You will discover in time that many of your teachers actually have similar commitments. But in your role as a doctoral student, who might become an assistant professor seeking tenure, the research focus must dominate while practice takes a hiatus for a few years. In fact, you won't be trapped by such a shorter-term focus. Moreover, your increased research prominence will give you the authority to intervene in policy discussions and proposals.

Scholarly research is committed to balance, objectivity, and empirical truth, all of which receive lots of doubt these days, but in fact they are real. You will be the champion of your ideas and research and scholarly insight. Professors serve on National Academy panels or go to Washington or the state capital for two years or more.

Right now you will need to focus your energies. Ambivalence will slow you down too much. Bill Bradley said that he practiced basketball all the time in college because he figured that when he was not practicing the competition was. In other words, there are other people who are focused and you want to be as strong as they are. (Other training tips: Manage and discipline your time and energy. Stop doing some things.

Take risks. And realize, again, that others are in the game with you, having the same stresses [*New York Times*, 15 January 2013, p. D5].)

17   *External Research Support in the Research University*

It is important that you prepare yourself for a career not only as a researcher, but also as an externally funded researcher – with support from foundations, federal and state agencies, and fellowships. Namely, you want to develop the skills for writing grant and fellowship applications, for finding and cultivating sources of support, and for delivering on the promises you made when asking for a grant or a fellowship.

1. Not only do you want to raise support for graduate students, for expenses, for travel, but you also want to buy out your own time, from teaching, so you have the time to devote to your project. Over the last 40+ years, a good fraction of my academic-year salary has been paid for by grants and fellowships. This is in addition to sabbaticals when I have held a tenure-track appointment. The range of subjects has been very wide. Virtually none of the monies have been used for summer salary. From my point of view that does not buy you time for research, unless you are desperate for money and would otherwise have had to spend your summers as a fast-food employee.

2. I have never felt that seeking and needing external support has distorted my research agenda. I may have had three possible directions and gone in the direction where support was available, but it was a direction I had earlier chosen. Moreover, external support is a seal of approval by those in the know that your research direction seems worthy. Of course, you may be the rare genius who knows better than anyone what are the right kinds of research that should be done, unrecognized by others – but I am not that genius.

3. So, you must learn to write research proposals and grants early on, and keep doing it. It's not just for scientists, engineers, and biomedical research. I have always had to do this, of necessity, so I think of grant-writing as dialing-for-dollars and in fact I get giddy when I first draft up a proposal. If I get half of my proposals funded, that's good enough.

4. There is no field of scholarly research for which no support is available. In the humanities, usually the support is in terms of fellowships or

grants to write your next book. In the social sciences, there is a much wider range of possibilities.

5. External support empowers you in the academic hierarchy. If you have strong support, you are more powerful than more senior colleagues who do not, more powerful than deans and provosts. Most of us are not so fortunate, but I have seen this power in action.

6. External research support does not mean you do less first-class research. When people say that writing grants slows down their research, I always wonder if the work they are doing instead of seeking external grants is that worthy. It's rarely the case. Moreover, serving on panels that review research proposals, visiting funding officers, is not merely about winning favor. It is about learning what others are doing, measuring yourself against others, and finding out where sources of support are going.

What you do not really want is "internal" support: your own resources are so rich you do not need support; you have an endowed position; your fellowship does not demand that you do research assistance or teaching. You want to be part of the system, you want to become someone's protégé (whether your advisor or a grant officer), you want to gain experience in the world. No one I know of has thrived on their own. If you have your own resources, help others to raise grants.

18   *Graduate Student Basics*

1. You do not develop a dissertation proposal by knowing all the literature. Rather, you find a problem or a site or a data set or whatever, and you work with that. You have a problem that demands from you what it needs, and you can meet those demands. You make a leap: it may not be right, but you will not know that until you engage it. So, how do you start? Think in terms of what you might do. That usually breaks the logjam. Show it to your advisor. The rest is work. Lots of work. But work is good.

Students I am supposedly helping become defensive about their ideas. They can just ignore my advice. There is no need to convince me they are right. The right response is, "Thank you." If you feel the need to say more, say, "I will take your advice into account." Find other helpers. I'm not the person you have to worry about.

2. A project description: Write a two-page memo telling me what you are doing.

A vita: Don't bury your achievements behind lots of weak fluff.

A literature review: Your first paragraph should say it all, rather than being a sort-of introduction.

3. Ambition and achievement go together. People can be extraordinarily focused, hardworking. They need to find a home department which does not resent their achievements and their success. Most scholars who do good work are not half so ambitious and so deliberate and focused. When you think of yourself in the scholarly world, keep in mind there are such ambitious folks around. They set the standard for those who want to be leaders. By the way, ambition need not mean being underhanded or greedy.

4. Office hours: Real professors are in their office only some of the time. They may be in their laboratories, they write, they serve on committees, they go to archives in Washington, Sacramento, or Seoul, and sometimes they even go to the dentist or the vet. *Most of our work is done outside the view of anyone,* even if we have a laboratory, and surely if we do scholarship of the more conventional sort – often nights and weekends. Just call and make an appointment.

Office hours are ritualistic, in that most students would prefer to see professors at other times. Make an appointment, show up on time, prepared (with a memo on what you want to discuss – so as to guide the discussion), and you will get more out of your teachers. Getting them "on the fly" as they are between things may be fine for a signature, but for real stuff they need to be focused on your problem, your concern.

19 *Being Autonomous*

1. You need to draft, redraft, and polish.

2. Show others your best work. Incorporate advice you have received on earlier drafts. Let it sit for a few days, and make further changes.

3. Be your own critic. You want to be autonomous. Hence, you need to learn to reread your work and improve it then and there.

4. Be resourceful. Ask a student; check the textbook; use the web. Use the "Help" in the computer application; search for tutorials; find the experts in the library.

5. Ask questions. In tension with #4, do ask questions of your instructor (or others). There are no dumb questions. But it will make a difference if you ask those questions after you have been resourceful.

6. No excuses. The cows do not want to hear excuses for why they were not milked today. If you do not show up, or show up late, the natural and necessary inference is that this engagement matters to you less than other engagements.

7. Do not blame others. You really do not want to say, "You told me so." You want to take charge, and say, "I'll fix it."

In the end you want others to think of you as responsible, delivering your personal best: resourceful, thoughtful, and respectful. Someday you will need a favor from others, and you want them to owe you, not you to owe them.

20 *Improving Your Work*

In general, you will get nowhere arguing with your instructor about the grammaticality of your writing, or whether your instructor gave you incorrect guidance ("you told me so"). On the other hand, if there is a misunderstanding, a clear memo stating your position can be very effective. But even if the instructor is at fault, you will do better to ask, "How can I make it better?" This is true in all situations where you depend on the authority of your boss/coach/instructor. It's not that the figure in authority is always right. Rather, you do not want the authority to have to prove to you that you are wrong (when you are wrong). So, if you are going to protest, be sure you are on the side of the angels. In a society rife with negotiation and litigation, we sometimes forget that not all positions are equally valid, that authority often is rationally grounded, and that you may well do better not by winning but by actually doing better.

Never submit poor work, either alone or mixed with good stuff. You will be remembered for the bad. It's like first impressions. You get a first impression of someone and then it turns out that the person really isn't as bad as you thought. But your first impression always looms in your mind. If by chance none of your work is what you think of as good, it is better to fix it and then submit.

21   *Learning the Material*

I wrote to a student: "You surely have the capacity to think through this stuff, since most of it depends on your basic intuitions about the sizes of things, and the credibility of the numbers your computer spits out – such as those large standard deviations you got at first. Trust yourself more, think whether something makes sense, and that will help. It's not at all about formulas, or about tricks. You knew something was wrong, and you have the capacity to figure out where to go next.

"But, it does take lots of time. In general, students are more than smart enough to do the work they have to do. But, often, they do not realize that problems may well require hard thinking, or that they need to write out an answer and see if it makes sense. Or many drafts, or many trials. Computer applications may have steep learning curves, and the only way you master them is by experimenting and learning from your mistakes. Yes, someone may know exactly what to do, but that someone may not be around when you are doing your next job or project. So you have to learn how to rely more on yourself, your own wits, and the occasional kindness of strangers and friends, as well as clicking on 'Help.' What you have to learn is how to learn more, how to figure things out."

Eric Clay wrote me, after seeing the above: "This seems to be the sort of learning moment when play and work merge into creativity. That is the sort of approach that happens when students are driven by a light-hearted sense of the importance of what they are trying to do, and they are fully aware that they do not know how to do it. The job of the teacher is to create an intellectual and emotional space where that can happen."

22   *How to Write Grant or Fellowship Proposals: For Doctoral Students*

1. You should never send out a proposal without your advisor working it over with you.

2. Funders say what they want in the grant announcement; often they list just what they want and in which order. Do what they say.

3. After you have written the proposal, your abstract should give away the main points. And the first paragraph of your proposal should do so as well.

4. Get help. Here's an example: Most of the proposals I have written have been for fellowships or grants from foundations. I have a collaborator from the Engineering School at the university who has lots of federal grant experience. It is not hard for me to write up a draft giving everything needed in the proposal. However, my collaborator takes what I give him and he converts it to National Science Foundation-ese. He'll need extra materials, and ask me for them, and he'll get them back from me overnight at the latest, if not by return e-mail. Of course, I read and change and edit the draft he produces, but what is remarkable is both how much of my original text is in the proposals, and how different it sounds after he has worked it over. The changes are subtle but significant. And my collaborator inserts lots of his own expertise along the way.

5. I have another collaborator who is not used to getting grants at all, since in his field consulting is the major source of fieldwork. He is very distinguished in his field. I interview him, take notes, and then draft the proposal. I show it to him, he makes suggestions, and then we send it off.

In both of the above cases, I could not make these proposals without my collaborators. We are jointly responsible for the work.

6. In general, what you want to do is to tag along on other people's grants early on in your career, and then have them help you go out on your own.

7. The best help comes from advisors, collaborators, and peers.

8. Finally, as you move up in the world, you'll want to make personal contact with the foundation staff, NSF officers, or Department of Defense funders. They want to meet you, and help you get funded in the directions they think are important. You need to visit New York or D.C. or the state capital or Kansas City and have lunch with people.

9. A good hit rate depends on the competition. Some fellowships go to 5 percent of the applicants. NSF and NIH competitive applications are at best 30 percent or so (and this is for first-rate applicants). Less competitive sources might be 50 percent. And often the grantor and you have been having discussions about what you both want, and the final

application has a very high chance of being approved. On the other hand, a hit rate of 10 percent is weak and too costly.

23 *Advice for New Students*

The university is an institution with some of the best faculty in the world. Your job is to find one or two or three of those people, and learn from them. What you learn will be about how to think, how to live an interesting life, and how to be a person of integrity and achievement.

Many of your teachers do want to talk with you, or correspond with you by e-mail. Do not hide.

(For undergraduates, your other job is to find something at the university that you care about passionately: the band, a team, a field of study, a research problem, an activity, a thinker. That will anchor you.)

24 *Qualifying Exams*

Waiting longer to take your exams does not mean you will do better. I am not sure when one should be ready, but ideally at the end of the second year or the beginning of your third is nice. Your advisor will guide you (or if not, get another advisor).

Respond to the exam's question. Have I answered this question? Is it clear that I have provided an answer? Is it obvious in the first and last paragraphs? And have I organized my answer so that a reader can be sure I have provided a response? Research references should suit your answer, and they should tell the reader that you are aware of the literature. Does the response read well? Can someone read it without going crazy trying to figure out your answer? This is not only grammar and spelling, but organization, subheads, topic sentences. In solving problems or doing proofs in the sciences and mathematics, make clear your motivation and your direction.

In your oral exam, you are welcome to ask for elaboration about a question if it is unclear. Then you should stop and think, and answer the question the best you can. The longer you go on without responding to the question, the worse it gets.

Your teachers are looking for evidence that you understand the main issues, that you have a sense of the research literature, that you can answer the questions (rather than just talk). If you are worried about the time constraints for writing your exam, you will have to face that here and now. Write shorter but clearer. As for the oral, remember, your committee would prefer to just pass you and let you get on with your dissertation prospects. Have you thought a bit about what you might do for your dissertation, literally what you might do, rather than some abstract idea? Discuss with your advisor and your student friends – ahead of time.

Your success or failure is a reflection on your professor. If you do well, that reflects well on your advisor. That you do less well is also a reflection on the advisor. You need your advisor in your camp, helping and guiding and teaching you. Some advisors cannot do this well, for some students. Find an advisor who can help you.

25   Writing It Down

If you are working on a project, it is useful to write yourself memos along the way: outlining your main ideas, summarizing your reading, proposing a structure for your study, listing potential main concepts. The memos should be short, at most one page single-spaced. If you are going to see a professor or mentor, you can share the memo ahead of time so you can set up the conversation so it works for you.

Do not be afraid to write it down. Writing it down shoots down bad ideas, and helps good ones become more substantial. You might wait a day or two, so you do not destroy ideas that are too nascent to survive – but do not wait too long. Actually, writing it down has never destroyed any of my ideas (but many have proven to be poor ideas in any case).

B. YOUR ADVISOR AND COMMITTEE

26   Why Does My Professor Ask Me to Write a Memo before He Sees Me?

A professor is always pleased to be consulted by students about their careers and their research. So why do I often ask a student to prepare a memo about the issues that concern them, before they see me? And then I read it, and get back to them by e-mail, still before they see me.

It is just what I do when I am about to consult others for advice or help. I show up, their having my memo in hand already. Or they write me a note, and the meeting turns out not to be needed. If I think things through, and write them down, even if they are contradictory or do not quite make sense, I am more likely to be able to figure out what to do – or better put, I am better capable of asking for criticism and help.

27   No Surprises for the Boss

If you are about to schedule a meeting with a faculty member or your boss, a meeting in which you are planning to discuss written materials (say a dissertation proposal or a draft), make sure the materials are in the faculty member's or boss's hands well before you schedule the meeting. This way, the person who has to comment on the material knows they will have enough time to read it. The usual experience is that the materials arrive the night before, by e-mail, typically at 1 AM – that is not comforting, does not allow for careful reading, and says something quite disturbing about you. Would you trust this person to deliver the goods for an important conference or grant?

Similarly, if you have a deadline to submit something, try to get it in a day or two early, especially if you are depending on the goodwill of the reader. Why press their schedule or their list of things to do?

This is also true for faculty meetings. If you want people to discuss a proposal or an idea, get them the materials well ahead. No surprises and no tricks, and be well prepared. You are more likely to be effective. And no excuses about how you just could not get the materials ready until that 1 AM time.

28 *Using Your Own Judgment*

I was asked: "I was wondering if it would be possible for you to look over my revised assignments. I made the changes you suggested but wanted to see if you could tell me any other ways I could improve. If not I will continue to revise on my own."

I wrote back: "It is important for you to take charge of your own work. I gave you whatever ideas I had about your work. If you have specific questions, I'll be glad to answer them. I realize this puts more on your shoulders, but that is exactly what I want to do."

My own experience is that I submit an article that I think is OK. The journal, if I am fortunate, says they are interested and gives me some suggestions for improvement (revise and resubmit), but they will not accept it then and there. I then revise, taking their suggestions into account, and with the passage of time since the original submission I may see other ways of improving the work. It still might get rejected, but the article is surely better. By the way, I do not recall ever having a paper or book accepted as is. And the guidance for revision has always been schematic. And sometimes (more than rare!) it was rejected in the end and I needed to find another venue.

In a coaching situation, you might receive ongoing feedback. And ideally we might do that with our students. Yet, the coach knows that the student must eventually go out on their own, and at some point the coach must step back. Students who do not develop confidence in their own judgment, even when that judgment proves incorrect, cannot be autonomous.

29 *Delivering*

The advisor says, write up this chapter now, yet the student is going to a conference and will instead spend the two months writing the paper for the conference. The advisor says, use this theoretical framework, and the student goes in a different direction. The problem is not whether you take your advisor's advice. Rather, again, the problem is whether you can deliver what you are supposed to deliver, on time, within constraints. No one can fault you for following your own path – if you deliver. (My one student who was most independent delivered, so I could only praise that student to the skies.) But if you follow your own path, and you do not deliver, then you are on your own: this is not the position you want to be in. How can your advisor advocate for you, when you are up for a job or a fellowship, if you have not delivered and you have not taken their advice (perhaps indicating the courage of your own path)?

Of course, you are still welcome to follow your own inclinations, but you now make it much more difficult for people to help you. At that point, you might well want an advisor who believes your inclinations are in accord with their intuitions.

How does an advisor get more out of students? Do not tolerate non-performance. If students are not doing what you want them to do, they need to know it. Egos are delicate, and students can be hurt by your being too sharp. But I find that most students do not get it. Namely: *It's the work, stupid.* Nothing else matters. They need to be told that the work must be done.

If a student disappears, the advisor will eventually assume they are nonperforming assets, so to speak.

Despite the myth that scholars do brain-work, most of the work we do is a matter of sitting down and doing boring but necessary stuff. The blocked artist or genius is not more useful than the blocked idiot. *If you do not produce, you do not produce. Excuses make you pathetic.* Perhaps you ought be doing something other than academic scholarship? (There are personal and family tragedies, but thankfully they are sufficiently rare that tragedy is rarely the cause. Clinical depression is more common.)

It may be you do not want to believe your advisor knows better than you how to do your research project or how to succeed. I keep discovering people who tell me they know better, when I tell them about what to do. Perhaps they do. But I have some experience, and unfortunately I am often correct.

30   *On Choosing an Advisor and Building Your Studies*

1. You are doing a PhD since you want to enter the research enterprise: academic, business, consulting, or government. Find out where your proposed advisor has placed their students in the past. Are the

places the kind of places you want to be? For more junior faculty, you will want to ask another question (see below #3).

2. Some doctoral students have an idea of what might be their research project. There is no reason to believe that their judgment is reliable – it takes years to build up that sort of taste. In general, you want to work within the research program of an advisor (who also fulfills #1 above). Some fields have fairly narrow ranges of acceptable research (where the data lie, where the major questions have solidified in their field). In general, if your advisor is not enthusiastic, pursue another project. (They might have very good reasons to think that your project is not likely to be fruitful.) Of course, there is always the case of the renegade student who really delivers.

Work on a project that suits your skills and talents, that engages you, and that is of interest to your advisor.

3. How vigorous is your advisor's own publication and research agenda? Do they regularly publish in the right journals, and do you find their articles compelling? Do they raise external research monies? Junior faculty are often at the edge of research developments, and their expertise and enthusiasm are very valuable. They probably know many people in the field, since they too are trying to build their reputations; they too looked for a job recently. They may not be overly burdened by administrative and external tasks. They may have time for you. On the other hand, famous people may or may not be attentive to their students. Find out.

All of these factors can be checked out by asking other graduate students, checking out CVs, going to seminars. You want an advisor who can give you the help you need, at all stages.

This is a more serious choice than marriage. While your being a graduate student is a four-to-six-year enterprise, your being a protégé is lifetime. By the way, this is why you want to do a spectacular or at least good enough job in your thesis research – your advisor's enthusiasm is crucial.

4. As for your coursework, the required stuff is secondary. What's crucial is your building up coursework that allows you to do your research, and also gives you some competencies when you try to teach. Get some teaching experience while you are a graduate student.

5. Those of you with multi-year fellowships are at a disadvantage unless you connect with an advisor early on. Start working with them on their research projects; have them become committed to you. That your advisor is not supporting you directly is the disadvantage. You are not at all a free agent; you are an "unmarried." (The exceptions to this observation are so rare, they are not relevant. YOU are not an exception.)

31 *Choosing Your Committee*

From A. Pappas, graduate student, art history, University of Southern California:

The Committee Overview:

1. How the student views the committee: Advisor is in charge of area of your interests. Second member of exam committee in charge of departmental minor. Outside member in charge of required outside area. Members four and five from department may work in related areas or with similar methodologies.

2. How the graduate school views the committee: Advisor is primary mentor and supervisor for student's project. Fourth and fifth members of committee enforce respectively department regulations and graduate school regulations (outside member). The graduate school representative also functions as go-between if difficulties arise between student and advisor.

3. How graduate school works, psychological aspects: Reenacts adolescence: pass your screening exams, get promoted to high school; pass your PhD exams, get a driver's license; turn in your outline, get the car on Saturday nights; turn in chapters, get your curfew lifted; get your cover page signed, leave home!

- Choosing your committee is like choosing
  someone to be your legal guardian.
- Your thinking will change as you progress – this
  may mean changing advisors, or moving to a
  new department or different institution.

4. The problem of limited choice: Small department – you may be stuck with a less than ideal advisor simply because they are the only member of your department with expertise in a certain area.

5. Other sources of information: Other graduate students who have formed committees and/or passed their quals.

You will have to balance the following factors as best fits your individual situation. Asking yourself these questions can help you decide which factors should be given the most weight and can help alert you to potential problems.

1. General strategy: Choose your advisor first. Present your advisor with your suggestions regarding other members. You may ask your advisor for suggestions as well. Remember, the final decision is yours. Build relationships with faculty members in your department, and in other departments, early – this will help you select a committee that can work together, that will enhance, not hinder, your intellectual development, and will help you avoid problems.

2. Outside member: Do not select this person for purely intellectual reasons. Remember, you may need this person's help if problems develop between you and your advisor, or between your advisor and other members of your committee. This person ideally will have tenure, will have served on prior committees in your department, and is someone who believes you are a good student. Under no circumstances should this person in any way be dependent on your advisor for professional favors or advancement.

3. Personalities: Can all these people communicate with each other? If you have a style of communication radically different from your advisor's, you may have problems meeting his/her expectations. If your advisor and one of your other committee members rub each other the wrong way, or if one of your committee members is so poorly socialized he or she continually offends the other members, chances are you will have to replace him or her, either for your own peace of mind, or at the command of your advisor.

4. Disciplinary divisions: Committee members with radically differing methods, premises, and ideologies may lend richness to your committee, but their diversity may also result in deadlock. Humanities students are particularly vulnerable here. If two members of your committee do not agree on what constitutes research, chances are you will have the impossible task of meeting conflicting requirements.

5. Availability: Is the person you are considering going to be available to you? For example, you will have grave difficulties starting your project

if your advisor is going to be away for a year doing fieldwork in Tierra del Fuego. Likewise, if your outside member is going to be away, he or she will have difficulty interceding for you, should it become necessary. You have to consider planned sabbaticals and research leaves when scheduling your quals – is it worth it to you to postpone your exams for a year while a committee member is out of town or overseas?

If the person is going to be in town, how many days a week are they at school? How often do they hold office hours? Are they willing to set up a regular appointment? If so, how often? Do they have e-mail? Can you call them at home? Do you have to pull teeth to get an appointment? When you have an appointment are you continually interrupted by phone calls, other students?

When you turn in papers or chapters, how long do you have to wait for it? A week? A month? In what form do you get feedback? Oral? Written? Is it vague or do you get specific questions and suggestions? Is the feedback uniformly negative? Is it balanced? Is it copious or minimal? If this person is a potential second department member, are they willing to chew the fat with you while you are in the incubation stage? Are they willing to read your chapter drafts?

Last but not least: Does the prospective advisor have tenure? Is the person up for promotion? Do they have offers from other institutions? Is the person being courted by another institution? What will happen to you if he or she takes a job at another school? Is this person near retirement? What will happen to you if he/she retires early?

6. Control vs. guidance: You need to consider the style of guidance the potential advisor provides. Do they have a hands-off, sink-or-swim approach? Do they provide more supervision in the early stages and less later on? Do they tightly oversee all areas of the project? Do they force their views upon the student? Is this person willing/able to learn from your growing expertise? Faculty members should be able to discuss their pedagogical philosophy in this area. What kind of guidance style works for you?

7. Support – financial and moral: How are discretionary funds distributed in your department? If by a committee, does your prospective advisor sit on this committee? If by faculty consensus, will your advisor be a strong advocate for you? Is your prospective advisor willing/able

to help you apply for outside funding? Is your prospective advisor well informed about such sources?

Has your prospective advisor supervised other dissertations? More experience isn't necessarily better – senior faculty members can be burnt out or consider graduate students a burden. However, senior faculty have seen the process many times and can be in a good position to demystify the process for you. Younger faculty members often have the benefit of youthful enthusiasm, but may be preoccupied with preparing for their third-year review or overwhelmed by new teaching or grant-writing responsibilities.

32 Firing Your Advisor

There was once a wonderful Mercedes ad: A woman is holding car keys, smiling broadly, and the ad says: Fire your psychiatrist!

Now, not all kinds of illness respond well to a Mercedes, but some of the time you do want to fire your advisor. You discover that this revered figure does not match you at all any longer, and the lifetime commitment you have made seems to be jail time. Do so graciously. First of all, get the car or the new advisor. Then make sure the psychiatrist does not feel rejected, but rather is now freed to find new patients whom he can charge higher fees. Lines such as: You have given me all and I am truly grateful, but right now we are not getting anyplace and it is time for you to devote yourself to other needs – and I will find help. But I do want to have you on my team, and I will let you know how.

If they insist on staying, be firm, do not be swayed, indicate it is for the good of everyone, and go forward. Remember that your psychiatrist is likely once to have been the guy you despised in eighth grade or even worse, so there are no gods here. Professors have spouses who know that they do not pick up their underwear, so to speak.

So get out the keys, go for a drive, and get the work done.

33 Memos to Your Committee

Every time you meet with a member of your committee, send a short note recapping what you discussed and what you agreed. This ensures no misunderstandings and leaves a paper trail in case of later trouble. In addition to projecting an image of competence, if you agree to do things by a certain deadline, you might well do them.

Memos are especially important after qualifying exams. Faculty often complain that students disappear into the woodwork after the exam. I would send a memo every three months with a list of things I've done, with evaluation of whether I met goals from the last memo, a list of upcoming stuff (conferences, teaching), goals for me to meet before the next memo (outline, chapter draft), and date of the next memo. I would also include grant application deadlines, so they will know a couple months ahead of time when I will need reference letters.

34 Success Is Not About Being Top-Ranked at a Top-Ranked School

It turns out that the top 1 percent of the law students often do end up at the topmost law firms, but of course not always. For the rest of the firms, leaders come from a rather wide range of students – once they have been admitted to a reasonably strong law school. The top of a profession is plateau-wide and has a very narrow peak. In other words, if you are reasonably strong, but not the very tip-top, you have a good chance to make it. What predicts success is hunger, a fire in the belly that makes you do your best, aim for the top. Law firms find that a strong student who comes from a "poor" background is the best bet. All of this applies to academia. Along the way you need to be adopted by a mentor (likely your advisor) and guided, since the system is not readily decoded, and the tasks to be mastered and done often are not stated explicitly.

35 Financial Support and the Subject of Your Research

1. Your advisor's research grants may well pay for equipment or space or paper clips, and for research managers, but a hefty amount may be budgeted for graduate research assistants – you! There is as well fellowship money, some teaching assistantships, and your own wealth. In any case, you will want to match your interests with the support that will be available for your research. If you are lucky, advisors will try to convince

you that you ought to study sewerage – even if you are interested in urban design – since they have lots of money for work in that area and they think you will be a person they might like to work with.

2. After your first year, you want to be sure that the work you do and the courses you take add to your degree, and are not merely diversions. Structured research experiences of increasing difficulty are the building blocks of a productive research career. Better this gets resolved by the end of your first semester. If you are somehow linked to an advisor who is not for you, see the head of your doctoral program and get advice. Of course, there must be a way for you to get support from your new potential advisor.

You may end up going where the money is. This may or may not be a good idea. You have got to make a living and get a job, and some fields are less well supported than are others.

3. In any case, faculty may court you with ardor, but in fact that does not mean you ought to respond in kind. If the situation in which you find yourself is not for you, see the head of your program and get help. The person to whom you are assigned knows that students need to find the right pond in which to swim, and understands that some people will leave them (while others will join).

4. Of course, there may be a field in which you want to work, and the advisor may not have large research grants. But often there are teaching assistantships, fellowships, university support, and other ways of getting money. Explore those opportunities actively.

For international students especially: American professors are just like other working people. They are not gods, not even demigods. They cannot totally control your future, since the American system is much too porous and varied for someone who feels angry at you to have much effect if you have other supporters.

If you are about to graduate: The mock interviews the career people offer should be of use with consulting firms and corporations, probably of lesser use with universities, and probably of some genuine value with foundations and government. Take advantage of the help. Remember, it is your life, and your advisor may not be able to help you here.

36 *Taking Your Mentors' Advice*

One of the curious experiences we have when people come up for promotion and tenure is that they have not followed their mentors' advice. We know they did not take the advice, since there is a memo in the dossier of the third-year review (halfway through the probationary period) in which the candidate is advised quite explicitly about what needs to be done. Here's the problem: Say the person has not made the kind of contribution that is expected – whether in publication, in method of research, in teaching. How can we then allow them to be promoted? They did not follow our advice; they did not perform adequately by their own methods.

You do not have to take advice. But then you want to discuss your reasons for taking a different path, have your mentors appreciate your reasons, and write it all up in a memo. *Why set yourself up?*

37 *How Responsible Should Advisors Be for Their Doctoral Students?*

As I read CVs and listen to job talks, review papers for journals, and serve on university tenure committees, I ask myself: How responsible should we be for our doctoral students? Here, I am not talking about dissertation supervision, guidance, job-finding. Rather, should we allow them to go out in the world inappropriately attired? What about decorum or alcohol use?

What is our obligation to them as they make their careers? As mentors and patrons, we might well want to be sure they are doing the right thing on the road to tenure, or even afterward. It is not unusual to promote your students for awards or academy memberships years after they have finished.

1. Should we revise their CV so that it conforms to the usual styles?

2. Should we make sure they give a practice talk in front of us before they give a talk at a meeting?

3. Should we edit any paper they submit to a journal or a meeting for proper form and for quality as well? At least read it over ahead of time, and give them advice?

4. Should we guide them carefully where to apply for jobs, where not to?

By the way, I am not claiming that we ourselves are experts on all of these aspects. And what if they choose to ignore our counsel? Knowing what is the right thing and practically doing it are separate skills. And some students are more readily mentored than are others.

38   *The Good Advisor*

Faculty can make it much harder for students to succeed. Some acts are just plain mischievous, such as sending in letters of reference too late, or not advocating for your students, or disappearing for a while and leaving the student in the lurch (not responding to their chapters, or their calls). Others are inconsiderate. In any case, some rules seem to be winners:

1. Always respond to requests immediately. You might say that you will get to it, whatever it is, in two weeks or a month. Then be sure to do that. If you cannot do something, even something you know you ought to do, say so and suggest alternatives. E-mail has escalated demand for responses.

2. Do not jerk students around. Do not change the rules midstream. If you have been saying that the work is good, or you have not suggested improvements in the chapters, you cannot then request major revisions at the end. If you cannot be their advisor, be direct and say so. If the student is weak, that is no excuse for there being no advisor for that student – if they have passed their exams. If they are not suited to graduate work, they need to be told that by the end of their first year.

Students should be insulated from departmental politics. Whether they are on your side, or against you, that has nothing to do with the help you give them. Better they should not feel that taking sides is their business. Obviously, this also applies to affairs of the heart, or the pocketbook, or the bedroom.

Students are enormously grateful to be treated decently, to have reliable advisors and committees, to be able to trust you to serve their interests. They appreciate your solving problems that you alone can solve, and solving them pronto. And they appreciate being protected from nonsense and idiocy.

3. You are obligated to help your students get jobs. You are not obligated to misrepresent their strengths; rather you need to set goals for them that are realistic and achievable. Great advisors always place their students; they do not place them all at the best institutions.

4. You will probably help rewrite the dissertation or the first chapter when it is published. One professor always writes the introductory parts of his students' articles, providing them with perspective and polish not available to beginners.

5. What you do or do not do will get around. If you help students, they will tell their friends. If you hurt them, in any way, they will perhaps tell only one friend (if they are afraid, or scared, or respectful), but then everybody will eventually hear about it. This will affect your career.

6. If you act like a jerk, so to speak, you will pay. For in the latter part of your career, you are in need of the patronage of those 20 years younger than you. They know all the stories. Tenure is no defense, and the power you have in that latter part of your career is likely to be much less than you imagine.

7. Say you have been shafted by your advisor:

Keep records and dates. If something has been promised by a certain date, you might even make an appointment for that date, or send a note indicating your schedule and how it will depend on others' schedules. Keep documents, copies of relevant e-mail. A diary is useful. Summarize phone conversations.

Consult with the dean or the associate dean. Come with a copy of your file, with records and dates, and offer to leave it for their perusal. Check with the outside member of your committee to see if your perception of things is reasonable. Once you do this, your advisor is unlikely to be contrite. Egos here are quite fragile.

In any case, no outrage. Play dumb, present the dean with problems and evidence, and ask, what should you do? Let them conclude you were shafted, from the evidence. "Is it usual for an advisor not to read the draft chapters for three years?" is a perfect question you could ask a dean.

Figure out a way to escape, find a job, and sometime in the next decade or two it will be payback time. If you are careful you can not only pay back, but also not leave a fingerprint on your doings.

39   Basics for New Faculty and Advisors: Avoiding "Internalization of the Aggressor" and Being "Good Enough"

Namely, *I would not want what [bad things that] happened to me to happen to others.* Faculty who are starting out need to be told the rules of the game, reminded of the rules early and often, and be told when they are off base.

There is a truck coming, almost always, and to ignore that is to be crushed. Faculty need to be focused and ambitious, and realize that their probationary period is the time in which they develop the habits of a lifetime. We live in a highly competitive academic world, and if you are not doing your best someone else is, and they will preempt you. Faculty who have the right habits and practices need encouragement nonetheless.

There are many innocent if pernicious influences that can derail even the most focused junior scholar.

Faculty need to have the highest of standards for themselves. Just because someone got promoted or rewarded for doing less than first-rate work does not mean others will get away with it. Faculty need to be reminded of those standards, and encouraged to pursue their scholarship at the highest levels.

In a university where the quality of the faculty has risen substantially over less than a generation, many of the most senior faculty will be less strong than the junior faculty. No one likes to say this, but it is both obvious and problematic. The seniors should see that their legacy is the quality of the people they appoint and promote, and the juniors ought be grateful for the vision of the seniors.

Again, the basic idea is that there is no reason to walk in front of an oncoming truck. More deeply, just because it was good enough for me does not mean it is good enough for my students. If I have suffered as a student or junior faculty member, why should they suffer? As the child psychoanalyst Selma Fraiberg describes it, mothers who say "if it was good enough for me, it is good enough for my kid" are "internalizing the aggressor" rather than saying, "I would not want my child to suffer as I did." The latter is the liberating move. *My advice takes from my own and others' mistakes, and counsels how to avoid them. By the way, it is quite hard to convince some people not to walk in front of oncoming trucks.*

My other way of mentoring is to listen to students, and respond to their real needs. The pediatrician D. W. Winnicott describes a mother who is "good enough," who responds to the baby's needs, anticipating them, is "in the moment" with the baby, "contains" that baby, and provides a chance for the baby to grow up by allowing mother and baby to be "alone together." I am not gentle, but I am direct. It may involve telling students unpleasant truths, but again they are less likely to walk in front of other oncoming trucks. My greatest strength is to see next steps and to see the main points of the work.

40   *Advisors as Scholars*

Students have a restricted view of the range and strengths of their faculty. You really do not want an advisor who is overly burdened or who is not an expert in your research field – especially if one of the faculty is such an expert or has great depth of experience. As for outside members of your committee, this applies a fortiori to the whole university.

How can you find out more? Of course, some of your classmates may have the information you need, especially about whether people are easy or difficult to work with. The web page of the school often has vitae for the faculty.

One of our graduates wrote a note to all the students, with advice that I think is much more specific and more wary than my own:

1. Looking at the eventual outcome (especially, employment outcome) of recent graduates from the program, I have come to believe that the most important task during the PhD program is to find an advisor who cares for you and understands you – your aspirations, weaknesses, and merits. Whether your advisor cares about your well-being is more important than whether he/she is an eminent scholar.

2. Even if your advisor is not an eminent scholar, but still is widely known, you are fine. You may be better off with this well-known person than with another person with better research skills. You can often learn

skills yourself, from courses and discussions with outside resources (including faculty at other departments). But it is so much nicer when you have someone helping you establish yourself. [Once a very-well-known individual from our school pulled me by the arm to a prospective employer from another university, saying, "Come, I will give you a job." I didn't get the job, but if I could have changed my committee, I would have taken that person as my advisor right then (no offense to my actual advisor, who was also great in some other ways).]

3. If you have strong beliefs or are very competitive, stay away from people who also have strong beliefs.

4. Ideology is important when selecting advisors and committee members. Some faculty members may be above and beyond ideological biases (or at least keep them dormant when dealing with students), but you cannot count on all. I experienced more ideological shocks than I thought possible.

5. If your prospective advisor is a very busy person, you may look for someone else. You want them to read your chapters as quickly as they can (weeks maybe, not months).

6. It is good to be organized. When writing your dissertation, try to document all comments from committee members. And do not be surprised to see new comments on old stuff (a chapter once okayed may not mean it is okayed forever – it may come back to you with new comments).

7. Look at your prospective advisor's (and committee members') research thoroughly. If they have mainly been criticizing other folks without putting forward anything constructive or original, you may be better off with another person. I think you will have more fun with an advisor or committee member who wants to square a circle than with someone who is apprehensive of presenting new ideas. Besides, if you have started with very little, you have to be bold enough to experiment with new ideas. Status quo will not take you a long way.

8. Find someone in the faculty whom you can run to when there is a crisis. If you are serious about things, you will have a crisis at some point – it is just a matter of time before it comes.

9. It helps a lot if you can find someone whom you genuinely respect. It gives you direction.

C. STICKY SITUATIONS

41 *Envy*

Students tell me that they do not want to publicize their achievements because they sense envy from other students, and even feel a bit ostracized.

1. The success of one of our students will help all of you – reputation matters.

2. Do not worry; none of you are so successful that you are worth envying – yet.

3. Ambition is essential. Ambition is often thought to be unladylike or ungentlemanly. Curiously, institutional bragging is considered OK, as long as you say we are the best (and therefore ambition is not needed). But it's just the reverse. Again, ambition is not about dominating others but about what you do.

4. Do not worry; you are not in competition with your fellow graduate students at Snooty U. The competition is out there, among the various institutions (worldwide, perhaps). Actually, the competition is also your future professional colleagues and coworkers.

42 *I Would Never Want What Happened to Me to Happen to My Students or to My Children*

From a student: "What accounts for the discrepancy between faculty expectations and student achievement? There is a particular reluctance to engage the institutional responsibility to address the emotional needs of students; the emphasis instead is almost exclusively focused on process, as if the machinery of sausage-making deserved more attention than the ingredients that go into making quality sausage. The Fordist enterprise of doctoral education has been in place for ages. The myriad issues and inexplicable delays that beset students and hobble departments' expectations could perhaps be expected – a consistent byproduct of a Fordist process in need of adjustment.

"Sausage is made with good ingredients and complementary spices; it emerges from the machine in a timely fashion and tastes good, too, when made with care. Churn the meat through the process too fast, or forget to add the spice, and inevitably there results a poor-tasting sausage with a lousy aftertaste. (Apologies to vegetarians and vegans everywhere for my ham-handed analogy.)"

Scholarly life is often isolating and discouraging, especially since it is so individual in many fields (but not in all). Many an assistant or associate or even full professor would find the above description applies to their current scholarly life. Isolated, lacking mentoring.

That this process continues generation to generation is striking. Psychoanalysis calls this "the internalization of the aggressor": If it was good enough for me, it is good enough for you, my kid or my student. If I suffered through it as a graduate student, my current students can surely suffer through it. The more humane response would be: I would never want what happened to me to happen to my students or to my children.

43   Competition

In the scholarly world, everyone feels pressure. But when crisis hits, the cows still need to be milked. All of this is true in any competitive environment, whether it be sports or business. And academia is competitive, at least at its highest levels.

44   Laptop/Smartphone/Tablet Decorum

You are always being watched and judged, and little idiocies can have long-term consequences. Your attention is a sign of respect, and you may not wish to indicate that you are "dissing" the lecturer or the chair of the meeting. And you could just be taking notes.

Now, you might fall asleep, or just daydream. These more conventional modalities are sometimes dealt with by your being asked a question, though people may also just let you be. You are welcome to edit the hardcopy draft of an article during a meeting.

If you go on a date and spend your time e-mailing on your smartphone, or responding to e-mail immediately, you will not be seen in the best light. And keep in mind that your boss may be years behind you in technology multitasking skills, and will take your open laptop not as a sign of your wonderful talents, but as a sign of disrespect.

Little of this may apply in a high-tech environment.

45 *The Experienced Student, the Military Veteran*

With the large number of returning servicemen and -women, and the midlife need to retrain for a second career, many university students are not late adolescents but are in their mid-twenties or older. Often they have deep experience sets, some of it unimaginable by their classmates. Moreover, they want to get through and get on with life. Most extracurricular activities, and most Mickey-Mouse-type class exercises, and most professorial pretentions just do not work for them. Even at the most demanding of institutions, they may well have a job as well as go to school, and often they have families and children, some of whom are college-age. Usually, they have more than sufficient discipline and character. Often, they are wonderful students because they now want to learn, to master new skills.

Great professional competence and great scholarly competence are not readily interchangeable. That is, good consultants and practitioners and good academic researchers have different skill sets. Do not confuse practical experience with matters scholarly. Usually, they are complementary. Yet many of the skills practitioners must have are just what the scholar needs – discipline, reliability, bureaucratic smarts.

As for military veterans, again they are likely to want to accelerate their time to degree, whether undergraduate or graduate. Collegiate activities are unlikely to appeal to them; their combat experience has transformed them. At the same time, most civilians do not appreciate the meaning of that experience.

Veterans may well want to seek out other veterans, who appreciate their shared experience. Martin Dempsey, Chairman of the Joint Chiefs, suggests that military people, even in retirement, ought not to be political (however that is to be understood). As for uninformed undergraduate opinionating, it's probably best to stay out of it.

Adult students present challenges to their classmates and their teachers. They are more likely to question not only the particular content of what they are being taught, but also whether this is what should be happening in a class. They may actually *know* something, as may other students. On the other hand, my experience has been that those students still benefit from learning to write, to master new fields, and to think analytically and critically.

It makes a big difference if the average age of your students is in the low twenties, rather than in the high twenties or thirties or older.

46 *Judgment and Grades*

When I see a transcript or a list of publications, I need to ask myself: Are these grades or publication venues indicative of the quality of the person's work? I know that it is hard to convey integrity, responsibility, perseverance, inventiveness – especially in a single grade or in a publication. So I hope that letters of reference tell me about these qualities.

Yet, hard work may not make someone a good surgeon or a productive mathematician or an effective manager. There may be a poor match between someone's talents and the work they choose to do. The best question to ask is: *Would I want this person to operate on my son, were the person a surgeon?* We want to know if the surgeon will do excellent work, not whether the surgeon has done all that his teacher has suggested. When students tell me they really need an A, I do not know what to say. I believe what they really need is to do the best they can.

Students sometimes ask for suggestions for improving their work. I do my best, but the work is often limited from the start by matters of natural talent and inclination, or inappropriate judgment on their part. They want to be sure that if they do all the right things, they will get an A. But the work is in fact "good" and a B+ would be an accurate grade.

Now, I have no problem writing a letter of reference saying something like this: "X is devoted, hard-working, reliable, and will always deliver. My course was not the best place for him to demonstrate his natural talents, and so he received a B. Yet, and this is crucial, I would rather have X in my team of researchers than many of my students who have received A's."

47   *Plagiarism*

When papers are checked through a search engine or a plagiarism service, an uncredited source may be discovered. Often, substantial quantities of a paper or project are lifted from elsewhere, perhaps with a general attribution but with no quotation marks.

There are people who make money not from selling papers and projects but from web searches to find items similar to what you are looking for (namely, Google, Turnitin). The search people are very smart, very motivated, and quite powerful computationally. Moreover, other "borrowers" leave their work on the Net, so that even if you have borrowed from a secure source, there will be footprints left by those less careful.

Professors are encouraged to use these search services, and the services are becoming much more automatic – and competition will make them much more effective.

By the way, there was a time when students would say that they did not know this sort of borrowing was not OK. It was part of their culture. Think here of what happens in popular music and mixes, or in sermons. (See Joanna Demers, *Steal This Music,* 2006.) Or look at the wonderful literature on book publishing's early days. Quoting from scripture or authority is often done in speeches, without acknowledgment.

But, at least in schoolwork and in scholarship, such unacknowledged borrowing is a violation of academic integrity and a form of theft. Acknowledged borrowing with proper references is in fact the nature of scholarship.

48   *"Steal My Ideas!": Impact, Originality*

"Do not worry about people stealing your ideas. If your ideas are any good you'll have to ram them down people's throats." – Howard Aiken, computer pioneer, at Harvard.

I encounter doctoral students and masters students worried that someone will steal their ideas. I always say that they will be lucky if others are at all interested in their work and their ideas, and thank the Lord if they are, so to speak, stolen. The problem is that your precious ideas may well be lost, with rather less interesting ones triumphing. (W. Brian

Arthur so argues from the economics point of view: increasing returns to scale create nonlinear sub-optima – that is, the first-est with the most-est may well not be the best-est.)

Get allies and recruit others. Footnote them and they will do the same for you.

More generally, in a competitive environment in which increasing returns play a big role (when there are standards, when the boss will send discretionary funds to your project if it looks like a winner, and it looks like one if you can show it is of interest to a number of others), probably you are best off giving away the farm and then being in charge of the county. Be grateful that someone is interested in it at all – for the fate of most work is to be forgotten soon after it appears.

There are genuine concerns of the professor stealing your work. Go to work, write an article for a journal, and go it alone. A professor inspired by your work may or may not be in the business of hurting you – he may feel that he is advancing your career. Do not get involved with that. Rather, do your scholarly work, acknowledge the help of the professor (perhaps profusely), and publish. *No need to make enemies.* Typical acknowledgment: "When I wanted to study Joe Schmoe's work, I could find no supporters until I spoke with Professor Socrates Ataturk, who has been an abiding supporter since. I am grateful for his guidance." (If you come from a Latin culture, there are in fact even further things to be said, or in the case of Japanese and German, it has to do with the honorifics with which you refer to the professor.)

49   Excuses

People have multiple obligations these days, and they make choices about priorities. Students will tell me about the demands of their job, and so their need to adjust their attendance at class. Or, that they needed to attend their grandparent's funeral and could not get in the work. Or, they needed to get a paper in for another course and hence they are late with the materials for this one. My usual thought is, why not do the work for my course and be late in the other, or why not tell your employer about the demands of school? It is, I realize, a different era than when I was in college and graduate school (the early '60s). Students used to have jobs, at least some of them, but they knew school was the obvious priority. Given the sense many students have that they are customers (this is supported by many administrative models), and we are suppliers, and that the customer is king, the rest follows. I suspect they feel the same way about their neurosurgeons, but I do hope the neurosurgeon has a more serious commitment to them.

In any case, we become the folks they come to with special pleas. Maybe that is the way things ought to be. But, again, they really do not want us to treat them as idealized commercial and economic agents, our devotion to them being merely a matter of their paying tuition. Of course, actual customers would hope to be treated more seriously (in what is sometimes called an implicit contract).

I do not know what to do in this case. I do know what it represents, a phenomenon which is nowadays universal. It comes up at tenure or promotion times, where people want both the transactional judgment about each case (Do I meet the "hurdle"?) and the transcendent value associated with the promotion (I'm really special and worthy).

Students know you might well get fired or dressed down and publicly humiliated at a job for handing in work late – especially if your boss were a martinet. We do not do that at the university except perhaps within the football team. Put differently, would the coach of the football team find these excuses acceptable? I suspect not. So, perhaps it is clear what to do, at least if we want a university the football team will be proud of.

50 *Toward the End of the Semester*

1. Copyedit carefully. Make sure sentences are grammatical. Make sure they flow.

Read the paper out loud or have a friend read it. You will hear its awkwardness or its grammar problems, since it is likely you speak in grammatical English. This counsel may be harder for nonnative speakers of English, but usually it helps a lot.

2. Tell the reader how your material adds up. What is the punch line or the story you are trying to tell?

Read over what you have written. Write down the main points you make as you go along. This need not be long. Then, look at this shorter list and try to figure out what you are doing. This is exactly what I do when I find that I have written lots, but cannot figure out what I have done.

When you figure out what you have done, then you need to be sure that you state it up front, and that your paper is divided up so that the main points are featured along the way.

3. Do not ask for more time since you have other papers due and "you want to make this paper really good." The paper is due next week. That other papers are due suggests perhaps you ought to ask those instructors for a delay on them, rather than ask me. More to the point, you can make a much better paper with a long rest period. So I would wrap it up now, take my advice on the draft you submit, and then make it into a much better paper in a few weeks or few months. Delay is the road to disaster for a graduate student. Doing a good enough job is a secret to success. You can then make it better. "Expressing your ideas perfectly" is the road to doom. Of course, once you have submitted this draft, you can improve it further. But at least you have submitted the work.

In formal work, as in mathematics or theoretical science or computer science, you have to do a proper ("rigorous") job. But if you have organized the argument, it's time to submit the work. You will learn in time how much detail need be provided to convince the reader you've not made a mistake. (Perelman's 2002 preprints on the Poincaré Conjecture were surely schematic, but what was crucial was that he showed the path and how to do the hardest parts.)

51   *Doing the Scut Work*

I received the following: "As a student who works full-time as an executive, most often we find that time is our most precious commodity. As such, it becomes overwhelming to learn to navigate through the school's various libraries to conduct basic research. Is there a service that one can access where one can provide a listing of publications to be pulled by support staff? Convenience and access being the two factors needed. I apologize beforehand if you find my question outrageous, given that the journey to locate such items may be part of the experience/discipline required to conduct the research."

I wrote back: "There is no support staff to do this. (They used to be called 'wives,' but now the wives need support staffs and are bringing home the family income.) You might hire an undergraduate. Actually, learning to use resources is part of the doctoral training. And it is the surprises in search that prove crucial.

"Your question is natural for an executive. But in the university, there are only two ways you are an executive: you are an administrator, and then you do not do much if any research; or you are a honcho who has substantial research grants that allow you to hire personnel, and then you spend lots of your time applying for grants. The rest of us are grunts, retail grunts. Professors have graduate students working with them, but they cannot be working for them."

From a colleague: "Unless you like the smell of books and the feel of paper much of what needs to be done can be done remotely. (And more and more books are on the web, whether as Google Books, or on amazon. com.) The university has a library portal that students and faculty can use. There is no reason why this cannot be used to gain access to journals. Books are a different matter (as are photographs, government reports, and the like). But a good start on research can be done from the comfort of your home.

"There is a more important issue here. Students need to learn how to dig into the literature. Having someone else do it for you might be convenient, but there is no guarantee that they will find what you need to find. I cannot tell you how many times a student will come to me and say, 'there isn't anything written on this subject.' It usually takes me (with the student looking over my shoulder) a few minutes to begin to dig through the literature – and it often takes figuring out what the right search terms are – and guess what, there are publications on the topic. If you want to play in the big leagues – heck, even the minor leagues – you have to know how to 'field the articles.'

"One of the best quotes I ever came across came from a leading scholar, who said, 'you have to handle your own rats.' The point he was making was that you have to know your data (not just rely on your research assistant), you need to know the literature (and know it comprehensively and critically), and you need to be able to think on your own. Lots of things can be contracted out, but not this."

52   *The Future of Data and Methods – Concreteness:*
Computation, Cinematic Arts, Statistics and
Economics, and Talking to Your Rats

Computation has transformed the research enterprise: writing (word processing, LaTex for scientific papers), calculation and simulation, statistical analysis and more recently visualization of quantitative data, imaging, DNA and textual analysis, sensing using smartphones, and many impacts I do not imagine. Big data sets are ubiquitous, and there are challenges to discerning information in those sets.

Yet, *you still have to talk to your rats* (and not only handle your own rats, as in the previous section). And *you will need to listen to what the rats say*. In other words, in many fields scholars have a distant relationship to the people and institutions they are studying, usually through already available data sets or generating their own. They do very little fieldwork or archival work – rarely "talking to their rats," so to speak. So, you might study the financial markets, for which there are enormous amounts of data, but never talk to a bunch of traders or bankers or lawyers or dealmakers through systematic interviews. You have powerful economic and finance and institutional theories, your intuitions, and schematic or stylized models, and you test your hypotheses rigorously. But what if these people tell you their world works differently than you theorize? You might say that what counts is their behavior, not what they think they are doing.Still, it is likely worthwhile to do those systematic interviews, if only to be aware of that mismatch of behavior and self-image, and more likely to have a richer theoretical structure about behavior. And just because you have years of experience as a banker or a lawyer in the field does not mean your intuitions will be a good proxy for those interviews. (Of course, for physicists and the like, there is no way to interview atoms or electrons. But here good scientists say they try to think like an electron – that is, imagine their being an electron with the forces an electron is subject to. And they examine in great detail individual events, as in bubble chamber photographs of particle collisions, to be sure that their ways of cumulating that data reflect what is actually going on each time.)

More generally, a more concrete approach to research, talking to your rats and listening to them (people!), going deeper into the archives, studying the historical context of the production of art and literature, is likely to provide you with a comparative advantage over the rest of the scholarly community, those who are neither handling nor talking to their rats. There is a Mexican expression to the effect that if you tell me the donkey is grey, you ought to have some of its hairs in your hand.

Another approach is provided through what is now called the *cinematic arts and screen language,* what is obvious to any undergraduate student. The cinematic arts are now employed in much of scholarly inquiry: gaming simulation, visualization, story as the metaphor for argument in much of social science, interactive methods and graphical presentations in statistics, collaborative team work (in business), the screen as the locus of work (standard professor in his office or home), immersion in decision-making and in molecular/drug design, montage in an archive, multi-media, -screen, and -sensory inputs and our capacity to navigate simultaneous images and sources, total design as in a film or a play. "Motion pictures" in effect summarizes all of this. (See E. Daley, "Expanding the Concept of Literacy," *Educause,* March/April 2003, p. 33.)

Some of the crucial features of what might be called cinematic arts:
- the screen and screen language – visualization, hypertext and hyper-reference (this used to be called scholarship), many cuts on the world
- story and storytelling, narrative, point-of-view
- time-based media (including reading!)
- editing, the cut, montage
- ambience (or background)
- interactivity (even in statistical analysis)
- immersion (being inside a molecule)
- simulation, games (SimCity, agent-based modeling)
- multimedia, multi-modal, the sensorium (e.g., real estate development fly-throughs), in which media are always together (sound, vision, ambience [for taste, touch, smell])
- total environmental design (as in a movie, or a photograph by Jeff Wall)
- multiple screens, glimpse and glance, exploratory data analysis
- collaborative production, joint work

Of course, many of these fit nicely under the rubric of computation, but it's no longer about numbers or calculation.

53   Data

Someone wrote me: "I am in the data collection phase of the dissertation and I am having trouble coaxing the data that I need from the public agencies that supposedly should have it. [My response: Not surprising. They may be secretive, but more likely they do not have the time or energy to produce it.] When I finally get the data, it is often not properly formatted, columns are missing, legends or keys are absent, units are inconsistent. [Not unusual in any such effort. You'll need the cooperation of the people involved to help you interpret the data format. You might indicate that you can clean up their data for their own use. Also, you may be working on a problem for which they have a real interest. Persistence is essential. They have to see your work as serving their longer-term interest as well. In general you have to make your research design fit the data you have. All my colleagues who use quantitative data need to clean it up before being able to analyze it. This is the major part of the work. Coaxing data from others is part of what it means to be a successful researcher. In other words, all these seemingly secondary factors are in fact some of the main parts of the work. Most quantitative methods courses make it seem like your job is to analyze the data. That is 10 percent of the work.]"

54   Incompletes: For a Class, for Tenure

Today, now, write a detailed memo or draft or outline of the required project, without doing further research, sitting down at your keyboard. You can indicate places that might require further inquiry, but I would bet that you know already how those places will come out. You may discover that you have the work in hand, and with a bit more work you might avoid the Incomplete. You can give your draft/outline/memo to your instructor or promotion committee (proofread and spell-checked) and show where you are, so that the Incomplete is actually well earned – and you have something to work with when there is time.

The work required to produce this draft/memo/outline should take no more than one or two days, total, maybe three to four hours. The idea is to put together what you know and understand in such a way that you can move forward when you have more time. If you have a rough draft or an outline already, can you move it up one level with a day or two of work? If so, it might be ready to hand in. The idea is to make sure that when you return to the work, you are not paralyzed by fear, but rather energized by the work you know you can now do.

Now, if life (romance, family problems) or your psyche has totally deflated and all is beyond help, then tend to yourself, make sure others appreciate the gravity of your situation, and if possible do as much as you can of what I recommend here. You'll still need to get back to the work.

TWO

Writing (#55–95)

A. FUNDAMENTALS

55   *Writing and Progress*

Learn to write clear prose, with grammar and diction that do not call attention to your writing. It is perhaps remarkable that some doctoral students cannot write straightforward sentences and paragraphs, but it is unimaginable that they do not learn as soon as possible how to do much better. I am told by colleagues in the natural sciences, engineering, and mathematics that these problems are present in their students, too.

The novelist Stephen King, in his book *On Writing* (2000): sit down, regularly, write, hold off judgment, and keep on writing. Writing or art is a defense against life. He ends the book with an account of how he started writing again after a very serious automobile accident in which he was grievously hurt.

Greg Hise to a student: "I can't state strongly enough how important it is for you to get out in the field, right now. It's the equivalent of a historian getting into the archives. No matter how sound and interesting your question appears, it is just that, a question. It is a hunch, one informed by your reading (the literature) and theory, but a hunch (or hypothesis) none the less. Begin with a place that is convenient to where you live or work, but begin. Test your methods, see what you find, refine your questions. Your questions may change, the literature may be all wrong; you may wind up comparing at very different places than you anticipated.

You may find these generalizations faulty. This is precisely the point, and why we do research."

Now is the time to write a memo to yourself and your advisor about what you have done this past year and what you are planning to do in the next year. It is time to sign up to give a presentation at an appropriate scholarly meeting, or if it is too late, to be sure to do so next time around. Organize a session with some of the best-known people in the field (you might present too, or be the session chair) – the trick is to figure out some topic about which they will want to talk. And you will have to ask them, so start with someone you already know.

To the field, to the writing desk, to the meeting.

56 Writing a Dissertation Is Chopping Down a Forest, Tree by Tree

Create space (on weekends, late at night, early in the day) to work on your dissertation, and follow through, though it's not always easy. Set deadlines for deliverables. Divide the project into smaller units. Chapters, sections, subsections. If you do each part, even close to its deadline, you will have a rough draft that you can then divide into parts for revision. Do not set unrealistic goals, too large units.

If the university gives you a fellowship, it is expected that you will devote yourself to your studies. The major cost of doctoral education is forgone income, and so the idea is to get through as soon as possible, so that you can go on to your next position.

57 Dissertation Proposals and Papers

1. Make sure it is easy to find your way around in a paper. Use subheads, and make sure that they make sense to someone who has not read the paper through. Make sure the first page or two is absolutely clear – and gives away what you plan to do and the main points of your paper. (Often, I discover that the conclusion is just what should be up front.)

2. Use simple typographic conventions. The following are mine, and I find them useful. They are old-fashioned, but, I think, still good.

- Use a 12-point type, something simple and easy to read.
- Double-space everything. Use one-inch margins all around.
- All paragraphs should be indented (rather than block).
- No need to skip an extra line between paragraphs.
- Skip a line between sections, and underline the section headings.

3. Sections should not be so long that I get lost in them. Probably a section that is 10 pages long in a 20-page paper is too long, but 10 pages might be fine for a 75-page chapter.

Your headings and subheadings should make up an outline (albeit rough) of the paper.

4. And if you want comments from people, put your e-mail address on the first page, and your telephone number as well.

58   *Forced Evolution*

During each of the four consecutive days in an intensive course, we discuss student papers, outlining them once more that day. Each day, including the first (they have even had time to do some reading or at least library browsing), there is a revised outline available at the beginning of class. Hence, at the end of four days we have gone through four versions, three of which are revisions.

Following E. H. Land, I call this "forced evolution." Land's idea was that you did not go home each day unless you tested out your ideas, and tested the next stage. It is better to find out now, rather than later. Think of ways of finding out vulnerabilities, and check them out now. If you have a bright idea, do it today.

Of course, you may need some help to do this. You are going to either do experiments, or go to the library, or do some bit of fieldwork, or develop an argument or a proof. And you may need a critic to help you think about where to go next.

59   *Setting the Agenda: Independence*

Write down what you are thinking, even if only in brief notes. Write yourself a memo outlining your current project, so far. If you are making a professional phone call, write down a brief list of points you need to get through. For a meeting, bring along a copy of such a list, give copies to the meeting, and go through it.

I want to teach you to be independent: how to be taken seriously; to have most of the resources to work out what you need to do. Combine your independent resources with the talents of others, when all of you are primed and have done your homework (written it down, practiced, shaped up).

60   *Storytelling and Focus*

One way to convince people is to involve them in a story (even for a mathematics paper), with all the detail you can muster. Stories get behind our defenses, balance yet incorporate contradictory sentiments and forces, give motivation to abstractions. Stories allow you to reconfigure your life or enterprise so that you can focus on what counts rather than on everything. The secret of moving forward, almost always, is not how to do everything, but how to do one or two things, and realize that some things should not be done or attended to. My files will never be organized, and dust accumulates behind my refrigerator.

61   *Using Design Skills to Write Research Papers*

In architecture school, students learn how to take a problem, figure out how to conceive it, and do a rough version followed by more detailed and revised versions, all the while breaking down the problem into doable parts and reconceiving it. The actual sketches, models, and drawings are the occasion for revisions and for seeing the meaning of what they are doing. And having done that revision, they again see what they are doing.

Moreover, they learn that there are real deadlines, and that a good enough version may be all that you have time for. You cannot spend all your time on conception, for the execution needs lots of time (hence the all-nighters). And you will be criticized along the way, and that criticism is just what you need to do a better job, no matter how painful it is. Some of the time the criticism is cruel and mean, but often there is a truth there.

62   Draw a Target around Where Your Arrow Hits

If you want to appear to be a focused thinker, draw a target around where your arrow hits. You do a project (your arrow), guided by whatever principles and expectations you may have. After you have done the work, review it and find out what you have really done, what is interesting about the work. Then write an introduction (this is the target) that says what you will do. Your project now seems as if it worked out perfectly.

63   Writing Advice

1. The passive voice does not work well for most of your writing. Moreover, you are not likely to be able to manage sentences that are ten lines long, especially if the main point is, German-like, sitting at the end of the ten lines.

2. Diction, your choice of words, gets in your way. Choose simple clear prose. If you want to use a technical term, define it. Fancy words usually defeat most writing.

3. Use subheads. Most of us cannot write more than five to eight pages without needing subheads to guide the reader. Make sure the pages are numbered. You ought to staple together papers under, say, 40 pages.

4. Make sure that if I only read the front page of your paper, I can find out what it is about and what you are claiming (your contribution).

5. Do not use cheap examples. (Are my references to oncoming trucks and to cows needing to be milked cheap?) You need to have specific examples, ones for which you have worked hard to gain evidence, if your claims are going to be taken seriously.

6. The structure of your paper should be apparent from the beginning. Not only the subheads, but how you number sections and subsections, and what you say in the first page or so all guide the reader as to what to expect.

7. Spell-check, always.

8. Sources: In journalistic style, one might say, "According to Joan Smith, scholar of meat at the University of Chicago . . . ," but for scholarly purposes, one would say, "Meat is the most eaten protein (Smith 1992)."

Of course, if you are studying a great thinker, then you will refer to them by name directly. *But professors are in general not great thinkers or great whatevers.*

9. Have a colleague read your paper before you submit it. Fix any problems.

64 *The Writing Path*

1. Plan and draft – see #9 below.
   · Submit (Usual Default).
Or, *Superior Default:*
   · Read over.
   · Fix pages 1 and 2, so they are not shockingly bad.
   · Use subheads to give it structure.
   · Fix first sentence of each section so it is not shockingly bad.
   · Spell-check.
   · Submit.
Or, *Much Superior Default:* Go on to #2–8.

2. Reread and outline what you have done already, and revise outline.

3. Cut and paste, divide into parts, so that it now comports with revised outline.

4. Read it over. Go back to #2 and #3 if it does not hold together. If it is more or less OK, go to #5.

5. Copyedit for sentences, diction (choice of words), topic sentences in paragraphs, paragraphs holding together.

6. Spell-check.

7. Submit – but see #8.

8. Serious work: Put aside for a week or even a day. Reread and do what is needed to make better.

9. A major problem early on is the morass of materials you have, the sense of being overwhelmed. So, put aside the morass, and write an outline of the dissertation or paper "out of your head." It can be a list of

chapters, or subsections of a paper. If need be, casually go through the materials, and then write. The basic idea is to embed yourself into the material, and then step away and organize it, and then go back in with your organization in mind and use the material to draft.

This list is neither final nor perfect. Its main job is to free you of the anxiety of keeping it all in your head. Type up the outline, stick it on the wall, and look at it in moments of anxiety and need. Now, do the same for each part (chapter, subhead). Sort your material into chapter parts or section parts.

65   *More Writing Advice*

1. If you use maps and photos, it will often be useful to give dates of the maps or photos, and scales for maps. This is especially the case if your scales change. Again, it is helpful if the orientation of all maps can be the same.

You are now layout artists in your papers when you combine maps and pictures and text. In general, put the materials adjacent to where they are discussed. If you choose to have figures in the back, be sure to number them and then refer to them by number. Make sure an overview map is available early on. Show people what they are supposed to notice. Label, and use arrows and encirclement to focus the reader's attention.

2. Do not use contractions in professional work. This way you will not confuse *it's* and *its*.

3. Do not use exclamation points (!).

4. Again, page 1 ought to be inviting and give away the whole story. In fact, for many of your papers the best paragraph is the last, and it ought to be first.

5. If you cannot properly use *that, which,* and *who,* break up your sentences into two parts.

6. Detail and specifics make for much more convincing essays.

7. Copyedit! Please! (Note how I used exclamation points here, the first time as in an imperative, the second as in a supplicant expression. But the exclamation points are not necessary, even here.)

8. In English, capital letters are used for proper names. So if you are referring to the Bunker Hill steps, you have a lowercase since *Bunker Hill* just modifies *steps*. But if you refer to Bunker Hills Steps, you are referring to a place as such.

9. You too often bury your ideas behind awkward prose, and leave the punch line for the end, when the reader is least under your control.

10. The semi-shiny paper you use if you are printing photographs makes it hard to read text. In the future you may want to consider this when handing in longer papers.

11. Please indent paragraphs, rather than skip a line between paragraphs.

12. Do not right-justify. Your right margin should be ragged.

13. When you copyedit, you need to be on the lookout for often-repeated words in adjacent sentences. This guideline does not apply to all such words, but often it is a matter of being aware that I have used *often* in these adjacent sentences.

14. It's = it is; its = possessive form. I know that your schoolteachers may well have missed this.

15. Sentences need to be clear about what the referents are pointing to (what does a *this* refer to, for example). In general, you want to be sure that the sentence is readily understood, even if a more complex sentence is grammatically correct. People should be able to read what you write without stopping to parse the sentence.

16. If English is not your native mode of working and writing, do not try to think in terms of your native language and then translate into English. Better to use simple sentences, ones that might feel primitive in your native language. Clarity and flow are worth a lot.

17. I keep finding spelling mistakes that I imagine most spell-checkers will catch. And it is sometimes (if not often) clear that no one has proofread your paper, or that maybe you did a draft and then marked it up and rewrote it and then did not check it over again. If you need to write something that is only two or three pages (or even one page), if you are to have the time to revise and rewrite, then write less but make it right and good.

66   *The Basics*

Spell-check and proofread anything you give to others – even memos or brief proposals. Make sure there is enough ink in your inkjet printer, the paper is OK, and even the stapling is OK. Why set yourself up?

Also, no excuses. You are, for better or worse, almost always being observed and judged.

Finish your draft tonight. Put it aside for a day or two. Then revise. I sometimes make the mistake of sending out a manuscript too soon, but I do not send out a first draft, ever.

I hope none of my advice is needed by any of you. (I know I need it.) I surely do not want to offend by suggesting that you are guilty of a problem. If the advice does not apply or seems wrong, you are welcome to follow another path.

67   *Usage Manuals*

If your *that*s and *which*es are being conflated, or you just like to see how language is coded so that it can do wondrous work, usage manuals are the places to see it all explained. For example, *collide* requires that both objects be moving – you can't collide with an abutment.

There's *Fowler's Modern English Usage,* and the adapted version *Modern American Usage,* and the *New York Times Manual of Style and Usage.* And there is the *Chicago Manual of Style,* which is rather more geared to the demands of scholarship and technical writing.

68   *PowerPoint vs. Analytical Writing*

Thomas Ricks points out in *Fiasco,* his 2007 book on the Iraq War, that in the Rumsfeld Pentagon PowerPoint presentations were passed down as war plans. It drove the actual planners crazy, since so much was left out, so much could be avoided or not thought out. Analytical narrative writing demands a level of coherence that most PowerPoint does not aim to deliver. Thinking things through, writing them out, is almost always the minimum needed to be sure that what you are saying makes sense. Publication, with its editing and peer reviewing, makes for better writing.

69   *Rewriting*

I thought some of you might be interested in what I did today. I have a book coming out. I am now preparing the manuscript so it can go to press:

1. Writing for permission to reprint parts of my own articles.

2. Writing for permission and black-and-white glossies for pictures I want to use. Also, preparing to have some diagrams drawn.

3. Making sure that everything in my bibliography coincides in detail with the endnotes. Is there a book I refer to in the notes that is not in the bibliography? And of course filling in all the lacunae in my references – dates, pages, spellings. And they had better be the same in the various references in the text.

4. Double-spacing everything. That includes the notes, but I had to figure out how to make this word processor do what I wanted.

5. Finding out who holds the copyright to some photograph I want to use.

6. Finding a passage in the Hebrew Bible I am using, largely in this case by looking at other places (Google) which led me to it.

7. Making sure the bibliography and notes are in proper form. Nowadays with publishers often setting type directly from your digital file, you have a larger obligation, even if there is a good copy editor.

8. Doing the Author's Questionnaire next – to help them sell the book. Then there will be those diagrams, and waiting to hear about the permissions.

9. And this is the fifth 90 percent of the work. (Recall that the book had to be written, and rewritten, N times. And I needed to find a publisher.)

Everyone who writes a book that is published does all of this, and more. By the way, if the book is to come out, all of this work is not such a burden, but in a way a delight.

70 *Writing So Your Work Is Accepted for Publication*

1. Always reread and edit before submitting. Long and fancy sentences, with highfalutin words, usually do not work – at least no more than wearing your uncle's tuxedo to class or your aunt's wedding dress to the first day at a new job.

2. Integrity: besides the usual academic integrity, there are other issues. If you have no sympathy for a position or a group of people, you are likely to show your hostility and distaste. You will do better, at least in the academic/scholarly context, to be sympathetic and show how the other positions or people might be sensibly motivated and credible (especially if you think they are wrong).

3. Again, it is likely that the editor or reader or referee is also reading tens of similar pieces of work. If they can't figure out what is going on in the first paragraph or page, you are in trouble.

4. When you submit papers to journals, if they accept your article subject to revision, in general write back immediately that you will do the revisions. Then do them soon (the editor might die or retire if you wait too long), and get it back to the editor. If you do not follow the advice about revision, you had better offer airtight reasons for not doing so.

71 *Editing Your Book Manuscript*

You have a book manuscript that needs to be edited.

· Put the manuscript in a loose-leaf binder.
· Separate the chapters with dividers.
· If you rewrite a section or reorganize, just replace those pages.
· Outline the book, and perhaps you can see what
   needs to be fixed or put in a different order.
· Do not worry about details at this stage. Note them in
   the margin, but your problem at this stage is to make
   the manuscript less repulsive and confusing.
· I work with hard copy, not the screen. For me, these
   are not screen problems. They require that I be able
   to heft sections. Your practice may differ.
· Use different colors of pencil to mark revisions,
   the latest ones in a new color.

· Do not worry if you think it is the worst thing ever done. It may be, but you do not know now.
· You are *not* allowed to look up things, check references, go to the library for scholarly purposes – at least now. Make a list of problems.

72 Fixing Your Book Manuscript

If you are lucky, you will have the benefit of a copy editor who cleans sentences, makes things flow. Nowadays, many publishers are beginning to ask for camera-ready copy, and do not provide copyediting.

In the last few days I have gone through a small mountain of stuff I need to read to be ready to rewrite a manuscript, taking notes on what seemed most important. Now I have a book manuscript in front of me, plus a much smaller pile of stuff I will need to incorporate into the text. What I have is a loose-leaf notebook with the manuscript plus my pages of notes for improvement, keyed to the chapters, plus a list of tasks (checking references, getting diagrams drawn, and permissions for pictures and quotes).

At the same time, I hear that a grant I have applied for has not come through. Perhaps there were competing interests, perhaps I lost out in a bureaucratic argument among board members, perhaps it was not good enough. I am disappointed, of course, but it helps that I am doing this work now. In a few days I will put myself together and continue on another grant application – I have lots of time before the deadline. (This book had earlier been found unsuitable – that is, rejected – by between six and eight presses, some of which had indicated keen interest in the past – but editors moved on, or the manuscript was not what they really wanted.)

73 What Is This Paper About?

It should be easy to find out just what is the contribution of a paper.

1. What did you do? How did you find out? How extensive were your analyses and fieldwork? What did you prove or discover or analyze?

2. What is your claim, your contribution to the ongoing research enterprise? That claim has to be said in the plainest language, independent of theoretical baggage or technical qualifiers (all of which are necessary, somewhere else in the paper).

3. And, how does what you did connect with your claims? For example, "In a photographic survey of over 200 industrial and manufacturing firms and sites within Los Angeles, what is most striking in this corpus of 10,000 images is the pervasive presence of manufacturing and industrial processing throughout the region in a wide variety of industrial classifications." The title of the paper might be, "Los Angeles: Still Defined by the Second Industrial Revolution." The numbers 200 and 10,000 say that this guy has done lots of fieldwork. Now there will be lots of theorizing drawn from French and German sources, stuff on Fordism and industry, plus a good deal of history and geography, not to speak of justifications for a photographic survey, for systematic surveys. But the main point is conveyed by that first sentence.

A reader should know what you have done and what you are claiming by the end of the first paragraph. The title must give away the whole story, not be oblique or just cute or a tease.

74 *The Big Idea, Lessons, Lists*

You've done a first draft of your paper. What next?

What is the big idea(s)? Very likely you have stated it only in the last paragraph, if at all. You need to reread what you have written. *What is the Big Idea?* Make sure that that Idea is stated in the first paragraph, as well as elsewhere.

Are there *Lessons* to be learned from your work? As with the Big Idea, you want to give away the Lessons early. You may need to reread your paper several times to discover the Lesson, if there even is one.

If you have surveyed a subject you may have a *List of Points.* Is that list clear, or is it so blended into the text that a casual reader might miss it? Use italics and subheads to make sure all readers get these main points.

Reorganize your paper so that the Big Idea, the Lessons, and the Points stand out.

Look for stuff you have left out.

B. BOTTOM LINE UP FRONT

75   Bottom Line Up Front = BLUF

I gather there is a principle in writing Military Intelligence Digests:
BLUF, Bottom Line Up Front. These are single-spaced, one-page memos
for senior decision-makers. And the main point has to be up front, even
for a short memo.

Begin with a bang, the main point, the stuff that you want people
to take home.

· If you talk about an area, you probably want
  a map at the beginning of the paper.
· You need to organize your report into parts, parts that are well
  defined. I want to be able to scan and find the relevant parts easily.

A good first sentence is golden. It should give away the main point of
a proposal.

76   *If You Can't Say It in Three Sentences, You Do Not Know What Your Script Is About*

There is a nice analogy between doing scholarly work you want others to
read and writing a movie script that you want to sell to producers. In an
online column, "Creating Bomb-Proof Loglines" (www.screenplayers
.net/loglines.html), Lenore Wright says:

> In some situations, loglines work better as a sales tool than screenplays do.
> Agents and producers [and editors] look for easy outs when dealing with
> unproduced writers. Loglines provide LESS for them to say no to than a detailed
> synopsis or a complete script does. This can be a plus.

The logline introduces the story to them, offering a taste of the movie
without forcing them to devour the whole script.

As an example of a logline for a character-driven drama, Wright suggests the following for *Rain Man:*

> A self-centered hotshot returns home for his father's funeral and learns the
> family inheritance goes to an autistic brother he never knew he had. The hotshot
> kidnaps this older brother and drives him cross-country hoping to gain his
> confidence and get control of the family money. The journey reveals an unusual

dimension to the brother's autism that sparks their relationship and unlocks a dramatic childhood secret that changes everything.

Here is a logline for a plot-driven comedy, *Some Like It Hot:*

Two male musicians accidentally witness the St. Valentine's Day massacre; to elude the mobsters who pursue them, they dress in drag and join an all-girl band headed for Miami. One of them falls for a sexy singer and poses as a Miami playboy so he can woo her; his pal has to dodge the amorous advances of the nearsighted Miami playboy he impersonates. Love conquers all – till the mobsters show up at the same Miami resort for a convention.

Who wouldn't want to read that script?
Checklist for your logline:
· Reveal the star's situation
· Reveal the important complications
· Describe the action the star takes
· Describe the star's crisis decision
· Hint at the climax – the danger, the 'showdown'
· Hint at the star's potential transformation
· Identify sizzle: sex, greed, humor, danger, thrills, satisfaction
· Identify genre
· Keep it to three sentences
· Use present tense

How can you pack all that into three sentences? If you think of your logline as a commercial for the movie you've seen in your head as you've been writing the script, then you'll breathe life and personality into those three sentences.

77   *The First Sentence Should Give Away the Whole Story; If Not, Do It by the Second*

I've just done that in the above title.

Most professional writing is for a busy audience: bosses, clients, community members, other scholars. They have lots to read and do. Or, as a lawyer friend told me: Do not assume the judge will read past the first few pages of the brief.

In your first paragraph, give away your main point. Do not promise, do not motivate (yet), do not tell me what you are going to do. Just tell me what you are sure you want me to know or do. Often, you discover this main point while drafting your memo or essay or article. I tend to discover the crucial sentence or paragraph in the conclusion or somewhere about three pages into the piece. Then I put it up front. This means you have to draft and redraft. Finally, you have *Permission to Enumerate, Subhead, and to Use Topic Sentences.* If you have several main points, number them. If you have several divisions of your piece, use subheads. And each section or division should begin with its main point: People should be able to read your piece in outline. I am told that is how students are taught to write legal briefs.

By the way, this is also good advice for talks and informative speeches. Tell me your findings in the first five minutes – before I doze off. I want to know then, not in the last three minutes of the talk. No promises, no teasers. Give it all away.

None of this applies necessarily to love letters, novels, or *New Yorker* essays.

78   *The Takeaway*

1. By the end of the first manuscript page, it should be clear what the paper is about, and the nature of its contribution. Moreover, by the end of the second page, I should know exactly what I need to take away from reading the paper. If I read no more of the paper, I will not be surprised by what you claim or find.

2. The research literature and the relevant argument might well be summarized in two or three paragraphs, with plenty of footnotes. Scholarship assumes that the reader is aware of the literature. Now, if you are taking apart another paper or argument, you might dwell on previous contributions, but in this case your contribution is that taking-apart.

3. Make each of your papers substantial, well worked out, developed. A bright idea demands lots of work if it is to become articulated and influential. I should not have to ask, where's the beef?

4. I want to know what the paper is about and what the takeaway is. I really do. So give it to me in the title. Most dissertation titles these days tell you virtually nothing about the dissertation's content. Yet the title could be sufficiently informative that search engines will find it if

appropriate, and researchers will know what is the main point of the dissertation. This is true of book titles, article titles, and most e-mail subject lines.

Bad: Poodles and Popery: Dogs, Ethnicity, and Neighborhood Culture

Awful: Poodles, Popery, and Property

Good: Residents' Dog Breeds Correlate with Neighborhood Characteristics and Ideologies

Better: Neighborhood Characteristics and Ideologies Extend to the Breeds of Their Residents' Pets

5. As for floods of e-mail: I do not open e-mail when the subject is cute or short or tells me to "update your whatever." My spam filter takes care of lots of the rest. I find I end up paying attention to less than one-tenth of the posters. Give away the whole story in the subject line (not a teaser). Maybe *all* you have to say is the subject line. Rather than links or attachments, paste the content into the message.

6. Again: Tell me the Story: If you have three main points, they should be in that first paragraph.

7. When you write something or prepare a presentation, whether it be a report, a memo, a love letter, or a speech – make a rough outline before you start drafting. You can start by listing your main points, then order them. You can attach to each item various sub-points or illustrations. Then when you write you can do so with confidence. It's also much easier. When you have a draft, let it sit for a bit, and then figure out if it flows appropriately.

8. Bullets (points) do not get through the Kevlar of most readers.

79   *"The Layout Was Hard on the Eyes"*

The acquisition editor of a university press that is considering a manuscript of mine mentioned in our conversation that "the layout of the manuscript was hard on the eyes." Of course there were other problems, but it matters if readers can read the manuscript readily with little strain.

80 *Why Papers Are Immediately*
Returned and Rejected by Journals

1. The paper is not appropriate for the journal. Check back issues to see if it fits. Is the paper insufficiently scholarly for this journal?

2. The paper is in fact a term paper that has not been revised. If you are early in your career, you ought to have a more senior colleague read your work before you send it out. Or, the paper is a first draft by a great person in the field – and it is embarrassing to read it.

3. It is difficult to find out what the contribution is. Be sure the contribution is clearly stated up front. The title should give it all away.

4. It is methodologically problematic.

5. You insult earlier authors, or other people.

6. The grammar is awful and the sentences are opaque. Readers cannot figure it out.

7. The paper is much too long given the average length of papers in the journal, at least absent of a serious justification for the extra material.

8. There are lots of stupid reasons: You have not credited previous work (some of which might be by a reader). You did not follow the recommended format for journal submissions. Your copying is awful. There are missing pages.

C. RESEARCH

81 *Reviewing the Research Literature*

1. The academic literature is a web, where any single contribution is linked to predecessors' work and is discussed in successors' work. This is indicated by notes (footnotes, endnotes), and the fetish we make of proper bibliographic form. It is in effect a great dialectical conversation. Moreover, that literature is a "graded" literature, with peer review almost always being the gateway to being included in it, and some venues (journals or publishers) generally recognized as more prestigious, reliable, and rigorous. Of course, very strong work may appear in less highly graded venues, and weaker work may make it into the top venues.

The lay literature is very different in its grading, and in general does not have the authority of the research literature. A book (that is, that physical object) is no guarantee of its being authoritative.

2. At any time, looking back, you can describe the lay of this webland, the main themes and arguments that have motivated a field. Often, very often in fact, there are surveys of the literature that provide some of this scholarly geography. Consult past dissertations; scan the library shelves in your area of interest. Key references may be pre-computer and not appear on websites at all.

3. There are particularly significant contributions to the conversation, perhaps not a single work but a sequence of papers (or a book), that epitomize past arguments and contributions and reset the discussion. Sometimes they are survey works; sometimes they are monographic studies.

4. A survey of the literature describes a scholarly geography, relevant to your own particular research problem. Likely, you will borrow from past surveys, rethink the geography from your particular perspective, feature some of the main conversations and describe the kinds of disagreement they contain, and say where we stand now. You'll still need expert experienced advice. The issue is not which sources to include, but which are more reliable.

82　Boring Work

Recently, I went through perhaps 2,000 of my photographs to make sure they were properly indexed and labeled, and selected a smaller group for a project. Most of the work required scrupulous care (wearing white cotton gloves) and being sure I was clear about what was what, and that everything was in order. Much of (research) work is not exciting, the greatest pleasure being when it is completed. I had resisted doing this indexing for a long time, but once started it did not take so long (four days), and I was glad to have done it. Of course, I should have done all of this along the way. Much of our work just has to be done; that's it.

83   *Craftsmanship and Film Editing*

Film editors create pacing, plot, and character out of raw material. Now, it is difficult to tell any story, and the facts and theories and data and fieldwork rarely fit together easily – and it is a great achievement to put them together into a story or a cogent argument. A film is such an achievement. To be able to find two such stories from the same raw stock is rare – usually what happens is that there are varying emphases on the material, and varying degrees of willingness to accept certain kinds of data and observations. To achieve a synthesis of different good arguments, showing how each accommodates the other, is a very fine achievement. To show that others have erred in their evidence and argument is a standard scholarly move. Of course, editors or scholars have to be careful, meticulously so, when they might be cutting out 80 percent, at least, of the film stock they get from the director, or maybe 90 percent of their data, usually more, and have to keep track of it all.

Film editors are part of a team endeavor. One editor says that *if you are going to make any changes or improvements, you have got to do it now.* If you leave it for later, then a two-minute job may well take impossibly long. All sorts of other members of the team (sound, prints, etc.) may well get hold of the material, and if you change it later the amount of work by others becomes much too large.

84   *Rereading Is Illuminating*

I was just rereading an article I have read several times. It is quite technical, and I skip around each time on each reading, although not over the same places. I had just drafted a chapter, and knew I had to go back to be sure that what I said about the article was correct, not so much in detail as in my general claims. Now, I have been thinking of the problems related to the article for a while. I am more aware of the issues than earlier, and now more aware of what I do not understand. And so when I reread it now, suddenly all sorts of stuff that I missed is now relevant, and I can see better what's up.

Thinkers are deep, meaning that what they say reflects lots of work and thought often presented offhandedly because they themselves finally understood something before writing. These are technical poems, not unlike the literature (poems, novels) that you were told to read carefully for hidden meanings when you were in high school and college.

D. PUBLISHING

85 *Grammar-Checking*

I am just finishing a book manuscript, and I have to hand in camera-ready copy to the publisher. No copyediting by the publisher. This is not good, but it is standard in the field I am publishing in, it seems. In any case, I took advantage of Word's grammar-checker. It proved helpful for "that/ which," and a few other problems. It also proved unhelpful, and much of its advice was not appropriate for my purposes.

86 *Publishing Your Dissertation Work*

Graduate students are so exhausted toward the end, they do not appreciate how important it is to publish quickly the results of their dissertation research. There is competition, and you want to be there first-est with the most-est. You don't want to publish the third of this year's books on the War of 1812 and cotton production. Also, if you plan an academic career, you must publish it (it is likely your only major research asset at this point). The major problems are:

1. Getting it ready to submit. If you plan to convert the chapters to articles, do one at a time. If it is a book manuscript, you usually cannot submit your dissertation without its being stripped of its dissertation apparatus (especially that survey of the literature). In any case, you will send a letter to an editor (preferably someone your advisor or your committee member knows; perhaps they can even write a letter on your behalf), with a summary, a sense of its market and competition, and perhaps a chapter.

2. Getting rejected, more than a few times. You are just starting out. You will make mistakes, the work will need improvement, and you do

not know the terrain. Senior professors get rejected, often lots if they take risks or publish in blind-refereed journals. Figure out where to go next, and send it out once more. You may learn lots from the referees' comments. If the editor wants you to revise and resubmit, do it now. Maybe the editor will die, retire, or change their mind.

Again: You will get rejected, more than a few times. Those who thrive in our business view this as a fact. Of course, you need good advice about the quality of your work, and the appropriate journals, and what you need to do to fix your work. If your advisor is not of any use, find someone who is. Never send out anything unless it has been read by two friends who can tell you the truth.

Again: *You will get rejected. But no one cares about that.* What they only notice, in the end, are the articles or books you have published, that they have read and learned from. They will wonder how you did all that work. In some fields the rejection rates are 90 percent; in others they are more like 20 percent.

3. You will get discouraged. Take the day off. Tomorrow you will be able to take on the problems with a clear head. This is lonely, often backbreaking work, with long-term payoffs that are uncertain. It is farming on the plains. If you do not like doing it, find another profession.

87   Collaboration

"You can make a lot of mistakes individually. But by collaboration, you eliminate a lot of dumb errors." – Epidemiologist Warren Winkelstein, *New York Times,* 6 August 2012, p. B10.

"People should work on their own problems." – Physicist P. A. M. Dirac, in G. Farmelo, *The Strangest Man,* 2007, p. 163.

1. Much real work in the actual world depends on teams, and with good leadership and tasking-out, things can work well.

2. There are likely to be some free-riders in any project. You must get the project done, and done well, no matter what. I have yet to hear a good excuse for not doing your part, and for not doing whatever else need be done.

3. In Wall Street firms, where teams of people make a deal go through, senior partners make an enormous effort to figure out who did what, who

just hung around ("touched" the deal). The annual bonuses have to be fair so that incentives work.

4. If you find that you cannot work in a team, and need to work alone, you need to find a job that allows this. By the way, Dirac may have been a loner, but he worked within a local and international community of physicists, especially during the development of quantum mechanics (1925–1935).

88   Substantial Contributions

Editors are seeing more early drafts of papers being submitted to journals. By "early," I mean less than fully polished papers, or papers by graduate students and junior faculty that have not been gone over and criticized by more senior researchers, as well as papers that might have been composed for courses or conferences but not thoroughly rewritten. Sloppy papers by senior researchers are also not so uncommon. The consequence is that more papers are rejected out of hand, or that revise-and-resubmit does not lead to acceptance.

While we now demand that the new junior faculty we hire have published some articles, my suspicion is that more energy ought to go into finishing the dissertation earlier, and perhaps writing one decisive and careful article setting forth the achievement of that research.

Similar issues come up in conference presentations. It would help if they represented substantial amounts of research. I realize there are enormous benefits to presenting at meetings – you get better known, people find out what is going on, your travel is paid for. But right now many researchers do not realize how much they are penalized for substandard work, a paper presentation which is then viewed as a waste by the people who got stuck in the room and could not leave.

What to do? Test out your drafts on senior colleagues. Do two or three drafts, at least. Let a paper sit in a drawer for a month, and then revise. And if you are senior, have your junior colleagues read over your papers – they know better than anyone what is hot at the moment, what is warmed over. You really do not want to have people avoiding your papers or your talks because they have tasted them before and found them lacking in nutritive value.

Many years ago, I was talking to a friend who was a member of a department replete with Nobel Prize winners. He said that his department asked about *the candidate's contributions,* not publications. In other words, having lots of publications that do not add up to a distinctive contribution is a no-go.

In any case, I now always ask, *what is the contribution of this work?* Does it advance the field? Is it significant? Does it add up to a coherent research program? What are the likely future contributions? Seventeen articles, each of which is epsilon (infinitesimal) in contribution, equal 17 epsilons which equal to zero in the end (remember when you studied deltas and epsilons in calculus).

When people write letters for promotion and tenure, what provosts in research universities are looking for is the nature of the contribution of the work. The problem with counting is that if we have lots of epsilons and we are told all about them, all it means is that the epsilons are perhaps doubly valuable. But in the end, two epsilons equal zero. On the other hand, there are those people, few in number to be sure, who write one article which then changes a field. If it looks like they might do this regularly, wow! (Again, Dirac.)

89 *Reviewers' Reports, Appropriate Journals, and Colleagues' Pre-Reviews*

If you submit a paper or a book manuscript, there will be referee reports on your work. Sometimes those reviews are wonderfully helpful, sometimes they are neutral, and more often than is desirable, they may be insulting and hurtful or misunderstanding or nitpicky or pushing you in peculiar directions.

Put the review aside for a few days. Then read it over and find the substantive comments. Make a list, triaged into *yes, maybe, probably not,* and in replying to the editor you need only summarize that list. Do not send back insult, hurt, or anger. If you know who wrote the hurtful stuff, do not get mad. You may not feel above it all, but you must give that impression.

In general, editors should not forward hurtful reviews to authors but summarize them in a more neutral manner. But that does not occur often enough. Your job is to be substantively responsive, now. Getting even can wait – your time will come.

You want to write a response that begins:

"I am grateful for the readers' reports, and for their many insightful suggestions. The following suggestions are right on, and I will revise while taking them into account. [Include here the middle ones of your triage. Do not argue with them.]

"The following suggestions are a bit more problematic for me. I believe that I have been misunderstood in some cases, and that means I must rewrite to make my position clearer to the reader. In others, the suggestions seem to be for a book very different than I planned, and I want to discuss why I am reluctant to follow them. On the other hand, it is important that the reader understand my choices, and that means there need to be revisions in the preface and elsewhere in the manuscript. [Here outline those revisions.]

"A scholarly community depends on the careful regard we have for each other's work. Thank you for your attention to my paper. Sincerely yours, . . ."

Do not expect to get away with not revising the manuscript as you have promised, and do not expect to have them like the manuscript just as you sent it. This is a negotiation where tact, responsiveness, and quick turnaround will help.

Comments that are wrongheaded, mean, obnoxious, and cruel are best passed over. If they are from a commentator at a meeting, the first thing you do when you reply is to be grateful for their careful attention. You then focus on the main issues, ignore all the nonsense, and do your best to respond to them. If you think a major revision of your position is called for, then acknowledge that. And at the end of the session, shake hands with the critics, and take them out for a drink or a walk. Most peevish critics are so mean and awful because they feel ignored. Once you pay attention to them, they might well become your advocates. ("Joe gave a paper in 1987, my comments were harsh, he took them into account and produced a much better paper, and I think his subsequent work has been superb.") *Power lies in graciousness, in generosity, and in taking charge of what is going on.*

If you are just starting out, get some guidance about the appropriate journals for your work, appropriate publishers for your book. Of course, you want to publish in the strongest venues, but the work needs to be up to their standards and demands, some of which are not about quality but about length, subject matter, degree of specialization, methodology. If it is the wrong journal, your paper is quite likely to be rejected.

Whether or not your manuscript is accepted, under whatever qualifiers, as I have indicated and I want to reiterate, you must take into account the reviewers' suggestions and revise accordingly. If you think the reviewers are wrong, you must figure out how to acknowledge their concerns substantively – that is, defend in your paper against their objections. Of course, you should have had colleagues review your paper before you sent it out the first time, so you might have avoided many of these suggestions for improvement, having already implemented them.

Just sending out a rejected paper without taking into account suggestions for improvement increases the odds that the paper will be rejected by the next journal. The paper might be sent to the earlier reviewer who had already suggested improvements.

90 Writing a Good Second Draft: Take Charge of What You Are Saying

Is the beginning opaque and confused? Make an outline of your paper, as you have it now. Figure out what you are trying to say. *Make sure that in the new first paragraph you fully summarize your paper's claims.* Often, you do a fine job of this in the last two or so pages of the paper.

Give your paper to someone else to read. Do they have problems following your argument? If so, make sure they can follow it, by using better topic sentences, subheads, and previews/summaries.

If you do nothing more than fix the beginning of your paper and fix the various formal aspects, you will be way ahead. This kind of fixing is not optional. Stop reading more material, thinking you do not know enough. Whether or not this is true, your job now is to make your work presentable.

If you have done what I have recommended so far, then: Cut out dramatic claims, ones which experts will challenge, and which you really do not believe (e.g., "this is the only . . . ," or "this is the worst . . ."). Is your version of the history of your country a scholarly version or what you recall from high school history? The latter usually does not hold up to scholarly criticism. Are your assumptions idiosyncratic and not argued for? Copyedit for repetition and flow. Cut out extra sentences or stuff that does not belong. This is hard work, and you may well need help from others. Edit for grammar; get help if you need it.

If you are quoting authorities, be sure they are authoritative. Just because a book is published does not mean it is respected. You might want to put all your bibliographic references into notes or even a bibliographic essay that is an appendix.

91 *Anxiety: Negative Reviews, Coauthoring*

From a colleague: "I remain concerned that the university does an unconscionably poor job of helping junior faculty learn to manage the publication process. And of course, it can be hard to understand why folks experience delays in getting their work out.

"When I think back on my early years, I realize that the main problem I had was the unmanageable emotional/psychological devastation when I received a negative review; it would take me months (or more) to be able to look at my work again. Indeed, I received what (in retrospect) was a highly encouraging revise and resubmit from an extremely good journal, but one of the three reviews was sufficiently nasty that I threw in the towel for more than a year on that particular article. (Ultimately it was published in Y, a good fit but not as reputable as the initial journal would have been had I known how to revise in response to the comments I received.)

"I got tenure absolutely by the skin of my teeth, in part because I hadn't a clue how to handle either the pragmatics or emotions of the review process, and partly because I wrongheadedly got involved in a long-term research project before I had finished publishing enough articles out of my dissertation. I remember being afraid to ask for advice on the matters for which I needed advice, and I recall receiving what seemed to be conflicting or confusing advice when I did ask. I did not know whose advice to take. I also recall being urged to publish while encouraged/asked to undertake tasks that detracted from publication. So my problems with the tenure process were mostly related to my own anxiety and lack of experience, partly poor judgment, and a little bit poor advice.

"Now my coping response to the emotional stress of the publication process is coauthoring, which mostly helps me to manage my anxiety (because then I'm not alone while under attack). Perhaps there should be some (not all, but some) coauthorship among our junior and senior faculty, which would help them learn the process by doing.

"The question then is how senior folks can help junior faculty learn how to manage the publication process and how to prioritize. There is a lot of tacit knowledge involved with success in this field. For example, academic conferences are places to develop networks of scholars with shared interests, meet with those colleagues regularly, and showcase work that is ready for publication. They are not places to get comments on horrific first drafts – get this advice from internal departmental workshops and feedback from close colleagues and research groups.

"Different folks have ways of coping with uncertainty and prioritizing how they place their work. Take W's advice to my doctoral class about writing and publication. He wrote prolifically and sent horrific early drafts to anyone he thought would bother to read them. (A story he told us was that he sent an early draft of an article to one of his colleagues, who sent it back to him with the note: 'From one . . . to another, this is utter crap.') [There is a cost to your reputation if people see such "crap." I would recommend not sending out "horrible early drafts." Let them sit in the drawer for a week and redraft.] He wrote and rewrote in response to comment and critique until he felt pretty satisfied with a piece. Then he would sit down and come up with a list of the four to six journals that he thought were most appropriate, ranked from best to worst. He would print out four to six copies of the paper, insert them into manila envelopes, address to the journals, and send out the first one to the best venue. When he got the first response, he would decide whether it was worth revising and resubmitting, and if not, he would put the next manila envelope in the mail, repeating the process until the article was placed."

92   *If You Write a Paper, Get It Published!*

All the strong academics I know publish often, and in the right journals. They almost never tell me that a paper they wrote was not really good, so they decided not to submit it. They fix the paper, make it better, and get it out.

When people tell me that they did not publish a paper because they thought it not of high enough quality, or when I am told by someone that they have had lots of ideas but they did not think it worth publishing them, I wonder what business they are in. Scholarship depends on the community's dealing with the work you produce, and what you do not publish is unlikely to enter the realm of scholarship. Telling me you have *N* working papers, but you did not push to publish them, tells me you are not part of the scholarly community.

Do not tell yourself stories about how there are people with real brains, and then there are the hacks who publish whatever they write. The people with real brains publish even more. More to the point, your reputation depends on your publications and their quality. Of course, you should be a good teacher, and do your service. But your major competitive job is to make your work part of the community's culture. Being smart and deep is nice, but being well published and recognized is better.

Yes, there are people who publish only gems. But most of us, all of us, are not so likely to lay only golden eggs. By the way, lots of the published literature, even in the strong journals, is not so very good. But at least people see it and can assess it. You are not above their judgment, even if they are not so bright.

There are a small number of scholars who "cannot write." Their colleagues and the profession value their insights, often presented as questions during seminars. They might well be the best of advisors to their colleagues about their research. Don't tell yourself you are one of these scholars. Let others decide.

If you have a bunch of papers sitting in a drawer or a working paper series, first get them all out and published. Then make claims about how the stuff doesn't count. Before that, your claim is unwarranted and seems like special pleading.

93   *Why Do People Write Books?*

I write books because I want to make sense of a phenomenon. I have to give an account of it and then develop a framework, with examples that illuminate that framework, that allows me to put what there is in a theoretical order. One example, or a bright-eyed classification system, or a rubric that everyone then adopts does not lead to much understanding – although it may make your reputation.

Books take a long time because when you have more to integrate into your account the amount of effort and rewriting and thinking goes up nonlinearly. More has to hold together, more has to be consistent, more is at stake. And, while books can readily disappear, never to be referred to again, they are more likely to be enduring than are journal articles in most fields. (Not true in mathematics or the sciences; sometimes true in the social sciences.)

Books tend to take up more intellectual space, take on larger problems, and make more intensive cases, and are more demanding, page for page. (But this is usually not the case in the natural sciences.) I just sent in the page proofs and index for my latest book. I am exhausted. I cannot imagine doing another book, but that only shows that exhaustion weakens one's imagination. The book was about six years in the making (with another book in between), involved at least three major rewrites and countless editing stages, and lots of life and death (of dear ones) in between.

A personal note: I began my work in the late 1960s writing articles. And over the years I continued to write articles, albeit many fewer per year as time went on. Some of the time, it made sense to group (mostly unpublished) articles into a book, since they in fact added up to a larger argument. That involved very substantial rewriting and editing (a year or more extra work). It was not just a matter, at all, of gluing together articles between hard covers.

I found that much of what I wanted to say needed longer forms. Either my papers were 60–100 book pages long (my first book consisted of one or two of these plus some others), and hence not suited to most journals, or in fact one needed a series of studies in one place to make the points I wanted to work out. The more theoretical and philosophic were my arguments, the longer the form. (This is not always true of contemporary academic philosophy, mathematics, or theoretical science, which are much more likely to be worked out, at least initially, in a series of discrete articles.)

94 Books or Articles

1. Different fields have different conventions about which are the appropriate means of publication of research work. In fields in which incremental contributions build nicely upon each other, or in which a complex study can be conveniently split up, the article tends to dominate. On the other hand, books allow for lengthy narratives and for complex arguments based on a half-dozen carefully studied cases.

2. In history and literary studies, the book has been the natural unit of scholarship. Detail is crucial, and one usually cannot use abstractions as a summative device. Explicating a long and complex body of work (whether in archives, or in the arts) demands the longer form. Sometimes this is the case in mathematics, where the synthesis of a field or the development of a subject requires the same sort of work. Often this is the case in much of the social sciences, especially if they demand lots of fieldwork or archival work. Articles may announce a major line of argument or inquiry, but are not the natural unit of scholarship. On the other hand, economics, political science, and sociology often are article-based.

3. In general, scholarly books demand three to ten years of sustained work. They are much harder to get published than are single articles, and if they are published by a reputable press they tend to receive quite close examination before they are accepted. People who publish books also publish some/many articles. People who publish primarily articles rarely if ever publish a book.

4. Here is a rough list of how things "count" in the academic world. Obviously, in fields in which research books are not the norm, many of the categories in my list do not apply. The significance and visibility of a piece of work may trump how it appears. You are best off aiming to be described by the contributions you have made to a field rather than by the number or kind of your publications. In general:

Books:

- · A monographic book represents several years
  of work, and is at the top of the heap.
- · A strong press with solid standards matters. A weak press
  substantially cuts prestige. Is the publisher reputable; does
  it charge $150 for a copy of a monograph? As for electronic
  books and journals, you are known by the company you keep.
- · A collection of your articles, in one book, usually
  counts next – especially if many have not been
  published before and form a coherent book.
- · An edited book, with most of the contributions by others,
  is much less significant as a sign of your achievement – even
  if editing may involve lots of work on your part.
  Better not to do edited books early in your career.
- · A textbook may represent enormous work on
  your part, but may not carry much weight in a
  research university. The case can be made that some
  textbooks are in fact research monographs.
- · A reprinting in another language, if translated
  by others, is a sign of your work's importance,
  not of extra work on your part.

Articles:

- · An article in a strong journal usually represents a good
  deal of work, but much, much less than a book.
- · An article in a weaker journal may involve the
  same amount of work but is less significant.
- · A sequence of cumulative articles counts more than
  the same number of diverse articles, but that sequence
  had better not be seen as stretching things.
- · A book chapter is in general viewed as an un-refereed article.

95   *Rankings*

What is the quality and depth of your contribution to scholarship? Your
book may be reviewed widely and positively in the popular press, but if it
is found lacking in the scholarly reviews you will not thrive in academia.

You may be on TV or the op-ed page, but in the end it is the scholarly judgment of your work that matters.

As for journal rankings, those rankings are only important if they reproduce the judgment of significant scholars. From the point of view of a scholarly community, popularity is no substitute for quality and significance.

Ranking journals and venues as A and B should not preclude evaluating the content and contribution of the actual work. We're in trouble if the actual contribution of the work is ignored compared to rankings of journals or counting citations.

In general, publish significant work in the major journals with the widest readership. If you publish in specialized journals, publish as well in the strongest main journals so that people in your wider field know about your work. You may be told to publish in the main journal(s) of your field, or even a specialty journal. Yet, provosts and the like are concerned that you publish in journals with even wider circulations. Their concerns may or may not be probative for you.

The main (disciplinary) journals have high rejection rates. But every once in a while, it would be good to do the extra work and make your work much more widely known. Similar issues apply to books. There are now specialty publishers; often, their books are priced at $125–250. I am unsure of their impact or quality. The university presses are the venues with wider readership.

THREE

Getting Done (#96–112)

A. FUNDAMENTALS

96 *Moses and the Promised Land*

Moses did not make it into the Promised Land, but it is better that you get done, file your dissertation, and get a suitable academic or nonacademic position or pursue your other goals. If you plan to have an academic job in the fall, you really need to be almost done by mid-summer, so you can have your oral defense. Looking for a job is demanding. A year early, you have the golden opportunity to make the big push on your dissertation so that you have something to show for yourself when people who are interested in you ask to see some of your dissertation. That is the latest time to go into high gear. (No painting your apartment, no putting in a new kitchen or bathroom, no unfocused activity.)

97 *Brilliant Ideas Are Already in What You Have Drafted*

Most writing is done under the regime of a deadline, sometimes self-imposed. Losing sight of your objective is a serious problem. Rarely do you have a revelation that is so new, so important, that you should alter your current plans, plans I hope you have already written down early on in a project. It is not that the revelation cannot suggest new avenues for work. But rather than beginning anew, you need to incorporate those new insights into your current plan. This is both practical and intellectual. Practically, you have to get done. Intellectually, you have worked very hard so far and it is likely that the new ideas are already present in what you have written (that is my awful experience, my "brilliant" new idea already there seven or eight pages away, having been written down two months ago). Getting done matters. In fact, *getting done is the only thing that matters.* I am not counseling doing a slipshod job. But for most of us, doing it "just right" is the royal road to not getting done at all. Or as one of my friends was told by her advisor, you can put that in your second book. Now is the time to finish the first one.

Of course, if you have not written a word, and only are planning, you can be rather more open to insights and new ideas. But you have to start writing, probably should have yesterday, and so get to work. My greatest discovery is how little is new under my sun, how much I have already incorporated into what I have written already.

98 *Working Hard*

· Working hard and sincerely on a project may not produce first-rate work. It is likely to produce good work. But not always.
· Your intentions and commitments to your projects will show, most of the time.
· There will be people who are able to do first-rate work but who do not work very hard. And there are people who do first-rate work and work reasonably hard.
· Most of the world is concerned with results. They might well care for your well-being. But in the end, what counts is the work you do, and the quality of that work. (For people with limited abilities, there are sheltered places of employment where their limitations are taken into account. Still, they must perform.)
· You are in a competitive world. If you do not do the first-rate work, perhaps someone else will – and their performance will set the standard. Some people do fine work consistently. They cannot help but do it.
· My job as your teacher is very different than if you were my son or daughter. One's children need love and support, although it also helps to be realistic about what they can do. As a teacher, I am trying to make you more capable, give you a sense of real

challenges, and grade you as the world expects. It is a disservice
to tell you the work is terrific, if it really is not even very strong.
· In general, the world expects you to be reliable, neat,
orderly, trustworthy, and honest. They really do expect
that there be no spelling errors, that grammar be OK, that
sentences follow from each other. Neatness counts.

99 _Catching Up and Getting Down to Writing_

You can get back to writing even if you are doing something else worthwhile just now.

In 2003, my book _Doing Mathematics_ came out. It was for me a _tour
de force,_ and I was exhausted. I was encouraged to publicize the work, and
I did write a summary article about the book which eventually appeared
in the most prominent place I could have imagined. And I even published in the same venue a translation I did for the book, now somewhat
improved.

I thought I was through for a while writing articles. I had received a
grant to photograph industrial Los Angeles, and in fact during that year
I spent about 112 days out in the field, going to 200+ different firms. Even
such exciting work can be exhausting.

In any case, I had to catch up on paperwork and other stuff that had
been put aside while I did my fieldwork. As part of my project I had to
archive and organize my photographs, something I had been doing along
the way. But cleaning up lacunae and getting things in order turned out
to be a big task – which shows that if you only kept better field notes you
would not have to pay for your sins (no one I know keeps good enough
field notes).

Lessons:

1. Get the information the first time. It is much easier and it fits into
your schedule better. Of course, you never get enough, but you will have
an easier time in the future.

2. Doing the Extra Work is perhaps worth it. The extensive indexes I
have produced, and the ancillary information I have gathered, add depth
to my project. It is lots of extra work, and if done retrospectively, it is
daunting. See #1 above.

Still, I had to face rejected articles and household matters. I happen not to like household matters, so rejected articles seemed most appealing. Various ideas for articles that I had written down became interesting. Talks I promised for the future suddenly seemed worthy of more than an outline (once I promise something like a talk, soon after I write an outline).

Much to my surprise I am in the writing business again. I worry about my getting back to fieldwork, and to organizing my archive of photographs, not to speak of household matters. But I am back in the writing business again. The writing business includes outlining, drafting articles, figuring out what to do with rejected pieces, thinking about the next book.

100 *Taking Notes: Reading Is an Active Process*

I use a bound notebook to take notes while I read, or to record my occasional ideas. What is most important is the analytic writing I do, where I try to link things up, try out ideas – which turn out to be brief essays in my notebook. My reading is rarely passive. I am usually up to something, so that my notes are part of an ongoing internal conversation. The stuff I read is part of the material I need for my work, or eventually seems to end up in my work, and so my notes and thinking-throughs are crucial to what I do later. I love having them in a bound notebook – no lost pages. But of course, index cards, computer systems, or whatever are also good ways. Every once in a while, I am outlining what I know, or the possible future chapters I will write, or plans for research. They too end up in the notebook, sometimes pasted in from other places. The main point here is that reading is an active process, and you are always in business.

B. FINISHING

101 *Finishing a Project*

It takes forever to finish a project, but only a finite time if you have a deadline. Some things will not get done this time around. Be sure that the writing is readable, the spelling is checked, the organization is clear, the message is manifest. Make a checklist of things to do, and check them off one by one. You may add to the list, but eventually it gets done. Or, at least, you say that is enough for now. The trick is to know when enough is good enough. By the way, *it does not always get better if you keep working on it.*

In software engineering, there is the "daily build." Each night someone compiles the monster program and sees if it works at all and holds together. Equivalently, you ought to have a loose-leaf notebook, with dividers labeled for each chapter, in which you fill in the chapters as you do them, or have outlines under each section. If there are diagrams or graphs or photos needed, put in pages with rough drawings of each graph and a caption. In other words, at each stage you have something that looks sort of complete. One distinguished social scientist I know actually has a sequence of different colored papers for the various drafts, so that the final draft is white.

Do form writing or dissertation groups, so that you have other students to share drafts and problems with. If you are having troubles with your advisor, others are too. And you can then figure out what to do.

Your dissertation title, book title, and article title should be informative (not cute), with all the keywords in it.

102 Getting Done

You do not become an intellectual in writing a dissertation. Do not worry about what you leave out. Worry more about what you can do.

Dissertations are composed of chapters, chapters of sections, and sections of subsections. There is also the abstract, the preface, the list of references. The way you get done is by doing each of these parts or subparts one after the other in any reasonable order. When you go looking for a job, they will want to see chapters of your dissertation, so the more ready you are by, say, 1 September or 1 December, the better.

Your dissertation is the beginning of your research career. So it need not include everything or even half of everything. What matters is that it include something, even one thing. You can always do more in your second book or in subsequent articles.

In general, you will not be able to get away with grand theorizing as practiced by some scholars until you have done enough so that people think you actually know something. Even then you may not be able to get away with it. Tenured professors with big reputations sometimes go off the deep end, but you cannot afford that early on.

Few of us are endowed with pure brilliance. What you want to have in your back pocket is your own handle on the world – the archives you have mined, the data you have gathered, the data you have analyzed, the theoretical literature you have mastered and can criticize insightfully, the technical skills you command.

103   *"My Professors Keep Asking for Revisions of My Dissertation Draft"*

Once you have written your dissertation or thesis, you then have to have it approved:

1. If possible, have your advisor read chapter by chapter, as you finish them. Your committee may be reluctant to do so, but at least your advisor should be willing.

2. Write down all suggested changes, and when you resubmit, include a memo with the suggested changes and how you made them in the revision. You might want to do this memo even before you make changes, and share it with your advisor with the comment, "I just wanted to be sure that you and I agree in our understanding of what needs to be done."

3. Your committee will of course see the whole manuscript when you come up for your defense. Again, carefully note any suggestions for revision, share the list with the committee, and then go forth.

4. Make the revisions. Do not argue with the advisor or the committee about whether they are needed. Just make them. Almost always they involve very specific passages or pages, and you can treat them as a checklist, as they do in construction. The committee and your advisor may be dead wrong, but right now you are trying to get your degree and get out of their clutches.

When you hand in revisions, write a memo indicating which revisions you have made (all!), and what you have done (even give page numbers – the committee may have forgotten what they requested, or almost surely have forgotten).

5. As for their clutches, committees are sometimes unwilling to let go of you. They keep having second and third and nth thoughts about revisions and changes, and they demand those revisions. Ideally your advisor will protect you, and negotiate a termination of the list. The outside member is supposed to protect you, but often they are either unwilling or unaware of their role. And your advisor may be either so desirous of your doing a really excellent job, or so unaware of the torture of constant revision, or so sadistic, that the advisor joins in the list of revisions and will not let go.

Now, *many rites of passage are sadistic.* You cannot do much, but realize this, make revisions, and wear out the committee. Keep track through the shared memos of what is being requested. Eventually, the committee's revision-requesters will look ridiculous. At some point, you need to enlist your advisor's help (even if the advisor is one of the chief torturers). I think advisors are almost always aware they are up to something fishy, and do not want the world to find out. So, you might say: "I have been making revisions now for M months. Here are the memos of revisions. Might we consider the project closed now? I will of course revise once more when I write things up for publication." What is crucial is the list of revisions, the memos saying you have done them.

6. Of course, you may well have done a rotten or unacceptable first draft. This is no shame. It is not even unusual. So perhaps you do need to make substantial revisions before they let you go. Perhaps you are so dumb you do not take their advice – then I have less sympathy for you, and have little counsel. But much more likely, the draft has gotten much better if you have been responsive.

People who talk about "standards" at this point are usually out of this world. You may well need the intercession of your advisor or someone on the committee.

7. Of course, there are formal procedures within the graduate school. These are last resorts. What you want to do is to have the advisor and committee eventually feel enough pressure to let go (here I assume they are not letting go for other than scholarly reasons, almost always the case), and then take ownership of how much better the dissertation is (agree with them, write an effusive letter of thanks), and hopefully they will help you for the rest of your career.

8. Remember that the academic research enterprise tends to breed insecurity into its members, including your advisor. They have been rejected often (journals), they have had problematic tests (tenure), and they have to endure not very responsive students. While it is too much to ask for your sympathy for your committee's situation (one you may well experience yourself eventually), realize it comes from experience which encourages them to internalize the aggressor rather than have sympathy for the other.

Remember, you are younger and sturdier than your committee. You will be around after they are dead. Whatever pound of flesh they demand is to be given with the pleasure of realizing that living well is the best revenge. And expressed gratitude is just what you need to perfect, for you are dealing with an authoritarian regime and sycophantic behavior is often rewarded.

104   *Have You Spent Too Long a Time in Graduate School?*

1. Each year you ought to write a memo to your advisor indicating what you have done this past year in your work and your plans for the coming year.

2. As for taking your exams, you should be taking your qualifying exams at the end of your second year of coursework (since by then or a bit later you will have the requisite number of units) or the beginning of the third year. This is usually honored in the breach. If you have thought about which are your fields of study earlier rather than later, you can plan to take the coursework and do the reading you need to do.

3. Be sure your advisor and your committee members know your plans. It makes no sense to ask someone to serve on your qualifying committee very late in the game, although that may sometimes be necessary. Have them committed to your education early on.

4. You are writing your dissertation. You may have given some first-rate conference presentations, but that dissertation is not getting written. Here's what to do: Get a loose-leaf notebook and some dividers. Get together all that you have written relevant to the dissertation. Figure out a reasonable set of chapter titles. Do not worry if it is just right – you

need some organization now. Then punch holes in the various bits and pieces you have written. Put them in the appropriate chapters. Usually you have some sort of dissertation proposal or grant application that can serve as your introduction. Your bibliography, prepared for qualifying exams, will serve for the moment as the bibliography for the dissertation. Some of the "chapters" will be very rough material; others will be more polished. Now you have something you can work on, fix up, put together. Consult with your advisor – bring along the loose-leaf – about what to do next.

5. Keep in mind the importance of getting done. This may well be the biggest project you have taken on, but it will not be the biggest in your life. You have better things to do than stay in graduate school.

None of this will solve your problems, but it may put you on the road to doing so. The most important thing to do is to organize yourself, your efforts, and your plans. And keep in mind that dissertations are written in chapters, chapters are written in sections, and sections are not very long. Do not be ashamed of being lost. The crucial task is to get the help you need to get back on track.

105   It Takes Twice As Long As You Planned

Over the last few months I have been systematically indexing and mapping the sites I have photographed over the past 18 months. Not all of my photographs are ideal. Some of them are underexposed, some are blurred, and for many the focus point is not quite right. They are not suitable for calendars or books. However, much of the information one might want to get from them is still there. In fact, if the wall is in focus but the person in front of it is slightly off, that might be OK (for you will then be able to read the poster on the wall, with its small type). In any case, it is better to have an imperfect photograph of something than to have none at all.

I spent perhaps 112+ days doing fieldwork during 2004 and 2005. What is impressive is how much homework you have to do to keep up – besides getting the film developed, there is storing the slides, labeling and indexing, mapping, and re-indexing, and retro-indexing what you had not indexed earlier, and thinking about what you are doing. I am told by friends who do other kinds of fieldwork or archival work or surveys that this is fairly standard. A ratio of 1:1 is conservative, and in the end the homework and the retakes take even more time (to make up for your mistakes, your left-out notations).

And of course you learn as you are doing things. You now know how you should have done it then. And you keep having this experience, for you do get more astute and capable, and you find new levels of excellence you wish to achieve.

106   *Focusing on Getting Done*

In conversations with my colleagues, what keeps coming up is how doctoral students need to focus on getting done. This is the beginning of your academic career, if that is what you choose. Not the end. What counts are exams passed, experiments or fieldwork or archival work completed, theorems proved, chapters drafted. It's nice to go to meetings, conferences, and graduate student workshops. But not if they get in the way of your getting done. (This applies as well to professors, the ones so busy they do not publish their research, or even get it done.)

Do not apply for grants unless they actually will help you get done. Maybe the application process will speed your formulating a chapter. But if the money is not essential, or does not help formulate a chapter, the application process merely gets in the way and takes lots of time.

Of course, you want people in the field to know about your work. One meeting a year with a well-presented paper is perhaps enough. When you are seeking a job, you will go to more meetings.

When you apply for a job, they might notice all those activities you have done on your way. But most likely they will ignore all of that, and ask: What does the advisor think of this person? How does the dissertation read? Will they be good candidates for being tenured?

You do not want to be known as a "slam" (i.e., slow as molasses, a drosophila gene that moves slowly). The university is well populated with them, unfortunately. I know this is the kind of advice that makes some people feel guilty. The proper response is to get to work. *Your past matters less than what you do now.*

107 *Do It Now: Displacement*

I was talking to one of our doctoral students, now finished. He held a job for part of the time he was writing his dissertation, and it took him longer than he would have liked. But he did get through, and I gather that his advisor thinks highly of his work. He said to me: I would get home at 6 and then have to work on my dissertation. Another story I heard is of a mother of three who would wait until the kids went to bed and then work on her dissertation from 10 PM to midnight (she also held a job).

I have been thinking of writing a paper on my photographing work. It would summarize a book I want to write and have drafted. About a week ago I made the roughest outline, and kept modifying it, looking over my notes. Now, I could have gone to the book manuscript draft and edited it down drastically. That might have produced a fine article. But I knew that I could not be so focused just now. I woke up this morning quite early, did not want to do all the other chores I had to do today (none academic, all around the house), and as a defense I started writing the paper. I just finished a rough draft, maybe seven hours later. I stuck in some of the book, and also part of another paper, but for the most part the verbiage is new. And I did not go back and fix it. I just went forward, followed my outline, and kept going. What I have now is almost surely awful. But I have something to work with. I can go to the book draft and see if there is stuff I left out. I'll need to get some references straight, put in some maps and illustrations, and surely when I show it to my colleagues it will need lots of work. *But I now have something to fix,* rather than an inchoate paper which is not even drafted, which somehow is supposed to compensate for the fact that it is not the right time to write another book. And it is time to put all my thoughts together, and tell the story I want to tell.

What is the lesson here? *Do it, now.* Prepare, set up stuff that you surely do not want to do so that the writing is an escape (it has always been so for me), and go to work. It helps that I have been thinking about this paper and the subject matter for five years, that I have written lots around it, so that it is in my blood, so to speak. But it helps even more that I was ready to get rid of it, even though I suspect that I will have to work ten times as hard to polish it off. Seventy hours actually sounds like an underestimate. What I gave up was being perfect, having everything lined up. In exchange, I got something done.

I recommend this strategy. It's saved my life – more than once. Not because the paper gets written, or the book. It's a terrific way of dealing with what you otherwise cannot deal with.

108 *Projects: Doing Better without More Work; Exemplary Faculty*

The following applies at research universities or comprehensive universities. If you teach at an institution where research plays a much smaller role than do service and teaching, there is corresponding advice, but with different emphasis.

Think in terms of one or two research projects and make sure those projects are substantial. What I note again and again is how people settle for less, compromise their ambitions, get diverted by little things. I note how colleagues dissipate their energies, rather than focus them. We are in a competitive environment within our universities, and the provosts know if we have much better or much weaker dossiers than our colleagues in other departments. Moreover, insofar as your field produces substantial research, the university's prestige will be enhanced: important books, significant empirical findings, inventive design solutions, broad-ranging theoretical innovations.

As I read dossiers on the university tenure committee, I am sometimes in awe of the achievements of some of my colleagues at the university or the people who will be joining us on our faculties. These are people who have mastered the discipline and focus needed to play at the highest levels. As far as I can tell, they are about as good teachers as anyone else, if not better. Their service contributions are usually substantial. (In other words, they are not getting away with anything.)

What are impressive are the focus, the ambition, and the choice of problems, venues, and outputs of the strongest people. As far as I can tell, they are not much brighter than most people, if at all, and they work hard but not to the point of becoming zombies or destructive to their families. What seems crucial is that they have *projects*, projects that are substantial (multiyear but usually not a decade), they build on their past achievements, and they are not much diverted from a cumulative research portfolio. They are not necessarily narrow, and they might combine a variety of interests in varying ratios in different projects. But they do have projects, they do produce regularly, they know how to take advantage of opportunities that come their way (grants and fellowships, chances to give papers). They may work in a narrow field, but by their devotion and invention (and these seem to be related) they enlarge what people thought was possible.

Now, they benefit from their past achievements, so that to those who have, come even more opportunities. So it may seem very difficult to redirect your energies in so focused and productive a fashion. But what is also remarkable is that some of these people, a small number, also find ways of entering new fields, fields in which they do not have much capital. So there is hope for the rest of us.

And these people have done a fine job of publicizing their work, giving talks, going to meetings, arranging meetings.

By the way, only a fraction of the dossiers that I have read are awesome. So there is lots of room out there for those who want to take up space in the biggest ponds with the richest opportunities. But you have to focus your energies, be ambitious, and know what you are doing. In the longer run, it would be nice to say that many dossiers are awesome. In very great universities (that are not too large), I suspect this is possible. In universities that appoint people to tenure only after they have had two home runs (or perhaps only one grand slam), the ratio can be higher. Good fortune helps, being nice helps, but in the end it is up to you.

Being barely good enough is the sure road to midlife depression, when the new generation of scholars arrives and they are much better and more achieved than you.

109 *Scut Work and Publicizing Your Research*

This morning I alphabetized about 150 pieces of paper about the firms I have been photographing. Sometimes I wonder why I do not have an assistant to do all of this for me. But:

· I learn a lot by being close to my own materials. Inadvertently,
I notice things on the pieces of paper, or the slides I am
filing, the Google or reference materials I am printing out.
I imagine if I had ten times the work I have to do, or if I
had an infant at home, I would need assistants. Of course,
I choose to do projects I can do in a modest way.

· I am not that busy with important things, and I am a
failure at conventional recreation. I do not do out-of-town
meetings. I am rarely on the phone. If you photograph as
I do, or write and edit articles and books, after three or
four hours, you are exhausted. So you do have time.

· When I have a student, I can usually find better work for
them to do. Others of my colleagues tell me that students
learn lots from scut work, and I suspect they are right.

· Publicize your work in (slightly) more popular venues.
Keep the deep ideas, but be briefer and less technical.

· You have to tell people your story again and again and
again. They never get it the first time. So there are different
venues of publication and lectures, and follow-up articles.
If you do this too much, however, you will get a reputation
for having only one idea and having become unserious.

110   *Moving to Associate Professorship*

1. You must publish in the visible, strong venues, with substantive articles. It may be OK if you come up for tenure with a comparatively small
number of articles (say, three or four, or five or six), but each one is in the
top journal, each reports enormous amounts of work, and each is part of
a cumulative contribution. (But still some departments just count. Find
out.) Otherwise, you need a wider portfolio. If you publish a book, it had
better be from a press that is reputable in your field.

2. Teaching is important, but few people are so extraordinary in their
teaching that they are as good as they think. They do not have innovative
methods; they do not transform teaching in the field.

3. And then there are those who think that service counts for much. Maybe for a longtime associate professor whom you want to finally promote. Maybe.

4. *Three mediocre achievements do not add up to one fine achievement.*

Do not tell yourself stories. Now, you might well get away with nonsense if you are sufficiently a lackey, but it is getting a bit harder to do that these days.

Why am I writing this now, once more, again? Every time I encounter such gross stupidity and idiocy, such willful ignoring of good advice, I am appalled. Surely, you will get bad advice from your seniors and advisors. But that is not the problem I see.

Maybe every two years, answer for yourself in 300–500 words:

1. What is my contribution to scholarship? How is it distinctive?

2. How is it being disseminated? Are these the most prominent and prestigious and authoritative venues?

3. How am I improving my teaching?

4. What should I *not* do for the next several years, so that I can have better answers to #1–3?

I received the following note:

> You have managed to scare me when I've read your stuff about true scholarship and "real work" (not just "work"). It makes me wonder if I'm really up to the task. It has been a relief when you say that there are very few successful scholars you have met who are geniuses. It makes me think that I may actually make it one day. The best advice I've heard from you (at least that has worked for me) is that our best tool as scholars (or would-be scholars) is our butts. That is, in the end, what gets the job done (and hopefully well done) is simply sitting in front of the computer and typing – and keep typing, no matter what. I've done that and it works magically!

C. REFERENCE LETTERS

111 *Asking for Reference Letters*

If you want people to write a letter of reference or nomination for you:

1. Give them lots of advance notice. It's rare that you hear of some award or job a week ahead. Usually it is many weeks or months. If it is

urgent, draft a complete letter, so all they need do is modify it. In fact, draft a letter or at least talking points in every case.

Let people off the hook: "If you cannot fit this into your schedule, I fully understand. Please just let me know." Even if they wish you the best and are your advocates, people resent being asked for letters when they are pressed and there is little leeway. You have got to be especially gracious. Moreover, almost no one can write an effective letter off the top of their heads. And rarely is a letter for one job suitable for another. The subtleties matter, for readers immediately pick up that you wrote the letter for Yale rather than Chicago and just sent Chicago a copy with a changed address. (By the way, this is also true when you write job application or graduate school essays and letters.) To ask for a letter is to ask for at least an hour of someone's time, often much more. If you give them lots of leeway, they feel that you are not imposing too much. If you give them little leeway, "Should I go to my child's drama performance or do your letter?" is not the question you want them to ask themselves.

2. Make sure they know you well enough to write.

3. Make sure they owe you something. If not, they may decide that other tasks are more urgent. (That "owe" means that years before you were a fine student, an excellent assistant.)

4. It is not at all fatal that the letter discusses your weaknesses. Gives it credibility. The crucial part is your strengths. On the other hand, plagiarism is probably a fatal flaw, although suitable contrition may be worth noting.

5. Good letters are either detailed and specific and extensive in their considerations, or they are much shorter but specific enough for the reader to appreciate the message.

6. As for dilatory letter-writers, to whom you have given plenty of advance notice, you might write them a note a day before the reference is due to ask that they tell you when the letter is sent out. That is both polite and reasonable.

Some people are not reliable and on time, and there is little you can do. Those are the same people who never turn in stuff to the deans and provost (their bosses) on time, either. So do not think they are "dissing" you alone. There may be medical reasons for their failure, but more often it is moral and characterological. I would avoid using them as references, since most faculty are anxious to promote their students and do the best they can.

112   *Writing Academic Reference Letters*

When you write a letter of reference (for an applicant, for tenure, for promotion) it is vital that the letter reflect your true judgment. Watching experienced readers of these letters has taught me that they detect bad faith, praise that damns the candidate, and lacunae. Moreover, the letter should reflect the needs of the institution: is it mainly a teaching institution, a comprehensive university, a research university, a research institution?

Be clear about your relationship to the candidate. Say whether they would be appointed, or tenured, or promoted at your institution, and why. (Often, they would not be promoted at your institution, but the reason may well make the candidate look good.) Make clear your assessment of their work, giving sufficient detail so that the readers believe you have carefully considered that work (whether it be research, teaching, administration, or public service). Contributions to practice are vital in some fields, and well-documented ones are important. Compare the candidate to others at the same stage of their careers.

And give your considered overall judgment, perhaps in the first paragraph and then in the summary. To indicate weaknesses is rarely fatal (at least no more fatal than the factual record itself), especially if there are strengths that are significant. In general brief letters from high gurus and stars do not help a case, unless the letter reads "this is the strongest scholar I know of in this area" and you give enough detail to indicate you really do stand behind what you say. Of course few letter-writers are so authoritative.

It is almost always better to be straightforward, direct, careful, and scrupulous in providing evidence for your judgments. Pulling punches decreases your credibility next time, and if the readers believe you have pulled punches your letter will be discounted or will even hurt the candidate.

None of this is news. People are more likely to be hurt by unwarranted praise than by balanced and fair assessments. By the way, vindictive or mean-spirited assessments or totally negative ones tend not to be taken seriously at all. And if you vigorously and in detail disagree with the candidate's work, and take it seriously, you are likely to help the candidate – clearly this is a formidable candidate to cause so detailed a response. (I once saw a ten-page single-spaced assessment letter, with chapter and verse comments and disagreements. It was serious and thoughtful. It ended with a very positive recommendation despite all the disagreements or because of them. The candidate was passed.)

As for the candidates themselves, your initial letters, or statements of purpose or career summaries, can guide reviewers. If you have a weakness you might well admit it: "I have published three articles, a smaller number than is usual. However, each has appeared in the main journal of the field and is now widely cited." Or, "over the past six years I have been given an extraordinary load of teaching and administration. My dean/provost knows of this and realizes that this has consequences for the number of articles I could publish." (You might want to exchange a memo with the dean/provost to this effect halfway through, or when you are given these extraordinary tasks.)

Make sure your strengths and your particular contributions are manifest. Deal with joint authorship issues directly. If there is something peculiar in your vita or your career, take charge of it. Hiding never works with the readers I have seen.

Your job is to make it easy to write a strong, forceful letter. People need to know you and your work. Good letters are detailed and specific, and they are more about the work and your character than about saying how wonderful you are.

As for the letters that are written about you when you come up for promotion and tenure: If you have been doing the right stuff, if your advisor and then the senior faculty of the place where you have an appointment have done their jobs to promote you, to make you and your work better known and appreciated, and to make you do a better, more professional and responsive job – then there will be a range of people who know of and appreciate your work, probably the leaders in your field. And while they may not want to write one more letter, they do feel an obligation to do so – it was once done for them.

Someone may decide not to write a reference for you for any of a number of reasons: they have written 35 of them already; they do not know you well enough; they are not experts in the field at issue; they have written a letter for someone else for the same job. Do not immediately decide it is because you are weak.

It is important to write thank-you notes to people who write your letters. It is just part of being courteous, since they are doing you a favor. But that is a favor they ought to do. It is our job to promote our students; their success is our success, and without our helping them in the ways we can help them, their lives will be much more difficult.

None of this is rocket science (neither is rocket science, for that matter). It is all about training your students so that you can support them, and their realizing that what they do reflects on their teachers, so that they cannot truly be free agents if they wish to be part of the society and the culture and have a job. A colleague says to me that he can spot the assistant professors who seem to flounder, and who are poor with their own students. And he knows they have been poorly trained by their advisors. That training by the way is as much about doing things on time, and doing enough of them, as about anything that might be called the techniques of research.

FOUR

Getting the First Job (#113–150)

A. FUNDAMENTALS

113 *Now That You Have Your Doctorate*

1. Our doctoral students are our most important exports.

2. What is crucial is that our doctoral students gain positions that they merit. Moreover, I am told by experts that for most academics "you end up where you started," so that first job is crucial.

Aim high for your first post-PhD position. If it is a postdoc, it is your gateway to a teaching/research university position if you choose that direction. If it is an assistant professorship, you want to be at an institution that is most receptive to your research contribution. And, frankly, you want to go to a higher-prestige university, if that is possible. In any case, you want to make tenure a doable goal.

You may choose to go to a teaching-oriented college, and for very good reasons. Then make sure you make contributions to teaching that are widely recognized (maybe textbooks, awards, articles about innovative teaching methods).

What is crucial is what you do with whatever position you find. Ideally, you will exceed the expectations of your new colleagues, they will be delighted to have you on their faculty or staff, and you will grow in your new position.

3. Geographical constraints may force you to seek a position close to home. Those constraints are honorable, and you will just do your best

within them. In the end, family counts more than prestige. (But not to the National Research Council.)

114   *What Do I Do with My Degree?*

Universities wish their doctoral students to become leading researchers and teachers in the field, take up positions at more prestigious universities, and join the academic profession. (Some doctoral degrees are professional certifications, and so function differently. But the prestige of your future appointments still matters.) Do they get jobs at peer or better institutions? Ten years down the line, do they retain such jobs, make significant contributions, and grow their own students?

Lots of students have other agendas. Some work in industry and consulting, others choose jobs that suit personal needs, and others decide they do not like doing research and would prefer to return to being a jazz musician. Or, rather than continuing to pursue a career as a research chemist, you go into politics and eventually become Chancellor of Germany, or you go back to school and become a rural physician. You have not failed as a chemist or whatever; rather, you have a new way of employing your talents and education. You want to make a contribution to scholarship, society, or government. Research training is powerful training. (I still live off my undergraduate and graduate training.) You learn about balanced analysis, critical views of others' work, an ethic of reliable knowledge. If you learn to produce reliable arguments and knowledge, you will have a very great advantage – if only to be able to see the flaws in the usual arguments.

As for our expectations, we do want you to follow in our footsteps, preferably in climber's boots able to scale higher heights. But the world is more varied than our imaginations. Let me make one strong recommendation: Whatever you do, put aside the time to write an article or book about your dissertation research, and get it published in a good venue, one where it is seen. You will be ahead of half of all doctoral recipients.

115   *Visibility in Graduate School*

You will want people to know of you and your work. Do attend the major meeting in your field. Organize a session and present your research at the meeting. Give a well-rehearsed presentation. People actually do remember, and are on the lookout.

You will want to build in some part-time teaching at a local college or university.

In any case, focus on getting out of graduate school, finishing your degree. Your progress may well be determined by other factors (family obligations, for example), but within those factors get out.

Seek model teachers, researchers, and presenters and performers and artists. Aim for the strongest achievements, rather than saying something to the effect of "if they can get away with it, so can I." You probably cannot, and in fact neither can they. (Perhaps no one says this, and they are just deaf to the calls for compelling excellence.)

Get to know the important people in your field, which work is admirable, which work you would like to be as good as. Do not worry about not being good enough. Good enough is usually a matter of hard work, focus, and scrupulous attention to detail.

116   *Job Talks*

When you go out on the job market and are fortunate enough to be invited to an interview, you want to keep in mind:

1. Do not offend anyone.

2. Your job talk must be well practiced, and its flaws pointed out by your advisors. It should be technically impeccable, it should be clear, and it should display your strongest work. If you are asked to teach a class, speak with the people at the institution about the level and audience. If people find that what you say is just wrong by their lights, by their scholarly lights, you are in trouble unless you can respond effectively. You have got to answer their questions, not avoid them, and not pull rank or expertise.

3. You are never too good for a job that has not been offered to you yet.

4. If you have to explain yourself, do so fully and in the context of the questions being asked. Do not stall or defer. They have the job; presumably you are looking for it.

5. You are representing your advisor. Make your advisor look good.

6. Give them something to take home: a basic idea, perhaps a chart, the chief points of what you are saying.

Of course, there will be disasters. And you will run into the propellers of someone in the department who believes that all candidates should be expert in their field, or who tries to show you they are smarter than you, or gives you the trouble they would prefer to be giving one of their colleagues. But you can do better, and that is all that you can do.

117 *Giving a Talk at a Conference (Or a Job Talk)*

1. Practice your talk and be sure it takes less than the allowed time, even 30 percent less.

2. Make sure your main claim or result is mentioned in the first minute or two. Titles should be informative, not cute. Make sure the main finding or claim is in the title. Give away the good stuff.

Your goal is to have some people be interested in your work, argue with you, take your work seriously. If someone asks, be able to explain your contribution to the joint work, your plans for future work.

3. Have a one-sheet handout (printed on both sides is OK) about your paper to give to all who attend. Include relevant data, an abstract, and your name/e-mail/website/way of getting the whole paper.

4. Have your CV with you at all times, in multiple copies, to give to anyone who might be interested.

5. Send copies of your papers to anyone who is interested.

6. As for PowerPoint, in general, it is sleep-inducing. If your spoken English is poor, it will help. If you have to use PowerPoint, maybe two or three slides every 15 minutes. If you want to show a data table, make sure the relevant data are highlighted or are in large type, and have the whole chart on your one-pager.

7. Questions are wonderful. You'll find people who are interested in your work. Speak to them afterward. If they find a problem with your work, perhaps they can help you resolve it. Thank them, and acknowledge their help in the published paper. If you do not know the answer, say so, and request that they see you after the talk.

8. Do not worry about approaching famous professors. In general, famous professors who are not surrounded by people are very unhappy. Their status always needs updating. This is an empirical discovery, not a psychological one.

9. Announcing that you did not have time to practice your paper – the data is so new and hot! – is to me a sign that I should leave the room immediately.

10. If you follow these rules you will do better than 80 percent of the people at the conference, including those famous professors.

11. Go to sessions that interest you and ask questions, so that you learn and people get to know you.

12. If you are shy, or too deferential (perhaps you come from a country where professors are treated as gods), then be sure to make your presentation excellent. It's not quite true, but quality does matter and can sometimes trump shyness.

13. If you leave the conference with two or three people interested in your work, you've done your job.

14. Do not get drunk or otherwise lose your good sense. Now is not the time to be a fool.

15. Shower every day, brush your teeth. Fancy clothes do not matter, but neatness helps.

16. If you go to many presentations, you will wonder how X, Y, or Z got tenure at first-rate universities. Some of the time, they were very strong but have lost their way, others do not show well, and others were mistakes.

118   *Speaking, Moderating, Commenting*

If you are giving a talk at the meetings:
- Be briefer than the allowed time. Prepare your talk, time it, and if you go over your time, be sure to cut it way down.

- Make sure you say your main point in the first
  minute. Repeat the point at the end.
- Answer questions respectfully. If you do not know the
  answer, all you need do is say so, and ask to speak to the
  person afterward. Repeat the question asked of you; it will
  help those who are sleeping or who did not hear well. Keep
  in mind that if the questioner is powerful and famous,
  they are more likely to have vision and hearing deficits.
- Come with a handout, perhaps one page, that has the essence
  of your talk, with your address and e-mail. Distribute to
  all. People like to take stuff home with them. Have some
  copies of your complete talk for those who ask for them.
  If you have business cards, take enough of them.
- Take a résumé or CV with you, maybe ten copies. You
  are in the job market – if not now, then in the future.
- Dress professionally, all the time. Bathe frequently. Good
  grooming matters. If you have streaked your hair purple,
  now is the time to wash it out. If you wear a toupee,
  be sure it does not show. Better bald than fake.
- Talk to people in your field, about your work or theirs. People
  love to have people talk to them about their work. No one
  ever feels overly attended to. The most famous academics
  are usually the hungriest for intelligent interchange about
  their work. Many appreciate unintelligent interchange.
- Do not tell people that you just finished preparing the
  talk as an excuse. I would walk out at that point.
- As for PowerPoint: If you cannot speak English well, use it as a
  helpful crutch. Be prepared for all your visual aids to die on you.
- Do not drink alcohol. Do not do drugs. If you have anxiety
  attacks, there are medications that are very effective.
- Do not sexually harass anyone. If you want to
  have an affair, be sure it is with someone who can
  give consent and is not under your power.

As for conveners and discussants:

· Politely but firmly keep people to their time slots. Bring a big clock with you. Give people a two-minute warning. The best line is that others need time and the audience needs time.

· Introductions are best short: Name and Title of Paper.

· Make sure there is time for questions.

· Encourage those who dominate the time to meet afterward.

· Never get into an argument with anyone. Just play dumb by following the rules. If necessary, pull out the microphone plug.

· If you are a discussant: Discuss *all* the papers. Keep well within your time limit. Be unfailingly polite. Emphasize what is strong in each piece of work. If the paper is awful, suggest how to strengthen the argument. "I found Professor X's argument quite engaging. Might I suggest that the argument would be strengthened if the evidence from study Y [which in fact contradicts X, no need to say this] were incorporated?"

119 *Job Talk Advice*

You are giving a job talk, which might be 45 minutes, or you are making a presentation at a meeting, which might be 12 minutes. Some obvious but often ignored to-dos:

1. Give away the main findings or discovery or main point in the first minute or so. People may fall asleep, or they may need to keep the main point in mind as they listen to the rest of the talk. Since they might come late, you might repeat the main point a few minutes into the talk. If you use PowerPoint, then show that slide again.

If you are interrupted by lots of questions or a fire drill, at least you have delivered your message.

2. If your conclusion has the main point, be sure to bring up the main point in the first minutes. Offer a preview, not only of where you will be going, but of where you will end up.

3. There are some times when the method used to do the analysis is of interest. But in general, what is of interest are your findings and discovery methods. Explain any esoteric method, so that it is clear. Use examples and analogies. This part must be in clear, nontechnical language.

4. If you can learn something from historical examples, or from previous research, do let the audience know that early on. You are making an advance on what everyone knows, so make clear just what your advance is.

5. *End early.* Never go over time. Keep in mind that the computer might die, or the projector bulb blow.

6. If you do statistical analysis of the data set:

    a. Be sure the data set is decent (too low a response rate? good questionnaire? proper sampling? biased collection?). If it is not decent, it still might be worth studying if there is nothing better, with the proviso that the conclusions may have systematic errors and not only statistical ones. Do you have internal consistency tests to show that the data set is better than advertised? Or worse?

    b. Statistical tests are meant to determine the reliability of a finding. But they do not tell you if the finding is important or the effect is large. Always indicate statistical error bars. If possible, indicate rough estimates of the systematic errors such as biased samples or low return rate – the latter requires some sort of simulation. Again, never show data without error bars. Explain any peculiar graphical convention.

As for importance, you need to tell yourself and the audience whether the connections are substantial in effect even if they are reliable. So, for example, if I regress X vs. Y, and they are nicely connected statistically, is the connection between X and Y large or small? Or, even if the connection is small, are the consequences small or substantial?

120   *The Content of Your Talk*

Do not presume your audience's sympathies. Always preempt the obvious questions, early on. Never give weapons to your enemies.

1. Why did you do this study? What motivated your development of this algorithm or technique? How does your contribution to mathematics fit into the enterprise? Why one more book on Shelly or on precursors to the First World War? How does your previous work lead up to this work of art, and how does it connect with others' work?

2. Give away your biases and prejudices. If you believe markets are the solution to all problems, say so early on. If you are a textualist in law, say so. You want people to argue, in your talk, about its details, not your general point of view.

3. Compared to what? If you claim that a number is large, compared to what is it large? Is there an analogy to a different time or place or subject?

4. It may well be important, even with large uncertainties, to know something. Say your data set is not very good, or that your analysis does not reveal too much. On the other hand, a small effect, measured with high precision, is interesting, but may not be important. (In much of natural science, on the other hand, a small effect measured with high precision may sometimes lead to a Nobel Prize. But that is because we have good theories about the exact magnitude of these small effects.) Preliminary studies may have poor data, but still be better than nothing.

5. If your contribution is technical, it is important to explain to others what that contribution is. Analogies and examples will help. In mathematics, and in other fields such as biology, there will be members of your audience who know comparatively little about the frontiers in your field and may well not be up-to-date with current techniques, terminology, or strategies.

121   *Job Search*

1. Be sure your job talk is shorter than people expect. It should be easy to follow; provide a handout, a sheet of paper with any charts and tables so people have something to take home. Practice in front of your advisor. Be clear what your achievement is, where it stands in the literature. At teaching (vs. research) universities, be open to the implications for teaching.

2. Many of you worry about your English language skills. Of course, it would be preferable for you to have worked on these while you were a graduate student. Still, there is much you can do to improve your chances. Prepare your talk carefully. Go slowly. Be sure the content is clear, your claims manifest.

3. Your advisor has primary responsibility for helping you find a job. And for good reason – the advisor knows the student best, and the advisor's reputation depends on the positions their students attain. But the doctoral committee is a backup. So you must let them know if things are not going well.

4. Think about what you might teach. Be flexible in terms of the needs of the college or university. Listen to what they tell you. Well before, be sure to have prepared two or three syllabi to help you work out your ideas and your potential list of readings and assignments. If you have evidence of teaching experience and quality, be sure they see it. Think about where you are going in your research. What might your next project be like? Where are you going to place your work?

5. Your performance on the interview does not determine whether you get the job. Your references, internal politics of the committee and the university, particular needs – all play dominant roles. But you can give it your best shot, and they will remember you.

6. Dress appropriately, do not drink alcohol even if they do, and be well rested. Do not worry about whether this is the job for you – until they make you an offer.

Some provisos:

Most of your teachers were hired under much less rigorous circumstances than prevail today – that does not mean they are less qualified than you are, but it does mean that the risks are now greater, and the competition is more intense.

International students should try for positions in the U.S. academic or industrial and consulting market. Whether or not you ultimately decide you do want to teach in the United States, you ought to have that opportunity. English language skills suitable for the U.S. job market are just the skills you will need for the international scholarly network (meetings, papers).

You will have to apply to as many appropriate positions as possible, leading to many, many applicants for each position. You and your advisor have to figure out how to stand out in the pack, including any influence the advisor might have so that they might look at you more closely. You must more carefully marshal your resources. Acknowledge that the folks who are hiring you may have had a much easier time than you will have, and go forward.

Volunteer to teach the largest courses (with teaching assistants, of course). When central administrations of major universities wonder where their money is going, they always look at the high-cost departments and schools, usually defined in terms of revenue per faculty member. Departments with lots of externally funded research or lots of students (especially lower-division undergraduates), which have reasonable-to-strong scholarly reputations, are usually bulletproof. Departments with small enrollments have small constituencies when budget-cutting time comes around. A department never wants the provost to even think that they are a target for cutting – so you want large classes, especially undergraduate courses aimed at all students. If the average class size is in the teens or low twenties (this does not apply to small colleges), you had better raise lots of external grant and gift money. In any case, seniority does not protect people from the demand that they teach large classes – at least nowadays. So if there is a large course, do take it on if invited. No, you do not want to be overloaded, and perhaps you can arrange some compensating time if the course is large enough, but why not make them indebted to you?

No one expects you to be a dynamite teacher. They do expect you to deliver, to be scrupulously responsible, to be discreet and fair. They do expect you to prepare well. And they will be flattered if you ask for help early on.

You want to be taken advantage of, so to speak. How else will they owe you rather than having you owe them?

Do not get involved in mudslinging departmental fights, especially when you are a junior faculty member. Often these fights have long histories, may reflect ambient dysfunctionalities, and are surely of no concern to your career. If you find yourself in what appears to be a diabolical situation, teach better, write more, and find another job. *Nothing ever gets better until a generation or two is gone* – unless a new chair is put in place with a mandate from the provost.

Every conflict you get involved with is perhaps one less major research paper you can publish.

122 *Job Hunting*

You cannot assume that you will get a first-choice assistant-professor job offer, or any offer, from one of the *N* applications you send out. You must have a spectrum of possibilities, so that if your first choices do not work out, you have some good second choices (rather than having to settle for fourth or fifth). Depending on your fields and research, these other choices may involve governmental or international agencies, private enterprise, consultancies, or practice in the field. It may be a postdoctoral fellowship or a one-year teaching position.

Realize that your job interview will reflect not only your contribution, but the recommendations of your advisors and others, and most importantly internal politics and particularities of the place you are visiting. You can do your best, but that does not say that something you do (or do not do) will not have adverse effects or especially favorable ones. Departments and schools are their own communities, more or less hospitable to outsiders and strangers.

Finally, there is no need to pick fights with those who interview you. They may be pugnacious, but more likely something else is going on. If you find out what motivates them you are more likely to find out what they are really interested in.

123 *Getting That Job Interview*

1. Will you be through with your dissertation defense by the time you ought to arrive at the new job? If not, you are much less likely to be invited.

2. In fields that have lots of articles as the means of publication, have you published some articles, perhaps with your advisor? In fields where books are what count, is your dissertation, as people have seen it, convincing as a piece of scholarly work? See #1 above.

3. Have you exhibited high degrees of industriousness, hard work, intelligence, diligence, and devotion? Can your letter-writers give evidence of this?

4. Have you made a (significant) contribution to scholarship?

5. Are you not only very bright, but also hard-working and productive and possessing integrity? Many fields do not depend on your being very bright; rather, are you systematic, very careful, solidly scholarly?

6. Your letter-writers should know you well, and be able to give detailed evidence of your strengths.

Now, all of this is a minimum. Your match to what the department thinks it needs, your performance when you interview (although what I am talking about is what is needed to get that interview), and intangibles you cannot anticipate (is there a conflict in the department where you are the bargaining chip?) all will affect how things turn out. But at least you will have a chance.

124 *Looking for a Job*

Now is the time to plan to finish your dissertation a year from now.

Now is the time to figure out one or two crucial meetings you plan to attend next fall.

Now is the time to cancel all other obligations so you do get done on time.

125 *The Academic Labor Market*

Our labor market is sticky and suboptimal. I know of several first-rate, very well published scholars who do not have permanent positions, or who have positions at places that are very poor matches for their qualifications. Moreover, every department and university realizes that it has made errors in promoting and tenuring some people – what is regrettable is that those people cannot find ways of retooling themselves or finding other positions, so they can become much more valuable and valued (it does happen, but too rarely for everybody's sake).

What this suggests is that desert and luck both play a role in the appointment process. Having a tenured position is a privilege, demanding that we live up to that role. (Some of us would be better off giving up that position, and going into work that would be more rewarding for ourselves.)

What this also suggests is that there are more than one or two people who somehow have been left out of our enterprise, when we would be better off having them inside. Their not being part of it is an indictment of our claims to excellence and merit.

I just noticed that the *New York Times* restaurant critic and now book critic William Grimes has a PhD in literature, of the vintage when there were no jobs.

126   *Finding a Job in a Particular Locale*

Given the nature of the U.S. job market, if you want to be in a particular location, whether for culture or family, you will have trouble getting an appropriate position. One should be flexible about geography, but over the years I have had friends who have chosen otherwise – right now one of them with six or seven books has never held a tenure-track job yet thrives nonetheless with part-time teaching.

An academic job is a place from which you build a career. While many of us might like a job at Best University (*however understood*), there will surely be strong new PhDs who will not have jobs at Best University. Since there is a good deal of arbitrariness in this process, a fortiori some of the people who have jobs at Best University are actually weak, and some very strong folks are at Mediocre University. My point here is that once you have a job, one that allows for a modicum of time for research (even a job that would appear to allow for little or no time for research), you are then ready to build your career. That means a focused research program, careful presentations at suitable scholarly meetings, getting to know others in your field (this is about having lunch, exchanging preprints and reprints, being interested in others' work). If you have a reliable advisor, the advisor will be looking out for your interests even now, available for guidance. (If your advisor is dangerous, try to keep them out of the picture.) You will work hard, and it does not get easier with tenure. You may not ever find the right job. Not enough people are dying or retiring or taking up the cloth. At Harvard one of your rivals will not let them consider you (so get a job at MIT or BU, if you must be in the Boston area). What is crucial is to continue your research work, maintain a dense network of scholars who know your work.

In some countries there are academic networks whose hierarchy is quite precise. The best people are at Primary University, either by definition or in fact. One of the consequences of the diversity of the United States is that that just does not occur with sufficient assurance.

What contributes to success is hunger, a fire in the belly, that makes you do your best, aim for your top.

127   A Market?

You need a liquid market if there is to be an optimal distribution of resources. Exchanges at a certain price are signals to others about what they ought to do. Hence, a university that does not have people leave on their own and move to other universities is likely to be suboptimal. You want a faculty that is hard to keep, although implicit contracts (you have been promised a new colleague, you are loyal to your dean) will make for sticky prices.

There are perhaps too few positions open above the starting assistant professorships for the liquidity of the market to be maintained (unless all institutions encouraged movement). Some fields are hot, and they are likely to have lots of signals; others are not and they are likely to be stuck. Still, it strikes me that many faculty would be invigorated were they to move midway in their careers, finding new homes and situations that would give their research and teaching careers a burst of energy.

A provost needs to know more about the value of the faculty, and one way of knowing is how they move in the system – although achievements are in themselves a good measure. The Nobel Prize winner who worked at Utah had left Harvard as an assistant professor since the department was contentious and he needed a less pressured, longer-term perspective provided by a less frenetic institution. So the sorting is sometimes more subtle than quality, often involving people being able to find environments where they might thrive. A stuck full professor is likely to find new opportunities at a new institution. Would we be better off with 20-year contracts, creating a secondary market?

128   *Being on the Job Market*

1. Get a job! You can work your way up.

2. Ambition counts. Do not "get a life." Realize the competition is working when you are not.

3. Gauge your quality by the strongest people in the field, not even the strongest people in your doctoral institution or the department where you have a job. You are unlikely to be on top, but it surely helps to know where you stand. Make a list of the top 10–20 people in your field who you would like to know about your work.

4. People are denied tenure because they do not publish enough work in the right places, and do not raise external grant money from the right sources. In general, this usually makes their contribution less significant, and in the end that is what counts.

5. Have your advisor read over your application letter, your CV, and whatever else you send along. Your advisor may decide it is worth calling up the hiring committee, or may not.

6. Your letter should suit the job. How would you contribute to the department? Be flexible but realistic. Make sure the main points are in the first paragraph. Indicate your research accomplishments and where you believe you will be going in that direction.

7. You may be interviewed by phone. Of course, be on time or early. Answer questions the best you can. If you do not know something, indicate you will get back to them with an answer, and then do so by e-mail. You may meet people at a professional meeting and interview there. In any case, have copies of your CV and your research work (proposal, chapter from dissertation, articles, whatever) with you to give out.

8. The university wants you to find an appointment at the strongest university possible. If you have place restraints, we understand but would rather you go to the best place. (It affects how everyone thinks of us. Placement counts lots in reputation.) But, of course, you have to get an offer. And you have to realize that search committees and departments are often quite risk-averse, and often the second-best candidate gets the job offer.

9. There are a large number of openings, in general, and an even larger number of applicants. You cannot know who will invite you, so apply to as many places as appropriate.

10. Research the department you are writing to. Find out more about the place. Are there questions you have? They are good for the interview, since you have to find out whether the place would be good for you.

11. If you get an interview: Be sure you are appropriately dressed, that you are rested, and that when you give your talk you talk for less than the time allotted. In fact, in the first five minutes, you want to say the main results of your work. No teasers. If you use PowerPoint, be sure that the slides are spell-checked. Practice your talk. Listen to questions. Answer the best you can.

12. We'll worry about what to do when you have an offer.

13. The most important thing is to let people know your strengths and your research directions and what you might teach. If you are going to a teaching-oriented institution, be sure people understand you appreciate that. If you are going to a government or consulting or RAND-type place, let people understand how you would fit in.

14. If you are not going to finish your dissertation by the time you are hired, you should not be on the job market. And the talk you give should have substantive results, not just promises.

15. Lots of people who violate these rules get jobs, and lots who follow them do not. But it helps a great deal to follow them.

16. It's best to be nicely dressed, business attire. Suit not needed. Why? It works better. You do not have to look like the MBAs in their black suits and strangling ties.

17. They'll ask you lots of questions. Many will have little to do with you, but will reflect conflicts in the department or showing off for the other interviewers. Just answer, be brief, and realize that your goal is to leave a positive impression of interest, research potential, and someone able to talk in front of a classroom.

18. Maybe your advisor knows some of the people who will interview you. Your advisor might make a call ahead of time, or introduce you at the meeting.

19. Everyone is nervous, including the interviewer.

20. Ahead of time, again: What would you teach? Where is your research or practice going? What kinds of other activities interest you (e.g., community work, innovative teaching, etc.)? When will you be done, realistically? They might even ask you for your weaknesses, so have some to offer up.

21. If they decide not to invite you for a visit, it may have little to do with your performance. *Hiring committees are like sausage factories, their internal operations best not known.*

22. More interviews give you more practice.

129 *Being in the Job Market, Always*

Although a first-year graduate student is obviously not in the job market, *you really are in the market for your whole graduate school career.* When you formally go on the market, you want to be sure that the people who may be hiring have heard of you before, since they have seen you at meetings, or you have cornered them at a meeting and struck up a substantive conversation about research you or they are doing, or they have seen an article of yours in print (or even as referees for a journal). You may have published a fine book review, one that is interesting (and not a putdown). Your advisor may have mentioned your work to others over the years (we are proud of you, you know!). Or perhaps it is a member of your committee who is high on you and your work. We may have heard from our undergraduates how you have been a terrific TA.

It works that way. *You are in business from day one.* Do not forget it.

And let me strongly encourage you to consider the variety of job opportunities. You may not want to be a professor, but perhaps you want the chance to think about the option – if so, you will have to apply for such jobs. And the same applies for other areas of opportunity.

1. Be able to describe your work (research and service/consulting) in a paragraph that focuses on your contribution to the field and scholarship. This should be straightforward and clear. You may well have to write different paragraphs to suit different jobs.

2. Rarely do search committees have the ideal candidate in mind. Some of the time, the ad is written to suit someone they plan on hiring

anyway. But there is no reason not to disturb their plans by presenting yourself as a superior candidate. Applying for a position is a chance to make yourself known to a much wider range of people, whatever else, and to suggest opportunities to the committee.

3. Read over the announcement carefully. Go to the website of the institution. Ask yourself how your talents, plans, and interests genuinely match what is being sought – without stretching things too much. If the match is weak, this might well be a pass for you.

4. Make a list of people who might write letters of reference for you. They might come from peer or better institutions to the hiring institution, but as important is that they know you and your work. You will need that list.

5. Go to meetings; get to know people in your fields of interest. This usually pays off years down the line.

6. In the case of cluster hires (and three or more in the same field might well be called cluster), can you imagine a cluster and offer yourselves up as a group? It might be a chance for several scholars who want to work together to be in the same institution.

7. Make sure your CV is brutally clear. If you are not the PI on a grant, do not imply you are. Do not mix un-refereed stuff with refereed stuff. People want to know, in the first two pages, your academic background, major grants and fellowships, and books (keep in mind that edited counts for much less than monographs). If you publish articles, make sure the list begins before page 3, probably in reverse chronological order. If there is mostly or lots of joint-authored work, in your application letter tell people why: for example, "I have superior access to fieldwork sites, but to fully exploit them I need collaborators, many of whom take charge of their part of the work." Or, "My statistical techniques are particularly suitable for this area, and I am sought out on many research projects." Or, "Joe and I have worked together for 30 years. We no longer know who did what. We have published more than twice the number of articles one would expect from a single author, so we are comfortable about the work."

One problem – what if you do lots of collaborative work, and then people start to count articles? It makes little sense to give each author full credit for the article, and not much sense to give the author $1/N$ credit.

Focusing on contribution helps. And "Joe and I" above avoid the issue completely by publishing more than twice as much as either one of them might do. Of course, some collaborative work demands enormous energy (e.g., some scientific experiments) producing few articles. Here, testimony from the leaders of the project will attest to your contribution and compare it with others in the field.

8. Finally, while the process is not a crapshoot, lots of internal politics, misperceptions, and nonsense play a role in these processes. So, if you are asked for an interview, think of yourself as fortunate but not necessarily more deserving than those not asked; and if you are not asked for an interview, you just have to keep pushing and learning how to do better.

Whoever is hired is never the best, and often is the least offensive reasonably qualified person.

It is up to you to fulfill the gifts you receive – by working hard and with focus.

Having the job, or even tenure, means there are other people out there who plan on out-publishing and out-contributing you.

You will find a good deal of repetition among these sections, as elsewhere in the book. Move on to another part of the book or chapter as needed.

130   *Job Search Advice*

1. Your advisor is key. They need to make calls, seek out opportunities, and sponsor you.

2. Your application letter needs to capture readers' attention immediately. And your cv ought to be simple, clear, and with no catches or nonsense. You should be able to send chapters of your dissertation or papers.

3. You ought to have spent the last several years at meetings getting to know people in your area. And having them know of your work.

4. Your job talk matters too much, unfortunately.

5. You need to be flexible about what you will teach, to be focused on what work you will do in the next two to three years, and also to have done enough investigation of the place where you are being interviewed

so that you can ask intelligent questions. Do you want to get a job at the best place, or are you otherwise constrained?

131   *Seeking a Job at a Meeting*

1. Have some CVs with you. If you have a nice description of your dissertation research, bring that too. If you have published a significant article, bring some copies.

2. Departments do not quite know what they are looking for until they see what is available. On the other hand, they are unlikely to hire a dentist when they are looking for an urban designer. The task is to find good matches between candidates and schools. If you are very research-oriented, some teaching-oriented places will be less interested in you. If you have strong service credentials, there will be schools that will value that (especially if they have cooperative extension positions), and others that will not know what to do with you. So when you interview, you are trying to find out if you will fit in comfortably in a place. You may want to ask junior faculty at the institution about how they are treated.

3. When you give your talk, some people in the audience will be looking you over. Some will snooze or check their e-mail.

4. This is an awkward and uncomfortable process. Most hiring faculty understand this and will try to put you at ease. They really do want to find out about you, what you might do, what you are doing now. But of course you really do not know what you will be doing two years from now. Asking the hiring faculty about their school will be illuminating, although you will want to check their answers with others.

5. Could you teach a wider range of courses? There are two answers, one based on what you have done, and one based on your willingness to take on whatever is asked of you. Rise to that occasion. (I taught a general education animal ethics course for two years, which would surprise all who know me, given my petlessness and my allergies. But it turned out to be very interesting and effective, the way I ended up teaching it.)

132   *Application Letter for a Job*

1. Cut out as much BS as possible. Be specific: about yourself, your experience, your interests, the place you are applying to, the match, and

your hopes and expectations. This means you will have to do some research about your targets.

2. You have about 30 seconds to make a first impression. That means your first few sentences have to be clear, cogent, absent of jargon and pretense. They have to say something.

3. Always remember that the people reading these sorts of materials have read lots of them over the years, and have the prospect of reading many this year. They are unwilling experts at smelling cant, braggadocio, fake claims, nonsense. It is not that they are trying to smell you out – rather they cannot help knowing when they are being diddled with. Of course, you might still get away with it – but do you want to play a game against a very well trained opposite?

And of course, proofread, spell-check, and have someone else read over what you will submit to see if it has big flaws.

B. JOB TALKS AND SEMINAR PRESENTATIONS

133 *Compelling Presentations*

Most seminars and presentations are awful or barely acceptable. When you attend one that is compelling and interesting, try to figure out what the speaker has done. You will learn lots. You will learn lots from the awful ones too – what not to do.

When you make a presentation, an oral exam, or a speech, or give a seminar or a talk at a meeting:

1. In the first minute or two, the main take-home points should be clear. You might repeat them a few minutes in for latecomers. Most people's attention will wander later, or they will be doing e-mail, or perhaps fantasizing about someone across the room.

2. Use PowerPoint as a complement to what you are saying, not as a repetition. If you want to give people a sheet of paper with your main points or even the text of your talk, fine. But people will again start not paying attention once they realize the PowerPoint is a repeat of your points. If you do not use PowerPoint, everyone will notice and it may well be the most positive move you make.

3. Make sure all visuals are easy to read. It's likely that the more influential people are older and have less acute vision. They may have less acute hearing, so be sure you are loud enough.

4. Respond to questions directly. If you do not know the answer, say so and ask to speak to the questioner later. Never be evasive or nonresponsive.

5. Finish in three-quarters of your allotted time. Everyone will be grateful. (Most of us are not eye candy. If you are, I'm not sure what to advise.)

6. Charts with lots of numbers, unless the crucial ones are highlighted, usually are disasters. Or, they will reveal your weak points. If so, take charge of weaknesses before anyone asks.

7. Good visuals – maps, videos, interactives – are now becoming easier to make, easier to make poorly, and more likely to be employed by others. So, you might have yours. A one-to-two-minute video is sometimes helpful. In many fields, visuals and videos are irrelevant.

8. Practice about three times. The first time will be a disaster. The second will at least make sure you are well within time limits. The third should be OK.

9. Look OK: You do not want people noticing your clothing, your face, your haircut. For natural scientists, a fancy suit is probably too much. For business, a well-cut suit is just what is called for. Some people will notice if the suit cost $150 or $1500, and if those are the people you need to impress, the $1500 is well spent. I am unsure what to recommend to women, but they are much more aware of these issues.

10. Allow time for questions.

134   *What Makes a Terrific Job Talk?*

My colleague Lisa Schweitzer has described a terrific job talk. What made it so good?

1. He motivated his questions brilliantly, drawing from the literatures.

2. He illustrated his points with clean, effective graphics.

3. He graphically depicted the different disciplinary perspectives on his research questions.

4. Although he constructed a fairly complex model with a lot of data and variables, you could read all of his tables and equations easily.

5. He responded to some pretty thorny questions with poise and reflection.

6. He briefly but effectively showed his robustness checks.

7. He distinguished between findings and policy/management recommendations.

8. He wasn't afraid to be controversial with some of his recommendations, but his affect was noncombative and intellectual.

The questions I ask myself: Is the candidate asking important and salient questions? Is she answering those questions in a focused, rigorous, and generalizable way? When asked about tricky points, is he able to answer with clarity and precision, or does he ramble in his responses? (This speaks to his ability to work with students and collaborators.) Alternatively, can she stand her intellectual ground with force and clarity when she is challenged, and can she do so without arrogance or defensiveness? Has he mastered the art of being civil – but controversial, taking us beyond the comfort zone of conventional thinking? Does the research demonstrate both originality of thought and rigorous training?

135 *Giving Your Best Talks and Oral Presentations*

If you give people the main ideas, if you do not take too long, if you answer questions, and if you are concrete and defend your ideas, you will be in command.

1. *What's the Big Idea? Where's the beef?* Make sure you tell them the Idea / the Beef in the first minute. Before you drag them through all the details. Make sure you repeat your main points at the end. Throw out everything that is not essential to telling your main points and why they are important.

2. Answer the questions you are asked. (If you do not know, say so. If you are unsure, tell us your best guess.)

3. There is no need to defend yourself. Defend your ideas. Be specific and concrete.

136 *Brief Presentation at a Scholarly Meeting*

There are always complaints about the quality of presentations at meetings. People have to present to get their way paid. They might be looking for a job, or even want to find someone interested in their work.

1. Practice. Be sure you are taking less than the allotted time. If it is 15 minutes, go for 13. If you go over your allotted time, stop then and there. People will be grateful. Also, be sure your display or slides or whatever work ahead of time. If they stop working during a talk, just keep talking.

2. If your language skills are deficient, use PowerPoint so that people know what you are saying. Also, have copies of your paper to give to people. In most hands, PowerPoint is the soporific of modern academic life, but it is better for people to follow your presentation than not understand it.

If you are shy, get help from therapists. Academic life is rhetorical and performative and combative. (Very few scholars can just make a splash and disappear and still be effective. You have to keep presenting and selling your work.)

3. Talk loudly and clearly. Face the audience at least some of the time.

4. Give away your main point in the first minute of your presentation. Do not save it for the end. I realize this is controversial, but given what I know of most people's concentration and patience, at least you have their attention in the first minute. Repeat that main point at the end, and maybe even in the middle.

5. If you use charts of numbers, be sure people can read the charts, or give people copies on paper. Use color coding on your slide so that people know what to look for. Always indicate uncertainty, whether it is statistical or systematic or just plain ignorance; if you have eight significant figures, I assume that is your bank account or an artifact of your computer program – you usually have about one or two significant figures, except in precision scientific work.

6. Cute titles are disasters. Titles should give away the main point.

7. As for questions: listen carefully, respond the best you can, say that you do not know if you do not know, and suggest you discuss it with the questioner after the session. And then take the questioner to a corner, buy them a snack, and get to know them.

8. If you are writing your paper on the plane or in the hotel room, you are likely to be in trouble. Maybe you should not go to the airport at all. The problem here is that your delivery may well reflect your lack of time to practice, and most of us are neither Moses or Jesus or Mohammed or Buddha or Confucius and able to sound wise always. At the latest, two days before you leave, practice your talk.

In general, well-prepared students will outdo their professors; well-prepared junior faculty will outdo their senior colleagues. It's no fun to watch people make a mess. More to the point, if you are seeking recognition, a job, or even just scholarly interest, *people are always watching you.* If you give a well-prepared talk, everyone will notice and be grateful. You might well survive a poor talk, even get a job, but that is playing odds that most people cannot afford. If you are the strongest person in your field, people still expect you to show up on time and be well prepared.

Dress neatly. No sneakers or flip-flops. Be well groomed, in casual business attire. Freshly showered and toothbrushed. Do not be drunk or drugged-out.

I'm sure there is more, but if you follow the above you will not be a disaster. If your work is average, and most of the work we see is, at least people will think well of you, and even recall your main point.

As for discussants: Find out how long you have been allocated for comments, and that will set your agenda. For each paper, figure out the most useful things to make the work better, and say that. Do not ever be cruel or demeaning, or smart-ass. Graciousness is part of the discussant role. Also, never advertise your own work, or your best friend's. Rather focus on the work in front of you. After the session, offer to take out the presenters for coffee and continue the conversation. In any case, surely take no longer than the time allocated. People would much prefer to hear your main points in five minutes, so that they can say what is on their minds.

137 Ways of Surviving a Job Interview

Be neat, clean. People have no capacity to separate image from substance. If your work is terrific, but they think you are a slob, they will say something like, "X wouldn't really fit in here." There are exceptional places, in two ways – either they want dumb slobs and you fit, or they believe they are populated by geniuses, and are quite willing to believe proper image is separate from substance and talent.

When you give your talk, never get into an argument with your audience. They may well be pompous, obnoxious, mentally unstable. Their colleagues know this. They do not want to be reminded of it, and more to the point they have to choose their own over you. Arrogance does not wash. Most academic departments act as bureaucracies, unwilling to really be happy with people who work too hard or are too successful.

Remember, they are trying to find a way to eliminate you – or at least some people are. Of course, if they (or maybe only the head) want to hire you, then you might be dumb, inept, and a boor and they will say there is promise, a chance for growth, and genuineness.

Departments are still subtly and not so subtly influenced by matters of class, style, gender, race. You cannot do much about this, but you can at least cut out the chance they have for cutting you out.

And remember, appointments are usually a product of group processes called faculty meetings. Such processes are in general known to be suboptimal, and at best satisficing with a least common denominator. There are wondrous exceptions, but it would appear that such periods last for 10–15 years at best, and then the department reverts to the usual behavior.

I am told by everyone that what you see is what you get, whether in marriage or in hiring someone. The dissertation or the papers are what you should expect more of, if you are lucky. You can't hope they'll become much better, or start publishing, or be good teachers if there is substantial evidence otherwise. People do not become more focused or thoughtful or deep. All of this is true in general, but there are wonderful exceptions. It is just not prudent to expect that you are a great handicapper unless you have demonstrated such skills consistently.

138   *Preparing for the Job Search*

1. If you become a college teacher, you will spend your career with late adolescents and some adults. A research university gives you greater access to a larger world of peers. But most of your time is spent with those late adolescents.

2. If you want a position that is not academic (such as foundation, government, university administration or other such administration, or corporate and private sector), it is likely that you will find your job with more limited help from your advisor. And there surely is an old boys'/girls' network. This is where the university's career services folks may be helpful.

3. If you do not have your doctoral degree in hand, when will you be done? You are unlikely to be hired without the degree – unless the market is so much a seller's market that the buyers are willing to compromise.

4. Prepare at least one job talk. It should be 30–40 minutes in length, at most 40 minutes. You should try it out, have well-prepared visuals (and be prepared for the computer to screw up, leaving you without Power-Point), and practice it at least once or twice more as you revise. The main points ought to be clear in the first five minutes (including your distinctive contribution and your findings or claims). If they are not there in those five minutes, you will lose half of your audience. Be sure your talk emphasizes your contribution and also indicates future work you might do (this can be at the end).

5. When you write an application letter, be sure to modify your basic letter (which you ought to share with your advisor) to suit the particular job demands indicated in the ad. Why would they want to consider *you*? Be sure you supply them with what they want (letters of reference, references, samples of work, CV). Proofread, copyedit, and spell-check. And proofread, copyedit, and spell-check.

6. If you are invited for a talk, be sure you know about the department and the research of your potential colleagues. An afternoon in the library or at the website is a minimum before you go.

7. Have some sense of where you will be going in your research, what you might teach, and even the kind of funding you might try to develop. You will meet students, a dean, some faculty. Listen, ask questions, be responsive. It is exhausting and inhumane. Do not drink alcohol.

8. Rest before you go. Take along extra copies of your work, your vita. Nothing should be done at the last minute. Your advantage is your being well prepared.

9. Your advisor and others should be consulted for advice that is more specific to the place and job. If your advisor is not too helpful, there is the rest of the faculty.

10. Your success is our success. If we can help you, let us know. And make sure that your advisor is in on all of what you are doing. A phone call from your advisor might make it more likely you are looked at, and perhaps invited. This exchange of students is of course fundamental to academic power.

139 *Job Interviews*

1. Even if you are dubious about the position, prepare well. Spend at least an hour or two on the website or reading other materials about the department and the university. Look over the research publications of people in your subfield. Your advisor may have helpful guidance.

2. You do not have to worry about whether the position is right for you until it is offered to you. Do not worry about housing, schools, or the weather – until you are offered the job.

3. If you have prepared well, you will ask your interviewers interesting questions about their department or their research.

4. Think ahead about the courses you might teach, and your research plans for the next five years.

5. If you have some problems in your CV or career, be prepared to answer questions or to preempt such questions. Your six months in jail when you were 24 are often hard to hide, but you are under no obligation to list them since they are not professional. If you did not get tenure at your previous institution, you have to be able to discuss that – even if you do not know why. Try not to say "politics." Put it more substantively: the chair changed and it was clear I did not have a future at the university, or, my field was not popular with the major professors, or, I had not published my first book in time.

6. If you think that an inside candidate or someone else is actually the shoo-in, think of the interview as a chance to show them they are wrong, or at least to make them regret their prejudice.

7. You only need one job offer.

140 *Interviewing for a Job, or in Fieldwork*

Say you have a chance to interview someone, say about a job, or for a paper, or for an informational interview. It is vital that you prepare for such an interview. If it is about a firm or an organization, minimally you ought to have looked over their website with some thoroughness. You might look at printed materials, or studies of the organization. If it is about a project, have you looked at the material that is out there about it, often available on the web or in libraries and archives?

Figure out what you want to talk about. What do you want to learn from the interview? If you have prepared appropriately, you will be asking questions that will be of interest to the person you are interviewing.

Think about what you want to convey to them about yourself. It is all right to send them a note ahead of time indicating what you wish to discuss with them, and information about yourself. (They may or may not have a chance to read it, but it shows your seriousness.)

What makes terrific interviewers on television is their deep knowledge about the person being interviewed (from memos prepared by their staff), their listening to what the person is saying, and so their capacity to match what they are being told with what they know already. They see openings for incisive questions.

Interviews work because the person learns from what they say and you say. I heard a discussion of celebrity interviewing recently, and the fellow said that interviewees control the subject matter and use their charm to convey what they want to convey. (For example, Nicole Kidman was supposed to be preternaturally sensitive, many questions down the line, to any questions that might eventually lead to a question about Tom Cruise being gay.)

So when you go for an interview, be prepared, be thoughtful and to the point, and know why you are there.

C. NO OFFERS?

141   *You Did Not Get a Job Offer . . .*

1. Some openings will develop, perhaps for just a year.

2. There may be some postdoctoral possibilities that are still open, or which have fairly late application dates.

3. There may be some teaching in the area's colleges and universities.

4. Some of us took a long time to find a tenure-track position, often doing administration or fellowships or part-time teaching. I would rather it does not happen to you, but it is far from fatal.

5. Search committees are notorious for their willingness to settle for someone who "fits in" rather than the strongest candidate, or for choosing a compromise candidate. You do your best, and your advisor does their best, but still it is more of an unsure process than we might like.

6. Your advisor is crucial. Do not hide from them.

I received this from a student:

1. Quality organizations are always recruiting – even when downsizing.

2. Sponsorship is one-third of the key to getting a good professional job (along with education and experience). Networking is like financial planning – start long before you need it and let it grow.

3. Yes, nonacademic work provides marketable and compensated activity during a possibly long academic job search, but it also consumes a great deal of time. If a student doesn't have the time to publish while in the school environment, he/she certainly will not gain more hours in a day by entering the professional market.

We want our students to have good productive lives, be responsible to their families and to their own ambitions. It is foolish to expect students to follow in our footsteps; in fact it is often unfair. Even doctoral students may be in school for many reasons other than becoming professors and researchers. People have real constraints – they need to support their families financially, they may have sick family members who need their attention, there may be political constraints, or in fact they may not like research. The idea that one is free of such constraints is one of those fantasies set up by "men with wives," so to speak, or those who "have money" to start with.

We have emphasized research work and academic appointments for our students in the PhD program because without that focus you will not even have a chance to have a teaching job in a research university. However, there are a limited number of those positions. That your teachers now have jobs may well reflect such processes or market conditions 20 years ago.

Few if any of your teachers do their best. They have many constraints on their lives; many are in fact sloppy, often afraid of trying to do their best. Yes, I love my work. But, perhaps, there were other ways of making a living (perhaps a much better living) that would have provided me with satisfaction and surely a lot less agony.

142   No Job This Year?

Do not be permanently discouraged by your not getting a job if you were on the market last year. Each year's market is a new one, for the most part. Search committees change. At the same time, think in terms of backup job, so you have a sense of real opportunity.

143   The Day Job

You need a good day job so that you can pursue your entrepreneurial project.

1. It seems that the headhunters now use monster.com and careerbuilder.com, and they pay heavily to use it to find candidates for positions. You'll need to polish your résumé so that it highlights your strengths. There's no charge to post, as far as I can tell. You could post your résumé today, and then revise it. Do not delay. (Whenever I have such ideas, I do them immediately – makes me feel better.)

2. You will want to find a headhunter in your field, in your town. Do that today.

3. You need to explore each avenue, because you then learn what makes sense next.

4. You only need one decent job. It does not matter so much if it is ideal, if it allows you to succeed. That success opens new avenues.

5. It is sometimes discouraging. You do not want to give up your entrepreneurial dream, so you do need to get a day job.

It must be a difficult time. It is. You have a terrific portfolio of skills. Someone should recognize them in just the right way. Of course, in many fields, the way you find a job is through connections, your teachers, attending meetings, going to the right events.

D. YOU HAVE AN OFFER

144 *The Job Market: Counteroffers and Market Signaling*

Decisions are signals to others about intents and capabilities. Poker players know this. If strong faculty leave your department with offers from other places (even ignoring the strength of those places), people will ask:
- Is this a faculty that is "hard to keep," it is so strong?
- Or, is this a chair/dean/provost that is
  not serious about being strong?
- Or, is this a chair finding a way of ridding
  themselves of faculty they do not want?

If it gets out that the administration did not make a preemptive or at least comparable offer, people will ask: What are the priorities of this administration or department? Should I, a faculty member, even negotiate with this administration?

What is most disheartening is to watch strong people leave because their deans did not respond aggressively. Or, even more ridiculously, on the decision day they receive a call from the president or the provost encouraging them to stay, but the counteroffer was nonexistent or weak. Or, several strong people leave one after the other.

When an administration sends signals indicating they do not meet offers or they do not meet offers from that (less prestigious) institution, it is as well to remember that pride goeth before a fall. If someone is important to you, don't be haughty: play the game for keeps.

Mistakes in hiring and retention are examined publicly for the next decade (as in sports as well). Nowadays, what with blogs and wikis and anonymous posts (and what the *Chronicle of Higher Education* has been doing for decades), much the same will happen to deans and chairs and provosts. It's not always pretty.

145 *Bargaining for Jobs and Fellowships*

It's the time of year when people start to get job offers and fellowship offers. It may be useful to keep in mind that what is most crucial in all cases are the conditions of work – will you be able to do the work you want to do, do you have supportive colleagues, and will they and the institution help advance your career, allow you to grow and enhance your reputation?

Now you may want to come to a place because it has good surfing, or you really want to be a screenwriter, or your true love works in the area, or you come from a nearby place, or your ill parents are nearby. About this I have little counsel, other than to say that you must be practical, know what you really want and need (very hard to know!), and understand there are consequences of choices.

Salary should be adequate, or even munificent, benefits OK, teaching appropriate. But you do not want to bargain at the margin (the extra 5 percent) if you have to sacrifice good working opportunities, fine mentoring, the right colleagues, prestige. The latter all add up in the long run to a much better life. (If you must have that extra 5 percent for good reasons, that clearly trumps my advice.)

And if you are bargaining and negotiating, keep in mind that at some point it sours the other party on you – whether it be in labor negotiations, or in asking someone to marry you, or in choosing an academic connection. People, in the end, must trust you, and feel that you will not go back on a deal, that you will not take all the change off the table, and that you are really committed to them.

Bruce Stiftel added: "Negotiation students will also think of problems from bargaining too softly: not asking for what you want, because you value the relationship more than the issues under discussion.

"So, if you forget to mention that you want to begin to work in forecasting, they may never know you could have been assigned to teach that subject. If you avoid mentioning that you need a specialized piece of computer equipment, you many have trouble getting later what would have been easy to give at the time you were hired. If you fail now to ask for a proper salary, it's likely to be years before that opportunity lost can be overcome.

"How can you increase the chances that your real needs are recognized and responded to, and your proper market worth is respected, while avoiding the pitfalls of coming across as selfish and untrustworthy? Homework has a lot to do with it. Find out what the market prices are for what you have to offer; find out what compensation and working arrangements are for current incumbents in the job grouping you would join. Of course I do not mean asking people how much they make. Use national data sources, and believable information you may have from others. Ask contextual and circumspect questions during the many private meetings you will have at the interview: How are teaching assignments determined? Under which rules? How are salaries determined? Do current assistant professors (or . . .) find that the resources available to them (and mentoring, and students . . .) are conducive to productive work? How does the administration expect you to be different from current faculty? (See, for example, Fisher and Ury, *Getting to Yes*, 1981.)

"Once you really understand what the system of resources and rewards is like, you will be in a much better position to make clear what you really need in a constructive manner, and to imagine what you can ask for legitimately and with likelihood of success."

146   *Jobs: Negotiating for a Position*

In general, salary is not your major concern as long as it is adequate for your needs and is comparable to that earned by others at your institution or in your field. Total compensation, which includes bonus, may be a bit more interesting. Benefits may be very important, especially if you are concerned about savings and retirement or have special health care needs (for you, for your dependents). Do not overly restrict yourself about location. First get a job offer, and then you can decide if the location is wrong for you. Decide what really matters: do not make a big deal out of a onetime benefit (say, moving expenses) if you can succeed on recurring compensation such as salary level or bonuses. On the other hand, you may need substantial computational resources to do your work, and you do want to make sure they are available at a price that accords with your resources. Job security may or may not be an important issue for you. Usually, if there is greater security, risk-taking and growth options are more restricted. Keep in mind that tenure in the academic world is important as a matter of rank. For the most part it benefits the university, not the scholar – for it informally takes you out of the job market.

You may want to have bragging rights about your salary or compensation. Do you really need these rights? The same may be true for rank.

What you really want is a chance to show your talents and to grow, to make a contribution and to be recognized and appreciated, and to be able to move into positions that allow you to show, grow, contribute, be recognized and appreciated, and move some more. Is this the right step, now, for you? Will it allow you to make a crucial next step?

Of course, very different considerations will apply to you when you first enter the job market than when you are in your later fifties and are thinking in terms of retirement, for example. If you are 50, and want to be sure you can write your next big book, make sure you do not choose a job that will preclude that even if it is otherwise attractive (e.g., a big raise, a nice named chair, and also, by the way, chairperson of the department).

I am amazed by how blind the various negotiators are. Faculty are often blind to their own longer-term self-interest, while deans do not figure out what would really make a difference (often, here, the trick is to offer a too-large salary or goody, since you really want someone, or perhaps the candidate has a special-needs child and you can help the family). And faculty and deans are blind to the imperatives that are on their opposite's mind.

Generosity is a sign of power. You want to get a position that will allow you to thrive, you want a faculty member or employee who will contribute greatly to your organization. As is usual in negotiations, have a plan in your back pocket that puts aside all the tendentious issues, allows everyone to save face, and gives you something you really, really want (you give up on that last $5,000 of salary, but suggest a substantial research account, say $3,500).

E. HIRING

147   *Mistakes in Hiring*

Keep in mind that the ones that get away might be replaced by others who are as good or almost as good. To avoid mistakes: Do not be too swayed by the job talk. *Read the work.*

148　*Hiring the Strongest in Any Field*

It may be useful for departments that want to move forward to think of advertising for the best candidates, regardless of field, or perhaps with a very wide range. You might get flooded with applicants, but an open-field ad will also bring to the fore candidates whom you would not otherwise see. There are legal reasons why ads are posed the way they are, but I am sure that these can be dealt with. Junior people can readily compete with senior faculty because the juniors may offer promising avenues the seniors have yet to explore.

149　*Quality: One A Is Better Than Two Bs, Unless You Have a C Average*

Most deans and chairs and committees should be counseled that if they offer excuses in a promotion dossier, they should be short and to the point. There are people who do perform, no excuses, and we have to ask why the university has to be satisfied with less.

In some fields, the university seems to be appointing or tenuring people who are solid Bs, largely because the A's are not available (we would presume). Sometimes it is argued that the department is at a C level and the Bs represent an improvement. It might make sense to spend twice as much as a B costs for a real A. Or give the A what they want if they are to come, as long as they are committed to improving the department.

I have read elaborate justifications for a low level of productivity, even with comparisons to other places and recent hires or promotions elsewhere. Or, it is said that A-quality people are infrequent. Still, for a university on the make, one real A is likely worth two Bs.

We might be skeptical of talk of "rising stars," or of arguments that if God chooses to collaborate with a B, B must really be an A. Skeptical of the papers-in-the-pipeline argument unless what is already out is substantial. There are slow starters, but strong scholars tend to be fast out of the block and to continue as such. Skeptical of the book-almost-done, although that may be a risk worth taking with assistant professors. Most such books could have been done 18 months earlier, but the candidate needed the tenure deadline to prompt them to finish. Anyone who needs this sort of deadline is less likely to be an ongoing producer at competitive rates. The rare case of slow productivity because a golden egg is being laid needs good evidence (chapters, sections of the paper).

Now it may be that a university is to be at best a B institution, but that is not what I hear out of the Central Administration Building of many institutions. Every B we appoint means that they are likely to increase the viscosity of the faculty and make it harder to appoint an A. Bs are not poor scholars. But they are not top-notch, and their ambitions are not great.

150 *Hire Smart, Keep Smart, Tenure Smart*

The hiring decision is the most important decision made by a dean. It makes sense to give very careful attention to hiring decisions, since at that point there is no emotional commitment to the candidate, no eventual problem of "endowment effects" (D. Kahneman, *Thinking, Fast and Slow*, 2011), where at tenure time you overvalue what you have.

The tenure recommendation is the second-most-important decision a dean makes. "Hire smart, keep smart, tenure smart" is a friend's slogan. Another friend says he wants "a faculty that is hard to keep" (since they keep getting hired away by Chicago and Stanford). As far as I can see there is no substitute for brains, defined not in terms of IQ but in terms of focused effort with good judgment and good discipline and high ambition. Entrepreneurial skills may also be part of this.

I mention all this because you want to be part of the solution, not part of the problem. *You want to make it easy for your dean to promote you.* You want to be focused, disciplined, ambitious, entrepreneurial, brainy, and careful in your judgments. This is a matter of getting guidance from the strongest people in the field, following through, not telling yourself nonsense, and having a sense of what you can do. If you decide that what matters to you is to live in X and devote yourself to Y, you may want to choose an academic venue that allows for that. But within that venue you want to be focused, disciplined. Find the pond that suits you and then swim like an Olympian. I always admire people who know what matters to them, and then go for it.

By the way, none of this is very different from what would be required in most corporate or bureaucratic environments.

People ask me whether I am writing about them – as if something that I knew about them is being made into a roman à clef *for public consumption. As in most novels, what I say is an accumulation and conflation and abstraction of past experience, and rarely if ever is any one particular person or event the source of what I say. If it fits you, it also fits lots of other people.*

FIVE

Junior & Probationary Faculty (#151–174)

A. FUNDAMENTALS

151 *Doing Your Best in a Bureaucracy*

Universities are bureaucracies. They provide for five-to-seven-year probationary periods for new professors (assistant professors), although a small number of universities or departments have longer periods. (And many European universities have shorter probationary periods, but much more demanding subsequent promotion criteria.) There is substantial pressure on probationary faculty: they must teach reasonably well, they must convert their dissertation research into publishable articles or a book, and then continue in further lines of research and publish them, and they must establish some visibility in the field. While this is often presented as hell, I think it is better thought of as training for the future, demanding focus, integrity, and hard work. Marginal passes of this process rarely bloom into significant scholars – hence my notion of training. To be a successful scholar/teacher demands the kind of discipline scholar-athletes have to exhibit. If you want to be chosen in the draft you have to exhibit commitment and talent.

Now, if you look at most major research universities, some faculty would seem to be much less focused and devoted. In some cases, they have made major achievements earlier – and it is hard to have a second no-hitter – and they do not know how to be journeymen. In some cases, illness has taken over (including chronic illness such as alcohol or depression or heart disease). In some cases, faculty are having a fallow period, surprising all when they flourish once again. And in some cases, they never did learn to be disciplined and devoted and focused – and so they do what they can. You should be aware that some tenured associate or full professors make salaries that are half or less the salaries of those in similar ranks or with similar years on the job.

Many if not most of us are journeymen. (Excuse the gender specificity.) This is a craft guild and while we may not be masters, we do a fine job. Some find their métier in teaching, others in research, others in service.

What is the lesson for you? The next seven to ten years of your career are your training ground. You can learn to be the best you can be, and have time for your family as well. Or you can try to figure out the system and see if you can succeed, in effect by pandering and finesse. The secret is that if you learn to be the best you can be, to be focused and devoted and careful, your career will be easier, the rewards will be (in general) greater, and the satisfactions will be larger. (I wrote "in general" because bureaucracies are in general not meritocracies – there are sycophants who do quite well, and some folks of the highest quality who do not do as well as they might. But thanks to the possibility of bids from other institutions, that may eventually be remedied rather dramatically – just do not count on it.)

152   *Focus and Direction in Your First Job*

I have been reading files for promotion and tenure, and I am struck again and again by the importance of focus and direction for the success of scholars. Rather than doing many things, they need at this stage to do one or two very well. Quantity counts, to be sure. But publishing in the major journals of the field counts even more. You need to make people in the field aware of your work early in your probationary period (send out reprints, invite people to join panels), and make your presence felt at national meetings. You have to realize that the most senior people want to know what the next generation will be up to.

If you are doing a book, you want to have it done and off to the press at the end of your fourth year or so, or even earlier, so it can come out well before you are up for tenure. Later may be OK, but it makes things harder.

Yes, some people get tenure with much less or with a more scatter-shot range of materials. Some get tenure because of less relevant reasons. But I observe that the demands in the major universities have become more stringent (not so much more demanding, but less forgiving).

153 *An Informal Guide for New Faculty Members*

You need to establish your reputation in the profession or artistic field, for the quality of your work and the significance of your contribution. You want to create significant scholarship and works of art and perfor-mance recognized as such by national leaders in your field.

You will need to focus your efforts, take full advantage of your doc-toral work (by publishing the book or the articles, or getting the grant) or of the work you did for your terminal degree, and then go on to establish the next project beyond your doctoral work. In some fields, you will need to finish up your doctoral work very quickly, and go in a new direction. In others (especially the humanities), preparing your first book (derived from your dissertation) will take some time.

In fields where performance and creative work are crucial, you will need to do much the same.

Talk with your chair, talk with your strongest colleagues, and pay attention to what faculty are doing in the top departments, so you un-derstand what are the signs of superb scholars and creators in your disci-pline: what kind of publications and exhibits and performances, in which premier outlets, and at what rate. Learn how important it is in your field to give presentations at other universities or at national meetings.

For many fields, *be careful about being sucked into working exclusively on team projects, or continuing too far in collaborating with your doctoral or postdoc advisor.* You have to make your own mark as an independent in-vestigator or artist, or as a leader of such endeavors. If you work in a field in which collaboration and joint publication is the norm, be sure you and others will understand and appreciate the nature of your contribution.

Research that is fun and exciting for you is likely to be seen as such by others as well.

As for books or journals, local vs. national venues, premier publish-ers and placements, consult with the strongest colleagues in your field.

If you deviate from the norm, there should be good reason for doing so, reasons that will appeal to others.

In fields in which you are setting up a laboratory or a team in order to do your research, you will need to attend to management issues: keep tenure in mind, and so formulate a five-year plan; create the lab culture you want and hire people who will contribute to it; manage your lab, do not let it manage you; learn and evolve as a leader.

Teaching: You will learn to become a stronger teacher. The sign of teaching excellence is the performance of your students, and not only or mainly your students' satisfaction. Pay attention to the student-teacher relationship, which includes mundane things such as setting up appointments, publicizing office hours and then keeping them, returning papers promptly, answering e-mail. Try to keep your teaching load reasonable and not to have too many new course preparations: if you think you are swamped, talk with your chair. Do not fall afoul of the rules against sexual harassment, and rules protecting privacy of student grades and other records.

Grants: If you are in a field that needs big grants to do your research you're probably behind already. Get that proposal in. What you are aiming for is continuous funding through whatever counts in your discipline as the really significant grants. And the grants that are credited to you are the ones where you are the principal investigator or the co-PI. (New assistant professors may well need to be incorporated onto others' grants, at least at first; it takes some time and often several tries to receive significant grants.)

Service: You have to be a good citizen, and your colleagues have to believe that on balance your contribution is positive, not negative. But you will not get tenure for your committee work, and you have to resist agreeing to do too much. Clinical duties will not get you tenure, either.

If you are part of an underrepresented group on the university faculty, you are more likely to be enlisted into university committees related to diversity issues (and more of these committees than your overrepresented colleagues). Whatever your commitment to these issues, now is not the time to focus on these committees. The best response is to indicate that your book or project demands all your time. (If they – the provost, your chair – insist, nonetheless, you might try to get compensating released time from teaching so that your research production does not suffer.)

Living a full life: At the same time, you are in world where there is little likelihood that someone can pick up after you – whether it be a mentor, a spouse or partner, or a departmental secretary (even if that helper is more talented than most of your scholarly colleagues).

You are likely to have major responsibilities outside your career: for your children, your parents. Family duties are real and important, and are essentially your main moral responsibility. If there is a crisis you need to try to arrange for extra time. You can talk with your chair or dean about rearranging your teaching load (perhaps teaching less in a time of crisis and making it up the next year), or you can apply to the provost to stop the tenure clock (extend your tenure decision deadline). Parents of a newborn or those who adopt a young child may qualify for a year's extension of the tenure clock on request, and ten weeks' paid leave. (You may have a legal right to additional unpaid leave.)

Strong academic environment: Say that you are in an ambitious research university. We constantly try to improve, so you ought to be stronger than at least half of your departmental or school colleagues, perhaps two-thirds. What you take for granted about the quality and expectations and ambition of the university are an achievement of the university over the last decades. The university is making stronger and stronger appointments. More of them are world-class spectacular scholars, clinicians, artists, and performers. They are capable of doing substantial amounts of the very best work and then some. Model your career after your most distinguished colleagues, and pay attention to what is being accomplished by your cohort or those a few years ahead of you at the top schools in the country. They are the peers to whom you will be compared.

An increasingly strong faculty serves your interests, but it also raises expectations. And those expectations are likely to rise substantially over the next several decades. In other words, unless you are willing to rise to the challenges, you will find that you will be falling behind. If this is too demanding an environment for you, there are many other environments that will provide satisfying challenges, probably better compensation, and high prestige. Be sure you want to be a scholar in a competitive environment in an ambitious institution for the next 25–40 years. (If you have trouble getting in your work on time and have had lots of late papers in school, you are unlikely to thrive in this environment.)

Promotion and tenure: Deans and promotion committees have to take into account these stronger appointments and expectations, and make a judgment that the candidate is likely to be a peer of the strongest faculty at the university. The dossier has to inspire confidence in the candidate and in the department's judgment. The university committee sees the full range of appointments, and is acutely aware of the strongest appointments (and the weak ones, as well). Carefully read over the promotion and tenure guidelines. They mean exactly what they say.

Mentoring and advice: The scholar's life doesn't have to be a lonely one. Talk about your work and your scholarly plans with colleagues inside the department and outside it, as well as your chair. Try to learn something from your annual and third-year reviews. But do not take anyone's word for it that your tenure is in the bag. As Yogi Berra said, it's not over until it's over. (And it is not over then. There are significant future decisions – promotion to full professor, salary raises, national and international awards, and offers from other institutions.) The tenure decision is not made before the provost makes it, and before that you will be evaluated at the university level and by external reviewers who are looking for the best. The good news is that you wouldn't have been hired unless your colleagues thought you could make it; everyone is rooting for you.

You will surely get mixed messages about the relative importance of teaching, service, and research. Research is likely most important in universities.

154 *Justifying Your Work*

· Taste: It helps to have good taste, to choose problems that are fruitful, to modify projects so that they are more interesting, to focus on what matters. It's not just having a good idea, it is having an idea that allows for development.
· Pride in workmanship: Carefulness, scrupulousness, timely performance. No excuses. You stand behind the work you deliver.

- Storytelling: You can describe what you are doing in a thoughtful manner; you can tell a story about your project that makes sense of it, even to those who are not expert or the cognoscenti. Your project itself is that story. And you can write well enough so that your grammar and diction do not get in the way.
- Intelligence, brilliance, and following the rules, what would seem to be required to do well on tests and in school, won't get projects done. Rather, character, perseverance, and commitment are at least as important.

155   *Your Personal Best*

Do a first-rate job – your personal best – the first time around. And if you get it wrong, do better the next time you get a chance. (Of course, you rarely know the criteria that will be used to judge you, even with those proverbial rubrics you had in school – but I do know that superior performances that just happen to be wrong still get lots of points.)

Often, we think that we have to manage our time and effort, trying for the regimen that gains us the best average grade or performance. Most actual performances in life are not about management, but about your personal best, about choosing your main focus or foci, and having a strong sense of priorities. You are much less likely to make trade-offs than sacrifices, and if you choose to make a sacrifice you try to figure out saving graces that justify your choice.

You have a seriously ill spouse or parent or child, and rather than trying to do it all (and some people can do it all), you may decide not to travel – something that will surely impact your career. But you also decide, or find that it is now possible, to write one book after another, for having focused your time and energy you actually have more time to write books than most of your colleagues (again, there are some who can do it all). Or, having been given a less than ideal academic position, you then figure out how to be much more productive and risk-taking as a scholar, again, compared to your colleagues. I know of both such commitments by different people. I am not suggesting that you do not pay heavily for following a different path. You almost always do. But at least you have saving graces that justify your choices.

You really want to ask yourself, *what should I not be doing, so that I can do my best at what I do choose to focus on?* You may decide that some things do not matter. Scholars or professionals may decide that having a fine-appearing home is much less important than their children and work (I recall one scholar saying they gave up dinner parties and dusting). But what matters needs to be done well.

Hence you do not ask, what do I do to improve my grade? You might ask, how do I perform so that my work is stronger the next time around? It's what coaches and teachers can help you do, in sports or surgery or musicianship. But they only pay attention to those who aim to deliver their best.

156   Assistant Professors: How to Survive

You have five to six years to show that you are a reasonably good teacher, that you can pursue an independent and well-regarded research program, and that you will be a good colleague.

Presumably, you have done a doctoral dissertation (or a law degree and a law review article, or performance, or artworks). Publishing or publicizing that piece of work should be your first priority, addressed in the first two years of your appointment. If you decide that it should be a book, can you get a contract now? If not, how long before you get the work in order? (Ten years? Then you will not be able to pursue that now.)

The major problem is a delay in publishing your dissertation research, thus delaying your starting another project.

If you start another project in year three, then you have about two years to come to the point where you can write up articles about it. It will take another year or two for them to appear.

The sign of trouble is when most of the articles appear in the year before you come up for tenure. There will usually be a bump in your articles or the appearance of your first book about this time. The question people naturally ask is whether you will stop publishing the day after you receive tenure. If it is a book, people want to see evidence that you are now pursuing another book and have made some progress. (In some places, tenure is granted well into the associate professorship, when two books are out or two major projects are completed or two NIH RO1s have been granted.

Or, perhaps one is done and the other is finished but not published. In these longer probationary period tenure cases, the timetable is different.)

If your department asks you to take on a significant administrative load (e.g., to chair one of the degree committees), you have to wonder whether they are setting you up for failure at the tenure stage. Most university tenure committees do not find the administrative obligation convincing, even if the department does.

What is most discouraging is to discover at the end of the third probationary year that the assistant professor has not made much progress, and often seems to think they are in good shape since so many of their seniors do not publish much either. A recipe for disaster.

If you expect that teaching will help get your tenure, make sure your teaching methods and quality are nationally recognized (not just teaching awards at your home institution), that you have written about them and published about them, and that you have a nest egg put aside for the good chance you will not be tenured. This does not apply at universities and colleges where teaching is the major activity, research being secondary or tertiary.

Stay out of departmental politics. This is best seen as a spectator sport at this stage of your life. When people try to recruit you to their side, say that you have to prepare an article for a meeting in two days, prepare that article, and go to the meeting.

Make sure people outside your university recognize your work. Make a list of likely referees, and make sure they receive reprints or preprints. Talk to them at meetings.

And, focus on what you are doing, so that your tenure case makes sense. The work should add up to a contribution or two that is well defined and significant.

I believe that almost anyone who is hired at a university could obtain tenure. Sometimes there is politics and evil (which is best dealt with by getting another job, living well, and leaving the idiots to their own devices), and sometimes you really are not up to snuff, but most often the candidate has left gaping holes in their vita, all of which could have been readily filled by careful focus and planning.

As for teaching, one ought to do a responsible job, listen to the feedback from students, invite colleagues to your class to help you do a better job. About service, again, that should be limited at this stage in your career. If they insist on putting you on the University Diversity Committee since you are an underrepresented minority, tell them you want a buyout from teaching, so you will still have time for your research. If they cannot provide that, respectfully decline, saying you have to focus on your research. They will get you later.

157 *Increasing Quality at Tenure Time*

1. Hire the strongest. If there are risks, note them and address.

2. Mentor regularly. Do not assume that the candidate knows what they should be doing.

3. Firm guidance helps to avoid mistakes.

4. Make sure the candidate publishes from their dissertation, or in non-PhD fields, that they publish work in the first two years. In the case of the creative arts, what have they been doing before being hired, and how can that be employed to produce measurable impacts? If grants are required, they need to be in process by year two, three at the latest.

5. Fix responsibility for mentoring and guidance and performance in a senior person. If the candidate fails, there are consequences for the senior. (This is probably a flawed strategy, but what I am trying to do is to make the unit responsible for failure, but not too responsible.)

6. If in the fourth year it looks like the dossier will be weak, what can be done? The fifth year is likely to be too late.

7. If there are teaching problems, address them in the year they appear.

8. As for the dossier: solicit arm's-length letters from the strongest places, include a clear statement of purpose by the candidate that highlights their contribution (not a survey of each paper in turn), deal with issues posed at each level.

9. Do not allow junior people to put their head in the guillotine. No one is above the conventional demands for quantity, for decent teaching, for reasonable collegiality, and for focused contributions. What is most tragic are those candidates who are manifestly of very high quality but have not produced at the requisite quantitative level. If mostly joint work,

there has to be more of it than if mostly singly authored work. Edited books almost never count.

10. Counsel the candidate to stop digging in the archives or mining the data or perfecting the performance, and write up the articles or the books and perform. You get better through practice, not through perfectionism.

158 *We Want You to Succeed*

We want you to succeed, and to be stronger and more prominent than the current faculty. It is in our interest that when you come up for promotion and tenure your case be strong, that your work be well recognized, that you have letters saying in effect that "if you do not promote her, we'll hire her away and promote her." (Letters sometimes say this; rarely do they mean it.) If there is something that you need to succeed and do well, be sure to let us know (we may not be able to get it for you, but perhaps we can suggest a substitute or an alternative path). If you are a "rising star" (to use the current fashionable term), how can we make you into a supernova?

No dean or department chair will say the following to its faculty: Could you get an offer from a peer or better institution that would tempt you to leave your current position? (It's time-consuming and distracting to be in the job market, so that is not your issue just now. Actual job offers are often quite idiosyncratic, since the market is so segmented and particular. Hence the "could you" hypothetical form.)

Do you (get offers to) give talks at the places where the scholars in your field operate? And again, do you publish in the right journals in your field?

159 *Junior Faculty Advice*

Write yourself a memo, now, indicating what you think is your major contribution to the field. If you want to have two contributions, fine. More than two almost always means you are in trouble. (Also, write down a list of readers or reviewers of your work – they ought to be at peer or better colleges or universities in the United States – and then try to make sure they know of your work. Send them preprints or reprints, and meet them at meetings.)

Is that contribution recognized? How can you be sure it is recognized? How do you deepen that contribution? (At this stage in your career, one fine contribution is an achievement. Your next project should deepen that contribution.) *A lot of epsilon contributions do not add up to a genuine contribution.*

Faculty need to publish in the prominent journals with the widest circulations. If specialty journals are the best place for your work, publish there. (But be sure that your mentors guide you about what counts.) That is actually a demand about quality and focus. Books you publish should be with a high-quality press (or if not, they had better get fine reviews).

Joint publication leads to a curious multiple counting of work – if three regular faculty work on a paper, it cannot count as one paper for each, but that is (sub)discipline-specific. If you do lots of joint publication, expect yourself to have many more articles than if you do individual publication. On the other hand, if your coauthors are your students or postdocs working under you, the paper counts as one paper for you and for the main student and/or postdoc.

Do not get caught up in many projects. Learn to say *no*. Keep your eye on the ball. A good excuse is: I'm working on the main projects for my tenure. I'd love to work on X when that is settled.

160 *Mentoring and Junior Faculty Leaves*

The junior faculty leave is valuable, but it must be supplemented by a no-excuses work plan. And the faculty member who wishes not to follow their mentor's advice has to understand that there may be problems down the line with their path (not because they followed their own way, but because their own way may not pan out). I am impressed by how wrongheaded junior faculty can be.

In the schools where they have an extra year or two of probationary time, they do no more than other comparable departments and schools with the usual probationary time.

161 By Year 2½

People who have not done what they must do in their first three years, will not then do what they must in the next two, making up for the lost time and doing the second half of the probationary work. They may still be promoted and tenured, but they never show the kind of focus and ambition of those who are on track when the third-year review takes place.

If you are an assistant professor, on a tenure track, and will be reviewed in your sixth year (in some fields, it is the seventh or eighth), you want to be sure that you are on track by 2½ years. By then:

You ought to have revised your dissertation work and submitted it for publication, and perhaps had it accepted. This means you will need to do revisions by the winter of your second year.

You ought to have begun another project.

If your dissertation work will lead to a scholarly book, then you have a longer time scale. But by this time, at year 2½, you ought to have done a revision. If you need to do further research, it had better be done by year 3½. (There are notable exceptions, for fieldwork in archaeology or archival work in the humanities, but be sure the chair and dean understand what you are doing.)

You cannot afford to let your first year of teaching go by without working on your research.

You ought to have applied for major grants, if that is appropriate to your field. In the sciences/engineering, where grants are crucial indicators, a much more proactive stance by departmental mentors and collaborators is indicated. The junior people need to be incorporated into grants early on, and their subsequent individual grant applications need to be vetted by their colleagues before they go out.

You ought to have figured out if there are major problems with your teaching, and addressed them.

Finally, your standards for performance should be those of the strong faculty at your university. Most of your more senior colleagues may well have operated under weaker standards. If X got tenure doing B work, five years ago, do not assume that doing B work will get you tenure. It may not.

Also, if your department loads you with lots of committee and service work, speak with the chair about your need to get your research done. Document the conversation.

Junior people must focus on their first project and get it done – publishing out of their dissertation, or a book. And they need to do this in years one and two and three, not later. They need to focus on what they must do.

Things do not end there. Successful junior faculty, who have a fine first book, often find it hard to finish their second monograph. They give lots of lectures, they may edit important collections or have collections of their articles and essays published, they may be promoted to full professor – but they have yet to do the close work needed to write another monograph or advance another major project. They may take umbrage at suggestions that they focus on that second big book or project, since they are now so successful. But in the end, they are avoiding the unique contribution scholars can make to the academy. Of course, their university may take advantage of them in all sorts of rewarding ways, distracting them from the big book. That's a major institutional failure. But, "After I finish my next big book" may scare off colleagues or the provost.

About expertise: The main point is that "to accumulate this body of structured knowledge, grandmasters (in chess) typically engage in years of effortful study, continually tackling challenges that lie just beyond their competence. The top performers in music, mathematics and sports appear to gain their expertise in the same way, motivated by competition and the joy of victory" (P. E. Ross, "The Expert Mind," *Scientific American*, August 2006). I think it is fair to ask whether this applies to historians or scientists, but I also believe the emphasis on "effortful study," going "just beyond," "competition," and "the joy of victory" is more universal.

162   *Subpar Performance*

People are hired and promoted to have careers with many books (or other projects or experiments or . . .), not just one. And to keep producing. That is what a professor is supposed to do.

Rationales for substandard performance:

1. In book-publishing fields, when the person comes up for tenure, or for full professor, the book is not done, or not out, or not reviewed. It may have taken a long time to be produced. We are sometimes assured that the work is pathbreaking, but there are no reviews, and no book. For tenure decisions, this is difficult. With focus and hard work, the manuscript could have been finished $1\frac{1}{2}$ years earlier in just about all cases. People with this sort of incentive structure are unlikely to be very productive and leaders in the field. Even if the work is terrific, will there be more of it in subsequent years? In the case of promotion to full, we might well wait until the book is out and reviewed. When there are retention issues, with offers from peer or better institutions, exceptions might be made.

2. In article-publishing fields, the problems are different, but more acute. In many fields, it would appear that the norm is now N authors, where typically $N = 3+$. Often the advisor is the senior author, and an argument is made that they could work with anyone, so that is a sign of the candidate's virtue. The number of articles is not at all proportional to N (or even $\sqrt{N}$), and in many cases the number of articles is $5–6$, and the number of authors is perhaps 3, the most significant ones done with senior authors.

The work of the candidate is sometimes technical, and highly valued, but it is not clear how much of an original pathbreaking contribution is the technical work. In effect, an article might well contribute to three persons' vitae and promotions. (In some fields in natural science, groups are very large, but then an entirely different dynamic is involved. Many hands are needed to make a contribution.)

If N people are authors, you might want $\sim N^{\alpha}$ times the conventionally expected number of singly authored publications, α being, say, $\frac{1}{2}$ to 1. But if the norm of the field is N authors, then the expected number of publications might be checked by counting those of the strongest people in the field; then there would be no multiplier. Leaders in the field have very many papers, their original contributions are strong, and there is no problem about N authors.

163 *Brief Guide for New Assistant Professors*

1. When you arrive to start your new job, please see your chair and figure out what they want you to do for tenure: kinds of publications, venues, appropriate numbers, grant expectations. Assume you will have to teach adequately, and probably do little service. You should be assigned a mentor-guide, and if that person does not work out for you, be sure to get another. *We want you to succeed, and to succeed excellently.*

2. Set up your life so you are sure to do what is expected. Also, make sure you go to the right professional meetings and make presentations, and get to know more people in your field, both your peers and the leaders. You might want to send them reprints. It's good that they know of your work already when your department decides to ask them to write a letter of reference.

3. Likely, you will be converting your dissertation work into articles or a book, unless you have had a postdoc where you have already done that. It makes sense to devote the first two years to doing this, and to submitting that work for publication. You'll need guidance about where to publish and how to write. This process can take some time, for even if your work is conditionally accepted for publication, you may well have to revise and resubmit. If you receive a rejection, have an alternative venue in mind, take into account reviewers' comments, and then send in the revised paper.

In your third year, you want to initiate a second project. This is ideal. There are lots of exceptions, for good reasons. Whoever is your mentor-guide in your department should be kept up-to-date with your schedule. In any case, when you come up for tenure, you should be well launched on this second project.

4. In some fields, one has to do a lot more work on the dissertation research before you can publish it. If it is a book, figure out a schedule so that you can submit the book to publishers no later than early in your fourth year. It can take a year for a publisher to make a commitment, and your first submission may not work out.

5. If you are going to need research funding, or you are expected to have it, you ought to be figuring out what to do in your first year. Again, this is not something you need do by yourself. You may find a collabora-

tor among your colleagues. In any case, be sure your grant applications are vetted by your mentor-guide.

6. Your third-year review should give you a good feel for your progress. The most important thing is to find out what you must do to stay on track. And do it.

7. When you are in your sixth year (or whatever year, or perhaps only when you come up for full professorship) you will be coming up for tenure. Ideally, you have published roughly the right amount and have more work in the pipeline. You want to write a personal statement that might be 1,000 words, maybe 2,000 at most, which describes the nature of your contribution to scholarship. And describe your planned future trajectory. The statement may well have technical parts, but for the most part it should be written in plain English, namely what any provost would understand. If your work is highly technical, give away the story in plain English in the statement.

You will also want the statement to include an account of your contribution to multiply authored papers. Were you a collaborator, or were you the teacher working with student authors? And if you have had some untoward events (illness, family crises, late start of lab), say that. If there is anything peculiar about your progress (say, you start publishing only in your fourth year), tell why. Not so much excuses as reasons.

8. Be sure your CV is scrupulously honest. If you were not the PI, be sure that is obvious. If the venue is not a refereed one, be sure that is clear. The basic idea is that you do not want a skeptical reader of your CV to find problems in it – for that diminishes the credibility of the whole CV.

Now, if you are in an arts field or a field where publication in scholarly journals or scholarly presses is the not the norm, make sure you do whatever it is people do in your field: exhibitions, concerts, reviews of your novel. If your school has a longer tenure clock, adjust my recommended times appropriately.

164   *Teaching Concerns*

Do not expect students to be enthusiastic. They may be cool or asleep or just enduring this required course.

Students do not know what is of interest to them. You have to figure out the hook onto which they can attach what you are saying. You have to talk to them, to their interests. When I teach humanities to engineers, I know enough of their culture so that I can hook whatever I am talking about to some example from computer science, circuit theory, or structures. *Knowing your students is the only way you will penetrate their defenses, defenses which are in fact sensible. They do not want to learn stuff. They want to learn stuff that has meaning for them. Everyone does.*

Arrogance is almost always a defense against being found out as stupid. So an arrogant student needs some extra attention outside of class. Invite them to lunch, and learn more about them. Let them do most of the talking, about their interests, their concerns, their careers. I suspect that the student will stop being so arrogant in the future. It is worth the lunch, even if you pay.

Humility comes only with age and experience. Your job is to make your relationship with students human. They will be more decent just because they cannot imagine being impolite to people they really know.

The secret here is that the instructor has a great deal of power, and the greatest power lies in finding out how what you want to teach will matter to your students. They want to learn, they want to get an education. They just do not know how.

165   *When Things Get Rocky in Your Department*

There is lots of turmoil in a friend's current department, but this is what she is doing – which I think is exemplary:

> I didn't want to get distracted when I was in the middle of all this. I thought I should try to get as many manuscripts as possible out and I did that. So far, I got one acceptance and I am waiting to hear from another editor. I expected to hear from this editor earlier but it is over six months now. I e-mailed the editor and she said she is waiting on one more reviewer (no one knows how much longer). [After three to four months it is reasonable to write the editor to find out how your manuscript is faring. After six, the journal is in trouble.] I thought if I should apply anywhere else I will have a better chance if I have a couple more papers published. So I did my best to publish this summer.

Note that the assistant professor focused on her work, not on the turmoil.

166 *Keeping Your Ears Open about Jobs Elsewhere*

In the 1950s and '60s, when universities were expanding rapidly, there were many job openings for faculty and fewer new PhDs or MFAs. There was lots of moving around, and perhaps the academic job market was efficient in valuing excellence. Undervalued people moved.

We are in a much less fluid time, and it is likely that many more faculty are inappropriately valued – they are not market-tested with any regularity. It's good for a department to have a faculty that is hard to keep. So it makes sense to encourage your colleagues to keep their ears open for opportunities that would improve their prospects. Yes, you will lose people, but you will then be able to hire perhaps stronger people. *Deans should be spending as much time improving their human capital as their pecuniary and material capital.*

You do not want to move around too much; it may be disruptive to your family until children leave the nest. But perhaps it is time to move again. You do not want to move just to change your salary by a few percent. You want to move to change your salary by 20 percent or more, to have new opportunities, to escape dying departments.

Schumpeter would have called this game of musical chairs a bacchanalian revel. Of course, there is much to be said for department solidarity – but in fields which are changing, or in which there are new cohorts of much stronger faculty, solidarity may not be so wonderful. Tenure binds you to your institution; it does not guarantee they value you.

167 *Getting Job Offers from Other Places
Is Good for Your Home Institution*

Even deans who are economists may not like to face competition for their faculty. But it is up to faculty to go out, get offers, and encourage their universities to recognize their strengths. This is especially true if you have been at an institution for some time, or you are young and a rising star. It will make your university better, whether you go or stay. You need to do this with finesse, not playing games with your dean. But, loyalty without rewards of rank, endowed chairs, and compensation means that the university is not at the leading edge or growing stronger.

168 *Taking Control of Your Career*

1. Be on time, deliver what is expected, and no excuses.

2. It is a competitive world. While you may not be practicing or studying or whatever, there are others who are, and they might well do much better than you will.

3. Figure out the norms and expectations of your environment and culture, and adhere to them.

4. Multitasking may be taken as disrespectful. Using your cell phone, checking your e-mail, doing other than paying attention – will be penalized in subtle ways you really do not want to discover.

We depend on the kindness of strangers – especially to write letters of reference. If you deliver, work hard, show a sense of decorum, and are respectful, not only will you be noticed, but others may well discuss among themselves how extraordinary you are. Otherwise, you might discover that the informal discourse is rather less complimentary.

There are those who are cutthroat schemers, and I have little to offer them.

B. PROMOTION AND TENURE

169 *You, the Candidate, Are in Charge*

You, the candidate, are the person with the most power over your tenure and promotion decision. If you have done what is expected, and others appreciate it, then there should be no problem. You have made a contribution to scholarship that is recognized as significant.

How do you know what is expected? Early on, speak with your chair and your most accomplished colleagues about that. Write a work plan. Share it with your chair. Take seriously the advice you receive in annual reviews and in your third-year review. If you are an associate professor, your best model is the strongest people in your field. If that is too demanding, find your peers and aim higher.

If you have done what is expected, your department, chair, and dean are less powerful. They could demean a good record if they dislike you, but they will look fishy. They might choose prejudiced letter-writers, but that almost never works – the writers' prejudice shows, and even more important, the writers feel they must indicate your strengths. The vote could be poor, but again your record indicates something is wrong with your department, not you. The dean might be lukewarm, but again it is the dean who would appear out of bounds. If all else fails, get another job and do your best. (If you are marginal, all bets are off, but: *Never give weapons to your enemies!*) If you do not have widely recognized scholarship, if you do not do a decent job teaching, you allow for much more discretion on the part of others.

The university committee and the provost must take into account the record in the dossier, and your strong performance is almost always probative. Again, if all else fails go elsewhere.

Still, you might wish for some forgiveness, for some of the kindness of strangers your colleagues have experienced. Perhaps you've made yourself weaker than you need be, you've become vulnerable, and people will often help out. But do you want to be in that position, or even allow yourself to come close to it? Do you want to be so marginal?

Often, dossiers suggest that candidates are good or good enough, at best. The issue of being sufficiently strong for the future of the university cannot be answered in the affirmative in many cases. Maybe it is OK to say that they will not get much better, so let's promote them now to full, but what does that say to the junior faculty?

If the candidate has sufficient publications, committees need detailed, textured letters and a good statement of the contribution. A case is being made, and committee members want to be convinced to act positively by the case, not by the fact that there is a dossier in front of them. The candidate's statement can make the case in terms of contribution, guiding the letter-writers. But often, the candidate does not make their own case in a substantive way, perhaps only providing a paper-by-paper tour.

It's difficult when a candidate is a protégé of some movement. Long, detailed laudatory letters containing little critical content, with no sense of the limits of the work, do not help. If you are lucky, one of the letter-writers indicates the limits of the work.

Think of the experience of buying a used car, or even a new one.

170 *What Do I Have to Do to Get Tenure?*

Say one is in a research-oriented university:

1. Have you been doing a decent job teaching? If it started out poorly, have you been getting better?

2. Have you been a decent citizen (serving on committees, doing your assigned tasks)? You should not be given major administrative responsibilities, at least during your first few years.

3. Have you raised grant money for research? If yours is a field where grant money is not relevant, then this will not dominate. But if you are in a field where grants are essential to doing serious work, then the demands on you will accordingly be more substantial. By the way, a good way to start is to work with senior people on grants, and then go out on your own.

4. Have you built up (early on, are you building up) a coherent body of well-published research, in which a well-defined contribution can be discerned? This should not be very difficult, since your first task is to publish your dissertation research, and your next task is to have a follow-on project that builds in a sensible way on your previous work. It is in general foolish to go off in a radically new direction. *Well-published* means published in the major journals of the field, refereed. *Contribution* means a substantial and substantive advance.

The rough schedule that works here – and it is not too forgiving – is:

Years 1–2: prepare for publishing the dissertation-related work, and get it accepted. It will come out in years 3–5. Make sure you revise promptly if a journal requests it. If you are turning your dissertation into a book, you need a revised manuscript by the end of the second year. This may be stretched a year or so (say much more research is needed or you expand your scope), but then starts getting sticky. Or, and this is less frequent, your dissertation leads to a contract, and then you have to revise.

Years 3–4: Start your next project. If you need lots of money, start applying earlier. By the end of year 4 I would hope you have some results you are writing up. Submit during year 5 early on, so that you are ready for tenure review at the beginning of your sixth year.

What about a *big* book or research project? At this point in your career the time it takes to do such work bumps against the decision time.

It is rare that such a big piece of work gets to the point, at decision time, where it can be fairly judged. It may be prudent to make that your second project.

How much to publish? A first-rate book that comes out in your fifth or perhaps sixth year is a fine achievement, especially if there is evidence of further projects being in process. At the best universities, the demand is more substantial.

For articles, in part this reflects the difficulty of doing your research. Does an article represent a year of work? If so, you will have few but deep articles. Some of those who publish five or six articles during their five-year probationary period are the very best. The question to ask yourself is, what is my contribution to the field? How does it compare with others of my cohort?

It is crucial to compare yourself to the strongest people, not the weakest-who-got-tenure.

The main reason people find themselves in trouble is that they are less focused than they should be. No redoing of the kitchen or learning a new language. I know very good people who have done one or more of these, have produced great work, and are esteemed members of the profession. But they are exceptional.

This is a deadly serious competitive business, and if you act as if you are trying to make partner in a law or finance firm, that will be a good guide. Many people think of tenure as a goal. It is not. Doing the work is the goal.

171   How Did X Get Tenure, Five Years Ago, When I Did Much More Than X Did?

I am asked: How did X get tenure, five years ago, when I have done much more than X did and my tenure did not go through? Other versions of this question: Y got tenure having done this much, with average letters; yet A did not get tenure, and A's dossier is manifestly much stronger. My colleagues are demoralized by this fact, in part by X's weak performance, but also by A's denial when he is so much better.

1. There was a change in provost in between.

2. Mistakes are made all the time. Hopefully not too many, but mistakes are made. Why are they made? Sometimes judgment calls turn out to be wrong, sometimes a dean makes a plea for someone who then does not pan out, and sometimes the dossier is very well put together or the reverse.

3. The university has become stronger in terms of its faculty. It could be that those tenured years ago rose to the occasion and en masse moved the institution forward. Or, it could be that the newest appointments and tenures are qualitatively stronger. Or both. And many of the past tenures have not moved forward. No one suggests that in general the past tenurings, given their records at that point, would now go through, although it might be argued that those people could have performed much more strongly at year six if the expectations had been higher.

Most people agree that demands at tenure time are more demanding than they were a decade ago. And there may be greater reluctance to give a pass to marginal cases. In part, we compare our candidates to peer or better places, and as the university has grown stronger, those peers are in fact stronger. More to the point, candidates are compared to peers elsewhere, not to colleagues in their own department.

4. Sometimes a more comprehensive picture may be revealing. Perhaps their whole department depends on Y's teaching. Perhaps Y is good at getting grants that support others' work. Perhaps there was a spousal hire issue, and the candidate was good enough but not stellar, but the spouse was the star they really wanted to hire. Perhaps there were retention issues, including preemptive promotion to keep someone off the market. Perhaps the actual letters, which you may not have seen, suggest the candidate does not deserve credit, or is much better than the record indicates. Or, someone who publishes lots has antagonized all of his colleagues, and so their votes may well not be strongly in his favor. Or, perhaps the research or style does not match well with the department, and the case is marginal, and so there is little enthusiasm for giving them a break. They then might go elsewhere and be considered prizes – since the match is much more appropriate.

In general, *what one should do is to focus on becoming stronger, rather than comparing oneself with weaker colleagues or tenurings*. You will then be in a better position to get offers from elsewhere, and your dean may have to pay attention. If you present a marginal case, and many do, you are setting yourself up for problems. Rarely is a strong case or a weak case mistakenly assessed. The best defense is an offense. And if all else fails, living well is the best revenge. Go elsewhere, thrive, and do not look back. Find a better match, where they appreciate your talents and virtues.

By the way, to prevent a marginal dossier: Do the work you are expected to have done by the time you come up for tenure (including having the articles or book in print), make sure you do a decent job of teaching, discourage your committee from getting letters from your advisor or collaborators or other previous employers (except to testify to your contribution to joint work, or your teaching or collegiality at a previous institution). You want your dossier not to have any flags that say, "something is fishy here." If you have had some untoward events in your life or career that affect your record, deal with them in a sentence or two in your personal statement. And the first paragraph of your personal statement should summarize your contribution to scholarship and suggest your future research trajectory as you now see it.

C. DENIAL

172   *When You've Been Denied Tenure*

1. Make a list of your vulnerabilities. Were your articles in the right journals, books published by good presses? Was your teaching at least OK? Did you mix with the rest of your colleagues? Almost all tenure dossiers have weaknesses. Be brutally honest about your weaknesses and vulnerabilities, at least to yourself.

2. Write a memo or grievance that details your specific concerns. You'll need to gain access to the dossier materials, including redacted letters. This memo should be factual, with no anger or indignation. Have a senior colleague or a member of the academic senate or a lawyer review it. If you compare it with other cases, make sure those cases are not too marginal. Lots of folks who are marginal get tenure, but they are not your best comparisons.

3. Keep in mind that provosts and deans need each other, while (all) faculty are in general cannon fodder. At a few institutions a strong faculty

member seeing the provost about a case can be effective, but in general deans have priority.

4. As for pursuing legal action beyond grievance procedures, you need to consider the costs, mostly in time and not only in dollars. I have friends who have been successful, with national committees backing them up.

5. Immediately go on the job market, where perhaps the persons who wrote letters for you can help. A smart dean or chair should help you as well. Consider different sorts of institutions. Consider a very different kind of work. Keep in mind that as a professor for the next 40 years you will be spending time with late adolescents and frustrated adults, and perhaps you want to play in a different arena. My basic point is that what is crucial are your family and your work, and there may be better venues than the one that has rejected you. My experience has been that any place I have left for lack of a future there, and there have been many, in retrospect looks much less desirable than the place and life I have lived subsequently. If they screwed you, they will eventually screw themselves. Just as it is difficult for abused spouses to leave marriages, so you will find it difficult – but ultimately you will be better off. Put differently, *my life has gotten better each time I have left a place that did not want me.* Perhaps it is because I am good at making lemonade from lemons. It's not that I am now in paradise – rather, *one can make a good life in a place that at least leaves you alone.*

6. Do not burn bridges. Just remember who has screwed you. In the next two decades you will have a chance to pay them back when they are older and weaker. A friend with a Machiavellian streak would promise to write a letter of reference for one of these guys, and he would write it, but somehow it got in too late – or he missed the meeting where his vote was necessary for the bad guy to get into a national academy.

7. Find a high-paying position outside the conventional arenas. Your colleagues may not say they care that much about money, but if they find that having been let go, you have enhanced your income and have good work, they will be envious. A note of gratitude to the dean and colleagues indicating that their decision forced you to look more widely and that now you are much better off is perhaps too much, but who knows?

Surely there is discrimination, viciousness, unfairness, and idiocy. If you have the energy to fight it, do it. But keep in mind that *what counts are your family and your work*. If I had gotten a regular appointment earlier in my career, I doubt that I would have my family and my suite of books and grants. A friend, age 65, has just joined Silicon Valley, Inc. Salary and stock options are very nice, but more important, she is highly valued and central to the enterprise.

Go someplace that values you for what you are good at. I am not trying to discourage protest and grievance and lawsuits and even righteous indignation – but make sure you take care of family and work first.

173   *If You Are Denied Tenure, Promotion, or Appointment – Unfairness*

Ideally, you have alternatives in your back pocket. You looked at other positions during the past year, applied for the appropriate ones, and perhaps received an offer.

If not, begin looking now. Living well is the best revenge, and usually you are better off going elsewhere and thriving.

Of course, you might get a second chance, or discover that the process was unfairly done. I would still prefer to have an alternative available.

As for a second chance, it is vital to have a sense of what was defective or missing, and preferably to have that information in writing, so that you can cure the problem.

As for unfairness: Are similar cases treated similarly? Almost always, "they" can show that the cases are not so similar, but that demonstration may well not be probative.

Were you given warning or guidance in your annual reviews? What did the documents say? Did you follow through, but still not get what you were presumably promised?

Was the review fair to your work? Did the reviewers have competence to judge it in its own terms, and compared to other competitive work? This applies not only to interdisciplinary work (there are always people who can judge it fairly, despite its being between disciplines), but also to work that is not so standard in your department. It is surely OK if some of the reviewers were hostile to your method, but not if most of them were.

Has there been discrimination that is unfair? (Affirmative action has mostly been applied to majority populations, in effect letting weak candidates through.)

Have you done your part? Did your dean or chair screw up the file? Are the external letters from the right sorts of folks? You will need allies in the department who can check all this without violating confidentiality rules.

174   *I Did Not Get Promoted*

1. Did you deliver on what was expected, indicated in your third-year review, or raised in conversation with your dean? If you did not deliver, you are already in a weak position.

2. While you might have reason to believe that prejudice was involved (race, gender, field of research, method, etc.), if you did not do #1, you are in a weak position.

3. Have standards for performance been raised since you were hired, say by the fact that your department or university has made appointments or promotions that are much stronger in that period?

That you are beloved by your students or valued by other units in the university is rarely probative.

Living well is the best revenge. You really do not want to join a club that will not have you as a member.

SIX

Grants, Fellowships, & Other Pecuniary Resources (#175–183)

175 *Incentivizing Research*

"Incentivizing research" typically means faculty bringing in sponsored research contracts and grants, time off from teaching to do research, research assistance, and, crucially, overhead. This may have little to do with much important work.

1. Much research is not about sponsored contracts and grants. In many fields, fellowships and grants from foundations may play a larger role. These do not yield overhead money but they are crucial to having the time to do the research.

2. The major incentive for doing research is the respect of your colleagues throughout the enterprise and the pleasure in doing the work itself. You may get promoted, you may get a salary increment, and you might get an honor such as a named chair. But many institutions do not reward research performance, especially if it is extraordinary, in any degree of proportionality. Institutions often value solidarity over excellence.

3. Say you are at a teaching-oriented institution. You have a larger teaching load than your colleagues at research universities. Still you can make a genuine research contribution. This requires extraordinary focus, a careful choice of project, probably slower progress, and good networking to stay in touch with the research enterprise. Quantity is no substitute for quality that is visible to others.

4. Teaching does not trade off for research. The best researchers are as good teachers as their colleagues, disproportionately better than you

might expect. There are researchers whose teaching is dreadful, but in general they are no more frequent than their colleagues who do little research.

176 *Applying for Grants, Fellowships*

You need long lead times to write your statement, and rewrite it, and rewrite it once more. Without time between drafts you won't make significant improvements. Show your statement to colleagues. Referees may not get past the first paragraph or two, so you had better be sure that you have the main point up front. What are you going to *do*? In scientific research proposals to places like NSF and NIH, not only are the readers expert, but they may look more closely at your whole statement.

177 *Raising Grant Monies to Do Your Work*

Ideally one gets external research monies from prestigious sources to do one's research work. In many schools, you will not be tenured if you do not get money from the right sources by the time you come up. Getting that money is a sign of quality and recognition.

Getting money from within your university is much less significant, and in general you are expected to leverage that grant into an external grant. If you do so leverage, then you are considered successful; otherwise you are not.

You may be supported by a research center in your school or by an endowed chair. Nonetheless you ought to seek and obtain external support from prestigious sources.

So, how do you get money? The first thing is to define your project(s). It should be substantial, but be doable in one to two years (or some well-defined part should be so doable). It should be manifestly a contribution and an advance. And it should appeal to the reviewers (which may be of different sorts for different kinds of sources).

Once you have an idea of your project, you want to find sources who might be interested. You might talk to foundation officers or to people who have grants in your area. You want to try out your proposal on experts in getting funding and listen to their comments and criticism.

In many fields of scholarship, one publishes one, two, or more articles a year if one is leading the charge, or a monographic book every five to ten years if that is the preferred mode. This is demanding, but not impossible if one is focused. What counts is not the number but the influence of your work and its impact. Nevertheless, do not tell yourself nonsense that your three articles are worth most people's ten. That is rare; such a claim is more likely an excuse.

Program officers at foundations and funding agencies want to meet you. They have to move money and so you represent a resource for them. *If you do not apply you surely will not receive funding.* Junior people might at first piggyback onto more senior people's projects, although promotion and tenure committees do ask if you have done it (the grant, the work) yourself.

178 *Getting Grants*

People who get goodies apply for them.

Some goodies are rare or hard to get. Guggenheims are of this sort. It is an honor to your university when one is awarded to its faculty. (The money is usually not so generous, and deans need to supplement it.) On the other hand, some goodies turn out to be easier to get. Not too many people apply, they are not so popular, they are wired, you are one of the few candidates – and sometimes this is a large grant that will only go to one of three people, high stakes indeed.

Some goodies are idyllic, such as the Rockefeller place in Bellagio.

Some goodies come with federal overhead rates. They may or may not be very hard to get. (Some are earmarked.) These are much appreciated by deans.

Some goodies do not come with federal overhead rates, or with much, if any, overhead. Many private foundations operate in this way. These grants may or may not be hard to get, to some extent dependent on your relationship with the foundation and the congruence of your ambitions and theirs. (I am told by program officers at foundations that it is often hard to give away money, just because many applicants are unlikely to deliver or their requests are outside the parameters of the foundation's giving.)

Some goodies are contracts, which specify what you must deliver. Some are grants in which you say what you will do – but it is much harder for them to demand that from you. In general, it is worth going where the money is and where the odds of making a hit are greater. For example, many scholars have ongoing relationships with foundations and their officers. On the other hand, honor and distinctiveness are also of much value, and it is worth going in that direction even if the money is not so generous or the odds are low.

In the case of grants and contracts with federal and state agencies, and with private foundations, it is often helpful if senior people bring along juniors as co-PIs or the like so that the juniors can become known and get to know that world.

It makes an enormous difference to deliver what you promised, on time and within budget. Sometimes this difference is merely legal and financial. Most of the time the difference is a matter of whether people come to trust you. Did you deliver that book manuscript in time so that when you came up for tenure the book was out?

Where to go to write a book, say for a year at a residential research center: National Humanities Center, Center for Advanced Study in the Behavioral Sciences, Institute for Advanced Study, plus ones in Europe, and other such places specific to subfields. Most of these have applications.

Ambition, whether it be competitive or a matter of your personal best, does make a difference, by the way. Having successful colleagues or peers or people you measure yourself against will make you do more, and get more. Being connected to the strongest people in the field means that your letters of reference will come from people with greater credibility and influence. Eventually you may well become one of those strongest people, and you might well feel an obligation to help the next generation. It is also a sign of your strength. It has been observed that even the strongest people have anxiety about their status, so that at some of the residential research centers, where people are away from their home institutions, many of the stars keep trying to be sure their shine is bright enough.

179 Do Not Do These in Your Grant Application

Do not fail to:
- Describe the problem: knowledge gaps.
- Clearly differentiate your contribution: competitive analysis.
- Offer a compelling value proposition: potential impact.
- Have a persuasive argument/structure: vs. poorly organized.
- Make your key point clear (rather than
  buried): vs. no highlights, no impact.
- Make it easy to read: vs. full of jargon, too long, too technical.
- Remove credibility-killers: misspellings, grammatical
  errors, wrong technicalterms, inconsistent format
  (from Dr. T. Pinkston by way of M. Heller).

All these come out of the experience of program officers. They are busy people, they want to move their money, and you have to make it possible for them to do so. Answer the questions; make it easy to find out what you are saying, and show respect through neatness and carefulness. If you misspell, there is reason to believe you may well do poor scientific work (especially in the age of spell-checking).

180 Preparing a Research Proposal

In the last few days I have been in the frenzy of preparing a research proposal for a small grant. The proposal has to be two pages long, with no small type, reasonable margins, and double spacing. Some lessons that may be of use:

I had worked on the problem in the past two years, but did not see how to make interesting progress on it. On campus, I knew of a faculty member who is expert on the techniques that interested me, the faculty member responded well to my ideas, and I saw how to make the ideas concrete. I wrote several versions of a preliminary memo (two single-spaced pages), shared them with several people who might be interested, and saw that I might move forward.

Now for the frenzy: I realized four days ago that I might get a small grant for a pilot project, checked the deadline, and discovered it was in a few days! So in the middle of the night I woke up and did four or five quick drafts redoing my preliminary memo and reducing it by half.

I gave a heads up to our grant people, and our dean, that this was coming down the pike, so that when they had to deal with it they would be ready and not be surprised.

I kept having ideas about how to make the proposal clearer and more straightforward, and I even woke up early the Friday after Thanksgiving (not to get to Wal-Mart at 5 AM to get bargains) with ideas about how to improve things a bit.

I'll let go in a day or so. The draft I had yesterday would have been fine, so the improvements are not so crucial, but I think they are helpful.

What are the main points here?

Revise, redraft. Again and again, if need be.

Keep within the length rules.

If you are on a short deadline, make sure all who need to know are warned.

It helps to keep thinking about your projects – you never know when opportunities will come along that will push them further along.

181 *Grant-Getting*

You do not get money unless you apply. Getting rejected half the time, sometimes more, is reasonable.

Repeat players do better. The funders know you and whether you deliver. So while the first time is hard, the second and later times often prove a bit easier.

Effort should be proportional to dollars. A $10,000 fellowship that requires a two-page proposal, double-spaced, is just right. Really large grants will require more pages, but not proportionately more.

The most valuable use of grants is for students and equipment and for released time from teaching.

Apply early and often.

Do not get money for stuff you do not want to do or that will not further your own program of research.

Do not let raising grants get in the way of finishing a major project. Assistant professors should not be in the grant-getting business unless it fits into their research plans.

Consult with people who have received grants or who serve on foundation boards.

I received this from a colleague: "I would add one other piece of advice from a scholar trained as a humanist. Partnering with interdisciplinary colleagues is a powerful way to use your training without taking on the entire risk of the grant-making process. My first big grant was with two wonderful scholars in the liberal arts. We then got a second grant together, and one of them is my partner on an NSF grant. In other words, try to find people who will help you do the research you wish to do. Do not join a group just to get money. Also, try to find people who do the work. I know it sounds silly – do not we all do the work? – but the cruel reality is that some people are much better to work with than others, and much more reliable.

"Clearly, working on these areas has broadened my research agenda, but my training has served me well in these projects. Telling a story, which humanists do exceedingly well, is something that not all economists and other harder social scientists do as well. I can't do a chi-square to save my life (although I now understand what they mean), but I can write up ideas and results that funders and journals seem to like pretty well. I can conceptualize the purpose of studies and question the methods by which results can be reached. Each of us has talents that can help a group, and we can be well served in return."

182   *External Research Support Does Not Corrupt*

People often say: there is no or very little external support available for our subfield; I would rather do project X, but I am likely to do Y because that is where the support lies.

1. Work that is not supported externally is no better than work that is externally supported. Also, external support may indicate that a problem is important.

2. The demand for raising external grants is serious in the schools that demand it. They view such grants as signs that the work is thought worthy by peers in the field.

3. Some forms of external support do not come with large amounts of overhead. And in some fields one does not expect lots of federal grants. However, in compensation many research fellowships are available in these low-overhead fields. External support is still there, and at least at many universities one is allowed to accept it even if it does not come with overhead if the grantor is prestigious (such as a foundation). On the other hand, such low-overhead places are quite willing to pay for support costs that can be itemized.

4. Endowed research centers should be seedbeds for external funding that enhances their purposes. They have a cushion, and that should encourage the faculty associated with them to take risks. Moreover, in a research university all such units should have vigorous research programs – or, if they are service-oriented, that service function needs to enhance the educational function within the institution.

5. Doctoral students are assets to their faculty advisor's research enterprise. Every student we admit should have an advisor committed to that student's career, and willing to support that student through assistantships from their research grants. In some fields we might make exceptions, but in general, the norm should be: If you want doctoral students, you have to support them (or help them get fellowships).

6. Scholars are not corrupted by having to gain external support for their research. This is the university's aspiration. If we demand that our more junior faculty perform at the highest levels, we have to demand that of ourselves as well. Money and external support do not corrupt; they are the avenues to excellence (although they do not guarantee excellence).

I've watched too many departments lose out, claiming they were above the forces of a research university. I've watched too many colleagues all over the United States claim that their research could not get support because of its field, when other colleagues in the same field at other institutions do quite well in getting external support.

183 *Low-Overhead Research Dollars from Fellowships or Foundation Grants*

While the university would naturally prefer that our externally funded research come with substantial overhead – those expenses for plant and equipment and administration are real – for some purposes it is rather more than grateful that we receive distinguished fellowships. Some useful facts:

1. You have to apply (for most of these). Not for Nobel Prizes (but even for these your friends have to politic for you) – but in general, you have to apply.

2. You have to apply on time. They do not have uniform dates, and some of them are early in the fall, others during the summer. So you need decent lead times.

3. You have to know about a fellowship. Often they are posted, or advertised in the *Chronicle of Higher Education,* or listed on the vita or bio of someone working in your field.

4. Your references and statement are crucial. Choose people carefully, and if they are in charge of getting in their letter of reference, make sure you give them lots of lead time, and that they will actually do so. Ask. As for your statement, it had better be responsive to what the funders want, be well within the length limits, be understandable by non-expert readers, and be impeccably presented. For even the most distinguished faculty, unless you have been requested to apply (it is "wired"), showing your statement to a colleague is a very good idea.

5. Be aware that the hit rate for fellowships may be less than 10 percent. Hence, to some extent this is a crapshoot. If they have a theme the year you are applying, if you are outside the theme you will be much less likely to be successful.

6. Be sure your application is believable. Have you a track record in this area? Are you so accomplished, though you are changing your direction, that people will be willing to bet on you? Do you have real work to do, or does it read as if you are just trying to supplement your sabbatical?

The crucial fact is that rejections should be the occasion for trying once more, perhaps with an improved application. I once applied on a sort-of dare by a dear friend, who thought I would be ideal. I knew of the fellowship/prize, but did not think that I ought to apply given my work. I applied, won, and paid a bounty to my friend (a first-class dinner). I discovered that I won in part because the previous winners were embarrassments – they needed a safe bet. The previous years they probably would have gone with the guys with the propeller-topped beanies (they did and learned a lesson).

There are also grants from philanthropic foundations, which often come with little overhead (but you can budget your direct expenses). But it matters if someone the grant officer knows can say that you are worth listening to. It will not get you money, but it will get you a more generous hearing. If you then screw up, you are not only in hock to the foundation; you owe your supporter, big time.

Your basic assumptions must be that the people who are reading applications are at the same time reading between 10 and 100 or more. They have to be able to figure out why you are worth a second look. Your vita should make clear your distinct virtues, usually all by page 3. Your personal statement must say why you are the right person to do this work and that this work is what is vital.

SEVEN

Your Career (#184–219)

A. FUNDAMENTALS

184 *You Are in Control of Your Career,*
Your Grades, Your Promotion

You are more in control of your career and grades than perhaps you imagine.

1. If you want to do excellent work, you need to do more, and with more care and attention to detail, than is normally expected. Excellent work is not just a bit better, it is much better. (If you think it is a matter of fulfilling a list of requirements, then you will not do well in the rest of your career. Excellence is always beyond expectations, in innovative and new ways.)

2. Same for your career. You need to deliver and deliver excellently, and you will be recognized. Yes, there is lots of prejudice and unfairness in the world, and you will have to work twice as hard if you encounter that. And through political action you might try to change it. But, in the end, what you have to do is to take charge of your work and your career.

3. As for tenure and promotion in a university, it's not rocket science. You are expected to do certain things, and despite all the talk, they are fairly clear. Publish, early and often, in the strongest journals. Do work that others recognize as significant and as a contribution. Be sure that if you work with collaborators, your contribution is clear and recognizable. You cannot publish in the important journals unless you do excellent

work, and then some. You have got to get the grants or whatever you need to do your work. No excuses.

People get A's in graduate school with specious work, move up in their careers because they are charming, and get tenured and promoted having done less than is expected. That's no reason for you to join this cohort. You do not want to depend on the kindness of strangers. You want to be in control of your career. Yes, the world is often unfair. Fight unfairness. But for your career, do more than you have to, maybe twice as much, so you can control what happens to you. And if you do not get the A's or that job or get tenured, go elsewhere, where they appreciate your strengths.

185   *Probationary Times*

The strong faculty do it all in the allotted period of about 5½ years. They organize their efforts and energies so that they do get the grants, publish in the main journals, and get the right publishers in the period allotted. The ones who might need an extra year or so are often fine people, but they are less likely to be league-leading players. In general, people who take extra years (here, I am not talking about medical or family reasons for extensions) do not show superior performance.

Still, five-plus years is an awfully long time to show your stuff. Especially since you have been working on your terminal degree's outputs for three to seven years. The strong people do it all, no excuses. Later bloomers, with their later articles or books, are rarely impressive. Again, there are exceptions – rare enough for a provost to deal with.

I have in mind my cardiothoracic-surgeon standard: in general you want someone who gets it right the first time, no excuses.

186   *Building Depth in Your Portfolio*

Your major problem as a beginning researcher is to convince others that you have something to contribute and that your work is worthy of their attention. Out there, there are lots of articles, presentations, talks, sessions, books. What you want is for people to think that your work is essential for their understanding of the field.

Some of the time, a single book or a single article will do that. You publish in the highest-profile journal (*Science* or *Nature* for biology, say), and that work leads to work by others, and you are known for your contribution. Or, your book is seen as pathbreaking, or showing a remarkable command of sources. Moreover, even if the published work has many authors, you are the lead author (and that is widely understood). It's not that it is your dissertation research and you are given lead authorship, but your collaborators and advisor attest to your leadership (remarkable for a new PhD).

Now, most of the time, you do not make such an impression. Your book does not disappear, and it is nicely reviewed, but it is a "first book." Your articles, while they appear in strong journals, do not appear in the top journals, or if they do they do not seem to resonate widely. You have to build up a portfolio of research. You need to build on your dissertation work, and then make sure your next project gets launched in good time. You'll need to appear in various venues – meetings, conferences, journals – if you have published a book (in part to expose your work more widely), and give talks at various departments at other universities or institutions. Immediately after the first appears, people are wondering when your next suite of work will come out, and may even start thinking you are a one-horse rodeo.

If you do collaborative work, you need to convince people that your group's work is significant, and that your contribution is vital and important. Publishing with different collaborators, giving talks on your own, writing some singly authored papers (this is sometimes not possible), having the work identified as coming out of your lab, all help. In fields with only multiple-collaborator papers, you probably will need more evidence of research than in fields with mostly singly authored papers. The multiple-collaborator contribution needs to be more substantial for a given number of years, or at least explained.

You want to have cumulative work, so that people are impressed with the depth and range of your scholarship, so that you mine your sources or experiments and so convince people that this work is substantial and interesting. (The problem is not that your ideas will be stolen, but that your work will be ignored or not be attended to. There are lots of people in your cohort who are aiming to take up space, and that space or attention is in fact limited.)

There are a few scholars who publish, one after the other, significant work in various areas, perhaps not even following up on their earlier work. If the work is not cumulative, few of these scholars are successful in convincing others of the value of their work (maybe others are jealous). But if you can have a series of home runs, you are rare and fortunate. In the monographic book world, I could imagine a series of fine historical works which would work this way. But I suspect that in the interim between books, you will publish articles on your previous or prospective work. And you will be invited to give talks on your work (and this is arranged to some extent by your initiative). People need to see your name regularly, in front of their eyes, or they will assume you have disappeared.

Most of us probably can successfully pursue two or three lines of work, sequentially, over a career. They may be in parallel, but that is a bit harder until you are well established.

People have to see you and your work again and again, be convinced of its significance again and again, and see the work grow in depth and range – for then you are a contender, someone they have to pay attention to. Otherwise, you are a footnote at best. You'll want to participate in conferences, maybe your national organizations, NSF or NIH or NEH or NEA panels. At the same time, if you spend lots of time on these activities, and you do not continue to produce scholarly work at a brisk clip, people may well respect your power but not your scholarship. It is a delicate balance. On the other hand, strong scholars seem to do it all. As far as I can see, they are focused, they do their research and writing and publishing, they are involved with their professional associations, serve on panels. I do not believe they are superpersons. Rather, they seem to be clear about what they are doing, do it, and get on with the next task. The people who do not are not less talented, per se. But they lose themselves and their focus.

The most remarkable scholars are those who have primary caring responsibility for their families – usually women, rarely but now more often men, and who do it all. I gather that they make explicit choices about what they will not do (say, worry about the spotlessness of their homes) so that they have time for their children and work. Keep in mind that women almost always have to bear their children (there is adoption or stepchildren), and that pregnancy and childbirth are for some women complicated, with lengthy recovery times, that infants usually receive most of their attention from women (this need not be the case), and that when a child is in distress it is almost always Mommy who is called. These are the most remarkable scholars of all. Their ways of doing it all are models for the rest of us.

B. AWARDS

187　Recognition, Awards, External Offers

You can't win if you do not apply.

If you are a member of a national academy or of an elite organization, your job is to get more of your colleagues nominated and appointed. You want your clowns to win, rather than theirs. Do not worry about worthiness.

Bonuses matter. Big awards should be bonuses from the provost, not just the deans.

Counteroffers should be always made for external offers (even if the other institution is less prestigious than your own – the issue is whether you wish to keep the professor) – unless you want to send a message to your school that you do not care. Preemptive measures may be needed to prevent your most desirable faculty from going on the market.

Strong placement of graduate students is very important.

If someone does leave, do they leave for a more prestigious institution? For a better situation? For a personal reason?

Even Jesus needed the Apostles.

1. Prizes have to be applied for. There are some which claim there are no nominations, but almost always there is a prize committee and they are glad for informal nominations – but if you know none of the members, or you have no friends who are their friends, you are out of the running. So be it.

Fellowships must be applied for. You want to have a list of letter-writers. Who owes you (rather than you owing them)? And you want to be able to write a short essay of application that highlights your strengths.

That essay will be used by letter-writers as well. And some will ask you for a draft letter of nomination (which you have written for yourself). You may want to give each writer a different draft letter, so that if they just copy the letter, the readers of the application do not become suspicious because of identical letters.

2. Prizes and memberships are much the same. Maybe one of your colleagues or friends or mentors will spontaneously want to nominate you. But from what I have seen it is much more likely you will have to ask them to do so, you will have to provide a draft nomination letter or give them pointers about your worthiness, and you will suggest a list of supporting letter-writers. Do not be surprised when you have to go through the nomination process more than once. Usually, there is no lack of well-qualified potential winners or members.

Politicking may be involved, especially for membership in national academies and the like. This is a very delicate but brutal process involving a full-court press that would appear to be casual. The literature on Nobel Prizes is richly suggestive of tactics and strategy, as well as of mistaken prizes. Or, to give an example, should John Nash, winner of the Nobel Prize in Economics, be nominated for the National Academy of Sciences in economics or in mathematics (his field of training, and where his work was originally published)? You might want to have him nominated outside your field so you can push your friend Joe Schmoe within your category.

3. Keep in mind that the problem is not whether you are worthy, but whether among all the worthy folks you are chosen.

4. At some universities, big prizes result in automatic and substantial pay increases. In general, I am told you will get compensating resentment by non-winners. But you and they should keep in mind how arbitrary is this process, and how those who win then win even more.

188   *Awards, Grants, and Honorifics*

You cannot win grants, or awards, or honorifics unless you apply or have others nominate you. Even Nobel Prizes and MacArthurs involve these processes.

1. If you miss a deadline this year, put it into your calendar for next year with a two-to-three-month lead time.

2. Have your application vetted by colleagues or teachers. If people have not won such awards, they are less likely to be useful – for this is a talent, not something intrinsic. Some fields have very successful people who do not get many if any grants.

3. Some awards are directed to you.

4. As for honorifics, you have to ask your friends or advisor to nominate you. People who want to be in the National Academies (Science, Engineering, . . .) have their friends nominate them and also figure out how to get enough votes. If you expect an award to just come to you out of the sky you will be disappointed.

5. You want to ask for awards or grants from those who want to give them to you. Hence it is vital to have a sense of what a foundation or granting agency is looking for. This is rarely secret, since the goals and agenda of the foundation or granting agency are almost always explicitly presented. And you can talk with the granting officers. They are looking for people to give money to – moving money is their business.

Do not apply for grants or awards that will not further your research agenda. Your agenda might be flexible, and you follow the money, much as university presidents have a variety of projects in their portfolios and when they make the ask, they choose a project that will fit the donor. But often people will get comparatively small grants and get caught up in research that does not serve their longer-term purposes.

6. Again, you will not get awards, grants, contracts, or honorifics without asking for them or having others nominate you for them. It helps, in the case of honorifics, not only to be deserving and qualified but also to be the least obnoxious person so qualified. On the other hand, if you get a Nobel Prize, the National Academies make sure you are admitted the next time around (if you are not already a member).

And, to them who have, more is given. Once you get on the gravy train, and you perform adequately, you are more likely to know how to ask better, and to be more likely to receive. The problem is to get on the train. It helps if senior people take you under their wing, if they incorporate you into grants early on and introduce you to granting officers, if they review your applications, if they write letters of recommendation. People can get on the train by chance, or on their own, but that is the hard way. And it is surely the case that some people on the gravy train are much weaker than those who are not: they are lucky, or they deliver on time (while the stronger persons do not), or they benefit from early success. The system is not at all optimal. But it is not perverse either.

Figure out what you might get, and then go out and try, and if need be get your friends and department to nominate you. And if what is available will divert you from your research path, perhaps you ought to finish the current project and only then apply for grants – the "unfinished" book or project is one of the diseases of academia. I note that these unfinished projects do not benefit from being delayed – people do not suddenly get deeper in the eighth or tenth year of a project.

189   *Too Much Pressure Here?*

Reading over these pieces, I am struck that for many of us the implied level of achievement is much greater than we are likely to deliver. There is not enough room at the top. So you will have to adjust this advice for your own situation and your own capabilities. Rather than be paralyzed by ambitions outside your likely range, you might be inspired by them, the off-scale scholars suggesting what we might do, even if that is not likely.

190   *Recognition, Academic Seriousness*

Again, aim for publishing in the major venues in your area, publish singly authored articles at least once in a while, publish with the university presses or other serious presses. Publish in wider venues than the subspecialty journals, so that your work can be more widely influential. Articles and books published in less visible venues are less noteworthy. On the other hand, and this is crucial, *what matters in the end is your contribution to scholarship* – and that is cumulative, substantive, and readily certified in letters of reference by the strongest scholars at the strongest institutions.

As for research support, the main reason why you want to get support from NSF or NIH or Guggenheim is that in such peer reviews, if you survive, your work is given an imprimatur that is otherwise unavailable. Overhead contributes to the desirability of the federal awards.

Even if you have your own slush funds to sponsor your research, or your own wealth to pay for it (as in political campaigns), external support justifies and certifies your strength as a scholar. Faculty recognition is not merely about publicity and puffery; it is also about authentic excellence. Always compare yourself to the top people in your field, the top three or four in your cohort, or to those whose performance is roughly like your own. You are unlikely to be a supernova, but you can learn how to do better from the stars.

I am surely repeating myself and perhaps hectoring you. But there is enormous external pressure on us to perform, provosts are acutely aware of what really counts in rankings, and standards for performance at the university rise as, thanks to the deans and faculty, the university hires stronger and stronger faculty. Those standards are not merely about promotion and tenure, but about the work we do subsequently.

191   *Campaign for Recognition and Awards*

Now is the time to think about getting some awards for your accomplishments. This may be a five-to-ten-year campaign, but you can't win if you do not apply or have others nominate you.

Aim for awards that have higher prestige. You'll need a list of references, who both know your work and have high visibility themselves. Apply for your university awards for research, teaching, mentoring. Some require dean's nominations, but the dean will be grateful for your offering up your name and all the nomination materials.

In general, if you ask people to nominate you, you will want to provide them with draft letters of nomination that fulfill the requirements. They can modify the draft, but at least you are asking them to do less work than otherwise. (Again, different drafts will prevent fishy duplications in the text of different letters.)

Junior people tend to get awards for their first book or a distinguished article; middle-level people, for projects; senior people, for lifetime accomplishments. You know which are the awards appropriate in your discipline or subfield. Keep in mind the deadlines. Keep in mind who might nominate you. If you miss a deadline this year, aim for next year.

Do not let winning awards become a goal in itself. Doing your work is what counts. You can't win if you do not play.

192   *Recognition – Awards*

Recognized contributions to scholarship come first, trajectory next. If someone is not on the playing field, usually they cannot win.

1. You want to be part of a faculty that is hard to keep. Offers from elsewhere are signs of the strengths of your colleagues. Students receiving classy job offers are another such sign. The places may be more prestigious, more suitably located, more on the make, more capable of recognizing faculty strength than we are, or offering opportunities such as administrative positions – or, all of these. The home university must make preemptive offers, often before people think they might be on the market, to keep its faculty – but once people are on the market they are more likely to leave.

2. Money counts. Even if your research does not require external money, the provost's office notices external grants, and often asks, Why no such grants? if there are none or few. More prestigious or competitive sources count. I've never heard a good excuse for why a faculty member does not get grants or fellowships.

3. Prestige matters: An award from your subfield is lovely; one from the field itself is much better.

4. Brag about what is strongest. Do not brag about stuff that is less strong or less important – it decreases your credibility.

5. You must apply or arrange to be nominated. The IBM Chief Scientist's job was to get IBM people into the National Academies, among other such duties.

6. Franchise matters lots: Publish in the strongest venues. Weak venues do not count at all.

7. Make sure the award is really important. Or is it a booby prize? If a university chair is in a narrow field, it is not clear the holder is really excellent.

8. *There is a substitute for first-rate work.* Lots of self-promotion and sexy subjects do count. *The experts are not fooled,* but most people are. In football this does not apply – which is why I keep saying, *we want a university the football team will be proud of.* On the other hand, first-rate work may take the long run to be recognized (and you might be dead by then), so it makes sense to promote your work.

9. Always hire and promote people who are much stronger than you. Would you want this person operating on your child, were the person a surgeon?

10. Fame is fleeting. You need to constantly maintain your assets, retaining faculty, getting money awarded, bragging, applying, aiming high, assessing realistically, and promoting yourself and your work.

C. IMPACT AND INFLUENCE OF YOUR WORK

193   *Impact and Influence*

You do not have to publish most of your work in the wider-circulation, high-prestige journals. Rather, imagine publishing one article every two to four years, summarizing the research and making clear how wide is the potential impact. That's the challenge.

Personally, an article I published in the *Journal of Philosophy* (one of the top journals in philosophy) was not likely seen by anyone in my field – but it was seen quite widely. My book published by University of Chicago Press, drawn directly from my work on urban modeling but about how physicists use mathematics, was unlikely to be read by most urban modelers, but such a press conveys prestige and impact that is worth having. (The article and the book derived directly from my work on decision-making and on modeling urban change.) No one in my field cared that I was the chaired visiting professor of entrepreneurship at a top-ten business school one year (or that I was a fellow at the National Humanities Center and other such joints). There's a big pond out there, and we ought to swim in it.

Incentives are not the only way most of us make decisions. We know the norms of our fields, we know much about prestige, and we are able to manage the complexities of incentives that may or may not encourage the right moves. That you will not get a gold star from your university for some choices does not mean you ought not to make them. And, most academic rewards come from without one's university, from the profession as a whole. And if you are not well rewarded locally, but are recognized externally, the market operates some of the time to make you offers from other institutions.

194   Impact Factors, Genuine Impact, Contribution

1. Do not confuse journal impact factors with your contribution and its impact on your field. It is the latter two that should dominate.

2. You want to publish your work in the journal with the widest appropriate readership, since it is hoped that your work will be influential not only over your subfield or field, but perhaps on other disciplines as well. Your contribution may well be more significant than those within these disciplines.

3. If the citation statistics do not accord with intuitions, try to figure out why. Often the statistics we use are inappropriate. (For example, perhaps one paper contributed enormously to the citation count, and it is a paper done as a postdoc with the lead professor in charge.)

195   Increasing Your Impact: Limited Room at the Top

In the end, what counts is the cumulative contribution to scholarship. My favorite story about increasing your impact is of J. Willard Gibbs (1839–1903), one of America's great scientists. He published in the journal of the Connecticut Academy – not a high-impact journal. He sent out reprints widely and to the right people. (He is the founder of much of modern thermodynamics and other parts of physics and chemistry and mathematics.)

1. Do first-rate work. Careful, scrupulous, significant.

2. Do cumulative work. Rarely does a single article or even a book change everything. Rather, a series of cumulative articles or a follow-on book makes a big difference. And your understanding will develop in that cumulative work, much as Einstein's did in his search for a theory

of general relativity (1909–1915), culminating in several articles, one after the other, as he figured out the right equations.

3. Talk about your work: conferences, visiting other universities. Travel costs are small compared to the real cost of promoting your work in other ways.

4. Send out reprints (or send preprints, or electronic versions thereof) to the 25 or perhaps 10 strongest people in your area. A simple note to the effect, "I thought you might be interested in these reprints," is enough.

5. When you go to meetings, talk to people who work in your area about your work, its problems and opportunities. Always have reprints, cvs, and preprints with you. People have time to read on the plane home.

6. Be tall or attractive or otherwise personally prominent. For better or worse, it helps. But if you are shorter and plain, do #1–5 and you'll do fine.

Yes, it matters which journal you publish in. And your promotion and tenure committees will ask, "Why not publish in stronger journals?" or journals with wider fields of interest – excellent advice and concerns. But if the most important people in your field think your work is important, that trumps everything. And reprints and e-mail get around all the publishers' hype re impact. In any case, if your work is not first-rate, is sloppy or poorly argued and supported, at least it will be well known. Someone, somewhere, may well think it meritorious. This leads to a final bit of tenure and promotion advice: When you are coming up, of course do your best. But also keep your eyes open for positions in other institutions: Your institution may not be the best match for your talents. I don't believe loyalty plays a role at this point in your career, although your colleagues may. Following #1–5 means that other places know about you. And, in general, I observe that people who move around find that the change is salutary for their work, even if it is disruptive. New colleagues, new norms, new environment and research sites.

In general, stronger journals and presses do a better job of vetting work and also editing it. In particular, the reviewers are likely to be stronger, and their advice will be more stringent. Not always, not often enough. The journals are likely to have someone copyedit the manuscript, so your minor mistakes are taken care of. None of this means that less strong journals may not do a good job of vetting papers and editing.

Second, who reads the journal? Who reviews the books published by this press? If it is a commercial rather than a university press, there is very likely no scholarly board that decides what to publish.

Is the journal or book priced outrageously? In many fields, books priced above $75–100 are likely priced for libraries. The same if a journal's subscription price per page is very high.

Edited books are rarely influential or widely read.

But, *the most important factor is the quality of the work itself.* Is it cumulative? Is it scrupulous? Have you sent reprints or preprints to the most significant people in your area? Have you published in some more widely read journals? Have you done original and deep empirical or archival work, or analyzed a data set or an artwork that no one has worked over before, at least in your way, or done a theoretical or mathematical contribution that builds on other work? That's what counts. Books matter, and not just your dissertation.

One last thought: Are you publishing and doing research just because you are expected to? Perhaps you have no real interest in the work you are doing – hard to admit, to be sure. Maybe you should be doing something else?

If you add up the number of scholars coming up for tenure in any field, and if you ask that they publish in the strongest journals or the strongest presses, the required number of pages vastly exceeds the pages actually published. Each institution has different expectations, and you want to keep those in mind. Institutions often say that they expect top journals and presses, but they seem to promote people who do not do much of this, and seem quite happy to do so. Other institutions never ask about publishing venue, because that is not their concern or because it is too demanding or because they believe they and their letter-writers can transcend any such concerns. Other institutions are on the make, and you must publish in venues much better than your colleagues.

There is a variety of excuses for not publishing in the strongest journals. I have read them all. None are convincing, in the end. The same for low publication rates. The same for no one having heard of the work before.

Two observations: First, institutions need to keep those limits of published pages in mind. If they expect people to publish in the strongest venues, they need to be willing to deny promotion on that basis rather than make excuses.

Second, in the end, *what counts is contribution and cumulative contribution.* Focus on that. Then focus on its influence and impact. By the way, the number of excuses for dispersed contributions is also varied and rarely convincing. And if the work is not good enough, are you willing to deny promotion? If not, perhaps some realism is called for.

196   Unrecognition

Geniuses and Great Innovators do not need the advice I provide. I observe that tenure committees readily recognize truly extraordinary cases, and so do hiring committees.

Of course, more ordinary folks suffer from mistakes and injustices. I keep thinking of at least three of my scholarly friends, as distinguished in their productions as most full professors at a major research university, who do not have proper appointments. I know of several denials of tenure who have gone on to very distinguished careers, perhaps more distinguished than those of the faculty members or provosts who denied their tenure.

My advice is prudent, useful for most of us. As for the errors of bureaucracy, my advice is set up so that one could make those errors less likely. If you think that taking undue risks is worth it, or that the institutions you participate in are so corrupted that their decisions are often wrong, I have little useful to say. And if you are a genius or a great innovator, my advice is helpful even for you. If you think you are a genius or a great innovator, but are not sure, the advice is doubly helpful.

197   Journal Rankings: What Counts Is Your Contribution to Scholarship

What matters in the end is the contribution you make and its impact on your field and the wider research community.

1. If you have been well trained in graduate school you have a decent idea of the main journals in your field. You probably know the main ones in your subfield. These journals published the most important articles you read in seminars and referred to in your papers. Similar issues apply to presses for books.

2. Of course, some very important work is published in less-than-top-ranked journals, and some fields are less pyramid-pointy than others.

3. In the end, the crucial question is the contribution and how it is recognized. So not only must you publish in the right venues, you must market your work: at meetings, by distributing preprints, and by sending out reprints – even in this day and age of digital everything. You can send out links or attachments by e-mail. At meetings you not only give papers, but you propose sessions around your special concerns, you are self-effacing and let others publicize your work, and you are also selling your work by talking about it to those who count. At some point in your career you start getting invitations to speak, you do that and you do it well, and then you get invited even more.

4. Moreover, you apply for and receive grants and fellowships. The committees that review these get to know your work.

5. There are many less strong journals, and there is much pressure to publish lots. One of our strongest assistant professor cases published a small number of detailed and lengthy papers in the main journal in her field. If you publish lots of jointly authored papers, and your joint authors are also faculty (at your institution, or elsewhere), you will need to take into account that someone will wonder about double- or triple-counting. What are the norms in your field? What is the performance of the strongest peers in your cohort?

198 *Productivity in Academia*

Recently I came upon the productivity index sheet for a social science–oriented professional school. Curiously you get 18 points for a new scholarly work, 16 if you are the coauthor, 18 for chairing a major departmental committee, 6 points for a journal article, 5 for coauthor, points for dollars you bring in, points for your work being consistent with departmental goals. Obviously there is little sense here of the work required to write and publish a book, for example. Or perhaps the department wants to encourage articles and chairing committees and discourage scholarly books.

There is a lesson, though. Anybody who does sustained serious work on a problem is not likely to accumulate many points. They are in effect too focused for the diverse productivities of this list. The list has about 75 categories.

I know of another department, in this case a premier social science department. The question asked is, what is your contribution to the field (independent of number of articles – lots of articles that in toto make no big contribution are therefore discounted)?

The productivity-index department will do everything but have very distinguished deep scholars. It will encourage "productive" scholars who are visible and very active. I believe that is their aim. Anyone who wants to write a big book, which means five or more years of work, will move to another university.

199 The Contributions Made by Your Research Work

Being a faculty member at a university that has some commitment to research is an enormous privilege. If the university is ambitious, and the faculty member shares that ambition, that privilege comes with the obligation not only to do research and publish it, but also to do important research. By "important" I mean research that makes a widely recognized contribution to a field, that the problems you take on are recognizably important to others (or you can convince them that the problems are important). You are in a competitive arena. You are not necessarily competing to be first, for your competition may be about the quality of your research and publications.

It is hard to know if research is important. Your senior colleagues may know, but sometimes they are not plugged into the most current problems. So it is good to find a mentor or a judge who can guide you to the strongest, most important problems, the problems where the payoffs might well be substantial. While funding organizations are not necessarily venturesome, they often have advisors and referees who are leaders in the field. Getting external support for your research may indicate that your research problem is important. (Not always.)

What you want to do is to publish significant work that is widely recognized. You want to make the most of your talents and your time. You want people to be able to describe your contribution to the field and how it has moved inquiry forward. (Listing numbers of articles or books says little about contribution.) Put differently, your time for research work is limited. If you choose problems that are less significant you are less likely to make an important contribution. The choice of topics and problems is crucial to your career and your sense of your contribution. (Of course, some of the time you will be mistaken.)

You are likely to make a stronger contribution if you focus your work on a small number of areas (one, two), and you build cumulatively on that work. At some point, you may decide to go in a new direction – since academic careers go for 30–40 years, this is natural. But, again, focus and contribution will enable you to be more effective. (Writing more articles, without focus or contribution, is not your goal.)

Now, you might like tending your garden, just the way it is. The questions of contribution and competition might well be put aside. But it is unlikely that your university and your career will be as fulfilling.

It is not just a job, it is a vocation. Listen to its call.

200 *The Value of Annual Reviews of Our Work*

Each year faculty members have to write up a survey of what they have done in the previous year, and also write a brief memo about their accomplishments and future plans. For example, in making a list of papers published or in the works, I realized that with a week's work (which turned out to be two or three weeks), I could get several papers out of my hands and on the way for (re)consideration by journals. Two proposed papers might as well be written now, so I did a draft of each. Some projects needed to be abandoned or at least scaled back. I would never really get to them. Others that I never saw as projects, such as my *This Week's Finds* posts, became larger projects for the next few years (eventually, this book!).

My point is that a regular review of what you have been doing can be quite salutary. It forces you to focus on work that might be done now, get various tentative projects off the ground, and abandon what will never happen.

201   *Writing for Wider-Circulation, Discipline-Wide Journals*

As you plan your projects for the next year or so, let me encourage you to think about writing for the main research journals. These journals have very high impact factors, and may well lead to your best-known work (whether or not it is your best work) for decades hence. The article may be about pathbreaking research or a survey of what we know in a particular area. In general, survey articles are not the province of more junior faculty (you will not get much credit for them, as they are "just" review articles), but they are ideal for more senior faculty. They increase visibility and they build on the specialized work you have already done. They are research articles, not opinion pieces or "comments" or editorials.

The hit rate for these journals is often low, and sometimes it pays to write to the editors with a proposal for an article.

One of the often-asked questions when people come up for full professor is whether they have written for wider-circulation journals rather than specialty journals. Not lots, but once or twice.

202   *Book Chapters*

A colleague wrote me:

> I think that you may undervalue book chapters. Chapters are sometimes part of quite influential edited books where the scholarship of the moment is brought together to make a statement. Such books cement together a movement of colleagues, and so they serve social purposes. These days, particularly because of the cost of such edited books, they are often carefully reviewed by multiple scholarly experts. The reviews may not be blind, but they often demand rigorous changes that rival all but the highest standards of peer-reviewed journals. Other books are invitational, and may be reviewed, but not as rigorously. Those, I agree, are less influential and less highly regarded. But in many social science and humanities fields an edited book of partly original contributions (not

previously published in journals) should be valued. And, such books may actually reach a much wider audience of scholars and the public. The question that is so hard to answer is how to decide the influence of such books.

I replied: I think your point is well taken, but I do not believe that is the prevailing wisdom. My advice is based more on the prevailing wisdom than on what I think is right. Here is the best way to handle this:

1. If you are an assistant professor, book chapters will not count for much in general. Editing a book is not a sign of anything significant. You should be spending your time on your own work, on your own monograph or further research programs.

2. You want to set the context in your personal statement. "The volume X, which has a chapter by me, has become widely known as defining the field of economic dentistry." Or, "The volume X is drawn from a symposium at the American Dental Society, the leading scholarly group in our field." Or, "The chapter X is significant for my work since it elaborates on the notion of occlusion, combining in an interdisciplinary way concepts from dentistry with those from psychoanalysis. In my subsequent article in the *Journal of Dental Psychoanalysis,* one of top five journals in dentistry, I work this out in theoretical detail." Now the chapter is seen as part of a research program.

So, yes, it is right that chapters might well be further valued. But early on they are not valued much; later on it is a matter of the company you keep and the influence of the work.

The provost does not want to be bamboozled or diddled. Make your claims be believable and appropriately modest; cut all the hyperbole unless you are in the top few percent, and even then let the work, the CV, the awards speak.

D. MULTI-AUTHORED WORK

203 *Why Do So Many Papers in Some Fields Have So Many Authors? They Do Not Seem to Be Much Stronger Than Papers in That Same Field with One or Two Authors*

In high energy physics, the author list for an experimental paper is very large – you need a village to make an experiment. I understand the four to nine authors on papers in medicine – the lab is getting credit, and the boss comes first or last. But it may be difficult for outsiders to understand the large number of authors in papers in applied economics (business, real estate, health) or social science. You do need people to massage and clean databases – but they are typically graduate students under supervision of their advisor. Do these multi-authored papers come from work as research groups? Are there proprietorship reasons (X has one database, Y another)? Are the results much more impressive than papers authored by one or two scholars?

Now it may be that there has been a transformation in scholarly work in some fields, where the skills needed to do work demand a team and multiple authors. It could be that the work required to do a paper is also much greater than it was decades earlier. Departments should make these arguments, comparing work by their candidate with the strongest in the field. That the coauthor is a student, or perhaps a postdoc, should be considered a plus.

It is notable that one of the earliest (theory) papers in quantum mechanics, authored by Max Born, Werner Heisenberg, and Pascual Jordan in 1926, was widely referred to as the *Dreimännerarbeit,* the three-man paper, one or two being the norm at that time. (There is also such a paper in genetics, from 1935, by Nicolai Timofeeff-Ressovsky, Max Delbrück, and Karl Zimmer, here about the gene being of interest to physicists.)

204   *Counting Papers and Books and Citations – Compared to What?*

There are two issues here: Is counting a good idea? And, how to count multiply authored articles or books? Whatever the answers, if we are counting, we need to know what other scholars do, whether in quantity or in numbers of coauthors, and this is quite discipline- and subdiscipline-dependent. So *if you count, compare.*

As for counting itself, it probably makes sense to count at the extremes. Having one or two or three articles or zero books raises flags about productivity. Very many articles or books, especially if the articles are substantive rather than comments or letters to the editor or micro-contributions, and if the books are monographs rather than all edited, are likely to indicate a highly productive scholar. In-between numbers are where the real issues lie, and it is hard to know if four or five or seven or twelve articles are enough for tenure, especially if there are many authors. Of course, assessing the nature and quality of the contribution made by the work, and the norms of the field at the strongest institutions, will be helpful and should be probative.

Counting citations, or employing various measures such as the h-index, can again be useful in the extremes. But in the humanities, citations are comparatively rare and may not indicate impact or influence. And journal impact factors may be meaningful, although they are often gamed and manipulated. In some fields, such as mathematics, where most citations are more than two years after publication, citation data and impact factors have to take that lag into account. Moreover, these measures are very poor statistics, in the technical sense understood by statisticians. Often the measures are quite skewed, so that averages and even medians are misleading. Whatever their shape, it is hard to get a sense of the equivalent of their standard deviations, or how significant is the difference between two people's measures, such as their h-indexes.

Collaborative work and coauthorship is an increasingly important fact of academic life. (Moreover, coauthored papers may receive more citations, whether because of quality or name recognition.) So, for example, mathematicians who once might well have written singly authored papers now more and more collaborate via e-mail with their peers. The problem of counting and credit becomes less clear.

At various places in these essays I am skeptical of counting a paper by N authors as a full paper for each of the authors. Some of the time a paper has a graduate student and their advisor as authors, and it may make sense to count such papers as one for each. In a big laboratory, with several coauthors, or in a piece of social science research with, say, four authors, it probably makes better sense to give full credit to the main author (if there is one), and partial credit to the others. My various recommendations of $1/(N-1)$ may be too schematic. But they do indicate a problem of counting the paper as one paper for each of the authors.

Now, we often say that one should not count, and should instead attend to the contribution. Still, who gets credit for the contribution is open to inquiry, and testimony from coauthors is often quite helpful.

One way of avoiding this problem is to see *what is expected of the leading scholars in the subfield at a corresponding stage in their careers.* If they are expected to have *M* papers, and most of those papers have *N* authors, then that settles the counting question in a concrete way. (It is sometimes interesting to compare *M* and *N* in one field with the numbers from another.)

As for counting books vs. papers, usually a field is driven either by books or by papers. A rule of thumb might be five to ten papers equal one book, but this is very field-dependent.

An oft-mentioned aphorism is, *deans can't read, but they can count.* (There is empirical work on this for economics and for law.) Quantity over Quality, but with provisos that the generalization may reverse under certain conditions. The interesting question is *how and what to count.* At the extremes it would seem not to matter. But in the middle, it would appear that you have to read.

205   *Teams and Interdisciplinary Work*

In big science fields, such as high energy particle physics (half-billion-dollar and more experimental apparatus), joint authorship (with many authors) is the norm. What is needed is a careful statement of the contribution of the candidate, and testimony from coworkers about that contribution. To lead a sub-team is one such role, another is to take charge of a major part of the endeavor, another is to be the theorist consultant to the whole project, and there are other such roles. Some of this comes up in statistical work in biology and medicine. In these roles, independence and contribution are readily discerned by those inside the work.

Usually, the problem in promotion dossiers is when these issues are finessed or little evidence is offered, or the number of publications is low. In the latter case, in fields where people count publications I wonder why we do not just divide by *N*–1 or some such. There are good reasons for doing so, or not doing so. I note that the multiple-author papers in many fields do not seem to involve more work than singly authored work, or surely not much more work. Again, student coauthors are not a problem, but a plus.

I have seen dossiers turned around by testimonials. Typically they say, we could never have done our project without Joe Schmoe; he took a major role in the analysis, and he has contributed more than his share to the project's formulation. (Lots of details follow.) When you have 30 members of a team, you need more information. When you have 3 or 4, the testimonials of the collaborators work fine.

There may be issues about who raised the grants, but even there grant applications might well be written by teams, honchoed by a committee.

In general, teams can be 2–4, 5–12, and 13–100. Different issues arise for each.

As for interdisciplinary work, the preparers of the dossier may make excuses, rather than finding the people who recognize the value of the work. Or, they make excuses for why the work is not published in prominent journals. If the work is valuable and a contribution, there are people of significance who will recognize it as such. So tell us why it is important.

206   *Multiple Authorship, Order of Names, Contribution*

The norms of listing authors vary between fields. Some are strictly alphabetical, while some follow the rule that first or last author is the main worker, and if you are in the middle of a list you are less significant. The first/last rule often applies when there are four or five or six authors, as in much of medicine and sometimes in life sciences.

There is a curious practice of putting the senior author on all work done in their lab – but unless they review the work and are involved with it, they leave themselves open to future problems if the work proves corrupt.

Students are in general given pride of place if the work is mainly theirs. But, again, it might be first or last author.

If there is an ongoing collaboration, you could alternate, as some collaborators do. Or you could be like a comedy act, where you are known as a coequal team: Dean Martin and Jerry Lewis.

People who read dossiers for a living, as in promotion committees, know how to interpret these lists of authors. But they usually ask for a memorandum about who did what. If you are coming up for promotion, your personal statement can say if you were the main or the coequal author. While letters from collaborators are never probative, they are useful in assigning credit for the work. Ideally, people focus on contribution rather than numbers of articles, but they will pay attention to the numbers.

Finally, if you do lots of collaborative work, you will probably have to do more publication than if you do singly authored work. Someone will divide the number of articles or books by the number of authors. Maybe the algorithm will be $1/(N-1)$, where $N>1$, rather than N. Eventually, the other authors will come up for tenure or promotion, and if they claim the same article that you did, it had better be work that requires twice as much effort as a usual article.

Collaboration and joint production functions are standard in industrial research or in banking and finance, as well as for armed forces. Collaboration takes enough in transaction costs to make for problems. But someone will ask: Might we get just as much important research from one faculty member as from two collaborating? Maybe that is not the case, and then you must demonstrate it.

207 *Collaborative and Team Work: The CV*

In many fields of inquiry and scholarship, projects are still done by individuals. Usually, monographs in history, literary study, and anthropology are single-authored; mathematicians work alone although collaboration is now increasingly the case (so that the articles listed in the nominating information for mathematicians who are seeking leading positions in the American Mathematical Society are mostly jointly authored). In other fields, collaboration among 3–6 scholars is the norm. And in other fields, the projects involve 25–600+, usually scientists.

The problem for the individual researcher is to be able to indicate the nature of their contribution to the work. Moreover, it is natural to expect less credit per article per author for multiply authored work, and hence there would be more papers or journal articles when there are more authors. This rule may not apply at all to large collaborative scientific projects. But it would seem to apply to fields like economics, business, biology, medicine, engineering. Of course, there may be a lead professor working with many students, and this situation accrues well to the professor and the students. More people working together to produce a paper may make for a wider range of competencies in the paper, and of course there are costs of collaboration and coordination. But in the end, more papers should be so produced than if each paper is singly authored. Hence, when people come up for promotion or tenure, just counting papers seems unfair to single authors, when multiple authors can each claim a paper as their own. Moreover, what we want to attend to is the contribution rather than just counts of papers and venues. (One way out of this dilemma is to compare production at the strongest departments with the candidate's.)

1. It is very helpful to write yourself a memo about collaborative work, indicating your contribution, others' contribution, and perhaps even a rough allocation of effort. The memo can be incorporated into the personal statement for the promotion or tenure dossier.

2. Your contribution may be distinctive and crucial. For example, "as a statistician, I have been able to extract the most usable information from a series of complex and messy experiments," or, "while I am not specialized in solving models, my distinctive strength is formally defining a model for particular situations," or "my name is on the paper because I am head of the lab, raised the research grants, and supervised the work, and I am taking responsibility for the credibility of the findings of less experienced scientists."

3. You probably want to have a range of collaborators, so indicating your independence. This may not be good practice for your particular research portfolio, and if so, you want to write that memo about collaborative work and also have the collaborators attest to your contribution. Testimony from collaborators (particularly from the PI) is always valuable evidence.

4. Often, scholars are encouraged to demonstrate their independence by writing singly authored papers. This may be good advice, but in many fields a single-authored paper is most likely to be a review article – which may or may not be impressive.

5. Say you can only work with others. You are terrific at doing analysis, but awful at writing up the results. You have great ideas, but heaven help you in the laboratory. I think it is important to indicate your contribution, acknowledge your dependence on others, and show how your

contribution is invaluable. What will be probative is the quantity of the papers you produce collectively, the nature of their contribution, the testimony of your collaborators.

6. Of course, you can start raising external grants, becoming a PI, and that will surely attest to your capacities – especially in fields which are hard to fund. You can take other leadership roles. But for most junior faculty, these roles will have to wait.

7. Finally, do not tell yourself stories about how much X did to get tenure or promotion. Rather tell yourself stories about your contribution, about the nature of your collaboration, and about your value to the enterprise. Also, people who are doing well show that by the end of their third year. If you take much longer, you will always be behind, or you will be the wonderful exception.

It seems likely that collaborative and team work will become more prevalent in many fields. So it is crucial to figure out a way to thrive given the environment and the judgment of your seniors.

208 *Multiple Authorship: How to Count Work*

For various reasons, multiply authored pieces of scholarly work appear more often in our journals and on our bookshelves. The work may involve the joint efforts of many disciplines, or it may be that people work as a team (one writes, one calculates, one theorizes), or that only team-work will accomplish the work (in very large scientific experiments). Or, the list of authors is the professor and their students or postdocs. How should we account for these efforts when it is time to consider promotion, tenure, or salary increases?

One might find out the nature of the contribution of each author, and then it might not be too difficult to give credit. When considering promotion, one might not consider articles, but contributions to the field in terms of substantive advances.

One might count articles or pages, with some weight given to the quality of the journal, and divide by some function of the number of authors. Such a mechanical procedure only implicitly measures contributions to the field and matters of quality.

Obviously, in actual consideration these two extremes are balanced, and one might well examine what the leading scholars do for a concrete comparison. Similar issues come up in deal-making in investment banking, where everyone seems to have a hand on the deal. When bonus time comes around, the senior partners have to figure out who really did the work. Their advantage is the smallness of the firm.

However, I suspect that many junior faculty do not realize that an article with four authors, one of whom is more senior, may be perceived as being about one-quarter of an article. A letter from a senior author saying the junior person deserves more than one-quarter of the credit will be valuable.

Finally, scandals where the senior authors put their names on papers that had dubious data by the younger rising-star coauthor are especially troubling. Say four people publish a paper where the methods are suspect, or one of the author's other papers turns out to be suspect, or one of the authors is found to be stealing Post-Its from the storeroom. How do we deal with claims of the other authors that they did not know? But given jointly authored papers those problems will arise.

209   *Individual vs. Collective Research Efforts*

It is not true that in the good old days most research was done by individuals on their own with no help. German universities depended on the Professor as the head of the research enterprise, and Japanese universities are perhaps still very much like this. There are groups of people working on projects. And American sponsored-research, in agriculture and for the military and industry, has often been part of larger coordinated enterprises. The professor who wrote a book all alone, without lots of assistants, surely was not unheard-of, but if one looks at most such efforts there is in fact a cadre of students (and of course the proverbial wife) who are part of the enterprise and without whom it would not go forward at all.

However, it is still true that some faculty and students tend to do projects on their own, at best with some research assistance, and almost never as part of some larger encompassing project. This is still substantially true in literature and history and philosophy. Some of our faculty write a sequence of books or articles, or both, with no collaborators, without being part of a larger project. Whatever happens with any strategic plan, or funding sources, they go forward as juggernauts. They may well find ways of funding their research through bootlegging onto various programmatic research funding sources or through fellowships or archival research grants. For these people the greatest benefit of university life is encapsulated in four words – *May, June, July,* and *August* (Daniel Bell's quip).

Some of our colleagues follow this loner path. They find support for their students in fellowships; they may well be distinguished members of their professional societies. But they are not part of programmatic research efforts. Their internal drive is supplemented by the rewards of professional recognition (book reviews, awards, articles in the right journals) and membership in invisible colleges, and not by overhead-rich funding per se (although as we saw in the salad days of the National Endowment for the Humanities, they were not averse to such sources).

Junior faculty are always tempted by various programmatic and strategic initiatives. For many such faculty, in fact, those initiatives allow them to amplify their efforts and achieve much greater impact and contribution than they would otherwise. But for others, they are false incentives, leading faculty away from the unique and distinctive contribution they can make. No one is above the temptations. None of us is without the need for support, hence the value of our greatest support, those four summer months available for our research work.

You are able to pursue your interests and writing if you are supported by a sufficiently wide range of sources. So, my book on religious figures and entrepreneurship was supported by the Lilly Endowment under their public policy program. I wonder if the Endowment had such in mind when it formed its public policy committee.

I write this note not so much to defend my own doings, whose main defense has to be the books and articles that are published and the students whom I have educated. Rather, it is to make sure that we encourage our faculty to make contributions in the ways that work best for them and for the university and for scholarship in general.

E. YOUR CV

210   *Evaluating Your Contributions and CV*

What you want to avoid is someone reading your CV and silently dismissing it, seeing some parts as diminishing the credibility of other parts. Experienced readers do this automatically, without thinking twice. You want people to believe that your CV adequately represents your achievements and areas of expertise. The same for any personal statement. There's no need to brag; the work should do most of it for you. If you are that good, do not worry: the CV will do the work.

1. If you are announcing that you have *N* articles, joint articles may not count as *N* full articles, one for each author. If you have one or two collaborators with whom you have worked extensively, you will want to detail your relationship. (Not on your CV, but in a personal statement.) Your advisor is fine as a collaborator when you first emerge from graduate school, but afterward you have to have a very good reason (and there are some) for so continuing.

2. Another double-counting problem is articles in press, articles published this year, and even articles submitted. It's always best to be clear about what's coming in this year, separating it from what is in prospect. Again, you do not want people doing subtracting or dividing to normalize your achievement. In general, mixing in first-rate contributions with much lesser ones tends to diminish the importance of the first-rate ones. You look like you are fluffing up your CV.

3. I would focus on the contribution rather than the number of articles. What is the substantive contribution of your work (and your personal statement can then footnote the articles that represent that contribution)?

4. Have you aimed for the right journals in your field? Consistently? Publication in the top journals in a subfield is often good enough.

5. What is the meaning of the author lists – are authors listed alphabetically, with first author most important, with last author most important? Again, the issue of contribution is crucial.

6. Funded research: Focus on externally funded research. It may or may not be prestigious to win some awards, but if you have to tell people

then it is not very prestigious. (Others can tell people, and they usually provide evidence of the difficulty of getting an award.) Internal university awards are nice, but they are viewed as being seed money. Did you then go out and get a big grant?

7. You will want to stop listing graduate student awards. More important, you want to be emphasizing the independence of your career from your graduate school training.

8. Quoting from student evaluations tends to be viewed as selective. Your student evaluation numbers are only meaningful when compared with your colleagues' numbers teaching similar-sized classes. Also, it is sort of like the A's and Bs students now receive. There is inflation.

9. If you give a list of talks or articles or grants, people check the dates and then ask: Did this candidate do much work in the last L years? Lots of stuff previously, but not so much recently? What about the hiatus seven years ago?

10. After a while, references cannot be your advisor or graduate school teachers, nor your new colleagues. Certainly when you come up for tenure they will have to be arm's-length scholars. (When you are in graduate school, and in your first year or two out, the advisor and other teachers are prime references.)

211   De-Fluffing Your CV

1. The first two pages or so are crucial. Do they list some of your most significant accomplishments: books, articles, grants? Do they mix in stuff that is much less significant? Many a c v has the most significant stuff at the end (or buried in the middle), where people are least likely to notice it.

2. If you are starting out in your academic career, you will not have lots to list that is important. Make sure what you do list that is important is not outweighed by much less significant achievements. In particular, submitted articles can be listed as works in progress with "Submitted to *Journal* . . ." But it makes much less sense to list articles you are writing as "To be submitted to *Journal* . . ." (It may be useful to provide this information for your mentors, though.)

3. If anything is in progress, you want to be sure it is "in press" before you give a completion date or a publication date. You might say that something is a "five-year project," since that promises much less.

4. When you list your fields of research or teaching, if you do, make them brief lists.

5. In general, date of birth, your home address, your marital status and number of children do not belong on your academic CV. Fancy layouts are unhelpful (this may be different for those in the design fields). Fonts should be totally uninteresting. And probably 12-point type given that many of the readers are over 45 years old.

6. Many readers will automatically count articles that appear in top-ranked journals vs. those in lesser-ranked journals. All will notice if you mix refereed with non-refereed journals or magazines (so have two lists: Scholarly Journals, Other Publications). If you are just starting out, no one will hold it against you if your publications are in student journals (rather, it is a sign of industry and commitment).

7. If there were periods when you did not do scholarly work (perhaps you played in a jazz band, cared for small children or sick family members, or did professional or administrative work), or during which you did not publish much, perhaps you can help the reader. I am not sure how to handle this. The point is that someone will notice and wonder. If you received your doctorate later than usual because you had an earlier career or role, a brief indication of that career is helpful. For the most part people begin to count the years from when you received your doctorate or other terminal degree.

212 *Your CV, for Those Who Are Just Getting Started*

Experienced readers of CVs, say on the university promotion committee, read a CV much as a radiologist reads an X-ray. Do not even think of trying to get away with anything, or bragging by fluffing it up. It just decreases the credibility of what you have done, and your good stuff gets devalued. Early on you do not have much to show. That is fine. On the other hand, if you have a Nobel Prize, you do not need to add much, but some people are curious about your work nonetheless.

If you are just starting out, or if you are new, of if you do not know the standard format and content, check with the members of your department about form and standards.

Separate out book chapters and conference proceedings from refereed articles (unless, as in computer science, conference papers in your field are refereed). Distinguish actual scholarly books from reports, even though the latter might be your claim to fame and distinction (as is the case for one of my strongest scholarly friends). If you are already an assistant professor, no one wants to know about your scholarships, your TA-ships. Your dissertation is not a publication, even if it is filed with UMI. If you have done lots of journalism and short pieces, separate them out into such a category. If you have done lots of joint work, be sure it is clear who the coauthors are and if you are an equal author. If you have presentations to list, be sure you list the important ones. If you have published three articles in the premier journal of your field, all coauthored with your advisor, people will wonder who was the lead author, so indicate who was.

Your areas of specialization, accomplishments, and special skills should be obvious, and important keywords should appear on the first page or two of text.

213 Stupid Résumé Tricks

· Do not be too crowded, or use too small type.
· Be sure the dates that you worked are clear.
· Telephone number? E-mail address?
· Cut out weaker jobs (for example, those of one month's duration).
· Make sure your list of activities does not include acronyms
   that do not make sense to the average reader.
· Some of you underestimate your talents and achievements.
· Do not list computer skills unless they are extraordinary.
· Better to have a CV that works for you than to copy
   your friend's layout. Alignment of paragraphs and
   indents makes all the difference in legibility.
· Do not use peculiar typographic symbols. Too cute by half.

· One page, not using the back of the page (for a résumé).
· Think of it as advertising, where your task is to tell a story that is compelling and true. Irrelevant stuff might be left out, but if this means there is a 20-year hiatus, you may need to explain it (you were incarcerated, you brought up a family, you were a stockbroker and decided to become a city planner).
· Be careful what you capitalize – proper names, but not important ideas, for example.
· You may want to adjust your résumé for different kinds of jobs.
· Spell-check, copyedit, proofread – twice.
· Use ordinary 20–24 lb. paper, white.

214 *Fluff in the CV*

I have just read over a vita of someone whose work I like. But the vita is filled with fluff.

Make sure that what I learn about you in the first pages is substantial. If you just have to list everything (including your Red Cross lifesaving certificate), do it farther down on your vita (and then delete it). Fluff devalues your achievements. Refereed publications mixed in with conference proceedings and presentations become less significant. If you have published a book, make sure I can see it pronto – not buried among lots of other stuff. If you have done lots of service and community and governmental work, list the big stuff up front. The lesser goes later if at all. Think of it this way – I am reading your vita page by page. My opinion of you cumulates. I would hope that you would agree that those cumulations ought to be big and positive, rather than infinitesimal and unsigned, so to speak.

215 *Curriculum Vitae – Format*

Fluff means there is something fishy. So:

Use a simple typeface, single-spaced is OK, with space between the sections. No bold, no varied fonts. You can underline or italicize titles and subheads. Ordinary 20–24 lb. paper you have in the standard copying machines, or just a regular .doc or .docx file.

Make sure your genuine achievements are up front: education, major fellowships and awards (but if you received them when you were in college, and are now applying post-PhD, they are not relevant), major grants in the previous five years, books (real academic books, not reports, not fluff), publications in refereed journals (accepted papers can be listed here too, but not those merely submitted, and not those accepted subject to revision), and then reports, book chapters. If you have major professional accomplishments they go up here, too. If you are a designer, your major commissions need to be listed, and then your portfolio is crucial.

For graduate students, if you have teaching experience, for professors, if you have supervised doctoral candidates, list this here.

Editorial positions might come here, but again be careful about fluff.

The organizations you belong to, the committees you serve on, the university talks you have given, all come later. I would choose the strongest ones, and leave out the less important – since every weak claim diminishes the power of every strong claim. Others would recommend complete lists.

More generally, when I read your vita I should readily sense your strengths and achievements, and at the same time I should not encounter flags that say something is fishy here.

Don't claim citation counts if you were a postdoc in someone's lab and the paper is very important (the laboratory head gets the citation credit).

Do not be encyclopedic. If you have written op-eds in the *New York Times* five times in the last year, it is better to say that, rather than list every one. Again, others recommend scrupulous completeness.

I do not have advice to give about professional résumés, or nonacademic positions. Straightforward honesty is crucial. And do not ever list your Boy Scout merit badges or the like. (Yes, people do that.)

By the way, people readily pick up that you did not publish for a long period, or that the journals are second-rate, or that the work seems unfocused. The people who read vitae for a living could also be reading spy satellite photographs for the National Geospatial-Intelligence Agency.

Edited volumes do not count for much, whether you are editor or contributor. But if this is a report on a major research project of which you are the PI, that is something else.

Your advisor's letter of reference will be helpful for getting your first job. After that, when you come up for promotion and tenure, it is not seen as objective and so is discounted.

Of course, you may not be able to fulfill all of these demands. Just be aware that the world notices.

F. CHANGING JOBS

216   *Should You Change Universities? Yes!*

Changing universities is a good thing. New colleagues, new challenges, new idiocies, all make a big difference. If you do not get an adequate salary increase, or promotion, or whatever, often it makes good sense to find another institution and move – for bargaining rarely solves the fundamental problems of your current department or school. (For deans who want to retain faculty, the lesson is act early and generously, and deal with recurrent problems as soon as possible. Your most desirable faculty are likely to leave sooner rather than later.)

If you do not get tenured, a new university offers a chance to re-configure your career. The new institution may be weaker, or not. But the important thing is that your strengths were not recognized at the old one, and now it is time to find a pond in which you swim just right. (Again, the lesson for the dean is to find good places for the faculty who do not fit into your institution – you get double credit.)

What are you to do about the people who will not leave, who make it difficult to keep your school or department from becoming weaker (they, in effect, repulse the people who subsequently leave). You can wait until they die or retire. You can find institutions that they would want to join. And you can, with the aid of the provost, bring in a cohort that presents a new opportunity. In any case, any mistake you make in appointment and promotion is likely to haunt you and your successors for the rest of the candidate's career.

Many people who leave, voluntarily or for non-promotion, seem to do better than many of their colleagues left behind.

When you come up for promotion or a salary increase or whatever, when you have just made a big splash with your scholarship, think in terms of a new institution. Ideally, your dean has anticipated this and made preemptive moves.

217   *Leaving Your University Position: Living Well Is the Best Revenge*

You just did not get tenure, or they did not try to keep you when you received an alternative offer, or you are unhappy at your institution, or there's no place for you at the institution, or you did not get promoted.

Do not spend much energy fighting. Too costly. Do not sue. (Others would strongly disagree with me. There are some quite successful cases, revealing shenanigans and prejudices that are quite embarrassing to the department.) If you do decide to sue, in the interim find another position and make the former department regret having let you go. It does not matter if it is at a "lesser" institution. Will it be a place where you can do your work and make a living and thrive? If so, thrive, do well, and show that you are in fact stronger than most of your former colleagues. Stay friendly with them as you thrive. The friendlier you are and the better you do professionally, the more they will come to see themselves as mistaken.

218   *Reinventing the Faculty*

The university that invents the way to improve the quality of its faculty – outside of better hiring, and incentives such as salary and promotion – will be able to do what no other university does. The issue is not tenure; rather, it is that tenure makes it very hard for faculty to think of alternatives just at the time of their lives when they might find terrific opportunities. Put differently, given all the talk that one does not any longer work for a single corporation one's whole life (a peculiar historical fact of slavery, and of the post-wwII era), I find it hard to believe universities will avoid this phenomenon.

219 *Why Do Faculty Leave?*

1. If they are junior, not yet tenured: they get an offer (solicited or unsolicited) from a better place (better because it is stronger, or it works better for them personally), and the offer has not been matched or perhaps cannot be matched given the situation. Or, they do not receive tenure, and then the question is whether they find another position (usually), and what is their long-term performance. Or, they move on to another profession, either because the research and teaching life is not for them, or because they are otherwise unhappy.

2. Once they are tenured: they do not receive a goody, whether it be a chair, a salary increase, or promotion to full professor; they get an offer much as above, but now they are not forced to leave but find attractive the features of another place – often a place which would seem to be less strong, but in fact offers specific inducements or strengths that are just what the person wants; they cannot stand the dean or the department, or the department is falling apart and it is time to leave before things get worse; personal reasons, whether they be spousal hires, better weather, different career line, divorce; they realize they are stuck and need to jump-start their lives and careers.

The major problem for the university is to keep some of its faculty off the market, the strongest ones in particular. For the faculty member, having offers is always a good thing. In other words, this can be an unstable situation.

EIGHT

Tenure & Promotion (#220–290)

A. FUNDAMENTALS

220   *What Tenure Means (for Lay Persons)*

Tenure is lifetime employment at your university (no guarantee of pay level or advancement), with an obligation to teach and write well, once you have proven yourself during a probationary period.

1. Say you are hired as a new assistant professor soon after finishing your PhD or a postdoctoral appointment or some other terminal degree (JD, MFA). You may have some publications, usually coauthored with your advisor. They may have helped you get the job. But this work will not contribute much to the tenure decision. (Faculty in the arts have demonstrated promising performance, evidenced not by publication but by venues and reviews.)

2. In the next 5½ years (more practically 5 years, and in some fields the time may be 7 years), what is called a probationary period, you need to show:

    a. that you are a good university citizen – this is usually
       least important, heavy service being something
       they saddle you with after you are tenured.

    b. that you are a decent teacher – if you have problems in
       teaching, work with your colleagues to solve them early on.

    c. that you have developed a research career that is recognized
       as contributing to the scholarly enterprise. At research
       universities, this is most important. You've got to be an

OK colleague, you have to be an OK teacher, but you
must be a distinguished contributor to your field.

 c1. You evidence this by your receiving grants that
 enable you to do your work. In some fields those
 grants must be of a certain size and come from highly
 competitive sources. In others, no grants are expected.

 c2. Your contributions become known to distinguished
 colleagues in your field, usually by your
 presentations at meetings, by your sending out
 reprints or preprints, by your correspondence
 with those working on similar problems.

 c3. You disseminate your contributions through
 publication in prominent venues: the most prestigious
 and widely read journals in your field and more
 generally in your discipline, books published
 by university presses or other such presses, and
 presentations at the right conferences and meetings
 and arts venues. The how-much questions, how
 many articles, are better answered by giving an
 account of how your work has made a contribution to
 scholarship – and in general one book or perhaps six
 or more articles in the right places might indicate that.
 But there are lots of qualifiers – is the book really good?
 are the articles coauthored with N other people, many
 of whom are using them to get tenured or promoted?
 what exactly did you do in joint work? But, in the end,
 it is the nature of the contribution that is crucial.

Some universities and some departments award tenure only at
the full professor level, associate professorship being a step on the
way. That tenure decision may be made in the eighth to tenth year, say.
In these cases, presumably marginal performance has been filtered
out by non-promotion to associate professor. Here the decision is
between the very strongest and the less strong; there is much more
evidence of research quality; a second NIH grant is likely; the second
book is done and perhaps out; and the candidate's work is more
widely known and evaluated. Candidates are likely to have offers
from other strong universities. The problem for the university is not

potential deadwood but recognizing sheer enduring excellence. The candidate takes up room at the top in terms of impact, venues, grants, and teaching. (Much of this book will not apply in this situation.)

3. When you are up for tenure, your department will ask you for a CV, some of your articles or your first book, and a personal statement that briefly indicates the nature of your research (and perhaps teaching) contributions and your future plans, and will then appoint a committee to report to the faculty. That committee will ask for letters of reference from arm's-length referees, and perhaps from collaborators (to find out who did what). They then summarize all of this for your colleagues, your colleagues discuss and vote, and your dean writes a memo giving a larger overview and the dean's decision. It then goes forward to the university as a dossier where it is reviewed by a faculty committee advising the provost, who is usually the one who makes a final decision, in fact the only decision.

In my experience the university committee is fair and unbiased, but they are looking for problems in the dossier, for this is a major decision and just as in the sale of a used car, the seller knows more than the buyer about defects and problems. They see a wider range of dossiers than just your department. They are asking whether this person will advance scholarship and the agenda of the university (to become much stronger) over the medium and long run. Those defects and problems may well not be important in the end, but they will be noticed. Hence, it makes sense for the department and school to send up a dossier that is honest, balanced in its considerations, and takes into account any problems (not by excusing them, but by putting them in context). I am not sure, but fewer than half the dossiers are obvious yeses, although probably five-sixths in the end are *yes*. (Keep in mind that some assistant professors leave before the tenure decision, and some weak cases never leave the department or school, so that five-sixths might be only half of all assistant professor appointments.)

221   *Lessons Drawn from Reading Hundreds of Dossiers*

1. All the research literature suggests that *candidates' performance in the probationary years is predictive of what they will subsequently do.*

2. There are *too many fishy dossiers:* not enough arm's-length letters, too many excuses for poor performance in grants or publishing. Perhaps each school should *appoint a devil's advocate who reads the dossier before the dean sees it, and indicates where the dossier is problematic, and sends it back for those problems to be addressed.* Maybe schools should have that devil's advocate drawn from another school.

3. No university will move up fast unless it takes on the fixed assets of the current tenured faculty. Much more *proactive mentoring* throughout the university would make a difference. I am not sure deans or chairs have the capacity to face these issues effectively. Perhaps some of the strongest members of a department might incorporate the weaker ones in their research programs.

4. The medical school at the University of Chicago developed a system for gathering data from candidates and evaluators that forced the right information through the use of electronic forms. Also, they *distinguished judgments of excellence from those of institutional need – and the promotion committee deals only with excellence.*

5. Here is a Tenure and Promotion Decision Checklist:

    a. Will the candidate make the university or the department much stronger?

    b. Did the department sandbag the candidate (too much teaching, service)?

    c. Red flags noticed when reading the dossier: Please list: _____

    d. Finished one major project and on to another with decent progress? Needed grants are there?

    e. Venues of publication are strong? Contribution to multi-authored work is clear?

    f. Contribution to the field is clear?

    g. Letters are from a fair representation of potential arm's-length writers? Letters discuss the work and its contribution? Letters indicate current visibility and potential of future trajectory?

    h. Committee and dean's memoranda deal with the issues? Do they present excuses? Are the memoranda balanced and considered?

i. What is your general impression of the case?

Good Enough .... Outstanding

j. What is the probability of this being a mistaken tenuring?

Mistake .... Sure Thing

k. Is the work significant? creative? imaginative? original?

1. (Looking back, four years later, has the candidate continued to be productive and to produce high-quality work?)

222 *Encouraging an Even Stronger Faculty in the Future*

1. Recognize the increasing quality of many appointments and promotions. Make faculty aware of it. Realize that an institution cannot
afford to have units that are much, much weaker than the stronger ones,
and units with faculty who are much, much weaker. Cut variance or at
least the left tail, raise quality.

2. Early warning system: For already tenured faculty, if there is a
problem it should be apparent within three years. For probationary, the
third-year review is most critical. In each case, assertive help is warranted: extra short-term support, guidance about teaching or research
by more successful colleagues, a set of goals for the next triennium, with
sub-goals for each year.

3. Move the standard for performance over slightly. For example,
the book should be out, especially for full professors. Same for articles.
The problems with teaching should be dealt with and worked out. Say
that the number of articles that is considered marginal is now about four
for tenure, with a few in the pipeline. Move that to five or six. And more
importantly: What is the contribution?

The change is in fact small, but more importantly, it makes decision-
making more reliable. The idea is to have many fewer dossiers that are
marginal, or at least to make the marginal ones stronger.

4. Fishy dossiers are sent back to the dean/department immediately.
If the letter-writers are not appropriate, it is much better for a unit to solve
the problem. The same is true of teaching evidence. If there is a problem
not dealt with at the appropriate level, send it back. Dossiers that are not
ready for consideration by the deadline will be turned down, including
tenuring – presumably the issues raised would have denied tenure in
any case.

5. Emphasize that most appointments have 25+-year consequences. Ask: If the person continues just as they are now, will that be acceptable for the future university we imagine a decade or two hence?

223   *Promotion/Tenure/Appointment: Very Brief Advice for All Involved*

- Mentor your colleagues, actively. Take the mentoring advice.
- You are master of your promotion. If you do what you are supposed to, and do it well, there should be few problems. Most denials are a consequence of your not having done what you ought to.
- Never compare yourself with the weakest in your department or field.
- Produce an honest dossier that takes problems in hand and explains (not excuses) them. If you write a letter of reference, be honest and detailed. (One colleague asked, "How did X get tenure?" I said, "When you were at your previous university you wrote a positive letter of reference." He said, "But I did not mean to be that enthusiastic.") If the case is weak, ask the candidate if they would rather withdraw and seek another position, thereby avoiding any stigma.
- Be honest in your expectations. If you are a comprehensive university, it is much harder for a candidate to do as much research as in a research university. Do you really expect them to publish in the topmost journals?
- You live with your mistakes for decades. If someone should not be tenured, help them find a job elsewhere. People are always pointing to X or Y and asking, how did they get tenure? X or Y would be better off at places that valued them more highly.

224   *Getting Tenured*

1. Get the book out, a year early if possible.
2. Publish in the main journals, at least once in the premier ones. For a much stronger case, publish several times in the premier journals.

3. If you do lots of collaborative work, you need to be sure your collaborators can say what your contribution was. It is sometimes recommended that you write some single-author papers.

4. Book chapters are never probative. Aim for the journals that are refereed and have high visibility. Do not let revise-and-resubmits stand around; turn them around immediately.

5. Do not get burdened by service or too many new class preparations.

6. Let people know about your work. Send out reprints. Attend and present and help organize sessions at meetings.

7. Make clear your contribution to the field. Write it down in one paragraph in clear language. This is not a list of your articles.

8. If you are not making progress, ask yourself whether you ought to be in a different institution where your talents are more valued.

9. Have faculty visit your classes and give you advice re teaching.

10. If you are very strong, the job market offers a way of your being sure your department recognizes your strength. It's good for your department to find itself competing for its strongest junior faculty. Do not play games; if you do get an offer and want to bargain with your current institution, be prepared to take that offer.

11. Get the book done. Publish in the premier venues. Understand your contribution to scholarship.

12. Keep in mind that there are others in your institution who are doing spectacular jobs at the corresponding stage in your career. Your provost will have them in mind when your case is reviewed, not the weaker cases in your department.

13. If grant-getting is natural for your work, start the process early.

225 *Avoiding Turndowns, for Tenure or Full Professor*

1. Some faculty are not savvy about when to be promoted to full professor. It does you no good to come up and get turned down; it hurts the credibility of the department and the school. So if a faculty member insists on being considered for promotion, it is up to the dean and colleagues to indicate the risks, and also not put the school's reputation on the line. The costs of being turned down are substantial, and need not be incurred. This does not mean you want to be overly conservative, but it

is usually apparent to experienced colleagues when someone is pushing the envelope without good reason. On the other hand, if someone has done important work, received the right grants, and published in the right venues, they ought be promoted as soon as that is achieved.

2. Junior faculty do not always know how to build their careers. They need to be told what to do, with guidance as to what is a strong record of achievement. Where to publish, what to publish, what is significant work. Eventually people learn, but sometimes it takes more than the probationary period. Again, it does no one any good to be turned down for tenure – it hurts the person, hurts the school. So, when someone comes up they should have done what they ought to have done, and if not they should gracefully move on.

3. Deans, with concurrence of the provost, may have idiosyncratic goals for a particular faculty member. Achievement of those goals, perhaps unusual as they are, would be warrant for promotion.

4. As for people who are given a chance to be reconsidered, there needs to be substantial new work, important grants received, recognitions that are significant. It's often hard to do that in a year, but I have seen it done – with panache. Stuff that was in the pipeline spurts out, and it is clear this is not just a onetime event but a sign of the future. The book is not only written, but now it is revised, much stronger, and has been finally accepted by a press. The NIH R01 grant comes in.

226   The Rising Tide: Your Personal Best Has to Be Superior, Not Marginal

1. What is changing in the university is the quality of the lateral senior appointments, and of some of the promotions. There is "compelling excellence," scholarly records that are so strong they demand our assent. The standards set by the strong appointments are impressive. These scholars and creative persons are productive and their contributions are substantial and widely recognized. And some of the promotions to tenure from within are similarly impressive. You have some junior faculty who clearly outperform their productive seniors.

One or two compelling performances would have little effect, but what is happening is that there are now enough so that as a whole they carry much more weight.

2. In a rising university, people who have had tenure for five or ten years say that they would not get tenure now. *Expectations have risen, but more importantly, excuses become less tolerable as stronger and stronger candidates come up for tenure and promotion.* If more of the stronger candidates are coming up, or being appointed, the effect is to make weak cases seem much weaker.

3. Teaching always matters. Evaluation should include class visits. Just as we expect research to be validated through publication in important venues, so teaching is significant if it influences practices elsewhere and leads to publications. Being a very good classroom teacher in a research university is no more important for promotion and tenure than is being an unpublished writer of fine manuscripts.

4. Promotion and tenure committees try hard to be fair. There is now less tolerance throughout the system for suboptimal performance.

227   *Promotion Guidelines*

Keep in mind that the university promotion and tenure guidelines are meant to help the university make its faculty stronger, and make the process fairer and more transparent. If something or some rule strikes you as peculiar, it is likely that it comes out of actual cases where things did not progress in a satisfactory way. While rules and regulations cannot prevent every problem, they can often help. The rules are rarely so rigid that good reasons for exceptions are not permitted.

Do not ask "whether X would be appointed/promoted in your department" when you write for letters of reference. Ask the writer to tell us which are the strongest departments in this field or area, and whether X would be appointed there. The former question often leads to evasions, while the latter seems to elicit real information that is quite helpful. Ask for letters from peer or better institutions; it is likely that faculty at those institutions have the kind of experience and standards that the university aspires to. Ask for letters from people in the larger field, especially for more senior cases; there is a commitment to having scholarly work have a wider impact.

Similarly, there is an emphasis on balanced appraisals of candidates. That a candidate is strong in some areas is very important, but they are likely to have weaknesses that are significant. *Hyperbolic praise implies poor judgment or worse on the part of the department or the dean.* But a balanced appraisal can say something like "X is a solid researcher, but they have led our department in revolutionizing education in the field, and those contributions have made the university eminent in significant ways." And the letters of reference can affirm that leadership. If grant-getting is part of the demands of a position, as in engineering or social work or medicine, there could be some candidates whose research achievements transcend that requirement – unlikely, but possible.

The guidelines do not make good bedtime reading unless you need to go to sleep. But they are useful for more junior colleagues, and for senior colleagues on promotion committees. But perhaps the greatest impact on the promotion/tenure process is the success of the faculty and deans in appointing extraordinarily strong faculty, and of colleagues in mentoring junior people who then come up for promotion with impressive achievements: compelling excellence.

228   *Professional Competence and Trust*

Ask, when you think of tenure or other such processes of judging entree into a profession: Would you want this person operating on your children or parents? Would you want this person diagnosing your symptoms? Would you want this person defending you in court?

If you ask these questions, then you want to be sure that the candidate is not only marginally competent, but reliably competent, at least. Will they continue to perform well, and for the possibly marginal case, will they improve enough? In the latter case, I am not sure I am willing to take the risk. For our responsibility as professors or in other professions is to make sure that people who have our imprimatur are reliable and trustworthy in their professional actions. In a research university, will they have significant research careers? If teaching and service is the major responsibility of the university, will they teach and serve well?

Different institutions will have different standards of performance, so I am not suggesting a single criterion. But you really do not want a butcher to be your surgeon, or even a marginal surgeon to be your surgeon. I've been told that surgery is different from being a university professor, but I do not think the question as I posed it initially is inappropriate.

I think much the same applies to professional degrees, whether MD, PhD, or master's. *This is a serious business we are in, and when we send people out who are marginal we endanger society.*

229 *Thinking about Your Promotion*

Keep in mind that nothing focuses the mind of a dean or provost so well as an offer of a position for you, or even a serious feeler, from a peer or better institution.

Make a list of potential referees. Do they know your work already? Do not include collaborators (a separate list) or your advisor or committee members. Are there potential referees whom you might not want?

Make a list of peers at other institutions. Where do you stand with respect to them?

Make a list of your strengths and achievements. Write a paragraph in plain English describing your contribution to scholarship. Make a list of weaknesses and problems. Write a paragraph about teaching, and one about service.

Compare your achievements and c v with the stronger ones in your school or department at the same stage. How do you match up? Comparisons with weak cases are unhelpful.

If you have done lots of joint work, write down your contribution to that work, and some rough fraction of the total work (this is impossible, but ⅕, ½, or ⅘ are probably distinguishable) for each major project. On the other hand, if a paper (joint or otherwise) demands much more work than most research papers, tell us and explain why (for example, a year to gather a data set – but then we hope you will write several papers from it or one very substantial one).

For better or worse, papers published in premier journals, or books published by top presses, get more attention and are given more weight.

Have your CV read by a critical person to be sure it is clear, to be sure it fairly represents you.

No excuses. Reasons are fine.

230   Do What You Must Do

If you have a mentor and they tell you to do something, you ought to do it. They may actually know something. Of course, your mentor might be corrupt or stupid or evil, but in general that is not the issue. If I tell you that your CV needs to be rewritten and this is what you need to do, #1–9, do not just do #1 or #2, but do all 9. Mentors do not have the time to argue that a truck will crush you when you walk in front of it. If I tell you that your dissertation proposal does not make sense, that observation is warning enough. Do not shop for someone to say it is good. *Do not think you will get tenure because you think you should.*

Unfortunately, rarely can you receive only positive encouragement. Cautions and demurrers are essential. Otherwise, that truck will crush you no matter how positive the advice. (I have not liked hearing that some of my work is crap, to use the term of art, from the strongest person in a field. But it is possible to recover and figure out what is going on, and to make the work acceptable.) If you can't take the heat, get out of the kitchen. Now, much of the heat is hot air, but some of it is steam and you will be burned to death unless you protect yourself, learning from even the most searing of criticism.

Also, do not whine, complain, blame someone else. It is unseemly. Do the best you can. If you think you have been unfairly treated, write the most anodyne of memos outlining your concern, and let others get excited. For example, you might write, "I have published one article each year in a major journal. I have tried to improve my rate of publication, but with my being assigned five rather than the usual four courses each year that has proved difficult."

231   Promotion: WYSIWYG

Reviewing the research literature in higher education on promotion and tenure:

1. *What you see is what you will get.* In general, the best predictor of future performance of an assistant professor, if tenured, is what they did during the probationary period. Much less often there is a late bloomer, much more often there is an early decline. (As far as I can tell, there is no systematic research on what happens to those who are denied tenure. Do they thrive elsewhere?)

2. *Associate professors are often loaded down with administrative work,* and that slows their progression to full professor, or delays it for a very long time.

3. The biggest problem is *the fishy dossier.* This is a more general problem in personnel administration. There can be misrepresentation of achievements (were you really the PI on this grant? is this book a scholarly book?) or suspicious letters of reference (people had not read the work, or they were pinkie-length rather than arm's-length, or members of a sub-disciplinary club), and perhaps the committee, departmental, or dean's memoranda do not take account of the problems. (The university promotion committee will have a member who happens to check up on things, or notices misrepresentations or letters that share a paragraph word for word. That stigmatizes the case, and often marks the dean as someone who is not reliable, from whom you would not buy a used car.)

Deans could be required to sign off on a dossier, as well as their dean's memo, à la Sarbanes-Oxley.

4. Publishing in the main journals and prominence: If you count the number of people up for tenure who are expected to publish in the main journals, there is not enough room in those journals for their expected number of articles. And if you count the number of places where people are expected to be among the leading two or three (or ten, or even twenty) figures in a field, again *there is not enough room at the top.* Social scientists call these "positional goods." I suspect that congestion pricing, as practiced in transportation, will not be popular.

232 Tenure Judgments: If You Have Any Doubt, Vote No

I have received this counsel re tenure judgments: If you have persisting doubts, vote *no.* The argument is that this is an unchangeable decision with long-term consequences. It would seem that those denied tenure rarely turn out to be strong scholars. This could be because they are denied a venue from which to work, although usually they can find a position at a good institution. Denials that are a consequence of internal departmental battles, the denial being collateral damage, may well find positions at stronger institutions and thrive.

As for marginal candidates, the ones for whom you have those doubts, but who are tenured nonetheless – empirically, few turn out to be strong, few publish lots of work, few become much better teachers. Remarkably few.

From the candidate's position, swimming in the wrong-sized pond is rarely a good decision, even if they feel there are others in the pond weaker than they are.

233   *Avoiding Tenure Mistakes*

We want to cut the number of mistakes we make in the promotion and tenure process. We make many more errors in tenuring than in not tenuring.

We could tenure people only where the evidence is overwhelmingly strong. (And perhaps only at the full professor level – risking their being bid away while waiting.) If we were explicit in our discussion about problematic features in a dossier, those negative signals, would that help us do better in the future, and also make a better decision now? We might study the cases where we have made mistakes (tenurings that did not work out well), and ask if we could have decided better.

We could have clawback provisions for departments – if one of their now tenured associate professor colleagues took (much) more than six years to come up for full, they might well have trouble going forward with new tenurings. Departments might keep the line and find a new candidate if they did not choose to tenure the current candidate.

Could our decision procedures be supplemented by an objective formula, so that problematic cases would be flagged?

234   *Making Multi-Million-Dollar Long-Term Capital Investments – Tenure, Promotion*

When you buy a used car you assume that you are not being told the whole truth, and you discount the price you offer, as well as have a mechanic check it out (G. Akerlof, "The Market for 'Lemons,'" *Quarterly Journal of Economics*, 1970). You may do the same with a house. Due diligence and skepticism of others' claims are natural. If the seller has a reputation for honesty, or offers a guarantee, you may be more willing to believe what you are told, but in general you check. At best: Trust, then verify.

If you are sending up appointment and promotion dossiers to the university, you are likely to find yourself in the position of the real estate broker or the car salesman. Your credibility is at stake, and your case is likely to be checked carefully. So how do you increase the likelihood that your proposed course of action will be followed?

1. Make sure the letters of reference are from arm's-length judges, that at least four to six of them deal with the work in substantial detail (rather than repeat the CV, or merely give their opinion of the reputation), and the writers are from peer or better institutions. Read the work yourselves, ahead of time, so that if there are genuine problems (the book manuscript has no introduction or conclusion, the statistical analysis is fishy), you are not blindsided by the letters. Letters that engage the work, but have criticisms of it, are more likely to be convincing than letters of praise where it is clear the writer has not read the work (more frequent than you might believe).

2. Deal with issues re teaching, service, or research early on. If issues identified in the third-year review are still unresolved, perhaps you should not be proposing the candidate for promotion. If you demand that a book be done and another in progress, or an NIH R01 grant, or whatever, be necessary for promotion, do not then justify much weaker performance as good enough. It is not, by your own standards.

If a full professor candidate has not yet published the books or articles, or their teaching is problematic, do not send up the dossier until these are dealt with. In general, there is no rush and if the candidate took an extra three years to finish the work, perhaps the university should be allowed a year to find out how it is assessed.

3. Counsel candidates who are not up to the challenge of a stronger university to find a position elsewhere, where their talents are likely to be better appreciated. More senior colleagues who choose not to meet that challenge might find a more satisfying position elsewhere. In any case, help your colleagues find the right position.

4. Problems or weaknesses might well be addressed in the personal statement or the committee report. Do not leave it to the chair's or dean's letter to bring them up. Then the chair or dean can put those problems in context – one way or the other.

5. Always keep in mind that your credibility as a department or school is constantly being judged. If you send up fishy dossiers, you will be much less credible when you want to make that extraordinary case. If your dossiers are seen to be fair and complete, your credibility is enhanced. Committee reports and chair's and dean's letters need to take into account the evidence and argument presented earlier, whatever their conclusions.

As for candidates:

1. Did you do what you were supposed to do with respect to research? Compare yourself with the strongest people in your cohort or the ones just before yours. It is self-destructive to say, weak X got tenure, therefore I should get tenure since I am better than X. If you have not done what you were supposed to do, if you have not dealt decisively with issues raised in your third-year review, you may want to find a position in which your achievements match the expectations of the institution. Your third-year review should be praising your research progress, rather than (as is usually the case) your teaching (too much) and service (too much).

2. Did your personal statement describe your contribution in brief understandable language? Did it deal with your contribution to joint work (are the coauthors your students, for example)? Do you give a credible description of your trajectory of work?

3. Living well is the best revenge. If things do not work out as you would like, find another venue, work hard, succeed, and thrive.

4. Do you owe them? Or, do they owe you? If you are coming up early, is there some reason why they should act now rather than when

they expect to act? While it is distracting to search for another position, if the position is at a peer or better institution it will change the dynamics. Be sure you might take the other position. Deans and provosts know how to play poker.

None of this is new or even peculiar. It applies with minor adaptations to buying a used car or a used home. The university cannot afford a sequence of lemons or a subprime crisis. Surely, they will make mistakes, but the above list is meant to decrease their number and likelihood.

Another take:

More than half of the promotions of assistant professor to associate professor with tenure, and perhaps the same proportion for promotion to full, are not strong. They may be adequate, but not strong. The candidates may be weak; the dossiers may be poorly prepared. Whatever the case, that makes it much harder for the provost to make decisions that are good for the university's future excellence. Mistakes are made, unfortunate ones. Too many ringers are tenured, and some very good people are let go. Note, this is not because we are unfair or too demanding or too generous. Rather, we are given insufficient reliable information, and then under such unknowns and uncertainties we still have to make decisions. Deans and chairs dump hard cases in the provost's and the university committee's laps, advocating for people who do not fulfill the dean's own stated requirements.

Associate deans, who usually prepare these dossiers, may well feel burdened. But they file their income taxes, and they do due diligence when they buy their homes. What's so distressing is that these multi-million-dollar appointment decisions are treated as if documentation and due diligence were not absolutely essential. The IRS does not assume that what you leave out will not favor you. The house you buy, you are stuck with, if the seller has done his work. Perhaps the provost should not always try to figure out the dossier – just send it back or deny in all such cases.

Perhaps I am insufficiently sympathetic to the plight of junior faculty, or deans and departments. On the other hand, presidents want to change the game, and some junior faculty can play the new game. Fifteen years from now the university will pay heavily for not pushing forward.

235 *From a Member of the University Promotion Committee*

Sure, I can make a judgment if I have to, and perhaps that is all that matters. But would I buy a used car from these deans? I think not.

1. Assume that the dossier writer and the dean have to stand behind what they write. Is it internally consistent, have you made substantive arguments, have you stayed on point?

2. There is no need to interpret secret ballot votes, so much as to consider the arguments presented in the discussion. Unanimity is not necessarily a good sign. Some dissent is perhaps more plausible.

3. There is no need to infer motives to letter-writers. You have chosen them. Focus on their arguments. If you think some are wrong, say why. To impugn some of your own witnesses is to impugn them all.

4. Keep out petty resentments from your memos. You want to be convincing and believable. Once you become cheap, none of what you say is valuable.

5. Everyone has strengths and also weaknesses. Few are geniuses, and most of us follow in a tradition with a well-worn and known path. What's important in the end are the strengths and achievements. Where does the candidate stand among their cohort?

6. That you do not like the work someone has done is rarely probative of anything. Keep to the judgments of the referees and the experts in the field. If the work is obscure or difficult to understand, the referees should be helpful. If not, get further referees.

7. If people have problems with teaching or service, or with their research, the university committee will ask: Why were these not addressed earlier? Did the candidate respond to help? Do not dismiss complaints; deal with them.

8. Rarely, there are personal animuses which need to be explained.

9. The book should be out and published and reviewed. The articles should be out and seen already. Surely there is a lot in progress, but that is not as convincing as what has been through the whole process. For first books, there may need to be some leeway; for retention cases, there may be the need for leeway. But in general, the message we want to convey is, finish the work, get it out there, have people appreciate it.

10. Letters from partisans (such as advisors and dissertation committees or members of a club) are not given much weight. They should not be solicited. If letters come from international sources, we need to have a feel for the eminence of the writer, and also their acquaintance with our standards.

11. It is getting much more important, in more departments and schools, that candidates have histories of external research funding. They may not be contracts or grants, but fellowships and prizes. In some schools, strong funding histories will be crucial to whether candidates are considered successful.

12. As the university becomes stronger, the external competitive landscape candidates face is stronger still. There are people who work harder, with more focus, with more funding. Will the candidate be stronger still as the university becomes stronger? Anyone who is tenured ought to be ready for the long haul of the next 20 to 30 years of competitive research, the competition becoming more serious every decade. Marginal candidates are unlikely to thrive under such a regime. Assessments of trajectory need to take this rising competition into account.

13. In a letter I read today from a candidate's colleagues, they went along, but said that the dean ought to tell their colleague to play nicer and play more with them, that their colleague's taste is not their taste, and that not enough class evaluations had been handed in (due to the School's error).

Do they get it that if a provost reads such a letter, any of the colleagues' doubts (which might well be warranted, although I think not in this case) lose all credibility? Kindergartners know better.

14. Examples of disasters waiting to happen:

The anthropologist is well grounded and terrific. But why do we get long letters from her dissertation advisor and other committee members?

The political scientist claims to be doing innovative work, but again all of this has been around a while. None of the reviewers compare the work with that of others who work in this field.

The book manuscript is filled with grammatical errors of the most simple sort. Will it be copyedited, or will the Press put it out as submitted? And while the articles appear in specialist journals, one might hope for some in the main journals of the field.

It's not that these people are unworthy. They might be. But, their dossiers raise suspicions.

15. In a dossier I read today, there was a secret ballot with one dissenting vote. Rather than just report the vote, as such, the chair then indicated that the chair thought they knew who the dissenter was and why there was a dissenting vote. Now, I have no idea how fine is the chair's clairvoyance. (The voting dissenter might be someone who is convinced of the original dissenter's argument; the original dissenter might have been convinced by the majority argument.) Also, if there were any expressed dissenting issues in the discussion, presumably they have been stated in the letter.

16. I read two dossiers today, each of which takes a good case and makes it worse. In one dossier, they dismiss the reviewers who do not say glowing things, impugning those reviewers' judgment. The problem is, why should I trust the other more positive reviewers? You really do not want to impugn your own witness. Deal with the substance of the concern. We're willing to hear arguments. Moreover, I wish more peer or better institutions were consulted. My suspicion is that the case would have been made stronger, not weaker.

In the second dossier, there is a real problem in teaching. Rather than having dealt with it – sending colleagues to visit the classroom, asking the candidate to modify their teaching if there really is an issue – we have a substantial number of student complaints dismissed and in fact not even dealt with in the departmental letter. The problem is not a new one, but has been noted previously. You would think they would have addressed it in the preceding four or five years. The candidate's research contributions are OK, if not so hyperbolically stellar as claimed. But the undealt-with teaching problems could kill the dossier.

17. Can we tell the deans (or the associate deans for faculty affairs) not to destroy their own cases? It's embarrassing. We might expect to be bamboozled some of the time, but at least have respect for our intelligence.

236 *Quality Judgments and Letters of Reference*

1. There really are very deep and inordinately accomplished scholars. They keep having home runs, or they have had a no-hitter in their

careers. There are others of us who are very strong. And there are others of us who are strong. Most universities would do quite well with strong scholars, including most of the top research universities – especially if most of their faculty were at least strong.

2. Letters of reference for promotion or appointment or tenure usually show remarkable agreement in their judgment of candidates. But there may well be one letter-writer or perhaps two who dissent from the otherwise-agreed judgment. Some of the time, they have an axe to grind, professional or personal. But often, the dissenting letter is quite rich in considering the work, detailed in its reasons, attentive to the actual work being reviewed. It may indicate weaknesses in the work or alternative paths – weaknesses and paths that might actually inform the candidate's plans. It may suggest that the candidate is strong rather than very strong, and that at the referee's university they only appoint very strong scholars, or that people with that style of work would not be appointed in their department.

Often promotion candidates' dossiers use elaborate arguments to dismiss the dissenting letter(s). Once you send out for the letter, you have to take it seriously. Rather than saying that the dissent probably indicates some areas in which the candidate is weak (and then arguing for the complementary strengths pointed out by the other letter-writers), the department impugns the person they chose to write a letter because of that person's authority and reputation.

A strong appointment is usually an excellent one. That the candidate is not very strong or deep may be relevant for named chairs, or whatever, but in general "strong" is very demanding. Many cases do not come up to that standard.

Once you have chosen letter-writers, you have to take seriously their letters unless they are egregiously unfair. That does not make it hard to make a good case for the candidate, because once you acknowledge the weaknesses you can also point to the strengths (and that is why you want to appoint or promote the candidate).

237   *"If I Did So Little I Would Be Ashamed of Myself"*

Universities are becoming less willing to go along with marginal cases in tenure and promotion. Members of promotion committees, coming out of their own publishing practice (early, often, and of high quality), wonder how the candidate could possibly be any good with such a marginal record: "If I did that, I would be ashamed of myself."

They may ask themselves, if I myself had this dossier would I feel justified in being promoted? And the answer often is *no,* given their own quality and productivity and impact when they were coming up. Of course, there are very successful members who exercise noblesse oblige.

People do not show sudden conversions to much higher productivity. Say you have someone come up for tenure or promotion. They have been going along publishing slowly and decently (but not publishing stellar pieces). You worry about productivity for the longer run; will they ever become really productive? Make significant contributions? And given the growing competition, will they just keep falling behind?

What happens in the several years after tenure? Often we have cases where people are marginal but very promising. The book is not done, the articles are not impressive, but the letters are strong on promise, and when the work so far is read, it really is promising. But we have to make a decision now. Do such scholars deliver? And what about their long-term contributions?

A five- or six-year sample, albeit it is a stressful time, tells you how people will operate the rest of their lives. And in marginal cases, there will always be that uncertainty. Those denied tenure rarely end up in strong universities (although it might be argued that the denial permanently damaged their prospects). That there are late bloomers, or surprises, does not vitiate these observations, so much as make us aware that we might want to examine marginal cases for hidden virtues.

238   *Marginal Is Not Good Enough*

Marginal work or marginal promotion dossiers are risky propositions. If standards rise, if a new administration comes in, if promotion dossiers are rising in excellence, you will be doomed.

If you want to be in control of your life, marginal is putting your head on a chopping block and asking the executioner for kindness. Not a good idea.

Marginal cases almost never result in excellence.

239   *Your Department's Credibility Is on the Line*

The committee members and the provost who read dossiers have enough experience collectively to figure out when you have not been forthright or have been deceptive. They'll check the h-index claims; they'll find out if NSF gives out grants in the field; they'll notice inconsistencies in the letters or the CV. Maybe not all will find them, but someone will. What amazes me is how often they find such tricks. Deans or chairs or letter-writers seem to feel they can get away with stuff. Maybe they are acting innocently, and that is even more frightening.

1. Letters should come from diverse institutions; the dossier should not have three of six or ten letters from the same place, no matter how distinguished.

2. Letters that have identical paragraphs (this happens!) indicate that there is an app for writing promotion letters, or that there has been collusion, or that the candidate or the department provided a draft letter to all referees.

3. If a candidate for full professor has made slow but steady progress since tenure, eventually they ought to be promoted. But at least be honest why. Strong contributions to teaching or administration may well be important at this level. But you probably will not be able to invoke all that until maybe 15 years after tenure. And the provost may decide that research contributions are the only ticket to promotion.

4. Lateral appointments should be terrific. But perhaps a senior member of the faculty needs someone, X, to continue his strong research program, and the appointment must come with tenure or at least an associate professorship. For the strongest faculty, it may make sense to give them the chance to make the case for such a lateral appointment. But it does not help to wax hyperbolic about X's independent research career, or X's grant-getting, or to make excuses for lacks. Rather tell the dean and provost and committee the real reason.

5. If someone who is non-tenure-track develops a portfolio of research and grants and publications that is quite impressive, it's fine to put them up for a tenure-track appointment if you have done a genuine search. If they are part of someone's research project and have always

been second banana, but that banana is wonderful, it might well be worth trying for tenure – with a frank account of why.

6. Grant support of a particular sort (for example, NIH RO1s) is not only about money but also about peer judgment. There may be surrogates for that peer judgment, for cases where the research is paid for in other ways.

7. A faculty should be allowed one peculiar case every decade. Not unqualified, but qualified in an idiosyncratic way. Maybe they know something. But this case needs the weight of the whole faculty behind it.

8. I am not sure how I feel about a dean's having such a peculiar-case privilege separate from that of the faculty.

9. Sometimes retention cases arise for candidates who do not have strong records. The other institution sees virtues in the candidate that are not perceived by your own, or perhaps they have need for particular strengths. If the dossier is not convincing to you, do not vote *yes*. Let the person go elsewhere, give them a good-bye party that is heartfelt, and everyone is better off.

Finally, your credibility is on the line. If you send up dossiers that are fishy, you begin to smell like old cod, and then in cases where you wish to really be able to exert your one free pass, so to speak, no one will give you the benefit of the doubt.

240 *Statistical Prediction for Better Tenure Decisions?*
Moneyball and Kahneman's "Cognitive Illusion"

Daniel Kahneman's book on decision-making (*Thinking, Fast and Slow*, 2011), the story told in the movie *Moneyball*, and Paul Meehl's *Clinical versus Statistical Prediction* (1954) all suggest that we might do better with some sort of objective criteria rather than relying on average professional judgment. Now, having a multiyear probationary period, external referees, and multiple levels of review may make the tenure process the most careful of personnel evaluations. The argument of Kahneman and others is that perhaps the most careful is not necessarily the most accurate. If we had information on tenurings that proved fruitless or denials that proved fructiferous, could we do much better in making decisions?

1. It would seem that behavior and achievements over the probationary period form the best predictor. If a candidate has done the research/publication as we expect in terms of contribution and quality, then OK. If not, no excuse seems to be exculpatory. The candidate will not become much better and may well decay rapidly.

2. The literature on promotion and tenure is concerned with how institutional culture affects productivity. Like produces like. There is a subtheme in much of this literature, that by production we should include teaching and service. Or maybe have a department in which some faculty do one, and some do another. Balance is a pervasive theme. But *the problem is how to increase research prominence and quality and quantity.* Life and family are here secondary (actually, research-productive people are no worse in their family lives than other faculty). This is not about being a Stakhanovite; it is about how to make our university stronger. The answer, it would seem, is to insist on high performance during the probationary period, no excuses, and then to figure out how to make the next period encouraging enough to continue that high performance.

3. You might find better ways of hiring so that it is more likely someone will be research-productive. There is evidence that postdoc performance is important in the sciences, though this is not so clear in other areas (especially if there are no postdocs in these areas). And you could read the dissertation with some care, and decide whether it is potentially first-rate publishable work.

4. *Moneyball* and Kahneman's "cognitive illusion": the job, as would be described by Kahneman, is to figure out who will be the strongest faculty in the future. (Some would argue that our job is to see if someone has "earned" tenure, a different perspective.) That is, *might we find some sort of criteria/rule/scoring system that would make it more likely we promote candidates with strong future performance, and much less likely we promote those who will wither, or "slams."* (I call them "slams" following the biologists' characterization of a drosophila gene: slow as molasses.) Put differently, might we do much better than the usual promotion and tenure procedures, a highly deliberative process?

5. Deans and departments are subject to what Kahneman calls "endowment effects": namely, overvaluing what they have in front of them.

Hence, one expects and usually gets memoranda from the dean and the department that would seem to be hyperbolic considering the evidence.

6. All the research on tenure suggests that *what you see is what you will get:* namely, if someone has been slow to produce, "slam," they will not change and likely will be a disappointment. And if someone has done first-rate work, they will continue to do so. If a candidate is in between, it is likely they will not change either. Again, in each case, will you be happy with this person's achievements over the next 30+ years?

7. *Too many dossiers are fishy.* Maybe the dean ought to sign something like a Sarbanes-Oxley statement to the effect that the dean stands behind the dossier. Maybe there needs to be a *devil's advocate,* in the tenure committee or the school, who examines dossiers and points out their weaknesses before the university committee sees them.

241   Would You Want This Professor and Candidate for Promotion or Tenure Teaching Your Child?

Say the candidate for appointment, promotion, or tenure were considered as you would a cardiothoracic surgeon. You are presented with a dossier. Would you want the candidate to operate on your child?

Everything is wonderful, but there are all these sponges that keep being left behind. But we are told that those are just complaining patients.

Everything is wonderful, but some of the reports from other physicians suggest that they would not want the candidate operating on them. But we are told that they are just too picky and do not like his use of chartreuse sutures.

Everything is wonderful, but no one has seen the candidate operate on their own – always senior surgeons are in the room helping or doing the tough parts of the surgery.

242   From Members of the University Promotion Committee

We are privileged to learn about the strengths of our colleagues throughout the university. New members always remark about the strength of some of the candidates, and the dossiers that present them: clear, compelling, no nonsense. We also know from our own schools and from reading the dossiers for our sub-panels that many dossiers are not so strong and are often troubling.

It may be helpful for us to convey our sense of the strongest dossiers to our colleagues and our deans. In effect, these are the real competition, setting the standards for the university.

Our impression is that many deans and faculty do not realize yet how strong are the strong cohort of appointments, promotions, and tenurings, how compelling are their dossiers. Even if a dean makes some of these strong cases, the dean may not realize how many similar strong cases there are – how these dossiers set a standard that is much higher than they generally apply.

243 *Being Conned When Reading Promotion and Hiring Letters and Dossiers*

You can only be conned if you rely on the good faith of the person who then turns out to be a con artist. Then, you will not pay too much attention to inconsistencies, you will be rushed into judgment, you will have too much compassion for the con artist, you will think the con artist is doing you a favor, and you will fear missing a great opportunity. All these are standard in discussions of con artists.

When evaluating a letter or dossier, you want to figure out if you can trust the source. Are the arguments too complicated? Does it seem that you are being done a favor but you cannot figure out why (e.g., a letter goes, "If you do not tenure X, we'll try to hire him" – often said, rarely if ever done)? Or, are you being let in on a secret that no one knows about yet?

Letter-writers, deans (or associate deans, who often prepare the dossiers), and departmental committees are not corrupt, nor do they think of themselves as con artists. Rather, they are trying to make their case, they know there are some killer problems, and they are doing their best. In effect, your job, as provost and university committee, is to help them realize the illusions they are under. It may turn out that the best case for departments is to admit the big problems in paragraph one, and discuss them further on, but provide a case for the candidate in terms of your needs and their strengths. So, if someone is not distinguished as a publishing researcher, but is a terrific leader and innovator as attested to by letters, has a range of deep experience, especially in the context of your field, and will enable a department to develop capacities that it deems vital, you might well advocate for the appointment in those terms. In a field such as cinema production, or the fine arts, or journalism, that may well be the right case.

244   *Tenure for Clinicians, Practitioners, and Teachers*

As for promoting and tenuring practitioners and teachers in research universities:

1. As in research, you are seeking people who make well-recognized contributions to practice or teaching, contributions that are thought to be significant and widely employed in other people's work.

2. So you must specify the contribution, why it is significant, and how it is recognized.

3. You have to make a case for a set of referees: important practitioners, for example. Their brief cvs should be impressive, and not at all parochial.

4. The letters have to say that the contribution is recognized, is widely employed, and is a significant contribution (and why) – in detail.

You do not expect to promote people for making insignificant, unrecognized research contributions, and so the same for practice or teaching.

If you are presenting yourself as making a contribution to practice, you have got to get out there and show it to important others so as to have it recognized and adopted elsewhere. To be a good practitioner or even an excellent one does not mean that your contributions are significant or widely recognized. Prizes and awards in recognized competitions are more important here than in research (for those prizes and awards tend to come much later for research).

It is up to us to decide what kinds of faculty we want. But excellence and significance are not options. And keep in mind that clinical or other such appointments may be the best ranks for some professors.

245   *Judging Work beyond My Ken*

Some work done by faculty is beyond me. I tell myself I'm not smart enough. This is not usually the case in math or physics or engineering, and in the case of the life sciences I get what's going on, roughly. I can understand most of the quantitative social sciences, and the fieldwork and case studies in anthropology or sociology, or historical work derived from archival research. Or so I believe. If the scholarship is in the humanities, most of the time I am OK as well.

However, there are species of work, often in the humanities, that use an intensely technical language. The sentences are oblique; the diction is foreign.

And, there are species that provide accounts of philosophers or mathematics, or at least mention them to justify the disciplinary work, where though I thought I ought to understand what they were up to (Heidegger or complex adaptive systems theory), I cannot connect the account with what I know. All these species need a different sort of reader, in part to judge whether they really are substantively faithful to the technical language. And when there is a philosophical or mathematical justification and some substantive disciplinary work, expert judgment is required to judge the justification, independent of the judgment of people in the field who might well be inadequate to judge the justification but quite capable of appreciating the substantive disciplinary work.

Of course, there is the need for plain English accounts of the work. Plain English is what a Standard Provost can understand.

246   *Doggie Comes Up for Tenure*

Say a dog comes up for tenure. For whatever reason, despite Doggie being a canine, you want to tenure him. You might give all sorts of reasons as excuses, such as that four legs make it hard to write papers, and barking rarely works in explaining things. And he had many new family members in the middle of the probationary period. Moreover, Doggie suffered from anti-canine bias from the allergic half of the department.

Do not go there!

Rather say that Doggie has proved to be a faithful member of the department, his teaching has transformed undergraduate education, and we have testimony from throughout the country of how a gentle lick makes statistics stick. Moreover, almost all the recent scholarly work for which the department is known has in fact depended on Doggie's collaboration. Professor Depressed has started to pump out papers at a prodigious rate, and is winning grants.

Then you say,

> We realize this is an extraordinary case; the evidence is idiosyncratic and well outside the norm. However, our department will wither and die without Doggie's presence, our students depend on his tutelage, and he is becoming our most high-profile member, known and admired throughout the profession. We put our reputations and integrity behind these claims. We want Doggie. Our dissenting colleagues are surely right that this case is outside the norm, and their votes represent valid positions. But from our point of view, a view shared by two-thirds of the department including some of its most distinguished members (including three Nobel Prize winners), the risks in this case are well worth bearing.
>
> We have been listening to Doggie's latest thoughts and reflections. They are profound, and are likely to transform our field. Of course, we may well be incorrect in our assessment. But we believe that the university will be well served by taking such a risk, and we plan to mentor Doggie so that his contributions are more readily appreciated throughout academia.
>
> We welcome the chance to discuss this extraordinary situation with you. Whatever you do decide to do, we are pleased we have had the chance to present our position in a forthright manner. And if Doggie must leave the university, several of us may follow him – not out of protest or in a huff, but as a rational calculation of what will benefit our contributions to scholarship. Our colleagues at other institutions have begun to inquire if Doggie might be available, and Goldman Sachs has already offered Doggie a position on its trading floor. Doggie loves the university, and we believe it will be possible to convince him to stay.

You make strong claims and put your reputations on the line. Offer evidence in letters. And the provost might even say, "If the three Nobelists want Doggie, I want Doggie."

247 *Hiring Grisha Perelman with Tenure*

Grisha Perelman (b. 1966) is a Russian mathematician who in 2003 proved the Poincaré Conjecture (actually Thurston's Geometrization

Conjecture) concerning the shape of three-dimensional objects in four-dimensional space, building on the work of Richard Hamilton. The Poincaré Conjecture had eluded the greatest minds in mathematics for a century. Earlier, in 1994–1995, Perelman had become of note to American mathematicians for a series of less spectacular achievements. Princeton offered him a position, as an untenured assistant professor. At that time he felt that he had shown his merit, and was offended by an offer that did not include tenure and full professorship. A few years later, after he had proved the Conjecture, Princeton again offered him a position, now as a tenured full professor. (Note that Andrew Wiles, who had proved Fermat's Last Theorem in 1994–1996, had already been a professor in the department for some time.) Now Perelman was further offended, since all they were doing, in his mind, was buying a certified great mathematician – and could they not see this earlier?

I suspect that the earlier untenured offer represented both some caution on the part of the mathematics department, in part because of his limited teaching experience, although they were willing to explore the possibility of tenure at that time, and a sense that it might not be possible to get such a tenure through the university given the small number of publications. (This case is *very* different from the Doggie issue described above.) However, if you have a very strong candidate for a position, it may make sense to use your credibility capital and push through the appointment. There are enough strong mathematicians in the Princeton department that the dean and provost and president might well pay attention to their collective judgment. (Of course, in some cases there may be doubters among the faculty that make such a push impossible. Would he continue to lay golden eggs?) (Masha Gessen, *Perfect Rigor,* 2009).

248 Ethos of Promotion and Tenure in a Strengthening Institution

I was talking with one of the newer members of a promotion committee, and he felt the burden of denying tenure to people. I suggested that we are advisory to the provost, who is capable of making decisions based on larger university considerations. Our job is to judge matters of scholarship, teaching, and service as we are presented with them. Candidates control their futures by the choices they make, the work they choose to do. When they choose to not do what is needed for tenure, our responsibility is to indicate such, not fix their errors.

Of course, we want to be scrupulously fair and procedurally proper. And we want to be sensitive to unfairness and improperness by schools and their decision processes.

Moreover, I think that many faculty who are marginal, as well as those who have clearly not measured up to tenure, would be better off in other institutions with expectations more in accord with their achievements. In the right institution, they will do better, and they will be more valued. If an institution is getting stronger in terms of its scholarly reputation and achievement, they are likely to fall farther behind – better to be someplace where they are in step and thriving.

I do not mean to be unsympathetic or harsh in judging candidates. But *tenuring or promoting people who are not up to the next 30 years of an institution's growth serves neither the candidate nor the institution.*

249 *Tenure Decision Errors*

1. Say a person who is being considered for tenure has published (or otherwise performed) comparatively little of consequence at that point. But a good deal is in the pipeline (drafts, submitted, revise-and-resubmit, in press?), and it is said to be of high quality and significance; or, they are said to be on an upward trajectory, for whatever good reason. Keep in mind that they know of the tenure decision date six years before it is set. Sometimes, tragedy strikes during this period – death of a spouse or child, a major health problem, whatever. The university responds by extending that date.

Now, performance is what counts, and if you cannot do it now, prima facie you are not up to the challenge. *Those denied tenure rarely go on to distinguished careers elsewhere.* The denial itself might be the cause, but it would appear that there was too much hope compared to actual prospective performance.

2. Late Bloomers. We are told that the candidate finally found their groove in year four, and is now on a very strong upward trajectory. There

are such cases, but they are rare in actual prospective performance. It makes sense to say *no* now, but to offer an extension with no promise as to the future. Discretion is needed in making this choice.

Still, sometimes it makes sense to say *yes* for more general university reasons, whether it be matters of field of specialization, or the needs of a department. But, then, it should not be expected that the candidate will bloom even if they are otherwise valuable.

If the book or articles that are prospective prove strong, there is still the risk that the candidate will never get their act together to be a strong faculty member.

3. Weak Performance Predicts Future Weak Performance. You are making a bet and the evidence is mixed and indicates weakness. If one in ten of such cases eventually proves strong, should you take the wager?

4. Mistakes Are Forever (or at least 30 years). *If you make a mistake, and the candidate is tenured, they are likely to be marginal for the rest of their careers. They are likely to advocate for other marginal cases.* Their standards will lower the quality of the department, pervasively. They may have other wonderful strengths, but it will not be as research scholars of a sufficiently high order that they can show off the university in a fine way.

5. We expect our university's football team to perform superbly this year, not next. We expect our top surgeons to perform this week, not next. Would you want a football player with this sort of dossier playing on your team? Would you want a surgeon with this sort of dossier operating on your child? Would you trust someone who assures you that the player or the surgeon is on an upward trajectory, but is not up to snuff now, and who urges you to put them in the lineup this week or let them operate on your child now?

6. Do I sound too harsh? Perhaps. It is your university at stake, your child, and your Bowl prospects.

What about the exceptions? There would seem to be no exceptions. The team loses, the students get poor guidance, and your botched operation is inevitable. Those promised prospective articles and books are disappointments, never so strong as promised, even if they do appear. The late bloomers I have referred to are quite rare, and perhaps another university will give them a second chance.

250   *Tenure Traps*

1. The university is serious about appointing and promoting people who are stronger than the bottom half of a department. This has implications for comparisons you make to others who were tenured or promoted ahead of you. It is not helpful to say that they were much weaker than you were and so you ought to be promoted. This is true for two reasons: they may have been stronger in crucial areas, deemed important by the university; or, your record may still not be better than the middle of the pack of your department or school, and so there is no compelling reason to tenure or promote you.

2. If you do joint work with others, expect to need to show that your work is substantial and significant. So if you have done eight articles jointly with three authors, think in terms of this equating to two or three articles. Not so impressive. Are the articles deep and complex, lengthy, summarizing a large project? Or have you published a number of little articles, drawn from one data set or one project?

3. How do you compare to your cohort? Is your cohort well drawn? Does your department find that you are "the best" by using enough modifiers so that you are the only one in the cohort?

If you do work with collaborators: Say you work with someone rather more senior than you, including your advisor. Someone is going to ask about your contribution relative to the more senior folks. That can be readily dealt with by letters and the personal statement (which must be confirmed by the letters). If you publish an article with a much more senior author in a major journal, much of the credit will go to the senior author. Again, there can be ways of dealing with that fact, but it has to be dealt with directly.

I am not trying to discourage joint publication, per se. But one has to understand how the world thinks, and that thinking often is in terms of individuals and their achievements, rather than teams. And universities tend to believe in "genius," an individualistic notion.

4. Do not fluff up your vita. External grants and awards are given much more weight than internal ones. If you are coming up for full professor, do not start talking about your dissertation research. Begin

with the work you did since receiving tenure. If you did 8 articles before tenure, and then 4 more, you do not really look like you have done 12 articles when you come up for full. Reports are different from refereed articles. On the other hand, as far as I can tell, a World Bank report can be as important as a book in some cases. So you will have to have your committee make the case.

5. Your letters should come from the strong people at strong universities. They should want to hire you. If they do not believe that you would be tenured or promoted at their institutions, that will affect how people think about your tenure or promotion here. Letters from strong people at less strong universities will need to be clearly justified, but need not be a problem. But having no letters from the strongest universities is likely to weigh against you. You must be sure to lay the groundwork for the letters by promoting your work at meetings, sending people reprints, and becoming a recognized contributor in your field.

6. When you write your personal statement, be clear about your contribution to the field. What advance did you make? What is the sustained line of inquiry you are pursuing? How has that been recognized? Is it impactful? Is it important? (A bad article can have lots of citations, but not be a credit to you.) If you have spread yourself thin, justify doing so. If you claim teaching excellence, think in terms of national recognition of such (rather than high student ratings). Service can be important (not for assistant professors) but it should be nationally recognized. (E.g., "While Joe Schmoe was chair of the department, he raised its visibility, hired the strongest people, and transformed it.") Just doing time and chairing some committees is fine, but not a big plus. I have of late seen "interdisciplinarity" used as an excuse for weak cases. Not a good idea.

7. If you want to get early promotion and the like, that is not a problem as long as your record is very strong. Good enough is not very strong. Get an offer from a peer or better institution.

Ideally *you are always on the market, at least implicitly. So every year the university has to think of you as one of their stars whom they must keep happy.* This is an almost impossible status to achieve, but keep it in mind. Becoming a fixture at the university is a sure way for them to take you for granted, especially as they aim to fulfill the university's ambitions. If you are essential to those ambitions, the institution should be making sure you are well rewarded.

8. By the way, it is not at all impossible to be tenured and promoted (maybe five out of six *who are put up* are tenured; some or many are not put up for tenure, and some or many leave for other jobs before tenure). Most people get in trouble because they ignore the obvious signs on the wall, get diverted by local nonsense. And some people make it through by mistake or favor. To those who study bureaucracy, none of this will be surprising. I believe just about all faculty can meet the standards. But it does involve focus, commitment, and hard work (but not killing work).

9. As for books: In general you want to publish a monograph (rather than an edited collection of others' work, which might include some of your own, or a textbook), and it should be published by a recognized strong (probably university) press. There are of course exceptions. And that book ought to be reviewed as widely as possible. In fields in which book publication is conventional, you might have to have one book published for tenure, and at least one more for promotion to full. At many universities, they ask when you come up for tenure whether you have another book well on its way (but some of these places do not give tenure with promotion to associate professor, and wait a while afterward). What people want to be sure of is that you have a strong prospective research career.

By the way, all bets are off if your work is considered of extraordinary import and influence. There are people who have published one or two articles and been given tenure and more – but those pieces of work have been pathbreaking, and immediately recognized as such (this is the rare part), and it is clear that they have many more works ready to appear. Or they have published books of extraordinary scholarship, and more are on the way.

Mistakes do not justify making further mistakes.

B. THE DOSSIER

251 *If You Are Chair of a Promotion or Tenure Committee*

Letters of evaluation should come from arm's-length referees at peer or better institutions, who have no connection (advisor, collaborator) with the candidate. The letters need to be substantive and textured, dealing with the work. A letter that argues with the work, but ends up saying that it is meritorious, is a very fine positive reference. Letters of general praise, or reviews of the CV, have little influence.

The considerations in the departmental faculty meeting should explicitly deal with problematic features of the case. In this manner, problems are discussed and analyzed. You really do not want a split vote because some people had problems and they were never dealt with.

Similarly, if there are problems in the letters, they need to be dealt with directly, not dismissed, by the departmental committee. It is much better that this committee deal with these issues, rather than a school committee or dean.

In some fields, including many of the natural and social sciences and professions, it is expected that candidates have competed for and won peer-reviewed grants (NSF, NIH). These are taken as confirmations of the strength of their work.

Candidates whose publication list is mostly multiply authored papers (except if they are the professor and the other authors are students or postdocs) might be expected to have a substantially larger number of articles than those whose papers are singly authored, *in that field*. In any case, in most fields one would like to see some singly authored papers. Moreover, at least some publications should be in venues that are not so specialized, and reflect contributions recognized more widely in their larger fields.

The personal statement is a good place for the candidate to describe their contributions to scholarship in clear nontechnical language, as well as in the jargon of the field. It will help the letter-writers, and the various readers of the dossier, to focus on those contributions. Lists of papers, one-by-one summarized, are rarely helpful.

If there are problems with teaching or collegiality, try to have them dealt with before starting the promotion process. Third-year reviews or annual reviews that indicate problems are the right time to take charge of those problems and solve them.

Probationary candidates who have not done the work – published the book or the articles, made strong and sufficient contributions to scholarship – might well be encouraged to find a position at an institution where their strengths would be valued. Promotions to full professor have no time line, and if a candidate is not ready, it makes no sense to risk rejection when a year or two later there might be a successful promotion.

252   An Ideal Dossier

An ideal dossier gives the reader a sense of the candidate's contributions, strengths, and weaknesses, and the vulnerabilities of the contributions. There is a detailed discussion of the candidate's work, critical and appreciative, indicating problems or disagreements. If there are issues, we are told about them in detail (and so eventually should the candidate be told). If one of the usual issues comes up, such as low productivity for a period of time, we are told why or that at least the department appreciates there is a problem there. Rather than hold back internal concerns, the department shares them – in part because those concerns are very likely to come up in the university committee, and it is better to deal with them ahead of time. Comments from members of the university committee who know the candidate are unlikely to be helpful, and letters from those in the university who want to support the candidate (no matter how prestigious they are, especially if they are outside the department) rarely help.

In general, almost all rave letters, almost all letters from advisors and collaborators (except to attest to who did what in the work), almost all unbalanced assessments hurt the candidate. The strongest recommendations are those that consider the work and the contribution, perhaps even engage it quite seriously and contentiously, and then in the end say, the candidate is terrific!

What always hurts are excuses, such as "this second-ranked journal is really important." (It's not that the excuse may not be true, but it smacks of special pleading.) If the work is good, that is the main issue, and if it is in a venue that is likely to be seen, that matters too.

It is better to give your true assessment of the candidate than to wax eloquently but incredibly. If this is the best book on Icelandic dentistry, it will not help to claim that Icelandic dentistry is a major field, but it might help to show that the analysis in the book has deeply influenced how people think of dental health all over. If the Icelandic dentistry book wins an award from the Icelandic Dentistry Association (or another two-modifier association, in which the number of potential awardees is typically one or two rather than twenty) it is unlikely to impress people to say that it is an award-winning book or article.

If the candidate does not get the grants normally required, saying that the standards have gone up or that the competition has increased and the hit rate has declined is an excuse. Presumably, your university wants to have candidates who have received the grants, not the almosts. Of course if the acceptance cutoff was 9 percent and this candidate stood at 10 percent, it may be useful to mention that.

Finally, while the number of stars in the sky is very large, on Earth the number of academic stars is rather more limited. The claim should be reserved and used carefully – at least if you want people to believe you when it really matters.

253   *Tell Us What Is Going On*

Say what is really going on. The candidate may be unusual, but for your school that is just what you need. Fine. If there is a retention issue, the dean can tell about the offers from elsewhere.

Reference letters should come from peer or better institutions. Reference letters should have dates on them. Explain old letters.

Science Citation Index (Web of Science) is the well-studied database. (Google Scholar is more reliable only in special cases.)

Articles in new fields can be published in the main journals of the main field. No field is too new to have impact.

Be sure your bragging holds up. Do not tell people the candidate published in PNAS (*Proceedings of the National Academy of Science*) when it was an editorial or a letter to the editor – that is not "publishing in PNAS."

Excuses are not convincing. Reasons might well be. Say the norm in the field is always joint work, and then provide testimonials or evidence of the contribution of the candidate. RO1s or NSF grants are absent, but the work is excellent nonetheless. Really not a researcher, but a superb administrator. Greatest achievement is two patents that transformed how cell phones work – have someone tell us the intellectual/scholarly contribution or how it has transformed modern life. World-recognized clinician or engineer or surgeon or politician, truly excellent, who should be part of the faculty. For most scholars publication is the road to excellence, but for some, especially in the arts and professions, practice is the way.

As usual, *contribution* is a powerful measure. Will it continue? How can that make a difference to the school?

254   *More Stuff from Reading Tenure Dossiers*

1. Can a university afford people who are likely to be longtime associate professors? If they are slow producers? Everyone in the profession knows of the great first book that does not lead to more, and in general there is no redemption for not having a second act. On the other hand, some first books or initial articles are so enduringly influential (or they lead to Nobel Prizes or Pulitzers or . . .) that the university is compelled to promote to full professor for the university's sake.

2. We have a tendency to think that deviant cases might well be great contributions if they work out. I wonder if we might get more great contributions from people who are more ordinary.

3. Cargo-cult professors, the ones who will save the department, are unlikely to succeed.

4. On the other hand, building from strength is possible.

5. Some departments that give us five publications by an average of three authors each as the evidence of tenurability ought to be taken to the woodshed. Others disagree with me, and say that one has to compare with other strong departments in the field.

6. Books need to be out and reviewed, which means that at the end of the fourth year you have sent the book to press. Hence, candidates for tenure in book departments might well be told they will not succeed unless they do this. (In practice, this may be too demanding.) And we want to see evidence of another major project.

As for journal article departments, if you do not have very substantial contributions in press at the end of year four, you are unlikely to succeed.

7. Deans and chairs, in their letters that are supportive, often kill the candidate without intending to do so. What's going on in their heads?

8. Letters that do not reflect the range of concerns of the research are unlikely to be helpful. It's much better to have one or two letters from those who are not in the cabal or club of the sub-sub-discipline.

255 Rhetoric of Promotion Committee Reports

It matters how you write the report from the dean or the promotion committee. A balanced statement of strengths and weaknesses with a judgment at the end is usually most helpful. We live in a legal and litigious environment, and the exact words matter, so it is crucial there be no hidden messages. Problems are not hidden; you have to face them. If those problems then become significant years later, you cannot say you did not know. Your report is much less subject to deflationary challenge if it is balanced and considered; the same is true for CVs. In fact, if you want to get away with proverbial murder, you'll want to do it under the umbrella of thoughtful textured analysis.

In a contentious field, often filled with hyperbolic claims and arguments, one has to be clear about what matters and how and why, which arguments are well supported, which are not.

256 Playing Chicken with the Provost and the University Promotion and Tenure Committee

People play chicken with promotion committees. People know what they ought to do, and then do not do it – in effect daring the department or the university not to promote them. And deans and committee chairs write excuse-filled memoranda. Most people who do not deliver are unlikely to fulfill your hopes. Better to say why there are these problems, and indicate future corrective plans. Indicate the case is marginal, but explain why one should come out on top.

Where did people get the idea that so few publications are enough? What were they doing in years two through four? I'm not just counting publications, but for most people few publications means small contribution. Moreover, if we let them be tenured at associate professor with a small number of publications, we'll get a small number when they come up for full.

Imagine if people were afraid to send up dossiers which were weak. They now figure there is no loss in trying. Of course, what happens is the loss of credibility of their unit, though they do not know it, and the stigma of failure. If you play chicken, in general you end up in a collision and die.

1. Typically you have five-plus years to show your strengths as a teacher and scholar. Try to front-load that performance in your first four years, getting the book published, the articles out, the teaching problems dealt with. Presumably, you've started out with a store of publishable materials from your dissertation, so get that done as soon as possible, and move on to one more substantial project.

2. "Early" promotion and tenure is rarely warranted by the record. (There are wonderful exceptions, but be sure you are one of them.) If you get an offer from elsewhere, and so can "demand" promotion, be sure you will take that offer. Your home institution might prove reluctant to make a counteroffer.

3. The quality of candidates rises noticeably every five years. Successful but still marginal candidates five years ago might not be so successful today. So your standards must be up-to-date, and you might compare your progress with those in other, comparable departments at your stage. Never compare your case with that of someone promoted five years ago, and never compare your case with retention cases. Moreover, very strong candidates, and there are more of them each year, tend to make marginal cases seem weaker.

The institution is making a long-term decision. Marginal candidates rarely move up to strong or even solid. We might expect short-term considerations to influence deans (rarely are they around as deans to bear the longer-term consequences of their decisions), but the university has to worry about the longer term. Mistakes made now (which become quite obvious 10 years down the line, the usual remark being, "How did X get tenure?") hurt for 25 years. You do not want to be a mistake.

4. Excuses never help. Yes, your research method requires lots of startup time, or is very time-consuming. Yes, you are a wonderful teacher, spending hours with students. Yes, the book got delayed or is almost published. But anyone who is making a serious multimillion-dollar

decision has heard all these excuses many times, and knows that rarely do they warrant a more generous assessment. Strong people deliver.

Do not be marginal. No excuses. Give yourself the chance to be one of the strong cases.

257 _Alt-A and Subprime Appointments and Promotions: Meltdown_

Alt-A loans were those made to borrowers who provided nothing more than their FICO credit scores (no income information was provided). It makes sense to believe that Alt-As are hiding something and are more risky. Subprime loans were to borrowers who provided sufficient information, and it was found wanting. Presumably, the loan rates were set high enough to compensate for the risks. Homeownership would flourish; the real estate market would be robust.

When the going gets tough, the Alt-As and the subprimes default at a much higher rate than do the standard loans. However, those who made those transactions do not get penalized – no clawbacks, although the institution may suffer.

Moreover, the basic idea of mortgage-backed securities (MBS) was that a mixture of mortgages provided greater certainty of returns than would any single mortgage – that is, lower variance. But this only applies if the random variables are independent, which in this case they surely are not.

The idea here is that MBSs allowed more investment funds to flow into the housing market, since investors now could treat mortgages much like any other security, with a risk and a rate of return. In general, this seems like a good idea. What was once a specialty market now is commodity.

But, those MBSs were inappropriately rated, with insufficient attention to problems of correlation and risk. Rates of return seemed to have little to do with the assigned quality of the MBSs.

Analogously: Alt-A dossiers have insufficient information, while subprime dossiers are wanting. Those candidates will become stuck at higher rates than would standard dossiers.

The idea that a departmental unit can absorb some of the Alt-As or subprimes, using them in effective ways, works about as well as the M B S s worked. It makes sense to take on these risky individuals since they allow a department to grow in useful ways, yet the risk is controlled to some extent by the organizational effectiveness of chairs and deans. That is, rather than wait for stars to be hired, rare and hard to get, let's try a new technology, the organization or bureaucracy, that allows for quality growth without stars.

The ratings we quote about departments are perhaps even less reliable than are the ratings for M B S S.

Moreover, deans and chairs get credit for hiring and promoting and for organizational growth (including research units, specializations in faculty focus), but *little clawback for mistakes* – often they are out of position by the time the dead wood rots. It is a good idea to develop organizational inventions, but you need to know the risks involved – and plan around them. But, in general, it may be hard to know the risks fully. To increase your tolerance for (now unknown) risk may be setting yourself up for a meltdown. A real options approach may be helpful.

There's no substitute for on-time delivery and performance, brains, and hard work. No organizational solution to a portfolio with lots of Alt-A and subprime people.

258 *Avoiding Getting Stuck with a Lemon*

In retrospect, a fraction of our promotions to tenure or even lateral tenured appointments do not work out well. We know that because those individuals become long-term associate professors, or if they do become professors they do not have vigorous research careers in subsequent years. How might we do better?

Most of the faculty are fixed assets, tenured and unlikely to leave the institution. Most of the schemes for mentoring or incentivizing the lost faculty seem not to be too effective, although for some of our colleagues that is just what they need. Perhaps it is time for the strongest faculty to take leadership roles, and form clusters of faculty so that the lost faculty find work within larger projects and feel the pride of colleagueship and success.

We might hire more advanced assistant professors, whose first books are already in production, who have some grant success, who have a number of articles at least in the revise-and-resubmit phase if not in production already. They would be tenured based on their second project being well along.

As for the promotion-to-tenure process, we have to assume that what we see now is what we'll get in the future. Slow production now will not speed up. Weak work will not become much stronger. The question we need to ask is, did the candidate do what they were supposed to do, whether it be the book, the grant, the articles, all in suitable venues? If the answer is *yes,* we can then ask about quality and trajectory. If the answer is *no,* tenure should be denied. No excuses. We might even ask, would I want this candidate teaching my children? Or were this candidate a surgeon, would I want her operating on me? There should be no surprises at tenure time. A mid-course review should have indicated expectations and problems, and if they are not fulfilled and resolved, the candidate should not expect promotion.

We need to know just what is the contribution of the candidate to scholarship or to the field. This should be in plain English, understandable by a provost not in the field. The letters of reference should support this claim. And if there is joint work, we need to know the contribution of the candidate to the work. And if there are multiple authors, and we are counting publications, we need to have a sense of how many more publications we might expect than if there were only a single author.

We need to ask, *Is this the best we can get?* Where does the candidate stand among their cohort in the field? Different institutions will have different expectations, but knowing where we stand should make clear the nature of the choice.

As for letters of reference, and realizing the demands made on the strongest people in a field, do we have enough substantive letters from strong enough people, so that we are likely to learn about the quality of the work? Letters that review the CV are not helpful; letters that indicate that the writer has not read the work are problematic. Balanced letters, with suitable demurrers, are most helpful. The demurrers should not be dismissed, but should be investigated to see how significant they are.

Fairness is essential. But that does not mean that we allow past mistakes as our standard. Rather, we might ask if the candidate is stronger than, say, ⅓ or ½ or ⅔ of our current faculty. Of course, we want to be sure that underrepresented minorities and women are treated fairly. (Primary responsibility for children [and especially, disabled children] or elderly parents may well warrant more than the usual one-year extension of the tenure clock.) Similarly, those who need to establish laboratories may have their tenure clock start when those labs are up and running.

As one reads the memoranda from the departmental and school committees, one wants to be sure they attend to problems in the dossier and do not dismiss problems because of something wrong with the letter-writer. The demurrers are canaries in the coal mine.

In the end there is the cover memorandum from the dean. They often see their job as selling the candidate to the university, and like the used car salesman they have much more information internally than would the provost. The provost might well discount the dean's memo, figuring that the dean was not revealing problems (again, think of buying a used car). Hence, it is vital that the dean consider the case in a balanced and fair way. It is fine if at that point, the dean says that the candidate's strengths are so important for the department, that the significant problems are worth overriding. Or the other way around. Hyperbolic praise or hatchet jobs, no matter how subtle, decrease the future credibility of a dean and a school.

As for candidates, you actually control your fate. If you do what you are supposed to do, you will be able to find another position whether or not you succeed at the current institution. To do what you are supposed to do, you almost surely have to start revising dissertation work, drafting and submitting papers, and applying for grants in your first year. And you need to say *no* to any diversions, whether they be book reviews, major committee duties, or external conference organizing. Get the work done.

259   *What Makes a Strong Tenure or Promotion Case?*

The really strong scholars are not built out of a Rube Goldberg of weak parts. They have a coherence and order, and the parts are themselves strong.

Your choice of work, and how you describe that work, can make an enormous difference. Your projects likely should be multiyear, with subparts if needed. Your publication venues, and presentation venues, should be chosen for their impact and impressiveness. To present at a meeting that is not significant, to take on a project that will not add to your contribution, may well deprive you of other opportunities. If you have done disparate projects, can you make a good case that they are aspects of a master project? And perhaps you need to write articles justifying that master project?

Good teaching matters, but it is rarely good enough and impactful enough to matter much. (This may be different in teaching-oriented institutions.) The same for service. If you are going to claim strength here, you need to be sure you have national or international influence. (Some people do change how a field is taught, or serve by becoming Undersecretary of Health or whatever.) You have finite energy or at least limited energy, and you need to keep that in mind.

By the way, it is never too late to become focused and effective. Senior people who have not published much for years can refocus and put out a fine and deep book or series of articles. Or perhaps their contributions are not well recognized by their colleagues, and they need to remind others of them. (I know of two persons who put together books of their consulting reports, lightly edited, which were in fact fine contributions.) More junior people can decide what matters, and make sure that what they do in the next five years is a coherent contribution.

Finally, as remarked elsewhere, letters should be from strong people at strong universities who know your work and who write letters that take that work seriously.

One or two other observations: It does you little good (at least until you get to court) to observe that X who was promoted or tenured recently had a weaker file. You have not seen the dean's letter, and that might be crucial. They may have received an offer elsewhere, or they may make contributions which the dean or provost especially values. You are also being compared, at the university level, with strong files from all over the university. Probably, no school or department consistently sends up the strongest dossiers, but some are known for the weakness of their dossiers, and others are known for the strength. And in fact, the quality demands are going up slowly and inexorably. A new provost might well change things dramatically, for the provost's experience and goals, and the fact that their aspirations are not yet compromised by the institution, might set the bar higher.

Even for interdisciplinary work, your letter-writers will still be answering the traditional questions about your contribution and your relative strength compared to your peers. It is rarely effective to say that the work is so advanced the strongest journals just would not publish it. Or that the strongest university presses would not publish it. Or, that the major sources of funding will not give you money for this reason. It is your job to solve both problems, those of innovation and of reception and reputation of your work. Institutions encourage risk, but in general will not support you if you fail miserably.

260   *Dossiers: Avoiding Disaster*

1. Whatever materials you send to the university committee and the provost, such as sample work, should be vetted by one of your faculty colleagues. Someone in the committee might actually read the sample materials, and if there are problems your case is much weakened. One school has people on the faculty read the various pieces and write memos about them, criticizing them, evaluating them. One piece per faculty member.

2. Unread books: A sure road to disaster is for no one recommending the candidate to have read the book or book manuscript with care, or the papers. In one case, it was clear that no one among the referees or in the department had read the manuscript, while they raved about its excellence.

3. Unmet objections: A university committee's concern re problematic citation statistics could readily be precluded by someone in the department checking out extreme numbers and the source of the citation statistics. Now is the time to catch problems, not when the dossier is in central administration. That supposedly rigorous folks are willing to let the candidate off, since the candidate is not in *their* field, is amazing. That they then would say that maybe it was the coauthor who made the error in the citation statistics is the kind of account that devalues all of the vita.

4. The committee must address trajectory issues, especially for tenured appointments.

5. As for reputation and publication venues and prizes, of course they matter, lots. But unless referees read the work – and many only read the cv and spit it back, rarely engaging with the work itself – their letters or the dossier are weakened.

The dean might say, I want X for purposes of school development. The dean takes responsibility for an exceptional case. But you do not want to use up your credibility, cred that might be spent on truly important cases.

The committees often have very astute members, who are eagle-eyed in reading the dossier, and as a group they find most of the problems quickly enough. They demand of others what they demand of themselves. They know which schools and departments tend to be reliable, and which are not.

261   Peer Institutions

What is a "peer institution"? A small number of institutions are so pre-eminent that they deign to designate as peers slightly lesser institutions, however *lesser* is defined. For most institutions, their peers are determined by public or private support, by religious affiliation, by academic excellence, by region or nation, by membership in associations (either academic or athletic), by size and history, by scale, and by whether they are community colleges, four-year colleges, comprehensive universities, research universities, or other classifications such as the Carnegie. Often, *peer* needs to be defined by general discipline (e.g., liberal arts and sciences, engineering, law, medicine) since most universities are a mixture of differently strong colleges, while for four-year colleges peers may be defined by their catchment areas for students.

262   Preparing Promotion Dossiers

If you are preparing a candidate's dossier for promotion/tenure/appointment:

1. Be sure the list of requested references does not include ringers (advisors, collaborators except for testimony about collaboration). Are they from peer or better institutions? Have they actually read the work?

2. Does the personal statement give us a good feel for the candidate's contributions? Is it much too long?

3. If there are problems (or issues brought up by the references), have they been dealt with by the departmental committee? If not, by the school committee? If not, by the dean?

4. Does the assessment appear balanced and fair? Weaknesses are natural. Have dissenting voices been given a fair hearing?

5. Have recent candidates received similar treatment in your department and school? If not, why not?

6. Has teaching been evaluated in a useful way (faculty visits to a class, for example)? If there are problems, should they have been addressed earlier?

7. Would you buy a used car, given that its mechanic's report was like this sort of dossier? You have more information on the candidate than anyone else, and you want to be sure you have conveyed that information to outsiders. Lemons, it seems, never get fully repaired. Moreover, your ability to sell your next car, no matter how fine it is, will be influenced by others' experience with this one.

8. If this is an extraordinary case, say so up front. Is there a real, competitive offer from elsewhere? Is it a spousal hire? Do we need this candidate to complete a major project? Does the whole teaching program depend on this person?

263   *Do Not Embarrass the Football Coach*

"I would like to build a University of which the football team could be proud." – George Lynn Cross, president of the University of Oklahoma, addressing the Oklahoma legislature justifying his budget request, 1951

Rankings are nice, but playing your personal best, contributing to a team's effectiveness, and staying in shape are fundamental. *We have a long way to go as professors.* The letters we solicit, the rankings we contribute to, our performance standards – all of them would embarrass a football coach, since often they are so undemanding.

264 *Real Professors' Performance*

Few people consistently deliver excellent work. At best, professors do good work, most of the time, and every once in a rare while they hit a home run. There are exceptional scholars, whose work most of the time is marvelous. *Most books and most research articles are good, perhaps having some influence, but likely to fade over the subsequent decade or so.* (I am told that mathematics has a longer life.) Doing good work demands diligence and professional skill, and that is quite an honorable achievement. Few enough rise to the occasion at this level. As far as I can tell, students are not very different from their professors.

If you read most reference letters, or many transcripts, you would think that the world is populated by consistently excellent performances and people. It could be that the only letters or transcripts I see are those of that small group of consistently excellent performers. More likely, we find it hard to say that someone's work is good or quite good, since that sounds like damning with faint praise.

Yet, I believe we want accurate assessments when we go buy a television or car or home, or choose a surgeon, or read a book review. Even as producers we need accurate information about the quality of our work, so we can find our niche in the market. It may be hard to accept that what we are doing is "just" good, but the world will likely find out the truth and our rewards will be commensurate with our performances.

Of course, this is not quite true. If we think we are excellent, perhaps we'll perform better, feeling better about ourselves. And the market is notorious for making incorrect short-term assessments of value. And games, whether in sports or life, may have surprising outcomes when considered one at a time.

It may be, as Garrison Keillor says on *A Prairie Home Companion*, that all the children in Lake Wobegon are above average.

265 *Blowing Your Own Horn*

In mathematics, they have shown how some journal was able to boost its impact factor above any other through self-references. Moreover, in other articles mathematicians argue that citation counts are poor statistics, having very unsatisfactory properties as statistics. (By the way, too many scholars seem to have four- and five-figure citation counts – who knows how?)

By the way, one problem of counting lies in multiple-author publication, and the possibility that the lead author is sufficiently known so that the tag-along authors inherit very high citation counts. Another problem when counting papers is that five single-authored papers appearing in a strong journal would seem, to me, worth more than ten multiple-authored papers in that journal. I know that lots of fields have multiple authorship as the norm. But it seems that studies (in economics) have shown that the production rate has not gone up even close to proportionately with N.

The best information is to be found in reference letters, especially if they are substantive, even disagreeing with the candidate (often these are the very best, arguing and pointing out flaws, single-spaced for pages, and concluding with a rousing positive recommendation). These letters can tell us the quality of the publication venues, the influence of the work. And most often the information is quite consistent among the letters, with of course differences of emphasis.

In any case:

1. When you publish an article, send out by snail mail printed copies of the paper to the top 10–20 people in your field (or at least those who would be interested in the paper). They'll actually be grateful. I know this sounds old-fashioned, but it helps.

2. When you give a talk, at a meeting, say, be sure that it is well prepared. In general, PowerPoint encourages sleep, so unless you cannot speak loudly and clearly use PowerPoint to illustrate your points, not as a summary of your points, point-by-point. Effective speakers have their PowerPoints provide accompaniment to what they are saying. On the other hand, why not hand out to all attendees (6 or 60) of your session a summary with the main graphs or charts (with your name and e-mail address on top).

Make sure that you say the most important stuff in the first five minutes, no matter how long is your talk. Give away the main points that are normally said in the last part. You do not know if you will be interrupted many times and never get to the main point. Of course, some people, probably a dean or the person you really want to hear the talk, will walk in five minutes late – so you might want to give this full preview five minutes into the talk.

In general, you will not get away with giving a talk on work in progress if you are early on in your career or too preliminary. Unless, that is, work in progress is what they want.

266 *Making Your Case for Promotion or Tenure*

1. Scholars and critics are professionally skeptical of claims made in others' work. Be sure that the c v, the personal statement, and the letters from committees and the dean make claims that are evidence-based, and that the arguments are sound. Problematic statements (in reference letters, in memoranda) should be dealt with substantively, rather than ad hominem. One should be sure that quantitative statements are credible. When evidence is lacking and when arguments are unsound or ad hominem, the dossier loses credibility.

2. As for venues: Aim for the place where the strong work in the sub-field is published or performed, and places with widespread audiences. Major journals or venues may be of either sort.

3. Each field has its own preferred venues and kinds of publication or performance and criticism.

4. Impact and depth are matters of quality and of cumulative quantity. Usually a series of journal articles are more influential than is just one. Almost no one publishes just one article that then makes their name. As for books, for assistant professors one published book may well be enough. But more senior appointments usually demand cumulative quantity.

5. Counting has become filled with qualifiers. When there are multiple authors to a paper, all of whom claim equal authorship, the number of papers we might expect is likely larger than in the case of single authorship – whatever the practice of the field. A field that almost always has multiple authorship would seem to demand greater quantity than one in which single authorship is the norm, since it is hard to believe that one paper should count as one paper for each of N different people.

Or, perhaps, nowadays a single paper is a much smaller (or, much larger) unit than it used to be.

It's best to compare with others in the cohort at other institutions.

6. Web publication is rarely a premier venue. (An exception might be peer-reviewed journals where additional materials are on the web.) In computer science, published refereed conference papers are equivalent to journal articles. Hypertext documents are likely web-distributed, but find out if they are peer-reviewed.

7. Web of Science is more reliable than is Google Scholar, with particular exceptions. The studies of the reliability of citation statistics have been done using Web of Science. In any case, the statisticians tell us that the statistics often quoted about citations, whether number or h-index, do not have well-defined properties (such as errors) and do not meet the usual standards of statistics.

8. About 10–20 percent of referee letters indicate substantive weaknesses of the candidate. The best letters argue with the work, present its weaknesses as well as strengths, and show scholarly skepticism.

9. It may well be the case that there is a rising number of dossiers that are impressively strong. Such outstanding dossiers and work might well be appreciated by committees and deans (who are likely to have been last promoted many years ago), so that their judgments reflect the profession's rising quality. Dossiers that might have been viewed favorably five to seven years ago may pale compared to the current crop.

267   *Personal Statements at Tenure and Promotion Time*

What you want to do is to direct people to your achievements.

Your personal statement should be no more than ten double-spaced pages. Will anyone read more than five or so pages? (Actually someone on the university committee will, and so be sure the later pages are in good shape.) In any case, divide up with subheads, and make sure the first paragraph gives away the main points. Here is how to begin:

"My research program might be characterized by [one sentence]. The major contributions of that research have been [three or four points]. In the future, I see myself as pursuing the following projects: [no more than two]." (The rest of the statement elaborates on this, taking on each of the points, and each of the future projects, with one paragraph for each – and with footnotes to papers.)

"My book came out rather late in the probationary period, although it was accepted three years earlier. The publisher then decided to get out of the field of dental hygiene, and I needed to find another publisher. A bitter divorce diverted my energies in the fourth year of the period. I believe I am back on track, as indicated by the second book manuscript in draft recently completed. [Here you have a short paragraph explaining any extraordinary negative aspects of your record. No excuses, be brief, and the facts should speak for themselves.]

"As for my teaching, my philosophy is to be a missionary, addressing students' needs at the stage they are at, rather than having preordained expectations. My distinctive contribution as a teacher is the materials I deal with, my lecturing style, and the projects I give to my students. [To be followed by one paragraph for each point.]"

268   The Promotion Bubble

The academic world is getting more demanding. Promotion dossiers that you send up now that are no less strong than the ones sent up in the last five or six years might well be rejected.

The bar has been raised in many institutions, and so we might believe that those of us who have been promoted or tenured would not be so promoted or tenured with the dossier as submitted in the past. Often, the bar is about at the same place, but tolerance for failure to meet it has evaporated. In part, this is due to the numbers of very strong dossiers that come through, showing that marginal cases might be rejected.

Many a university has gotten much stronger in the last 20–30 years. Those of us in our 60s are in mean perhaps less strong than those in our 40s.

Strong dossiers are now characterized by: No-excuses lists of publications (right number, right strong venues); letters from premier places; letters that discuss the work in some detail, whether or not they agree with it; good personal statements. The school's and dean's statements are rather less important except insofar as they summarize substantively the letters, and indicate matters of fit and trajectory.

These dossiers stand out, and make you proud to be a scholar. Put differently, the publications must be in the significant journals or the best university or other presses, the letters give you a real feel for the contribution of the candidate, and the candidate has a well-defined trajectory of future work.

Many of our past dossiers would not fulfill these requirements. That they went through is a sign of a "promotion bubble" which has now burst. Hyperbolic letters, excuses for less-than-expected performance will not work well. Service or teaching are important but only in extraordinary cases will they be probative.

All of this should make those of us who are quite senior a bit uncomfortable, and those promoted in the past five years a bit more unsure of our virtue. Of course, all that means is that those of us who are tenured need to work much harder to justify the faith the university has placed in us.

269   Expectations for Tenure: Is There Enough Room at the Top?

What are the expectations for getting tenure? Are journal articles more valued than books? Or is it the other way around?

Different sorts of universities tend to have different expectations. For example, community service or teaching may play a larger role, getting along with your colleagues and doing your share of the scut work, publications venues, major contributions, and so forth will be differently valued.

In a research-oriented university, however distinguished, what you want is to have a tenure portfolio that will get you hired by a peer or better institution. This is the safest, most powerful position to be in. Second, you want to have made at least one well-defined, recognized contribution to scholarship. Most likely, this will come out of your dissertation work. And you want to have started another line of research that is promising.

As for numbers and venues of publications: If you work with collaborators, you should in general have greater numbers of publications than those who work alone in your field. *If all the people coming up for tenure were to publish in the top journals, we'd need more "top" journals.* So, clearly, you will publish in a variety of venues, some suited especially to your field or subfield (and those journals may in fact be very demanding and prestigious), some more widely seen, and some that are less prestigious.

As for numbers, that is something you have to ascertain from your departmental chair. As for books vs. articles, again this is something for you and your chair to discuss. The problem is that "a book" published by a comparatively weak press will likely be much less recognized than an article in a strong journal. But, more importantly, a book represents a coherent presentation of work, but in some fields work is always presented in articles.

I have not answered these questions precisely. If a knife were at my neck, I'd say a book published by a university press or a half-dozen articles in the main journals qualify. But contribution is more important than numbers.

One other thing: You may need to show that you can raise research money. You can support graduate students, you can have time off for your research, you can help fill the coffers of your department or school. And the money ought to come from high-prestige or high-competition sources, to validate your work. At first, you may be under a PI; later you will be the PI or co-PI.

Finally, what's crucial is what others think of your work. Make a list now of the 10 to 20 people in the field you would like to think well of your work. Maybe you can think of only 5, but as time goes on the list will grow. Make sure you get to meet some of them at meetings, discussing your work and theirs. Send them preprints or reprints.

270   *Time in Rank*

We need to appoint people to the appropriate rank, whatever it is. Usually, one makes those judgments based on the CV and the reputation of the person. If a new PhD is qualified as a full professor, we might make an assistant professor appointment to be sure about teaching, but promote to tenure and even to full professor as soon as possible.

As for waiting six years in rank, and the like, again this is not written in stone. Assistant professors can come up whenever they are qualified for promotion and tenure, but most candidates need every month (and then some) of that probationary period.

Most of us have gone through the ranks and process by the book. But I would think we would be pleased to have colleagues who are so productive and impactful in their work that we would want to promote them more expeditiously. What the regular schedule allows is for ordinary scholars to build up their contributions and reputations, so that they might be promoted. Some scholars need more time as associate professors to build up the national reputation they would aspire to.

Most academics end up in the place they started out, their first jobs. You must be sure that your dissertation work (and postdoc work) makes you eligible for the strongest universities. *You have to play for keeps from day one.*

271   *What Counts for Tenure and Promotion*

1. Whatever you do, it should be recognized by scholars at peer or better institutions, and often by critics or practitioners and clinicians. It may be published in the main journals of the field. Or it may be recognized by awards, by replication of practice in many places, by others' books. It should be seen as a contribution that advances scholarship and practice. Do not mix in weak contributions with strong ones, for that weakens the whole case.

2. Whatever you do, it should be seen as advancing your school or university's mission. Your dean is the one who testifies to this: We need Joe to teach psychiatric dentistry, since we want to lead nationally through our highly popular and remunerative rigorous master's program in this area.

3. Whatever you do, the letters of reference should provide comparables with others who do similar work, ranking and placing you among your cohort and others in the field. If your work is peculiar, I believe there must be people at peer or better institutions who do similar work. If you do not rank at the top, however that is done, what people want to know is where you stand. They will make their judgments based on your institution's standards.

4. The letters of reference should come from people who are nationally recognized as authorities. No ringers (dissertation advisors, people from your own institution unless they are testifying that you did the work), no friends, no people of lower rank than the one you aspire to.

The best letters attest to your contribution, in detail, substantively. They can even think you are incorrect in part, but if the letter is detailed and serious that matters a lot.

5. At some institutions, it might well matter if you are someone's boy or girl, someone's protégé, and that someone is on your faculty. That is, they view you as their successor, or they see you as really terrific and they are willing to put their reputation on the line. And, at your institution and nationally, they are viewed as authoritative.

Most places are bureaucracy-driven rather than patronage- or sponsor-driven.

6. No excuses. Reasons, and accounts, are better.

7. Sometimes mistakes are made.

272 *Dossier Illusions*

· Often candidates are referred to as "rising stars" of their field. Once in a while this is an accurate description. Most of the time these are, at best, planets without their own source of energy, that shine by the light of another star (advisor, collaborator, puffery).

· Teaching is a valid reason for promotion if it is a contribution to scholarship attested to by the letters of reference. But it must be a widely recognized contribution: innovations in instruction, significant textbooks, curriculum leadership. Being a good classroom teacher, even a spectacular one, is not a contribution to scholarship – and many of the best researchers are as well fine teachers.

· We have in front of us someone who knew that at the end of Y years they would be evaluated. Yet they did not produce much, or at least not enough. They might well continue to produce as they have for the last two years, or the last Y might be the right time line.

What we demand of student athletes, that they perform at their personal best, and that they be competitive, is just what we should demand of our faculties. And just as we demand that athletes also do reasonably well as students, so we ought to demand a full spectrum of achievements of our faculty.

We might argue that the candidate is about to do terrific work, and we do not want to lose them. Would it not be better to have someone who did terrific work in their probationary period?

More to the point: Marginal cases rarely turn out to be strong scholars. They may be good, but they are unlikely to escape the limitations that haunted them during their probationary period.

273   An Epitome of Concerns re Tenure and Promotion

Over the last several years it is likely that your university has appointed more and more stronger candidates, as evidenced in the dossiers. They reset the bar for your colleagues; in particular they make marginal cases appear much less appealing. Similarly, some promotions are very strong and again reset the bar. And this influence cuts across the schools, so that a school's marginal cases appear marginal in part because of the strong cases throughout the university.

Put differently, we expect our faculty to be as strong as our football team. Or, putting it in yet other terms: Would you want a surgeon with these qualifications (similar to those of a given dossier in some other field) operating on your child?

A number of concerns:

1. Due diligence: Letters should come from strong institutions; they should not come from collaborators or advisors (unless to testify to who did what in joint work); they should deal substantively with the candidate's work vs. recitals of the cv.

2. Don't put up associate professors for full professor perhaps two years early. Too many articles are under submission, or the second book is not out and reviewed. Of course, retention may be an issue, and then there is no problem. Otherwise, deans can offer salary increases for strong work and assure candidates that they will come up when their dossier is really strong.

3. We see few if any marginal tenure cases bloom into true excellence. We have very few errors of denial of tenure to those who then become outstanding elsewhere. Rather, we make the other sort of error (How did X get tenure?).

4. Longtime associate professors, say 14 or more years: If they continue to do scholarship, publishing their work, even if not in the best venues or the most obvious sort, it's time to promote. Chairing departments or being an associate dean is not a reason to promote. Outstanding administrative work might well be. The stigma of "longtime" is enough of a disincentive to those who are more ambitious.

5. It may make sense to have four-year reviews of associate professors, if only to prevent #4.

6. Lowering the dean's rhetoric might serve the university. "Genius" and "rising star" are all too present, and all too absent in actuality. Most such claimed "rising stars" are merely planets illuminated by a sun.

274 *Promotion Dossiers as Excuses*

People look at the rules or promotion guidelines and then quote them to justify what they do. So people will say that we ask for five or six substantive letters, and then they will have just six, most of which are formulaic. Of course, they then do not quote the rules when the chapters/verses are not quite suited to their purposes. We ask for peer or better institutions, but then we get not-so-peer institutions, and an argument that all the people at these less eminent institutions are really very strong (which may well be true, but what if there are no letters from peer or better institutions, or it is said that X used to be at Wisconsin even though he has moved to Montana?).

We now routinely ask external reviewers to identify the schools where the candidate's type of work is done superbly. There should be a sufficient number of letters (with supporting details) that have come from these places.

There are the book manuscripts of accepted books that are not yet out, not yet reviewed, for promotions from associate to full. The candidate has taken $6+M$ years at associate professor. What is the rush to promote? Surely, this makes sense if they are being attracted elsewhere, but that is rarely the case when M is, say, 4 or more. If M is zero or negative, I have no problem thinking this is a real case, but when M is 4 or more it seems the candidate has taken their own time, and we are meant to rush.

And in the background are the dossiers of the strong people hired or already at the university who perform superbly, on time, with great impact. They now set a standard much higher than the proverbial "hurdle." In fact, I would think that we want hurdlers who can do well with a raised bar.

275 *Benchmarking, Reviews, Citations, and the Disciplines*

1. Usually, reference letters compare scholars at other institutions at roughly the same stage in their careers.

2. In fields in which a book is the standard contribution, impact and contribution are not well indicated by citations in the subsequent two years, so they are not useful for tenure and promotion purposes. Impact is better indicated by book reviews, how many and their venues: main journals in the field vs. specialized ones; many vs. one or two. In the journal-article fields, citations indicate something about impact, but for substance, it is useful to rely on the letters.

3. Books tend to take a while to be influential through citations in journal articles, and even longer through other books, times too long compared to when decisions are called for. Often, one has to rely on reference letters for first books when promotion to associate is on the agenda.

4. For journal fields: Citations are helpful for promotion to associate, crucial for promotion to full. Again, there are issues of delay, but much shorter delay than for books.

5. Some fields demand a book and several articles. (Often this is honored in the breach, by the way.) The articles here are previews, almost always. To evaluate the work, people are waiting for the book.

6. In all fields, it should be possible to explain to a professor layman and the provost what the contribution is and its significance, even if the field is technical or has a specialized diction and discourse. Moreover,

letters can be substantive using lay language in describing the contribution clearly.

For a university to become stronger, many of the lateral external appointments must be very strong, as should be more and more of the internal promotions. They set the standard, they benchmark. Strong cases make weak ones seem untenable, unless there are institutional reasons that are overriding.

276 *Preparing Promotion Dossier Materials*

1. Bragging rarely works. Do indicate your achievements, and the committee and deans can assess their importance. If something is particularly significant, and they are not likely to appreciate it, let them know (but think about why they would not recognize it). There is likely to be a dossier that happens to be read before or after yours, where the candidate is rather more modest and the achievements are rather greater – hence, you will be discounted.

2. CVs need to be brutally honest. If you are the PI, fine; if co-PI, fine; if on a list of collaborators, fine. But do not conflate these. When you list your writings, separate un-refereed articles from refereed articles and conference proceedings. (In a few fields, refereed conference proceedings are considered the equivalent of journal articles, at least.) Have your CV approved by a senior colleague.

3. What is your contribution to scholarship or science or art or the profession? This is about the impact and importance and significance of your work, not the inputs or the fact that you are a pioneer. Context is the most important thing. Your personal statement should make this clear in the first paragraph or on the first page, in a short paragraph.

4. Make sure your letters of reference come from the strongest institutions and the strongest people at those institutions. And rarely should there be more than one letter from each institution. What the committees want to know is the judgment of people who are their peers or stronger. That you might be promoted at a much weaker institution is not very helpful. Since letter-writers are mostly chosen by the committee, all you can do is have your supporters encourage them to find strong people.

And if possible some people outside your subfield might be consulted to give an idea of the impact of your work more widely.

In any case, substantive letters about your contribution are very helpful. Surveys of your CV rarely are valuable, even if they are enthusiastic.

5. There is a curious problem of joint authorship. If you and others agree on your contribution (#3), then it is less of a problem. In some fields, jointly authored papers with more than two or three authors are the norm. Two questions come up: Did you do much or are you just listed? Can you work independently, at least in the sense of finding another group of coauthors? While you are often encouraged to do some singly authored papers, in some fields that makes little sense except for a review article. What's crucial is that the committee or the department chair indicate the culture of joint authorship, indicate that they have information on your contribution (#3), perhaps gleaned from interviews or phone conversations with collaborators, and so take charge of the problem. If there is just one joint author, the other person might be asked for a letter about contributions to the collaborative work.

If there are N (>2) authors, someone will count each paper as $1/(N-1)$ papers. In some fields this makes no sense since experiments or projects have few papers, the number of authors is large, and the effort required of each person is very substantial. Again, this is what should be discussed in the personal statement or the departmental report. But in some fields, if there are three authors, a paper should count as half a paper – and so you should have twice the number of published papers as those who work alone (controlling for quality and placement). Again, an account of contribution can go around this. And norms of the strongest candidates at the strongest departments at the strongest institutions will avoid counting dilemmas. If all of this is too demanding, *strongest* might be replaced by *strong* above.

Some people are always in a collaborative role, since they may do crucial but what is conventionally taken as secondary work. And that so-called secondary work may demand great skill and scholarly competence, and only be demonstrated within applied contexts – and the research would not happen without it. You may not be tenured at the very first-ranked universities, but you are likely to more than pass the requirements at other highly ranked universities. Again, what is the contribution?

6. Do you really want to be an academic? Maybe you would be happier in a different work environment. Are you going to write your second and third books? Finish them and publish them in good time? Will you keep getting grants to run your lab? Are you engaged with the problems of your field? If not, maybe you ought to think about finding a pond in which you will both thrive and feel authentic. I am not so much worried about senior academics in the last few years of their careers, but about those who are in the middle of their careers and could make dramatic shifts.

277   What Is the Contribution?

Usually, we can figure out the nature of the contribution, even in fields such as mathematics or biology/medicine or philosophy. The candidate's statement, the various committee reports and dean's memo, and the letters usually allow us to get a handle on what is going on. That handle might be schematic – X has solved this longstanding problem vital to the field. Often, we can get a more substantive sense as well.

But if we have a club phenomenon, where there is a mode of discourse that the candidate, the dean, the committee, and the letter-writers share that is not open to others, there may well be a problem. Are they all part of a cabal, so to speak, uncritically advancing their movement?

We might ask for a memo that explains the contribution in plain English. I do know that if I can talk to the members of the club I can almost always figure out what is going on by asking questions. What I am looking for is a model or a picture that translates between the club and the world.

278   Writing Your Personal Statement

When you apply for a fellowship or a job or for promotion, you often have to write a personal statement. It may be addressed to people in your field, or perhaps more widely (as in some fellowships, or for promotion).

- Write it in plain English. If you have lots of technical stuff, at least the first paragraph should make sense to lay persons.
- Do not brag. If you are the world's expert, let others say that about you. You can tell about awards and prizes, but usually they are listed separately. If the awards are obscure, you might say something about them. You might say: "My work has been recognized by a number of awards and by my giving several invited plenary lectures at meetings."
- If you have lots of technical stuff, say explaining your work on cell processes, and you have illustrations or charts, terrific. But, again, the first sentence or two of that paragraph should be in plain English.
- What people are interested in is your substantive contribution to scholarship, at least if you are a professor. In effect you are saying, *the field was in the following shape and then in my work I moved it in the following direction.*
- Also, you want to indicate your plans for the next few years. Be realistic about what you can do. You might say what your long-term goal is.
- If you are promising a book or article, be sure that what you have done – a few chapters or a draft of the article – is available.

279   *Promotion Dossier Checklist for Preparers*

1. Looking over the dossier, do you believe others should rely on it?

2. Letters are independent, textured, from a wide range of peer or better institutions. There are no ringers, such as the dissertation advisor. Collaborators are asked to testify just about joint work and the candidate's contribution to that work.

3. If the letters indicate problems, the administrative memos deal with those problems substantively (rather than dismiss the letter-writers). All referees are taken seriously. The arguments of those with whom you disagree are addressed substantively.

4. Have you aired your department's dirty linen for all to see? (Do you want to?)

5. There is a statement of the candidate's contributions written in nontechnical language. Their relative standing among their peers is described.

6. Interdisciplinary work has an audience and peers to evaluate it, and venues where it is published. Relevant departments have also been formally consulted.

7. Criteria of the department are consistently applied among dossiers (such as a home-run paper, or a second book published, or citation counts).

8. The dossier deals with its internal conflicts and inconsistencies, rather than leaving them unaddressed.

9. Reasons and substantive argument, rather than ad hominem insults and excuses, characterize the dossier.

10. The membership of various administrative committees is fair and manifestly unbiased. For example, a collaborator is not head of the faculty committee.

11. You report internal disagreements and votes in a unit or a committee and discuss them substantively. Rather than imputing motives to dissenters, you present us with their arguments and why you disagree with them. Secret ballots do not permit reliable interpretation.

12. Problems with teaching, collegiality, and research quality have been addressed well before starting the promotion process. The candidate's classes have been visited by their colleagues. The chair has spoken with candidate about their uncollegial actions.

13. The dossier considers strengths and weaknesses.

14. The CV has no major problems, such as un-refereed work mixed in with refereed work, or unclear PI status.

15. If a candidate has done joint work, you have discovered the nature of their contribution vs. that of the other authors. When you count up articles, you do not double-count multiply authored papers (giving full credit for each paper to each author).

16. The dossier you present will be compared with other dossiers, and your candidate stands out for the quality of their scholarship. (They are well over any "hurdle," and in fact are superior.)

17. The personal statement is not too long, nor is it sprinkled with excuses and whining.

18. You do not play chicken with the promotion committee, in effect daring it and the provost to approve a candidate whose dossier is defective. This is unfair to the candidate.

280   A Credible Dossier

1. My experience of university committees suggests that they try to be fair and flexible. They are especially aware of issues of underrepresented groups, and try to be sure no problems creep in.

2. Imagine that you are a parent whose child brings you a mechanic's report on a car the child wants you to purchase for her:

    a. You want to be sure the mechanic is authoritative, and not in the pocket of the seller of the car or of your child.

    b. You read over the mechanic's report and you want to be able to understand it; if it is purely in terms of automotive engineering language you are not sure what to make of it.

    c. The report of the supervisory mechanic should be balanced, reflecting the mechanic's reports, indicating both problems and virtues.

    d. Your child's argument should reflect all the previous reports, but might well bring in their special needs or desires.

Everyone would appear to be committed to your buying the car (or your child would not be showing you the report), so you have to be skeptical. But it is likely your child would not want to have a car that broke down after 1,000 more miles.

3. In general, the big question is, what is the contribution to scholarship (or the arts) made by the candidate? While this may well be described in technical terms in some of the letters of reference and even in the personal statement, it matters that the contribution be described in ordinary terms so that a judgment can be made. If no one describes the contribution in ordinary terms, you might wonder what it is. In general, it does not help the case if all the letters are highly technical, especially if it is apparent that none of the writers have actually read and absorbed the work.

Numbers of publications depend on the field, and having lots of publications but no discernible contribution is unlikely to work. If a book published by a major press is the norm in the field, it must be there.

Personal statements that explain the meaning of the work and provide a credible account of the trajectory (past and future) are helpful. Bragging never works. And if you speak about a book that you are writing, you might well be asked for the manuscript so far.

4. The candidate and dossier need to be compared to the strong appointments or promotions at that rank and in that cohort at the university – in all fields. Finding someone who was promoted who is as weak as is the candidate is rarely convincing.

5. The impact is usually clear from the letters.

6. As in #2 above, assessments by interested parties or unbalanced assessments (good or bad) are rarely effective. Letters have to be credible, substantive, disinterested, and clear.

7. Did the candidate do what they were supposed to do: raise external grants of the right sort, publish the book? Many schools have standards that are honored in the breach.

8. When people come up earlier than expected, they should have a strong case. That others with weaker dossiers at other universities ("better" than our university) have been promoted is not probative – perhaps a mistake was made elsewhere?

9. In general, deans and committees are the guilty parties in making a case problematic. Memoranda are biased, dossiers employ unbalanced advocacy, claims lack substance, internal inconsistencies abound (within a dossier, among dossiers from a single unit).

10. Keep in mind that there are strong, effective dossiers, even for candidates who are not the most distinguished. It's all about honest assessment, a good account of the unit's needs, a good sense that the dean knows what they are buying. Candidates, departments, and schools are the most powerful people in promotion and tenure, for when they prepare an honest dossier they are likely to prevail.

281   Ringer Letters, Weak Trajectory, Uncollegial Behavior, Early Full Professorship

1. Third-year reviews are the occasion to flag problems and seek corrections: teaching that has deficiencies, slow publication rate, no grants, uncollegial service behavior. Most problems show up by the third year.

2. Letters from the candidate's advisor or doctoral institution are unlikely to be helpful. Multiple letters from the same institution are unlikely to be helpful. Letters from collaborators are useful in indicating the contribution of the candidate to joint work, but not in evaluating the quality of the work.

Moreover, the tenure committee is seeking textured letters that indicate the writer's intellectual involvement with the work of the candidate. General praise, even from prominent people, is not very helpful. We expect the writers to have actually looked at and in general to have closely read at least some of the work we send along.

Dossiers stuffed with ringer-letters, even ringers who are prestigious, are an insult to the candidate, indicating a perceived weakness by the department.

3. Trajectory is important. Most candidates have long careers ahead of them. If they have slowed down in producing research, if they have slowed in grants, if they have serious problems in teaching and service, there has to be reason given to expect a change in trajectory.

Comparatively weak candidates are likely to face a much stronger university in the next decade, and more so as their careers move forward. Will they be left further behind?

There is no rush to promote candidates to full professor. If there are problems in their dossiers – weak visibility, low grant rates, problems in teaching and service – then it is a good idea to encourage them to improve, and then send up the dossier. This might well involve a delay of more than two years. But there is no reason to risk a turndown, and this will become more likely as more of our full professor dossiers (both internal and lateral) get stronger.

4. Marginal tenurings that are approved need to be supplemented by careful mentoring for at least a decade. The problems need to be worked through. The candidate will benefit, and so will the university. Of course, demurrers might well be delayed until after the initial information about tenure approval is conveyed.

And spectacular tenurings need to be conveyed to the candidate, to indicate to the candidate how much the university appreciates them.

5. There may be good reason to have a very strong research/creativity person on a faculty as long as their poor behavior (in teaching, in service)

is adequate. And each university needs people who are outward-looking for prestige, even if they are, at least at this time in their careers, not particularly fine university citizens. The strongest faculty often do it all.

282   *Promotion Dossiers Can Self-Destruct*

Promotion dossiers can self-destruct, taking a good case and making it worse.

1. Say you dismiss the reviewers who do not say glowing things – impugning those reviewers' judgment. The problem is, why should I trust the other, more positive reviewers? You really do not want to impugn your own witness. Deal with the substance of the concern. Moreover, you want more peer or better institutions consulted.

2. Say there is a real problem in teaching. Rather than having dealt with it – sending colleagues to visit the classroom, asking the candidate to modify their teaching if there really is an issue – student complaints are dismissed. The teaching problem is not new, it would appear. You would think the department would have addressed it in the preceding four or five years.

The candidate's research contributions are OK. But the undealt-with teaching problems kill the dossier.

It makes no sense for a school to destroy their own cases, when in fact they want a positive outcome. It's embarrassing. The provost might expect to be bamboozled some of the time, but at least have respect for the provost's intelligence.

283   *Dossier Phenomenology*

1. Marginal cases are almost always poor. This is obvious when one reads a good case, and then the difference is apparent.

2. We still do not know how it happens that longtime associate professors then lay golden eggs.

3. There are schools whose dossiers are much more reliable than others, and this seems to be always the case.

4. There are schools whose dossiers are much less reliable than others, and this seems to be always the case.

5. Bait and switch. We are told that we have to appoint X if Y is to come, and then Y does not come. X is often marginal.

6. Excuses for weak performance are almost always lacking in credibility. The excuses weaken the case.

7. Assistant professors should never edit a book; they should write another one.

8. Comparisons are only credible when the field is considered widely.

284   *Problems with Promotion Dossiers*

The deep insight is to read the work, consider the dossier as a whole in context, not get caught up in counting. Think in terms of the quality of university, the message sent to other faculty (especially probationary or mid-career). Cases are cases, not examples of generalized rules. Outplacement may be good for the candidate as well as the university.

285   *Excuses You Really Do Not Want to Employ*

1. Our faculty have low citation counts, and their work is in weaker journals, so we cannot criticize the candidate for that.

2. Everyone in this field comes from less strong universities, and writes in this intricate way.

3. The committee composition was inappropriate (said when the report comes out), even though someone was given a chance to object to the committee when it was formed.

4. We are making a Type II error, rejecting someone who will turn out to be terrific. The work in progress will be much better than what we have seen already; there will be as much of it in future years as we have seen in the last two years (albeit there was little in previous years). They are a "rising star."

5. The important people (in this field) are so overwhelmed with letters (as am I), that they never write detailed, thoughtful letters. We rarely even have time to review the sample papers we receive.

286 *Might Departments or Schools Be Allowed
to Make Their Own Tenure Decisions?*

It has been argued that a strong department should have a natural interest in continuing and enhancing its strength, and that it is recognized as strong means that the department is qualified to make its own tenure decisions. That might well be the case. However, it is the university that guarantees the tenure and remuneration of the candidate, and so the provost might not like to have the university's money spent by such agents. Moreover, many departments are not so strong, and others are known for prejudice and self-dealing.

What surely is possible is that strong department tenure recommendations will be given weight that is often probative. What they still must do is provide promotion dossiers that are convincing to their colleagues throughout the university, if only to retain their reputations as strong.

C. MORE ON DENIAL

287 *Unfairness*

The academic labor market is denominated not only by quality of work, but also by quality of life, family ties, and other such, not to speak of prejudice and unfairness. Most research and comprehensive universities, and most colleges, have very distinguished members of their faculties who are unlikely (and for good reasons) to move to stronger institutions. Similarly, because of matters of style and method, strong journals turn down papers that turn out to be outstanding, and often publish weaker papers.

What saves this whole system is the diversity of venues for work and for publication. There is also enough arbitrariness that the system is shaken up. What is remarkable is how well we do given the possibilities for snafus. People do not get anything close to the rewards and positions they deserve, but what helps is that diversity, and the possibility of disrupting innovations.

The best way of dealing with unfairness to oneself is to acknowledge it and then go out and do your work, find new ways around the idiocies, and outlive your opponents.

288   You Don't Want Your Colleagues to Write This Sort of Letter to the Provost

Dear Provost Anna Smith:

We are writing to express our dismay at and deep dissatisfaction with your recent decision to deny tenure to our colleague Robert Pied.

First, this decision belies the official University rhetoric stressing support for innovative research and graduate programs, particularly those involving trans-disciplinary study. Robert Pied's scholarship can best be understood as making the subjunctivity between theorists and practitioners visible and understandable; it thereby exemplifies precisely the kind of critical scholarship our field requires at this point in history. Yet, this is the second time in the past few years that the School of Podiatric Medicine has put someone forward for tenure who is actually doing such cutting-edge scholarship and whose tenure has been delayed or denied. Both dossiers were evaluated by members of the university tenure committee from traditional fields that are not particularly knowledgeable about or receptive to these modes of experimentation. But in Podiatric Medicine we believe it is absolutely crucial to recruit and retain faculty who are both willing and able to guide students into a set of fields, industries, technologies, and pedagogies that are rapidly undergoing transformation, and we can think of no scholar who is better able to perform that role than Robert Pied.

Secondly, this denial of tenure ignores the unanimous support of the Podiatric Medicine faculty from all divisions, a unanimity based on a wide range of professional expertise. This trans-divisional approval demonstrates Robert Pied's ability to do outstanding work that meets the rigorous standards of many different approaches.

Third, when tenure is denied to a scholar like Robert Pied, one who has been instrumental in developing and directing a new cutting-edge doctoral program like iFOOT (Intersectoral Foot and Other Orthopedic Transections), it demoralizes the students and undermines the program itself. If Robert does not receive tenure, the iFOOT students may well wonder, then, what are the chances for them once they receive their own degrees.

For these three reasons, we urge you to reconsider this decision because we think it is striking a serious blow to the future of Podiatric Medicine and to its most innovative programs and plans.

289 *Tenure Due Processes*

Of course, you would like to know the reasons you were denied tenure (or granted it), and indications of your strengths and weaknesses as identified by letter-writers, committee reports, and dean's and chair's letters. You might like to know which scholars you were compared to; in any case, you probably can make a decent guess as to the members in that cohort. As for the votes at various levels, one of the problems is that the vote itself without detailed knowledge of the discussion may not be sufficiently informative. And the discussion at the meeting may have various devil's advocates, who then vote in ways very different than their comments would suggest.

You might like to have your department's decision be probative. But what if the chair does not agree with their colleagues' vote? Perhaps some departments are strong enough that their decision dominates other considerations. On the other hand, one of the purposes of the tenure and promotion process is to blunt arbitrary and biased departmental decisions.

The university tenure committee is advisory to the provost, who usually makes the only decision. (It may be the president or board of trustees, but usually this is a formality.) No provost will listen to a committee they do not respect.

You surely want more proactive mentoring, and at year three a better indication of where you stand. You want reports from departmental committees and deans that fairly present your strengths and vulnerabilities, and do not weaken the case with lame excuses. And you want the university to be fair when it asks that you be a top scholar, if in fact it does not acknowledge the capacity of the university to field a team of such hitters.

290   *What to Do If You've Been Denied Tenure*

1. There are people on your campus who know what your rights are in this case, what procedures to follow. Maybe your Academic Senate.

2. The institution may stonewall, but that is not your problem. Find out what you are allowed to see, and send formal notes to the right people about it, with copies to the provost. Hire a lawyer to make sure you retain your rights.

3. I would not fight it too hard, though. (Others strongly disagree with me.) Too costly to you. You know your publication record, and I suspect you know how strong your work is. *Now is the time to find another position, at a place that needs what you have.* This is separate from #2 above. Pursue both. You have a year before your contract is over, so this gives you time. *You might even withdraw your application for tenure, so it is never denied you.* Check with wiser heads.

4. Assistant professors tend to write articles drawn from their dissertation and their first independent project. People grow, they change over five-year periods. Most full professors, with distinguished careers, started out as assistant professors writing those articles.

You've been given a blessing. Now is the time to find another place, maybe of a very different sort than where you are now. I know it sounds stupid to use the word "blessing." But in my experience it has been.

Ask yourself, am I as strong as half of my colleagues? If not, go elsewhere. If so, go elsewhere gleefully.

Sorry to be so positive.

NINE

After Tenure – Associate & Full Professorship (#291–307)

291 *What Did You Do This Summer?*

What do professors do during the summer, when they are not teaching? They are doing their research. Since most are on a nine-month salary, they may well be spending the time at their summer cottage, or their lab or an archive, or their office and the university library, working. The kind of busyness that characterizes our lives during the school year has to yield to intense focus. Daniel Bell, the sociologist, said that four words characterize the benefits of academia – May, June, July, August – when he would draft one of his long essays.

Of course, your life may be falling apart, the kitchen redo is in its sixth month, or a newborn or late adolescent child is precarious. And if you happen to have a major illness, get help.

By the way, I know some of us are just running our lemonade stands. Most competitive people are at their desks. If you do not deliver, they will.

292 *You've Just Been Promoted by the Skin of Your Teeth*

Say that you have just been tenured and promoted to associate professor, or that you have just been promoted to professor. What next? Keep in mind that you have family and personal obligations, that you cannot do everything, and that choosing what to do (and what *not* to do) will give you the freedom you need. Also, that you are part of a large organization, the university, and a larger enterprise, the academic world. *Your contribution is always within the context of others' contributions.*

Likely, the university's standard of quality is rising. In other words, if you do not continue to grow and develop you will fall behind. What is your trajectory? *Are you spending too much time on your e-mail? Going to committee meetings? Commuting? In other words, are you doing things that consume enormous amounts of time, but prevent your getting to what you think is most important?*

1. Perhaps yours is one of the 5–10 percent (or more, in some institutions) of dossiers that are stellar. Of course, you will want to continue in your current path. What more or different can you do? You can mentor your junior colleagues and your senior colleagues so that they can be more effective and productive and successful. If there is a promotion and tenure vote, do not assume you are unique. Others should match up to you.

2. While it is nice to be the biggest fish in the pond, there is much to be said for being one of a school of such big fish.

3. Perhaps you are not in the minority of dossiers that are quite strong. What you want to do now is to figure out how to do better. Find out what the external letters said about where you are weak (there should be no problem in getting a summary of their contents) and where you are strong. Have you spread yourself too thin? Should you think about refocusing your work in a different direction? Think of this as a five-year project. No rush. Is it time to seek more external funding? You will surely be recruited for more service to the university. Can you say *no* to some requests, while contributing significantly to others?

4. Perhaps you are in the residual category of those who would not receive tenure and promotion or at least would be rather more iffy were your dossier considered ten years from now. Of course, ten years from now you might well have upped your performance to meet the new standards. You have been tenured, or promoted to full. But unless you figure out how to redirect your work you will fall behind decade after decade.

Some of you might well consider a change in career. It is not too late. Is there something else you would rather do? Is there a different sort of university where you would thrive?

Others may have chronic illnesses that have prevented them from doing their work as well as they would like. Can those illnesses be more aggressively treated? If not, can you arrange with your dean for a more effective contribution to the university? If you have family obligations, say children or ill parents, which have a significant effect on your ability to do your work, figure out with your dean how to make things work as best they can. No one expects you to instantly bounce back from a serious debilitating disease. Again, plans and working with your dean and colleagues will give you the room to recover and resume your duties the best you can.

Some may well have discovered that they do not like writing or doing research, preferring teaching or service. Or that they really want to be a dean. Now is the time to find a position where you can follow your interests without thinking of yourself as failing in a research university.

If you are going to make a commitment to teaching, can you make that commitment nationally recognized? Think beyond textbooks. Might your ways of teaching become the new norm throughout your field? Make sure your dean and colleagues understand your commitment, that it is not seen as failing in a research university, and deliver on that commitment. There is lots of external grant money available for teaching innovation.

But say that your commitment to research is strong, but it has not produced the kind of outcome that is as strong. Now is the time to talk to your more successful colleagues, get their advice, again discover what was advised in the external letters. You may have been promoted even though you did not follow the advice you received in a third-year review. That advice might still be good. Make a written plan that you share with your dean, and then over the next five to seven years deliver on that plan. You will want to focus your research, you will want to be sure that it is more widely recognized, you will want to choose topics and goals that others will appreciate. If you are following an idiosyncratic path, say because you think this is the most productive way to go, then let your dean and colleagues know that, indicate what you think will be good goals, and argue for them. Perhaps there is a way of connecting your work to the mainstream. It might take a year or two of hard work to make this connection, and several follow-up years. But the payoff may be well worth it.

In five years, you want to be able to describe your significant contribution to your field, where whatever doubts that accompanied your promotion and tenure are seen as resolved. Again, if you are not suited to the university should you be somewhere else where your style is more highly valued?

If you have reason to believe you are in this residual category, figure out how to make the most of your talents. Do not tell yourself stories about what's wrong with others. The university will not go along with those stories after a while. The strongest people on our faculty are not only the best researchers; they are also fine teachers, and do much more than their share of service (locally, nationally, internationally). You may not be one of these people, but you can make sure your personal best is something you and the university can be proud of.

293   *You've Just Been Promoted or Tenured*

Your dean calls you up, and tells you the good news. You've been promoted or tenured. What is most interesting, and you will have to ask to discover this, is what particular problems and insights arose in your dossier and your case:

- The letter-writers were insufficiently arm's-length, and so were less convincing than they might have been.
- Your personal statement never made clear what your contribution was.
- Your teaching had problems that might have sunk you.
- You have not been as productive as you ought to have been.
- Your work is very highly thought of by the readers, and one or two wrote wonderfully detailed letters that had important insights about your work, its limitations and problems, and areas you might work on.

Not many cases are so clear-cut, with so few problems, that there is nothing to learn from the promotion and tenure process. *Most of us have limits,* but those limits or inadequacies were not judged to be so significant compared to your contributions and teaching. *To have an understanding of those limits will allow you to grow.* It would be unusual for those limits to surprise you. You probably know them already. But it would be helpful to have an idea of what the readers thought, and even what the promotion committee thought.

It is not too difficult to summarize the important points of the letters, especially those that comment critically and helpfully about your work. But someone will have to do it, and your dean may be reluctant to try. Putting the request in the context of making your work stronger may make for a more cooperative dean.

294   *For Associate Professors: Grants, PI-ship, Fellowships*

When associate professors come up for promotion to full, promotion committees ask about their grantsmanship. This is perhaps less important in some fields, but even there external fellowships are important.

For many fields, you are at the right stage in your career to become a PI in grants from NSF or NIH or NEH, especially if you haven't done so already, or to apply for year-long fellowships to pursue your work. This is not only about money, but about external validation of the quality of your work, and about not only summer salary but also time off from teaching during the year to allow for more research, and to better support your students. The idea is not to add to your load, but to make better use of your time – so that time invested in grant-getting pays off in much more time available for actual research work.

A fine publication and research record is the background for going out and becoming a PI on a substantial grant.

295   *Bureaucratic Drag*

Many long-time-in-rank associate professors are produced by deans and, more generally, the academic bureaucracy. Work needs to be done, someone has to do it, and if a faculty member is not too resistant they end up with that work. Unless you are very determined, you can be inducted into this army. The only effective defense is to be doing lots of research, traveling lots for scholarly reasons, and essentially passive when there are crises. Some people can do everything, so it appears that drag is not a problem for them.

People are subject to these temptations and drag. I do not see any institutional effort to control or reduce drag; it has become stronger over the years. Either we should find a way of reducing drag, or we should not tenure people who cannot resist it. More generally, if a faculty member cannot focus on research (and teaching), especially in their first dozen years, they should be encouraged to find a different career where their strengths are valued more appropriately. And we need to create institutional means of restarting people when they have been slowed down by drag, by illness, and by family crises.

296 Laying Golden Eggs: Long-Time-in-Rank Associate Professors

Long-time-in-rank associate professors may well lay golden eggs, fully deserving of promotion to full. Really strong, impressive, well-recognized achievements. This may be too strong a requirement for all long-time associate professors, but it is testimony to a faculty's capacity for renewal.

297 Getting Sandbagged and Slowed Down

If you are in a research university, and your promotion/tenure depends mostly on your research contributions, then when you become tenured and an associate professor (if that is the progression in your institution) you will find that you begin to get substantial service obligations, and maybe some greater teaching obligations, maybe grant-getting and more doctoral supervision. This is natural. But *you do not want to delay your getting to full professor.* So: If you are burdened with tasks that have extraordinary impact on your research time and contribution, make sure your chair and dean (and provost?) understand they are contributing to your being a longer-time associate professor than they would wish. And compensating released time to pursue your research should be built in. Also, you do not want to be dragged away from your longer-perspective research endeavor by too many short-term service obligations. Put differently: You are surely responsible for your work, but if the institution puts major roadblocks in your way they should so acknowledge and compensate you with the time you need for your work.

298   *Getting to Full Professor – Stoking the Fire in the Belly*

1. Continue to teach reasonably well, and if there are problems with your teaching, address them. You will surely have new service obligations, but there is no reason to have them overtake your research work. If they are so onerous, make an arrangement for future time off for research. Ahead of time. "I want to be sure to continue my research productivity and chairing the department is sure to kill it, so I want a semester off after two or three years." *Get it in writing,* and if you can get a year off, even better.

As for your research so you can be promoted to full, you need to do one more book, or one more suite of articles, or receive one more major grant and follow through on it. The venues are important, for you want your peers to notice your work. Peer recognition usually stokes fires nicely, and may even lead to some rewards.

You want to become more visible and recognized for your achievements, so that you now are sure to have a national or international reputation.

2. If you were tenured to associate but it was a marginal case, you want to show the world that you appreciated their faith in you. Lots more real work, nothing marginal this time around. *Clear the decks; focus on a major project.*

3. If it was a mistake that you were tenured, and you really do not have a research career ahead of you, find another position at a place that appreciates your strengths. *It's no fun being a longtime associate professor.* Do not worry about prestige; focus on what will make the best use of your strengths.

4. It is crucial to realize that having achieved tenure, you are expected to do even more, to accelerate your contributions, especially if your university is ambitious. If you cannot keep up the pace, find another position where you fit better.

5. You'll want to get the kind of mentoring you already have received as an assistant professor, or should have received, to help you move for-

ward toward full and then upward. Find that sort of mentor. You may not have the right intuitions about what to do. The most distinguished members of your department or elsewhere can be helpful.

6. If you have been successful, but others think you are undeserving, for whatever reason, just keep doing your work. You may well not be terrific, but continuing to be productive is a powerful answer to doubters and troublemakers. And in five years those others are as likely to fade away and a new audience will appear. In the end *the fire in your belly is best fed by the all-consuming work you do.*

299   *Becoming a Full Professor*

Assistant professors, in universities with real tenure tracks, have a period to show their independence (from their doctoral training) and their capacity to contribute significantly to the scholarly endeavor. Rarely do they do their best work during this period. But by the end they should evidence that independence and contribution. They should also evidence that they can teach well enough so that they are likely to become stronger in time. And that they have a promising research trajectory.

Typically, the full professor is someone with a national reputation, with another substantial contribution above and beyond what they did for their tenure and to associate promotion, whose teaching is reasonably good, and who has served the university and wider scholarly community. If grant-getting is part of the position, they have gotten the right grants from the right places. If they are going along in the usual six-year associate track, teaching and service may not need be given much weight, but if they are spending 12–15+ years in rank, all sorts of other considerations may play a role.

If you do really important work, at any stage, or if you get offers from peer or better institutions, all bets are off. The offer reflects an appreciation of your larger impact on the field. As for really important work, it is sometimes hard for deans to recognize this, but in fact the external world does so quite readily. In fields where books are important, if you publish those books more swiftly and the reviews are strong, there should be no problem in promoting you early. The same is true for articles, although prominence of venue and impact of research matters.

Ideally, one continues being productive as a full professor, although some people do not fulfill their promise. (In the University of California system, with its steps, the evaluation process continues until retirement – and you can be "decelerated," your progression delayed. Other universities indicate growth and development by salary increments, and your salary might stagnate.)

As for people being ready for full, think in terms of a rich vein of publication and research beyond their assistant professorship. Deans have promoted people without that rich vein since they took the promotion to be a matter of time in the rank of associate professor and reasonable performance. Nowadays, that will not fly.

300 *Promotion to Full: Your Personal Statement*

What is essential is a well-defined and well-developed nationally recognized contribution to scholarship in your field. *There is no rush about promotion to full,* so committees will tend to ask that you do what you should, and not make exceptions. Take another year or two, they might say. If you have a job offer from a peer or better institution, then we have a different situation. They may go all out to keep you happy. Earlier performance standards, set minimally by some people promoted over the last decade, are not relevant.

They want to see:

1. Independence and leadership.

2. Visibility. When we write to letter-writers, we really do not want to discover they never heard of you before.

3. Books or articles that have been out, for a while, so their impact might be assessed.

4. A clear justification for promotion. There is less reluctance to ask candidates to make up for deficiencies and come back in a few years.

5. *Clear achievement.* Write yourself a two-paragraph description of your contribution to scholarship since you were tenured. Describe your contribution to joint work.

6. The number and placement of your doctoral students.

301 *Social Promotion*

There might be an argument made that the person is tenured already, and that after a while we might as well not hold them back. But, one wants to send the right message to more junior colleagues. Senior lateral appointments are often very impressive. And many internal promotions are impressive as well.

302 *Promotion to Full Professor*

1. Have a national reputation for your contributions, recognized in letters from distinguished scholars at major institutions.

2. Contributions are well defined and deep. There is a substantial contribution since tenure, or the tenure contribution is so preeminent that we recognize that (this is rare, but quite possible – the great first book that becomes a classic, and the author is stuck, yet is more highly recognized than most full professors with many books).

3. Clean up your CV.

4. Aim for some publications in a wider venue than specialty journals.

5. Obtain external funding or fellowships, with leadership in such. Awards, perhaps.

6. Teaching is OK, same for service. If there are problems, they have been dealt with. If teaching or service are primary contributions, are they nationally recognized? Is there a reason for local contributions to be extraordinarily recognized?

Teaching includes mentoring doctoral students and placing them in strong institutions.

7. Standards rise. We might imagine a candidate who is caught in such a rise and who will not catch up. A dean might delay promotion for a while. Or if the junior faculty is stronger than the seniors, make sure salaries reflect that. You probably do not want to promote associate professor X whose résumé is less distinguished than that of assistant professor Y – or Y might get the message that Y should go to another institution.

303   What to Say to Senior Faculty When the University Is on the Make

"Some of our more junior faculty are resetting the bar: grants, article venues, quality, awards. Many of them are poised to become very strong – perhaps they need a few years to develop grant historics, deeper research records, greater independence. They are launched. We believe you are able to contribute to the advancement of the school. Let's think together how you can be part of the school's growing excellence. [Implied is that they will otherwise be left behind.] *What should you stop doing, and where should you focus your energies?* Let's make a goal list for the next six months or year, and meet to be sure we are meeting those goals."

304   No Faculty Member Is beyond Redemption

Some faculty members get stuck, for whatever reason, and do not move forward in their research or teaching. Find out what happened, talk to them, deal directly with the issue. Perhaps the university can enable them to get back on track. Maybe they can collaborate with their colleagues. Perhaps they can take on university administrative duties where they might make a contribution. All will feel better about themselves.

It is not a matter of being brilliant. Most of us cannot be brilliant. But we contribute to the research and teaching enterprise with high professional skill. If we cannot do that, both we and the university are best off if we find another role.

305   Retirement: Moving to Another Role Elsewhere

For some faculty, retirement or moving elsewhere are well-planned processes, reflecting a sense of what they want to do next and their financial capacities. But for many faculty, it is not easy to decide about retirement. At some point you may find that teaching and research do not motivate you. It is perhaps time to look elsewhere. You may want to die with your boots on, but your current boots hurt your feet. Or you may be ready for a less pressured life, with greater control over the demands you place on yourself. What's crucial is to realize that retirement and moving allow you to do new things – but of course, what are those new things? For many of us, there is no good answer to that question and we might not discover an answer, if there is one, until we retire.

All of this is bromides. I wish I had better wisdom about retirement and changing roles.

306   *Appointing Star Professors and Those with Unconventional Careers*

1. Stars know everyone, so the letters of reference will not be so arm's-length. For perspective, it would be helpful to find out how the star is perceived as weak.

2. Often, the main issue, and this applies more generally, is unconventional careers. If someone is first tenured at an institution, and then leads one of these unconventional but successful careers (in government, in management, in foundations), we surely will promote them. So the issue is about new appointments.

3. Stars sometimes lack a second line of research or a major monograph beyond the dissertation. There are two cases here: those who promise one, and those who do not. In the former case, it is vital that they be encouraged to deliver.

Consider the following cases I am aware of in medium-ranked departments:

- Adams – no second line of research yet, though promised ("promised" here means anything from a few chapters written to a good complete draft). Very high profile.
- Brown – no second monograph yet (but chapters available). High profile, major contribution to the institution.
- Crockett – published lots including second major project, brought to university by deans, enormous energy to organize new research unit in her field.
- Dawn – no second monograph yet (manuscript available though), enormous energy in innovative work beyond the first project, big contribution to university.

· Elton (brought to the department's attention by dean) – lots
 of writings, but work is more popular than scholarly, in
 effect a successor to Vance Packard or Thorstein Veblen.
· Fonda (brought to department's attention by dean) – after
 first monograph changes career path, no second monograph
 likely (although there is talk about one), national institutional
 presence is wide and currently at top of the heap.

People examining these departments would consider these scholars
as prime assets. At the same time, more junior people might feel that
these people are getting away with murder, not having done what the
junior people must do to get promoted. These unconventionals receive
angelic dispensation for having done something of great distinction,
having taken a risk most people do not take. And the university probably
figures it can do better with such angels than by trying to always have
more conventional scholars. The more conventional plodding-scholar is
the foundation of our fields, often produces very important scholarship
several times in their career, and is devoted to the field and the institution. They are only plodding compared to the stars, but they really are
what we are in the business of fostering.

307   *Senior Faculty Visibility*

At research universities you get promoted to full professor because you
are now highly visible. You have published that second (or third, or
whatever) book or kept that continuous stream of federal funding and
scholarly articles. People in your field cite your work and regard it as important to the future of the field. You are also expected to have become a
successful mentor: of your PhD students (did you get them through their
dissertations? where have they landed jobs?); and, increasingly, of junior
faculty. Being a good teacher and good citizen is expected.

If you were once highly visible, you are likely to stay that way, if only
by your past reputation. But you will be dismissed by the cognoscenti if
you keep doing the same research (which you consider deep and others
consider repetitive), if you have become a dean or head of an organization (being known for your leadership is OK, but the junior faculty will

still dismiss you as not doing real research), if you spend your life in the Academic Senate, if you have not published important work regularly, if you have become a successful screenwriter and you were once a professor of English (in Los Angeles this is a distinct possibility), if you reside far from the centers of academic power (the flyover cities) and have not been present and effective at meetings and published lots, if you now run a successful consulting firm and make lots of money.

You now need to do what you once did: the fieldwork, the research, the thinking, and the publishing. This means that every 10–15 years or so you are likely to change your focus; you carve out time to write even if you are dean/Senator/Oscar-winner; you go to the major meetings and actually deliver scholarly papers; your students do the same and they get premier jobs and publish as well; you write articles and books drawn from your consulting work. I imagine if you are Henry Kissinger or Condoleeza Rice, you do not care for any of this advice, as you have other ambitions.

If you want to restart your research career, you have the advantage of experience and judgment and tenure and security. So you can take risks. You have to work as hard on your research as you did when you were starting out, but with less anxiety. And you have to allow two to four years for it to bear fruit. Most deans and provosts, when informed of this sort of strategy, will be delighted and will try to help you.

What matters is discipline, focus, and ambition. *Just go to work.* Start a new project, do the work, give papers at meetings about it, publish the articles (and endure the rejections by journals).

This is a highly competitive enterprise. *People are coming up all the time, and they crave your reputational assets, and they are out to kill your achievements by overshadowing them with their own.* They honor you, but then they bury you. Still, you have an enormous advantage over your junior colleagues and you can take advantage of it.

The great part is the library, the classroom, and the laboratory. *We're lucky to have jobs in these institutions.* What we need to do is to take advantage of the possibilities they offer.

Now, you may have significant obligations to others such as children and parents, you may have chronic illness or disability or depression and the like. You may suffer from substance abuse and alcoholism. You may have fallen in love, finally. (Or gotten that third divorce.) Tragedy may have struck more than once over a short period of time.

It's hard to do much of what I suggest at these times, although a regimen of regular work may well be the equivalent for you of jogging. The best discipline is to do the work regularly, promote it suitably, stop answering your e-mail, and have a sense of what comes first – the work and the writing and the fieldwork.

TEN

Scholarly & Academic
Ethos (#308–391)

A. FUNDAMENTALS

308 *No One Ever Does It on Their Own*

Some of you may wonder if it is you or your professor who gets you a job. First of all, no one in academic history ever got a job purely "on their own merit." Others who had authority had to put the weight of their experience and authority behind them. Second, there are many strong candidates for any single position. The chosen one is to some extent arbitrary. Put differently, many are deserving, but you do not necessarily get what you deserve. And sometimes someone who seems less qualified gets the job (mistakes are made; people may not say what they really want). Finally, you may well be one of the mistakes who are chosen. That is of no matter, for then you must live up to the expectations of the position, and presumably you will do so.

So, you ought to be grateful for the support of your advisor or others who have helped you. It mattered enormously. But it is you who are being hired and it is you who got the job.

309 SEND *and Die*

Of course you should act on injustice, unfairness, and wrongs. But: *Never give weapons to your enemies.*

If you have given them weapons, immediately sue for peace, make abject (and if necessary public) apologies, and hope for the best. Your enemies, if they are smart, will graciously accept your apologies. But do not be surprised if ten years later you find that you end up in a cul-de-sac, with none of their fingerprints on it.

If you write a letter to someone in which you say things you eventually regret, you can express your apologies, you can hope they accept them, but you can't take it back. At least with letters, you might tear up the letter and not send it. With electronic mail, we tend to be less circumspect, and so we are more likely to say things and in ways we might well regret – and we usually hit the SEND button before we have a chance to delete.

If you broadcast the letter or e-mail, you will find it much harder to recover.

Do not make threats unless you are willing to follow through on them. If you plan to go to the boss, be confident the boss will not summarily throw you out of the office.

If you have done this before, assume people have long memories, and are quite willing to bring up your past behavior. You don't want to give weapons to your enemies.

310   *Trapped in a Seminar*

1. The best seminars I attend are disciplined by the presence of other colleagues, many of whom are very smart. But most of the time, ten minutes into a talk, I want to be someplace else. I ask myself, Why am I here?

2. There are many reasons to attend scholarly meetings. But it would be wonderful if we could just look at the papers ahead of time, and then meet to ask questions and argue. Much the same is true of university meetings, where a well-prepared memo would set things up for discussion.

311   *Feynman on Conference Disasters*

From a letter of the physicist Richard Feynman to his wife: "Remind me not to come to any more gravity conferences" (*What Do You Care What Other People Think,* 2001, p. 91).

He refers to discussions in which:

1. The work is completely un-understandable;

2. Conclusions are vague or indefinite;

3. Something that is correct and obvious is worked out by a long and difficult analysis;

4. It is claimed that some obvious and correct fact is in fact false (the author being stupid);

5. An attempt to do something probably impossible, but certainly of no utility, is in the end shown to fail;

6. The work is just plain wrong.

Now this was about general relativity, but the list applies elsewhere as well. He describes participants as being like worms trying to get out of a bottle by crawling all over each other.

312 *What You Should Have Learned in Graduate School*

1. *You are always being judged.* In your classes, in your papers, in your class presentations, in your interactions with others. If you do first-rate work, people actually notice. If you are sloppy or impolite or unprepared or mediocre, people also notice.

And there are always a few people who actually do a first-rate job, so the standard is set and it is quite high.

2. *You are always expected to deliver.* If you make an appointment, plan to show up early. (This way, there is no story to be told about traffic or weather.) If there is tragedy in your life, you are likely to be cut some slack. But it is up to you to take charge, let people know how you are dealing with the delays.

Do not tell people that what they expected of you was less important than something else. If you have one overarching task, you may not be able to reliably take on another.

3. The connection between being judged and your delivering is that *people will not rely on you if you do not deliver.* And if they will not rely on you, you will have fewer opportunities and less desirable ones.

4. We do live in a busy world, with many countervailing pressures. And many people can multitask quite successfully. What you do not want to do is to do a mediocre job where you believe it counts. You prob-

ably will have to cut down your list of tasks to those that really matter. (I find that I can do teaching, writing, and family. That's it.)

313 Sabbatical Means Always Having to Say No

If you are on sabbatical, you are likely to have a well-defined set of tasks, set by the memo in which you requested the sabbatical leave. *The big secret to getting your work done, the tasks you set yourself, is to say no whenever you are asked to do anything else.* Almost everything else you are asked to do is worthwhile and important, and even urgent and compelling. But the set of external demands is unending, and you will not finish even a fraction of your tasks if you ever say *yes*.

Most people do not do most of what they say they will do on their sabbatical. In part, there is a natural urge to exaggerate one's potential achievements. But they also say *yes* too often. You do have to tend to your doctoral students. And you do have to write letters of reference. But after that, what you have to do is the tasks you set yourself.

Note that personal and family issues may also come up, and they are unavoidable and must be attended to. (They are not part of your sabbatical.) So sometimes you will not get to all your tasks for these reasons.

314 Taking One's Own Advice

A colleague pointed out that I would be better off taking my own advice. I like to think my advice is not merely compensation for my own deficiencies, but is objectively useful.

In any case, advice offered abstractly is just that, abstract. One makes a complex set of choices, and balances prudent advice with other prudent advice.

315 Machiavellian Advice

If you are in a bureaucracy, where schemes are hatched and people play for keeps, and some people are likely to be two-faced or diabolical or viciously prejudiced:

· Play Good Boy (or Girl).

· The fewer opinions you express, the better.

· Every opinion is a black check.

· Opinions are expensive.

· Sugarcoat all.

· Tell them what is politic.

None of this will save you if *they* are out to get you, if they feel that you are "not one of us" and want to send you on your way. And of course you will have decent and courageous colleagues who will try to do right even if that proves unavailing.

316 *Human Tragedy and Compassion*

There are circumstances where with your best efforts things do not turn out the way you planned. Foolishness, vanity, and stupidity are frequent enough in our lives. Death, divorce, love gone awry, and the like will affect you for very long times. We discover that we have chronic illnesses, or soon-fatal conditions. They can be devastating. You do not just "get over it." And there are many events and times which are merely not good.

Not everything can be cured or even much ameliorated. And of course, there is the sublime, the sacred, or the just plain fun.

These are facts. It is how you handle them that will denominate your life and your sense of yourself.

Still, much of your everyday life cannot be put on hold. On farms, some of the time people cannot meet the challenge of everyday life, and their neighbors come to their rescue. Religions have formal mourning rituals, often forbidding your doing any everyday work for a week, say, while your neighbors come to your aid and consolation. So the issue is never absolute.

And *the trucks are coming*. Some of the time people actually get hit and go splat. You do your best, but some of the time you cannot get out of their way.

317   *Resilience, Focus, Direction, Perseverance*

You are going to get rejected, you are going to be tempted by lots of interesting projects, you are going to have too many of your own, and you are going to get discouraged by your own projects – everyone I know is in these situations some of the time. You will succeed if they do not defeat you. Brains or technical skills are no match for depression or brittleness. So, if you are resilient, can focus your energies, and persevere, you are likely to do much better than your very smart but more brittle colleagues.

318   *Patience, Resilience, Courage*

"There are many brilliant people . . . but those who end up having sustained artistic careers are not necessarily the most gifted. . . . The ones who survived combined brilliance with more homely virtues: patience, resilience, courage." (Joan Acocella, *New York Review of Books*, 15 March 2007, p. 31)

319   *Is There a Substitute for Brains?*

When I read a fine piece of work, whether it be in history or in natural science or in literary studies, this "off-scale" work knocks me out. It is so terrific.

On the other hand, most of scholarship depends on our collective efforts, bits and pieces adding up, checking out each other. A dean might mobilize the existing faculty to do better, and perhaps to work together or more coherently to do much better. And you might train your students to be more effective so they get better jobs. You have sunk costs in your tenured faculty and current student body. It pays to develop organizational solutions much as Adam Smith describes in a pin factory.

And brains need to be focused, on time, disciplined, of high integrity, professional. (A few of the most successful people are also scoundrels and toadies and opportunists, but let us ignore that strategy for the moment.) At the highest level of play, sheer talent surely matters. But, again, it pays to show up on time, be focused.

There are many sorts of "brains" or intelligence. I am not arguing for any particular form of intelligence or even for smartness. (Mike Rose's *The Mind at Work*, 2005, describes a variety of such skill-intelligences.)

320   *Untreated Illness and Work*

If you have untreated illness, it is likely to make it much more difficult for you to do scholarly work, work that depends on our ability to focus and act autonomously. Get the help you need. Some illness can only have palliative care, but that is worth having. Under-medicating is often worse than no medication. So you have to be a compliant patient. And some illness is tragic, with consequences that are overwhelming. There is nothing simple to do.

With chronic illness, or illnesses that last for more than a week or two, you have to acknowledge that they do affect what you can do. And then you find ways of doing what you must do. Some just push their way through. But at least for many of us, it is best to acknowledge there are limits, and to then work within those limits. Some disorders, such as anxiety, are treatable with medications or various therapies. There's no romance to schizophrenia. The same is true for alcohol.

Chronic illness or fatal illness is not a sign of poor morals or divine intervention. They might be treated, to some extent, the chronic nature of the illness being something you learn to cope with. Work can be a powerful defense against some chronic illnesses.

321   *Failure and Bouncing Back*

Hitting bottom might well crush you, but it might be the occasion to bounce back. The problem is to find the right pond, the place where your talents and inclinations work. People who do not do so well as artists end up thriving as journalists or movie executives. Universities have many faculty who are unable to move themselves out of their tenured positions to find places that would be more rewarding for them. The veneer of success and respectability many of us wear may well hide genuine hardwood (albeit for a different role), not just a foam core and a rotted soul.

322 *Creativity*

You are more likely to be creative if you have mastered your craft, know lots of examples, and have lots of experience. Systematic hard work, delivering on time, perseverance, and carefulness also contribute. Bright ideas usually have been expressed before, so it helps to have a good feel for what people already know. The real trick is to take bright ideas or applications and push them forward, to adapt them to new circumstances, and to persist in the face of boredom, disinterest on the part of others, and apparently overwhelming difficulties. It helps to be less bound to convention for whatever reason. It helps even more not to be worried about being original or creative.

323 *Whatever You Need Is in the Room. Do Not Go Home without Testing Out Your Ideas*

Edwin Land is said to have recommended that you should not go home from the lab without that very day testing out your newest ideas. And that whatever you need to do your work is in the room. You ought not to wait, but to find out if those ideas are fruitful, then and there.

Do a pilot study or a rough draft now. You will know better if it is worth doing more.

324 *Pronto Prototyping*

I had just begun a new photo documentation project. I had an idea about how to do it, and had seen some models by others that were inspiring. What I did, immediately, was go out and spend a day, actually a few hours, doing some experiments. I had the film developed and printed that day, and I could immediately see what was going on, what was good about my idea, what needed to be changed. Not that I know what I am doing, yet. But I am much further along.

My point here is that if you have an idea for a project, go out and do a pilot or a test as soon as you can. Better to do it before you go to sleep than to wait a few days. You will learn lots, discover which ideas are misconceived in their current form, and make room for new ideas and hypotheses. (The risk is that you reject good ideas too soon.) Still, the more precious the ideas, the more you should check them out pronto.

325   *Basics for Getting the Work Done*

1. If what you are doing is not the one thing you should be doing, you can't look effectively for the right one. Other people are, and they will beat you to the punch.

2. You have to give more than you receive. You want others to owe you, rather than you owing them.

3. You have to be low on crises, financially stable by being frugal, and low on drama. Then you might actually get work done.

4. Half of what you have to do is not enough. You might be trying, but no one has time to wait.

5. No excuses.

6. For the moment, ignore #1–5. Just do something, and get it done.

326   *E-mail and Your Reputation*

Your reputation is always on the line. Do not set yourself up. People are tired at the end of the day, and so they send out messages that do not serve their interests, but aggravate their problems. People decide to show that they can hurt others as much as they feel they have been hurt, rather than figure out what they really want to do and achieving that.

In general the best strategy when one is the recipient of such e-mail is just to ignore it, or to respond to it as if there were a more cogent message buried behind the unhelpful stuff.

327   *We Get Paid to Show Up*

We get paid to show up for faculty meetings, committee service, graduation, and other such ceremonial occasions, as well as for students, seminars, and talks. We also get paid to show up early or on time, and to say *yes* to the dean and provost. It is not OK to plan your trip, even your research trip or lab experiments, so that you cannot make it to graduation.

You always want to be in a position that they owe you, not the other way round. You want people to feel gratitude toward you, not resentment. It's not that you will not get promoted, although in some schools resentment seethes. Rather, you want to be on the side of the angels, so that when you need an angelic dispensation people will feel they owe it to you. And we all need such dispensations.

328   A Deeper Career

1. Describing the work of a mathematician (who passed away comparatively young): "I will never forget Tom's lecture at Princeton, in which he simultaneously solved three outstanding open problems in this area, not previously known to be mutually related. Tom published few papers, but several of them went as deep as the human mind can go" (C. Fefferman, quoted in T. H. Wolff, *Lectures on Harmonic Analysis*, 2003, p. vii).

2. In reading over some letters of reference, there is a uniform theme that I think is powerful (at least for this field): One is expected to publish a first book that shows the capacity to use original sources and to integrate what you discover with what is known, and in your book (almost surely based on your dissertation) to make a genuine and perhaps innovative contribution. However, it is your second book that shows your capacity to be deeper, more profound, more capable of taking on a big problem and producing master work. You have a wider range of references, better judgment, and more courage. You take on demanding and serious problems.

What does this mean for the dissertation student or the assistant professor starting out? Your dissertation and first papers are a windup, a practice, a first time, and your first book will seem flawed when you look at it 20 years hence. It is the quality of your subsequent projects that proves you. Your task is not just to get tenured, but to have a deeper career.

329 *Judgment and Maturity*

Timothy Gowers, in his *Very Short Introduction to Mathematics* (2002, p. 128), points out that what Andrew Wiles of Princeton needed to prove Fermat's Last Theorem was

> great courage, determination, and patience, a wide knowledge of some very difficult work done by others . . . and an exceptional strategic ability . . . a matter of careful planning: attempting problems that are likely to be fruitful, knowing when to give up a line of thought . . . being able to sketch broad outlines of arguments before, just occasionally, managing to fill in the details. This demands a level of maturity which is by no means incompatible with genius but which does not always accompany it.

These are matters as much of character as of knowledge, of thoughtfulness as of energy: courage, determination, patience, and careful planning and follow-through. They might say, "He's just a really smart guy, and people know I like really smart guys." But in the end, does your colleague deliver?

330 *Doing What You Are Supposed to Do*

I have over the years not done lots of things I have been supposed to do. I am a survivor, so to speak, of many mistakes, a fortunate survivor. But my path is not recommended.

331 *Awkward Letters and Memoranda*

1. Reference letters: One is evaluating, comparing, discussing the significance of work. These are judgments which you are entitled to make. There are almost always stronger elements, even for weak candidates, in every dossier as well as weak elements. It is up to the departmental and university committees to balance these considerations, so what is needed is the factual statement of your judgments and why you make them. Whether someone would get tenure at your institution is a judgment, as is your comparison with other scholars. Those judgments should be supported by evidence, but they are not claims larger than your judgments. Yes, letters have to be substantive and supported by evidence. In fact,

having provided the reasons for your judgments, which presumably are sensible ones, you insure yourself against liability.

2. A memo to the dean or provost saying that their request that you serve on one more university committee will get in the way of your doing an article on T will at least make that person aware of the facts. And if it is in your file, even with no reply from the dean or provost, it will be effective. More to the point, to say how you planned to use your time to do the article, and saying that the extra task precludes it, is evidentiary. Such a memo can be written in a tone that is not legalistic, but rather elegiac about lost opportunities. ("I am glad to teach a fourth course this semester if it serves the needs of our department. But I hope the university appreciates the fact that as a direct consequence, the article I am writing on my current research will not be done in time for my tenure review." Or, "I will need to have released time from teaching next semester so that the article I am writing . . . will be submitted and reviewed in time for my tenure review.") Finally, minority or women faculty members, who tend to be put on more than their share of committees, ought to request compensation in released time from the dean or provost or chair. Actually, deans ought to offer that without being asked.

B. EXCELLENCE

332 Excellence and Politics: Playing in the Big Leagues

Be aware of your competitive position within your department, and the position of your department in the university, and the university among other universities.

The way you get stronger is through decisive and blunt judgments that allow you to redirect your energies more fruitfully. *Better the humiliation of a corrective than going down a losing path.*

Try hard not to get publicly involved with internal politics. (You may well need to get involved, but maybe you do not want to leave behind your fingerprints?) *You are always better off being so strong you do not need your institution.* Do they owe you? Or, do you owe them? On the other hand, you do need *an* institution.

333 *The Rules of the Game*

Over the last decades the university has been more demanding of its faculty, and as a consequence the quality of the university has improved (in research, in research funding, in quality of students, in jobs those students get in academia). That trajectory is likely to continue and perhaps even be accelerated. And our standards for promotion and tenure have become correspondingly more sophisticated. Senior people say they are not sure they would be tenured were their dossier to come up today – although I believe that given the more sophisticated standards those people would have risen to the occasion.

334 *Reputation: You Have Only One Chance*

As a student, you really had only one chance. People may well reschedule a missed meeting or give you an incomplete. And if you submit work that is extraordinary, they might even forget your missing the deadline. But once you are shown not to be available, how can others rely on you? You may have good reasons for not delivering or showing up, but did you call ahead to announce them? Did you leave early for the appointment? (Humility, and a sense of their own failings, might convince others to be forgiving. But, again, how do they know you will be reliable?)

If you come up for tenure or a third-year review, and you are not up to snuff, yet they give you a pass, will you deliver in the end, or will you always be late, with too little, and with excuses? (Again, there are remarkable exceptions.)

Of course, you can change. You can become scrupulous in delivering, being on time, in quality and rigor. And people will forgive your past behavior. They may even forget. America is a nation of second marriages, or new starts, and the frontier.

You are likely to pay for your past lack of diligence. (I know I have.) But at least you can go forward with head high and a sense of your own integrity and value.

335 *Goldman Sachs Described*

Terms used in several 2007 *New York Times* (15, 19 November) articles about Goldman Sachs, the Wall Street firm: elite culture; sense of close-knit partnership; bright people; weeds out people ruthlessly; personal coaching; pursuit of excellence; building a culture; manage risks with a strong controller's office; smart people.

Several years later, those terms have a different valence.

336 *They're Judging You All the Time*

The world of work is judging you all the time, perhaps unfairly. Present yourself so that you have the best shot at being seen in the best light. Do not set yourself up for disaster. Have people feel indebted to you, so they go the extra mile for you. They may never have to go the extra mile, but it is that extraordinary help that makes the difference in your life.

337 *The Impression You Make on Others*

Your reputation for quality and integrity is always up for grabs. You don't want to appear sloppy and inconsiderate. Always be prepared, on time, tactful. None of this should be surprising. It is what you must have been taught by your parents. And if you have made an error, admit it and do your best to get back on track. People are forgiving most of the time.

338 *Your Reputation Is on the Line Each Time You Make an Appearance*

I am impressed by how vividly and precisely one is evaluated. Every time you make an appearance – in writing, in a talk, in e-mail – people are evaluating you. Minor errors do not matter. And even major mistakes or calamities need not be probative – if you do not repeat them. But in general if you are on time with your work, it is polished, and you are focused – and you are consistently so – you and your reputation will benefit enormously. As a friend who survived the fascist regimes of the '30s and

'40s would say to me, Never give weapons to your enemies! I would only qualify this by saying that you do not want to give plutonium cocktails to your allies either.

This is serious. It was obvious to us when I was a student. My teachers were not polite. Nowadays I think we are more polite – but do not mistake politeness for forgiveness or being nonjudgmental.

339 *Work That Matters*

You will be asked two sorts of questions in your first job interview, when you come up for tenure, and years later. What is your contribution to scholarship, to the field, to the practice? What do you plan to do in the next few years?

Letters of reference need to be authoritative and detailed. Train people to talk about you and your work in the ways that you find most effective. That means they need to be able to answer the first two questions about you for themselves. Give your letter-writers lots of lead time. Make it easy for them to help you. *Do not give people a chance not to be able to help you.*

You will develop a stronger reputation if you do substantial cumulative projects rather than bits and pieces of all sorts. It will serve your interests to make your next project have a natural connection to your previous one (perhaps methodologically rather than in subject matter). Cumulation and coherence make it easy for people to understand what you do. The artist Frank Stella has done a series of about 150 works, one for each chapter of *Moby-Dick,* over a period of about ten years. The works are diverse, but there is a mode of putting them in a series or sequence or whole that then gives a sense of cumulation and achievement.

Fear and anxiety about a task can prevent you from trying. Try to do what would appear to be a monstrous task to see if it is actually at least doable in an approximate way. Allow yourself to play, to have a chance to try something without claiming you really know what you are doing – of course, eventually, you'll have to deliver the goods, but that is eventually. And as is my wont, once I have a first draft, I can go to work.

340   *Academic Assets, Reliability*

Make sure your contribution is clear and distinguishable from previous contributions by others. Make sure you have a real asset in your work. You can know stuff that no one else knows because you went and looked, did the modeling, ran the programs, and did the proving.

Now, if your work becomes interesting, others will want to be sure you are right, especially if they disagree with you. They might go back to the archives and check out what you quoted from. They might ask if your numbers are too sensitive to your parameters. They might look closely at your data set. You really do not want to have your doctorate revoked or to lose your professorship.

341   *Fairness and Rewards*

When it rains, the drops do not choose to land on you. You just happen to be in their way. It makes sense to do a very good job in your work. But the rewards are rarely proportionate or even in step with your achievements. People who receive lots of rewards and are very successful are likely to be deserving, but there are many folks at least as deserving who do not receive those rewards. Hence just because you are successful, does not imply that you are especially deserving.

You might wonder why you did not get a job for which you were particularly suited. The most likely hypothesis is perhaps unsettling. Appointments are made through committees and discussions among members of a faculty. In general the second-best candidate is more likely to have great support given the variety of criteria and concerns of a group of people. Such a group rarely makes an optimal choice; rather it chooses the most qualified, least obnoxious candidate.

342   *Pushing for Excellence and Preeminence*

1. Increase student quality – especially by going around the GRE, SAT, and GPA measures. Seek out exceptional talent, experience, focus.

2. Faculty is a sunk cost with no short-term way of being altered. Triage: identify those who perform exceptionally well, and ask them what they need to get to the next level; those who perform weakly, and figure out who can be moved up, who might be encouraged to find another position; those in the middle, who need more careful guidance about what is expected.

3. Raise the bar: stronger students mean that weaker ones have to meet new standards; same for stronger faculty. Tenure-track institutions will surely tenure people who are not so distinguished. So the standards might well be raised by external senior appointments. If you bring in someone who publishes twice as much as most of the faculty, they reset the standard. Same for national prominence. If you bring in three or four such faculty, you can raise the bar with greater confidence. Then you need to help the less strong faculty move up. But they may well never move up enough.

4. These ideas are draconian. It all depends on what you want to achieve. If it is a football team, my ideas are modest. If you are running an institution where solidarity always trumps excellence, I have little to say.

There is no substitute for brains, for focused energy, for publication in premier venues, for impactful contributions. *Doing good enough is not good enough in a competitive environment.* For while you are doing good enough, some of the competition is more ambitious, more focused, and more serious about excelling. Most faculty and students can move up at least one level or rank in their work.

Strategic plans tend to be corporate and bureaucratic. But if you are going to be Google, you have got to have a killer app, and you have to have first-rate people. I do not believe in corporate solutions (starting a research center, the strategic plan) unless they have behind them first-rate-plus people. Preeminence may be so far from where we could get in ten years that we may have to make more incremental steps.

343   *Excellence – How to Make the Football Team Proud of the University*

In a bureaucratic environment, standards are set for decent but not extraordinary performance. You do not want to stress the system too much, for then there will be errors and mistakes. You might be able to speed things up, but then you have problems of sabotage. This is as true for professors in a university as for workers in a factory or a coal mine. On the other hand, in sports for example, one expects the personal best from people as well as superb teamwork. Good enough is not good enough. This is also true for extraordinary music, fine arts, scholarship, and so forth. Hence, there will be people and teams and departments that are truly excellent, outstanding, they will have an ethos, and people who share that ethos, that demands focus, devotion, very high standards, a keen sense of the competition, hard work, and talent. And *coaching needs to be sensitive to individuals' limits and capacities. You don't want to push excellence to the point of demoralizing your faculty.*

Most people in college expect to be graded as if they are in a bureaucracy. The can ace a course by suitably figuring out the teacher, doing what is required in the syllabus, and not much more. They are not trying to excel, they are trying to ace the course. Or they aim for a C, with similar devices. Of course, they would like their neurosurgeon to aim to be excellent, superb, much beyond standard expectations. They want outstanding excellence. (It's not good enough that the surgeon just passed the specialty boards. The surgeon should be much better than that.)

I give assignments and teach and coach my students so that they have a chance to do truly superior work. That of course depends on their taking up the challenge, realizing that I do not have preordained standards for judging the work – rather the work they do demands my assent to its excellence (or not-so-excellence). If you expect me to tell you if the work is good enough, it may well be good enough and deserve a B. Some students have greater talent, are more coachable, or choose projects that give them a greater chance to do significant work. By the way, this is true for professors as well.

Some people work harder, or are less satisfied with what they do, than others.

We choose the arenas where we expect ourselves to truly excel by dint of our devotion to the problem, and arenas where good enough is good enough. A great sports team or a great university department depends upon unflinching honesty about where you really stand, and about what you must to do to be so excellent. You might not succeed, but if you tell yourself that you are excellent but are in fact not so, you will get nowhere. You might say something different in public, to sway the fans or the provost or deans, but if you tell yourself lies you will not be able to grow and develop.

344 *For Faculty Who Want to Do Well*

If you have recently been appointed or promoted, your dean and provost are thinking: Congratulations. Now it is time to prove that you are worthy of your new rank – get the book out, start publishing two to three papers a year, propose a major project and give me a time line for getting it done. You have the potential to do much stronger work than you have been able to do so far. We want to make it possible. Make goals and timetables and review them every six months. Drive, Focus, Achievement, Outcomes, and Good Judgment matter enormously. As for small or epsilon contributions' we know that N times epsilon is still epsilon no matter how big N is. What is your five-to-seven-year plan for making one or two substantial contributions to scholarship? If they are in teaching or service, they have to be major and nationally recognized (as we demand for our research). Keep in mind that at an ambitious research university, your external reputation is important, and that reputation has to be based on formidable research accomplishments.

If you do not want to play in the big leagues, now is the time to go to another university more suited to your ambitions. You will do better that way.

345 *Playing at an Extremely High Level*

Every person who plays one of the positions on a contending team plays at "an extremely high level." Note: this is not a matter of being sufficient, but a matter of excellence. "An extremely high level" makes concrete what we want from our faculty without using words such as *genius* or *brilliant* or whatever.

A competitive nature and a culture of personal best characterize the most serious academic circles. Doing just enough (getting a book published) is not enough. Is what you have done performed at an extremely high level? And have you continued to perform?

By the way, you can choose to play in B leagues or C leagues, since you have other values than those required to play successfully in the A league. Still, in your own league you need to play at an extremely high level.

346   *Bonuses*

1. Bonuses paid to Wall Street types are supposed to reward them for successful risk-taking, encourage their doing their best instead of resting on their laurels, and invest assets in the people that earn the biggest returns. People might game the system, or their risk-taking may bankrupt the firm next week or three years down the line, so we might have clawbacks. Say the university froze faculty salaries, and then made all increments bonus-based, going up or down depending on performance in the last five-year period. Note that the competition is not your close colleagues, it is the whole university's faculty, and indirectly that of all other peer universities. Right now, probably no more than a third of the faculty contributes to the highest production. Many people would benefit from focusing their minds.

How do we become stronger as a whole, and how do we maximize the performance of our fixed assets of people? The gap between the strongest faculty and the middling is very large. There is lots of solidaristic rating, where everyone goes along to get along. (I would love to be assured that I am wrong about all this.) But this does not help a university's reputation. I understand how morale can suffer when people feel unappreciated. What we need is the stats pages of sports sections, but with appropriate measures.

2. We might encourage an outplacement program for faculty who do not have a strong future with us. Other places might well value them more highly.

3. We are in a competitive business, and top performance demands that we remain focused. Others are monitoring our performance. Every time the administration talks, that wanting to win big (in football, in

scholarship) is their theme. This is no sweet family when they are talking about the football team or the prominence of the university – for family solidarity, a wonderful virtue, will not make you preeminent. It may give you resilience and inner strength, and great values – which the provost and the president talk about too. And it may make for a good community. Those are important. But, again, they want to be number one.

347   *Global Warming of the Quality Temperature*

As a university gets stronger and attracts or retains more faculty with strong dossiers, what happens to the faculty and schools who do not keep up? In effect, we have global warming, the ice melts, and those lagging elements will be underwater in ten years. I suspect they could do much better, but they have to realize that the university's quality temperature is rising, and they will be inundated unless they find higher ground. The standards are not set in your department or school, nor are they set by the strongest people in your school or the average – they are in effect set in the national marketplace, and most immediately in the provost's office when the provost and committees review candidates throughout the university, and strong candidates reset the bar.

If you get time off from teaching for administrative duties, then you ought to have as strong a research profile as those who do not. *Research cannot account for less than 50 percent of your time in a research university.* (Probably this does not apply to full-time administrators.) The secret words are *May, June, July,* and *August* – what are you doing those months but your research? We live in a highly competitive academic world, and your university may want to be number one or two, and we are the team on the playing field. Whatever you may think of past promotions, the standards for the future are rising and are out of our hands. If this scares you, find another university, one that is less ambitious. If it excites you, realize that the university will encourage you with all its might.

When you make your list of references, cross off collaborators, teachers, your colleagues – all pinkie-length references. Just have arm's-length ones. People who can compare your work with the best, or with an appropriate cohort, and whose judgment will be seen as unbiased. When you review your CV, in general do not count articles in weak journals or book chapters. It is probably too stringent to say that if you have multiple-author publications with N authors, count each article as 1/N unless your coauthors are students or there are exceptional circumstances. Presumably the other authors will also want to count it as a publication. Write a two-paragraph description of your contribution to scholarship. If you have published outside the mainstream (other countries, other fields) are they in the right venues? Have you published in the premier journals, the best presses? Or, at least the recognizably appropriate specialized or idiosyncratic venues? And if your work has had little impact, why? You have to be the person who knows your strengths and your weaknesses – given the expectations and ambitions of your university. Weaknesses are not a problem as long as strengths are real. If you have had problems with teaching, have you addressed them aggressively? And, again, that someone with a weaker record has been tenured or promoted will not justify your promotion.

If we do not change, we will be underwater in ten years.

What I am saying is meant not to scare you, but to give you the information you need to thrive over your career. But if you do not like what I say, just ignore it. Perhaps I am wrong. If you follow my advice and I am wrong about your university, you'll be able to get a superb job elsewhere.

348   *Your Comparative Advantage*

If you read the artist David Hockney's autobiography, what is clear is that he took up the challenges of art school as the occasion to do first-rate work, in his own terms, whatever most of the other students were doing. Hockney's grade school report card was not in term of grades, but in terms of standing in his class. And sure enough he was first in art and rather more middling elsewhere.

Excellence demands minimal qualifications over a wide range of skills, peaks of quality and performance, and character and courage. Excellence demands your personal best. You are not competing with those in your classroom or your cohort. You are competing with a much smaller group of people who will excel in just those areas in which your advantage provides you with the chance to be excellent.

349   *Fame Too Late*

". . . he made many contributions in this area usually credited only to M. H. Stone. . . . His exclusion from his share of the limelight is due in part to being in Japan during the second world war, and even more to his insistence on using his own special terminology and failing to relate his work to that of others" (*Handbook of the History of General Topology,* vol. 1, ed. C. E. Aull and R. Lowen, 1997, p. 251).

If you are in a relative backwater and you do not adapt to the dominant mode of talking, your work is most likely not to be recognized. It is "too hard" to read; there is a community of others who are working the mainstream together; people wonder why you talk "funny." Moreover, every paper you publish that is marginal or not part of a coherent program of research is not so likely to be noticed and will not contribute to your reputation. *It does you little good to be discovered after you are dead.*

350   *Whether the Work Is Any Good at All*

Maybe the paper is not at all awful, but it is not good. So, polish up the sentences, so that one does not trip over your choice of words, and tell me up front what you are up to. Fix it the best you can, and then get criticism and help.

In reading a student's or colleague's paper, I tend not to make evaluative judgments. What is needed is craftsmanship and quite specific advice. The twentieth-century physicist Wolfgang Pauli said that some work was not even wrong. Usually, that is not the problem.

You may have a high IQ, but you are unlikely to be a genius. Dedicated, hard-working, thoughtful, and passionate about your work, but not a genius.

351   *Craftsmanship*

Academic craftsmanship has much in common with carpentry or plumbing or welding. Were we to have the ethics of the trades, we might understand better what it means to do our work. Do not delude yourself.

Welders have tragedies in their lives, they are busy. But the metal awaits them. You do not want the carpenter to use sawdust and glue rather than cut the hardwood to fit right.

If you are supposed to build houses, building lots of cute chicken coops does not count (i.e., writing a bunch of unrelated articles rather than conducting a coherent program of research). If you do not deliver, why should anyone want to give you a promotion, tenure, or whatever? I am sure you feel that way about your plumber. You should feel that way about yourself, and about your colleagues.

352 Annual Reviews

Your annual review statement cannot be exculpatory – excusing nonperformance. State in one paragraph your goals and contribution.

The strongest venues do not have room for all major articles and all monographs. Hence the demand for prominent venues will often be honored in the breach. (Note that book chapters, edited books, or reports do not count for much early in your career. If one of them is widely influential be sure to say that.) A list of publications is impressive when the publications are in the major journals. Do not delude yourself about which are the major journals.

353 No Complaints

Do the right thing, the first time. Everything counts – your showing up, your tasks, your remarks, your attire and grooming, your dissimulations, your gaming of the system.

Everyone has been treated unfairly, is too busy, and may well be angry. If you need to let off steam or complain, try it out first on a friend. No broadcast e-mail. If you have an idea for a project, test it out immediately. Write it down, check the literature, tell a friend, see if a small pilot study will tell you more. Never go to bed with an untested idea. Force the evolution of your work.

354   *Thanking Everyone*

I received the following note from someone who has been helpful to me in my work. I did not intend to slight his work, at all. But in scholarship, where your name is the signpost of your value, people are naturally quite sensitive if they are not explicitly recognized again and again.

"I saw your article in the *Journal.* I have to say I do not appreciate my contribution to a paper reduced to 'and collaborators.'"

I wrote back: "I am guilty. I would be glad to write a note to the *Journal,* and I shall do so. It is no excuse, but the sentence/paragraph I wrote referred back to the earliest papers by M. Ideally, I would have been able to have lots of references, but they wanted few and in fact there are none.

"In my book, of course, there is ample reference and naming, with some attention to the subsequent work by yourself. In the article, I do indicate in several places the role of your contributions albeit without naming you. And it must be especially galling to be elided over in a semi-popular presentation, where no one who is not expert would know who did what in what is a major discovery. The only compensating fact is that the work is referred to in the context of one of the richest lodes in science.

"You have been very supportive of my work, and I have been grateful for that. I do regret the elision. I'll do what I can to make up for it."

C. ON TIME

355   *How to Be on Time*

Arrive early, be prepared early. This may be five minutes early for a meeting, one day early for a presentation.

The only persons who are allowed to change the schedule are your bosses. Your peers are disrespectful and waste your time if they change the schedule, without notice well in advance. Bosses should not be flippant in changing schedules, but they are bosses.

You are always overbooked, and thereby always falling behind. But that means that most of what you are doing is unimportant. Do what is important, do not fit in stuff that need not be done, and always respect others' time and schedules.

No one should have to wait for your call to make an appointment. Rather, make an appointment and keep it. Not "Somewhere between 4–7, and I will call you at 3 to confirm." Cell phones have made people careless. It's not enough to call five minutes before you are scheduled to arrive and announce a one-hour delay. Even worse, someone wants to see you, but they cannot commit to a date and time and place a week ahead.

If you are on time, or even early, most of the time, the times when you are late will be excused. By the way, traffic is never a good excuse. Leave early. Bring materials to work on if you are early in arriving.

If you are often late, do not be surprised if people start to assume you are going to be late and begin without you, or leave for the evening before you arrive. Do not be surprised if your boss starts to leave you out of considerations. Do not be surprised if your dates find new partners. Maybe the Queen of England can get away with being late – but, as far as I can tell, she is always on time.

All of this is about common courtesy. In times when clocks mattered less, when life was "simpler," these concerns were not serious. But complex society depends on coordination, and clock-time is the device for doing so. There's competition in the world, and thems with the first-est most-est will trump you. Do not worry: someone does show up on time or early, they are ready and able, their work is excellent, and they are on to the next job.

All of this applies to friends, or to your family, as well as to work. If you have divided loyalties, then you had better figure out which ones will have to suffer and then expect to bear the costs. Or, you have to drop some of your obligations so you can fulfill the ones that matter. Again, do not worry – someone else will figure this out, and show up on time, always, with what counts.

It is not uncommon to find people in authority violating these rules. They are boors. The boss who shows up late for meetings, because he was on the phone, is a boss who does not win loyalty and support from the staff. Essentially, as Hegel said, the knight's failings are known to the servant.

You do not get away with anything. It's not karma. It's just that someone somewhere notices, and your reputation is besmirched.

356   *Nobody Procrastinates Their Way to the Top*

Now, you may not want to get to the top, but would settle for halfway up. The real issue then becomes, will you settle for one-tenth the way up? Universities will become less forgiving. There is a plentiful supply of scholars coming out of the system. If you are slow early on, there is little reason to believe you will speed up. That does not mean there won't be surprises, but you have little reason to expect them. Universities see themselves as competing in larger markets, and hence face tougher competition. What might have made for a fine local or regional institution, in 1955, is very different from what makes for a fine international institution today.

None of this is about killing yourself. It is about focused work, with well-defined goals, and a sense of your competition and mission. It does mean that you have to say *no* to lots of requests you make of yourself or others make of you.

357   *On Time vs. Late*

I am late because I do not stop doing something else sufficiently early so that I can be on time for my next obligation. What might you conclude from my being late (and perhaps from your own being late)? That I am not so good at managing my time, and I do not respect you very much or I am angry at you.

Yes, there are times when you are unavoidably late. But these are in fact rare. If you are consistently late, you have to ask yourself, how have I arranged my life to be late all the time? You should never be "too busy." "Too busy" means you have little sense of priorities, that you do not control your life at all, that the people you are dealing with do not count much to you. Being on time is a cultural phenomenon, and there are many cultures in which being a half-hour late is just fine. But clocks and being on time are part of complex bureaucratic societies, as they allow for coordination of many different activities and actors. It's the way we live now.

D. OVERLOADED?

358 *Focus*

Not everything has to be done, and the trick here is to say *no* to most opportunities, so that you can deliver intensely on what is most significant. That involves planning, having a sense of what matters, and learning to say *no*. Meetings and departmental retreats demand substantial time from the many participants, yet each of us has about 2,000–2,500 (maybe many fewer) work hours each academic year, without taking account of vacations, family emergencies, and commuting.

359 *Overloaded?*

Write a draft of the paper, now, without finishing all the work, so you have something you can work with. It may mean settling for less than perfect or ideal, so that you can get done. It may mean not doing everything. You want to shift yourself from overloaded to having lots of work, work that can be done piece by piece.

I am not counseling doing second-rate work. I am suggesting that if you are really overloaded, it is much better to do adequate work than collapse completely. And if you do a draft now, perhaps you will have time to fix it a bit later. Get in a decent job on time, even if it is not as good as you might otherwise do or like to do. It can have missing parts, but try to have it hold together as it is. Now you are in a more powerful position.

Your power lies in being in charge of yourself and your work. You do not want to ask for small favors; if you have to ask for a favor, you want to ask for a big one. And if you have been reliable and on time, you have built up the goodwill that makes granting the favor more reasonable. Your most precious asset is autonomy. Do not give it up.

360 *When the Task or Work (the Dissertation, the Book) Is Too Much*

If your book project is too much, perhaps it is time to write a summarizing article (do not even look much at what you have already written) that highlights the main point of the project. Aim for a broad audience in your field, make sharp statements, use poignant data or examples. You are unstuck, and you have put out a piece that will be important for the reception of your book. Give away all the main ideas. You can then go back to the book manuscript. This almost always applies to dissertations, unless the strategy is a way of avoiding finishing your dissertation. And if you need a book for tenure, start now!

If you have a series of articles in mind, just write one of them, now, and shepherd it into print. Right now, you need something doable.

361   *May, June, July, and August*

The most important words for a professor are *May, June, July,* and *August.* Now is the time to set reasonable goals for the summer. Do not piddle away the time with redoing the kitchen.

Summer is the time to start anew. In the end, *what counts is the work you do.* You discipline yourself by that work. Do not set yourself up. Match yourself to the work. I love writing and teaching and thinking – even rewriting, rewriting, rewriting (well, not always). If this work is for you, now's the time to reaffirm it.

362   *Time*

Of late I have had to think more than once about what I can do given the time I have available. Some of us may have more hours to devote to our work than do others – because our obligations may or may not include our parents, our family, service to the community, and so forth. It may not be difficult to discern those obligations (whether we wish we had them or not). We are welcome to violate those obligations, but then we usually pay – often immediately, sometimes in 20 years.

The crucial point is that the world (our colleagues, students, departments and deans, the community, scholarly societies) will lay claim to us as much as we are willing to give to the world, and then some. Yet, much scholarship depends on husbanding one's energies, focusing one's efforts, and saying *no* to much of the world, even if we are saying a big *yes* to some aspects of it. Scholarship need not be lonely, if your work is collaborative, but often it is – whether in libraries, at the desk, in the archives.

I keep discovering that I have to shed massive amounts of load – again and again. I do have a sense of the main projects I am working on. But, always, lots more legitimately begs for attention. And sometimes it may be appropriate to take it on and sacrifice either one's family or one's primary scholarly work. Still, there is the moment a few months later when you realize you have sold your soul, usually gratis. So you have to regroup, carefully figure out what matters, and gracefully exit from some of those secondary projects. Everything will not be fit in; some things need to be put aside.

It is awkward and perhaps even dishonorable to exit some projects. But in the long run, you must as a scholar be committed to your primary projects, those that you alone can do, those that contribute to the growth of knowledge and art and a better world.

The advantage of having a good sense of what you are up to is that such a sense acts as a compass. Still, I eventually let down my guard, or consciously take on projects that I feel are important even if they are not my primary ones. *So the processes of exit and load shedding are rather more recurrent and humbling that I would ever have expected.*

The good part is that over the years you do the most important work; you make the contribution that adds up, that does not lie undeveloped and unfinished. (Few of us can expect to have someone go over our unfinished manuscripts or projects and finish them for us – after we are gone, one way or the other.)

To play in those bigger leagues, you have got to do the work. If you do not, someone else will, and they will take up your shelf space without your having realized it.

363   *Time Management*

If you have to do something for tenure, do it now. If I get a grant and I have promised something, I try to be sure I have some version of that promised object sooner rather than later, and preferably much sooner. (By the way, *I have made every mistake in the book, and then some. If I talk to you about mistakes, I have surely made them, more than once.*)

The world is rich with possibilities and temptations, and it is your job to figure out where you must go, and how to say *no*. The best line is, "I am writing chapter 2 and need to focus on getting it done." If you can do it all, I have no objection. If you write between 8 AM and 12 noon each day, I really cannot tell you what to do the rest of the day, as long as you are back at your desk at 8 AM the next day and are ready to go back to work. The same is true for your lab, perhaps 8 AM–6 PM. Most of us are not quite so disciplined. And, usually, we need the rest of the day to be ready to write tomorrow.

364   *Scholarship and Community*

We are a community of scholars. We have to rely, in the end, on the integrity of our members, when we read their work, when we base our own work on theirs. Members whose integrity is problematic make that community much less effective. So, for example, in the natural sciences and the social sciences, faked experiments may mislead others, wasting their time as they try to find out "what went wrong" in their experiments. Claims without error estimates or sensitivity measures are of little value, largely because we do not know how reliable they are. In mathematics, a colleague who is not scrupulous finds that their work is no longer accepted (people want to have others provide proofs). And in philosophy if we discover that someone is reprehensible we wonder about their arguments and theories.

If a colleague holds to an ideological position that I find wrong but not reprehensible, I might still be concerned about whether their scholarly claims are reliable or whether they are unfairly selective in their evidence.

E. THE RESEARCH ENTERPRISE

365   *Success in This Life*

You work in a community of scholars who judge your work. You want them to appreciate what you do. You really do not want to be appreciated after you are gone. What this means is that you must connect your work with others' work, you must attend meetings and sell your ideas, you must keep in mind audience and venue. It pays to advertise. At the same time, it does not pay to antagonize folks gratuitously. Gracious criticism and blandishments, if they are not too obvious, are part of the enterprise.

If you are willing to be a lone soul, none of this advice applies. I have met virtually no one who is so willing, at least if they become scholars. I suspect that about half your time will be devoted to spreading the word, the other half to writing it.

Of course, you do have to do the work.

366   *Scholarship and Opinions*

1. If you publish on the op-ed page of any newspaper, no one expects your claims to be accurate and fair – even if you are a scientist. This is an opinion piece: presumably you have not libeled anyone, but surely you are entitled to strong opinions, supported by suitably woven evidence and quotes. Readers should be skeptical.

2. If you publish a book with a scholarly publisher, expert referees have vetted the manuscript. But if you publish a book with a nonscholarly publisher (and this includes most publishers), even very prestigious ones such as Norton or Knopf, there are no such guarantees. Presumably you stand behind your argument and footnotes, but outsiders cannot know if the text has been vetted. Reviews in the scholarly journals may be helpful. Academics also publish books, such as novels (and they are not professors of writing), in which their expertise as professors is not the main point.

367   *Scholarship Is a Competitive, Resource-*
Driven ($, Time) Enterprise

1. You are in an enterprise that is quite competitive for the top positions and prestige. *If you aren't working hard, your competition is.*

2. You have to raise money for your research. Never tell yourself you are in a field that does not get research support. If you are going to have graduate students, you are going to have to raise lots of money to support them.

3. Whole departments have been eliminated or folded into other units when the provost discovered that they did not raise lots of research money, their faculty was not the world's best, and they did not teach lots of undergraduates. Fields that justify low publication rates are then subject to comparisons with related fields that have much more robust publication rates. If you are in a department in which everyone has a well-endowed chair the pressures are different. When people say that research grants are not needed in this department since we are so robust financially (say, endowment, student income), they are not realizing that external research grants represent validation of one's excellence.

4. Excuses do not work. They do not bring you support. Excuses bring out the sharks, ready to eat you alive. What works is performance, job offers from other institutions, external research grants, restricted and big endowments.

368   *Politics: When You Have No Influence*

The economist Albert Hirschman spoke of *Exit, Voice, and Loyalty* (1970) as responses to difficult situations. My friends who have left their departments or universities for other departments or universities have chosen Exit. Usually Voice did not work, and Loyalty became difficult as they felt little influence in their former homes. A friend, who is also a dean, once said that he wanted to have a faculty that was hard to keep, where faculty members received offers from peer or better institutions and sometimes they did leave. More often than he would have liked. In fact his faculty were quite happy with their department, but a variety of factors (prestige, family needs, maybe money or honor) allowed them to Exit with honor.

Deans do not much like it if their faculty are looking for jobs elsewhere, especially their strong faculty. They can announce they will not meet offers (as one told me he did – but none of his faculty was about to leave for money; they left since Voice was impossible). But if you are not a player in the academic job market you will surely find the consequences undesirable in the long run.

Ideally when you come up for promotion, tenure, or whatever, you have in your back pocket a potential offer from another place, an offer you would take seriously. Or, you have gone out and looked and discovered that where you are is best for you. Or, you have gone out and looked and found a possibility you had not imagined but which bests your current position (with that promotion) for various reasons. You do not want to spend too much energy on such searches, but I imagine it makes especially good sense after you have been at one institution for, say, two decades, and you are still likely to have two more decades of productive career.

Most people do not move around much if at all. There is much to be said for a stable faculty in a university, but there is much to be said for the exchange of faculty among institutions. The fact of the matter is that you want not only to have a good job, but also to be appreciated. You may have to find a different pond in which to swim, if only because the pond you swim in now is murky and you are not appreciated much.

There may be much to be said for loyalty and commitment to an institution. But after many years your situation may have changed and it is time to move on. And for some faculty there is a period when they are offered many alternative positions, and they are right to appreciate that that period may not last.

In any case, do not lose touch with what really matters – teaching and scholarship. In the end, what matters are the students you teach and the productive research programs you pursue. Your classroom is more important than the curriculum committee. And your study or laboratory, and your books and articles beat arguments academics have about running departments or salary structures. Writing books, doing experiments, crafting articles, and proving theorems, as well as teaching students, is the best revenge on bureaucratic nonsense. In the end they are the only thing that matters.

369 Academic Tantrums

I recently had a sobering experience of the academic tantrum (AT). Tantrums are "fits of bad temper." I received a written communication attacking me ad hominem for my scholarly judgment. I responded in a conciliatory manner. No good deed goes unpunished, and I received back another AT, still ad hominem.

What to do?

1. There is much to be said for tearing up or deleting the original communication, and going on with life. ATers tend to CC their messages far and wide, usually to authorities. It still might make sense to just tear up or delete, but your reputation has been maligned in public. On the other hand the ATer is well known as such, and so perhaps your reputation has been enhanced.

2. You cannot win. Those who tantrum do so because they feel impotent, and they will continue to do so. They see the world as revolving around themselves. Mild paranoia, perhaps even warranted, goes along with the AT.

3. The ATer has much more energy for battle and engagement than you do. If they read a memo such as this one, they are sure you are writing about them (who else could be so righteous, so clear about your faults?).

If the ATer has decided you are their enemy, never give weapons to your enemies. Never respond at all. Delete or destroy the original message, be as anodyne or even obsequious to the ATer as you can be, and just wait.

370   The Cost of Gaming the System

Those who game the system believe that if they are smart enough, there is little harm in trying to get away with something. The worst thing that happens is that you pay a fine or you get your hand slapped. Why not ask for what you have been told you ought not to get? You may actually get away with it. But if you develop a reputation for gaming the system (and people seem driven to brag), you lose people's trust and willingness to rely on you. They become much more wary in dealing with you, putting up barriers and defenses, legal and procedural. They become less willing to go the extra mile for you. If you are known to skate the edges of good form, behavior, or gratitude, you will find that some people know how to very politely deflect all your requests while being generous to others who are not such game-players. Often, you rely on those people to get your work done or to get through life (and they are formally under your command – but not in practice).

Optimal bargaining theory suggests you want to leave some goodies on the table even if you win big, for you'll never know when you will need to rely on the goodwill of others whom you have just taken to the cleaners. (Some people get known for being sharks, and perhaps they get away with it until they die. But *Schadenfreude* wins in the end, and in how you are remembered, it would seem.)

When you act too big for your britches, or when you start throwing your weight around, what you may discover is that your britches will split down the middle, and there are others who have a lot more weight they do not need to throw to knock you off your feet. Again, this is nothing new.

371   *High-Concept Titles of Papers and Books*

High concept is a term of art in moviemaking, for a conception of a project that is self-explanatory: Danny DeVito and Arnold Schwarzenegger as *Twins*. Titles of scholarly work, outside the natural sciences, are obscure or too cute. In effect, they do not have high concept, a title that gives it all away.

Journal editors might ask: Does the title of your paper give away your main findings and its subject matter to those not in the know? If not, please fix.

372   *Strategy*

"I have developed three criteria to determine my selection of an issue; I ask myself first how important it is; second, what kind of contribution I can make; and third, how many people are already working in the area." – Ralph Nader (quoted in McCoy and Wu, *The Two-Dimensional Ising Model*, 1973, p. xvii)

373   *Scholarship*

Scholars are particular experts in small areas, and are usually able to reliably evaluate a somewhat wider area of work. At some point in their careers they may have larger visions and syntheses, and they offer them to their scholarly community with suitable warnings and sources in the notes. At another point, they may write popular books – books that might well be written by journalists and writers – that convey their synthesis. These popular books may not stand up to scholarly scrutiny since they leave out the qualifiers and counter-explanations that are the sign of scholarship. A curious example lies in preaching. In matters of biblical interpretation, one might want to consult those who have mastered the original languages and know the previous arguments about the texts under consideration. We want board-certified physicians to be our surgeons. And we want them to have extensive experience in this sort of operation. As much as you would wish to have an experienced board-certified surgeon, you would want to have a scholarly source. You really do not want to die on the operating table or be bamboozled by the popularization.

374   *The Scholarly Bottom Line*

What matters still at the university and in the scholarly world are cumulative contributions to knowledge published in peer-reviewed venues and in scholarly monographs (published by presses that have sophisticated review processes) that will be reviewed in the major research journals. There are corresponding demands in the arts and the professions. Contributions are recognized by peers, argued about and with, and grow in depth over time.

There are other significant contributions. One may develop methods of teaching that become nationally recognized. One may make service contributions that are widely recognized. But, in general, it is research contributions that are most influential in peer judgments.

Organized research units, such as "centers," become known for the richness and depth of the contributions of their members. They may be known for the research dollars that flow through them, but it is through the contributions that they are judged.

For many areas of research, external research funding is absolutely essential; previous performance and contributions are indicators of future performance and so whether funds flow in your direction. It is the research contributions that matter. Most peer reviewers are quite willing to separate grantsmanship from scholarly contributions and distinguish the two.

In the end, *there is no substitute for brains, focus, and hard work devoted to the production of scholarly contributions to knowledge.*

375   Focused Work

The successful professors are those who not only work hard, but are focused in their endeavors, who are capable of convincing others of the quality of their work or at least of their industriousness, and who are politically astute. *Brains may matter, but they matter a lot less than do industry and focus.* I am quite willing to believe in the genius of the very top people in any field, but once slightly off the top, hard work dominates.

376   Reliability

If you have not built up credibility with years of scrupulous and proper behavior, you may lose points rapidly, happily setting yourself up to go over a cliff or to be hit by a truck. The world is not mean, but the world is filled with people whose respect you covet but who are unwilling to correct you.

It is gross malfeasance to allow someone to continue in professional training, or to graduate with a master's degree, or to become tenured unless one has an unambiguously positive assurance that the person will be competent and scrupulous. If you cannot do the work and provide positive evidence of your reliability in your trial period, why should I take the risk of having you work in my body politic? I do not find what I say here attractive, but I know of no way out.

377   Recognition:
(Specialization → Productivity) × Visibility = Compensation

Recognition has an important influence on Compensation. Productivity is not the simple variable that leads to Compensation, the conventional scholarly explanation. If you specialize you tend to be more Productive, and if you are Productive and also Visible then the rewards flow to you (E. Leahey, "Not By Productivity Alone," *American Sociological Review*, 2007).

378   *Grade Inflation?*

Whenever one sees rising prices one has to adjust for the quality of goods to get a believable measure of inflation. The history of higher education suggests that only about a third of undergraduate students have been there for what might be called an academic education (the grinds and the scholars and the premeds); the rest have attended primarily for sports, social life, or politics and the arts. So if we have an increasing number of students who find they need better grades to make it in the world (the above two-thirds did not), they might actually be working harder and hence some of the GPA increase might reflect actual quality improvement.

379   *Rejection and Recovery*

The reason I have not always gotten published or received grants is that there were other articles, books, or proposals that were more meritorious, more suited to the journal or the foundation's agenda. One of my colleagues suggested that appointments/chairs go to the qualified least-objectionable person (mini-max, sort of). I do not know if this is the case, but if it is, most of us were second-best. Once in a while, journals, grantors, and tenure committees make mistakes or exhibit prejudice or unfairness – rather more rarely than one might expect given what we know about human perfidy. In general, it's better to look to one's work to find the reason for rejection than to look for conspiracy, unfairness, or whatever. (But some of the time, still, there is egregious prejudice. Check with friends who know more.)

On the other hand, the economist Paul Samuelson said that the reason that he was not appointed to Harvard early on in his career was that they were too parochial to appreciate his contribution (not that he was Jewish).

You may well leave an institution that makes no effort to retain you. Soon after, or even contemporaneously, you publish the first of your pathbreaking articles or the first of your *N* books, and you receive major fellowships. In fact, maybe the institution could not figure out how to retain you (not enough money or a position, or you were not a good fit for their culture). No need to blame anyone. The best thing to do is to go forward, thrive, and tell people how wonderful it was to be at that university. Things worked out nonetheless, and you are grateful for the chance to be at U, and even for their rejecting you.

I know nothing about litigation, conspiracy, or prejudice. I know that there is lots of unfairness in the world, and historically people of color and women, and Catholics and Jews, have suffered from them. I once asked a distinguished African American scholar if he was angry about the prejudice he encountered in his career. He told me, no, he always knew he was better than them. Maybe most of us cannot be so secure or maybe we are not better than them. But we have our strengths, and if we exercise them we are better off. (None of this says that campaigns to ensure equity and fairness on the part of journals, grantors, and universities are not vital and worthwhile. If we do not do that, the institutions we care for will wither away and become vestigial.)

380   *Taking Charge in Group Work*

If you have to make a team presentation, and some members disappear on you, or do not respond to e-mails, or cannot help because there is an emergency in their lives, write them off and go forward yourself with whoever is there. The show must go on.

Similarly, if you are on a committee and it is going nowhere, perhaps you can do the committee's work (say, draft a working memo) with one or two others and get going. If you are chair of a committee, it may well be that you will have to do all the work. The good part is that you will not have to deal with the dead. And if the dead come to life, have them do work.

Finally, there are some people whose main job is to sabotage you. Some of the dead work this way. They throw fits, threaten, call you names, justify their positions by means of tortured arguments meant to help them get their own way. At some point, they will have to be jetti-soned. To give in to them for the sake of peace means you are condoning infantile behavior in the name of cooperation and the like.

By the way, none of this applies if the dead have all the power. I have no good advice here, except regicide or tending your own garden. There are good tactics, ones that are more modest and often quite effective, and they involve a good deal of device. About that I am not expert. The powers of the weak can be substantial, since *the strong depend on the weak more than they allow.*

381   *What Counts in Scholarship*

1. Articles in scholarly journals count. Good articles in strong jour-nals really count. Articles should build on each other. You should circu-late your reprints to the relevant people, simply writing, "I thought you might like to see this article. Sincerely, X."

2. Edited books and textbooks do not count so much. Books from publishers who price them at $150 are suspect in any case. (But books in law and science and mathematics, from the most reputable of publishers, sometimes have fairly high prices.)

3. Vanity presses do not count.

4. For those who are doing what is traditional work in the humani-ties, what counts is a book published by a university press or equivalent.

5. Promotion to higher ranks goes with increased national/inter-national visibility and deeper work. Hence build on your past achieve-ments, and get involved with the important scholarly meetings and organizations.

6. Teaching counts, more and more.

7. Do not make enemies of your dean, provost, or president. This should not be difficult, but I am amazed to discover how often people do this without being aware of the consequences. Be prepared to resign and take another job if you cause a brouhaha and then lose, or go off to the countryside and write three books, never showing your face for five years.

8. Do not expect to get away with two-facedness. There is too much communication in a university for a misrepresentation to survive.

9. If you drink and profess, get help now. You can also get good help for schizophrenia, bipolar disorder, anxiety, obsessive-compulsive disorder, and depression. They do not increase creativity, and in fact possess no charm whatsoever.

10. You live in a legalistic and litigious regime, not one where your authority can trump your past behavior and the e-mail you leave behind. Do not expect to get away with arbitrariness or prejudice.

11. You did not get to your current position based on your merit. It helped, but so did gender, race, connections, and brownnosing.

12. This is a terrific business. Teaching is wonderful. Writing and research are rare privileges. Universities have always been corrupt, but still offer the only place in town to teach and write if you have to make a living as well.

382   *Scholarship: Scholia, Advances*

Historically, scholarship has often been an effort to restore and edit ancient texts, to gather and organize material artifacts, to translate important works (translation often involving high philological skill), and to carefully explain the meaning of these texts, artifacts, and works. Such contributions were crucial to the preservation and transmission of other cultures, earlier or in distant locales. They made it possible for us to appreciate esoteric texts whose natural associations are otherwise lost to us.

More recently, we have come to identify scholarship with publications of articles and books that "advance" the field. This is much influenced by a model of natural scientific inquiry. For many purposes it is a fine model. And, in general, this is the path to follow for a doctoral dissertation or subsequent research in your academic career.

But keep in mind that fashions change, and one way of doing research in a field may be superseded by another. So some advances are in effect throwbacks.

383   Do We Read What Is Published in the
Journals and Presses We Publish in?

Do people actually look at the journals they publish in, regularly? Do they subscribe? Do they regularly check the tables of contents? Do they find articles they wish to read? If it is a matter of books, do they buy books from their press? Do they read the catalog?

Have journals become places to put articles, but not places to actually learn from, to keep up with work you respect, to mold content through editorships and reviewing? Similarly, are some presses for publishing your books, but not the ones that publish other books you read or buy, ones whose fact of publishing a book indicates to you that the book is authoritative and worth checking out? Are its books reviewed regularly in the main journals you read and publish in?

Some journals are priced out of reach to be sure, and so are some books. This is itself a problem. We might even argue that people learn of relevant work from preprints, from online services, from working papers, from references in articles they read, not from looking at the journals or the books themselves.

People do subscribe to the journals that come with membership in societies, but they are much less likely to subscribe to others, and they do not spend time in the library or online scanning the latest table of contents of most if not all the journals they publish in. They do not buy many books. But it would be a useful way of determining which are the A-level (to use the term of art from business and economics) journals and publishers in each field. Some of this depends on the field. Scientists and engineers (and some of the more "scientific" humanities such as philology) are probably most assiduous about checking the journals. Or do they, too, just find the relevant articles from online sources?

384   The Research Literature

Professors and scholars and scientists do work. When they write it up, they indicate the relevant previous work by footnotes. They rarely discuss that work in detail, unless they are doing a review article, or they are pulling apart that work since they think it is wrong. In any case, the best scholars avoid personal attacks, even if they are pulling apart someone's work. Rather, attack on the demerits.

To be a scholar is to know the literature, that is, the previous work relevant to your field and subfield. By your referring to the right pieces, you so indicate.

You have to assume in scholarly work that people who work in your area of concern will read your articles, be on the lookout for problematic and virtuous contributions, and also note whether you cited (their) work that is relevant.

Before it is published, scholarly work is almost always reviewed by people who are like the people who are writing it (peer review). Hence there is something like a seal of approval if and when it is published. More prestigious venues (sometimes they are conferences; more likely they are journals or university presses) have (or claim to have) more rigorous peer reviewing. That an article is published is no guarantee of its quality, but the higher the prestige of the venue, the more likely it is reliable work.

There are many places to publish, many of lesser prestige (publishers, journals), and while excellent work might appear there, in general the work in these venues is less strong and less reliable. If you publish work in a weaker journal or venue, people are more likely to be skeptical of it (whether or not that is warranted).

Students begin to get a good handle on the research literature in their field. If you are entering a field without guidance, the best places to go are the strongest journals and the major university presses. Recent work almost always refers to previous work, so if you skip backward in time you will get a good overview.

385 *Rereading the Hard Parts of a Source*

I recommend to students that they not worry too much about difficult passages in reading on the first or even the second reading. And the same is true for writing. *You can come back to it later.* This is true and I think good advice.

However, I am writing a chapter right now, and in fact I did skip over many passages in the works I am studying, in part thinking I understood them. I wrote up the analysis of the works, as part of the chapter, and in my first draft it all seemed right. But in this draft, as I was reading it last night, I knew something was wrong. First of all, what I wrote did not make consistent sense. Then I realized I had not understood the relevant passages in the works, at least not understood them carefully enough. I had the basic idea, but not the details that make the argument actually go through.

After several hours of reading, thinking, and confusion, it all became clear, the rewritten sentences in my chapter are now correct, and no reader will notice the hard work (I hope!). Again, this is perhaps two sentences, but they were wrong – and their error might have only been noticed by the experts, the ordinary reader skipping over it. Or perhaps not.

You do not always pay for your sins and errancies. Hence I do recommend skipping. But sometime you do pay, and if you are lucky you can pay with a second notice at high but bearable fines.

F. CONTROVERSY

386   *Bureaucratic Survival*

All people are responsive to the bureaucratic demands of their positions. The biggest demand is that each problem just go away. Personal and professional sympathies are dominated by genuine fear as well as by timidity. If you are seen as trouble, in general you will be wished away – and if some demagogic bullies are doing the troubling of you, and no one stands up to them, then everyone seems to collapse forthwith.

Assistant professors should tend to their work. This is actually quite reasonable considering what they must do to earn tenure, in purely scholarly terms. But tenure and further promotions do not protect you from bureaucratic imperatives. You have to have lots (lots!) of allies and political savvy to survive such battles. The lesson of course is to build alliances and watch the operators who succeed.

387   *Reviews of Your Book or Article*

It probably does not matter what they say about your work, as long as they are talking about it. There is some truth to this, even in the academic realm. It may be useful to keep in mind the following.

1. Book reviews of your work that appear in scholarly journals are usually under the obligation to be fair and honest, in effect to be capable of being peer reviewed. People are sometimes quite vicious, but in general that is not proper.

2. Book reviews that appear in the popular press should be taken to be advertisements for the book – what they say is almost irrelevant compared to the fact that the book was reviewed in the *New York Times* or *New York Review of Books*. Reviewers tend to be rather less scrupulous in the popular press, but also less vicious.

3. In some fields, mathematics in particular, there are review journals that survey all the literature and those reviews are done by experts in the subfield. Again, what counts is that your work is being brought to the attention of those who might well be interested in it.

4. When you are being considered for a job, the reviews that appear in the scholarly journals are the ones that ought to be paid attention to.

You surely want all the publicity for your work that you can get. But in the end, what counts are the opinions of a small number of very distinguished scholars. I am not sure this is always good, but that is what happens.

388   *Accusations and Innocence*

Barbara Chase-Riboud sued filmmaker Steven Spielberg over the originality of the *Amistad* story. Now it turns out that in Chase-Riboud's second book she took stuff verbatim from a nonfiction book on some historical event, without attribution, for her fictional one – and she said that all these sources, encyclopedias, nonfiction, are in the public domain anyway (which in fact is not at all true). She was found out, it would seem, when a *New York Times* reporter chanced upon the coincidence while researching a very different topic. Chase-Riboud says the Dreamworks lawyers fed the information to the *New York Times*. In any case, the taking of the passages is undeniable.

Of course, this does not mean that Spielberg and his writers are innocent of the charges. But Chase-Riboud will have to do more than she has to make her case.

389   *You're 42, a Postdoc: What to Do Next?*

You are wondering if there'll be an academic job for yourself. It is too hard to get an NIH R01 grant, and without it you are a servant on others' grants. What you need to do, now, is to generate some options. Since you once worked in sports medicine and know a good deal about knocked-out teeth, maybe you should check out the possibilities of working within an institute for sports dentistry, one that is sponsored under the Department of Defense (for many of the same reasons that breast cancer research is sponsored by the Army; teeth are knocked out in war). And since you worked for a pediatric dentist who had you set up a bite tester, maybe there is a future in medical devices. Make a list of the three to five people you know who might give some good advice, and call them up immediately and arrange a conversation: "I'm thinking that academic positions do not offer me a chance to apply my interests, and perhaps I need to work in translational research, in sports dentistry, or perhaps infant occlusion. How might I go about finding opportunities in these areas?"

Maybe the academic job will come along, but if not you want choices. Do not worry if the choices seem strange. First get the job offer, and then think about whether you want to accept.

390   *If English Is Not Your Native Work Language*

One of the valuable aspects of coming to study in a foreign country is the opportunity to learn better the language and culture and history of a place. If that country is a dominant world force, there is always the mixed feeling of being at the center of things, of gaining access to what is otherwise not available back home, and of resentment of the hegemon's arrogance. Such is the content of much colonial and postcolonial literature.

If you can improve your English language skills so that they are more natural, that skill will serve you well in subsequent years. Scholarship is an international endeavor, ideas and practices from one place moving to other places. In international meetings, English may be the only language most of the attendees share – so your ability to learn and to proselytize will increase insofar as your English is clear and effective.

Take advantage of your instructors' efforts to correct your English. Rewrite the parts that have been corrected, then and there – not for a better grade, but to learn more about the colloquial and everyday. Make sure you spend much of your time in the United States not talking in your native language to your co-nationals. Watch television, especially if you can have both sound and the subtitles.

Do not get discouraged. And do not worry about losing your own national skills and language – they will always be with you. None of this reflects on the real value or strength of any particular culture. It is merely a practical strategy. The foreign language requirements for the American doctorate (two in my case) were about gaining access to other nations' achievements – not about the moral quality or virtue of those places.

391 *Finding Out about the World in a Reliable Way: Fishing for What's Going On*

"I was doing observationally driven research. That's the kiss of death if you're looking for funding today. We're so fixated now on hypothesis driven research that if you do what I did, it would be called a 'fishing expedition' . . . That's the 'fishing,' because there wasn't a hypothesis. Well, if you do not know anything, you can't have a sensible hypothesis. I keep saying that fishing is good. You're fishing because you want to know what's there." – Janet Rowley, cancer geneticist, about her work, *New York Times,* 8 February 2011

ELEVEN

Stronger Faculties & Stronger Institutions (#392–420)

A. FUNDAMENTALS

392 *College Admissions*

The Shape of the River (W. Bowen and D. Bok, 1998) is about selective colleges and race-sensitive admissions. College admissions at non-selective colleges admit any qualified applicant; at selective colleges, admission is based on a very wide variety of factors, academic qualification being in effect a minor factor. Post-college success is directly related to the selectivity of your college. People with lower scores than you got in, when you did not. (Half or more of the highest SAT group do not get admitted.)

Jerome Karabel (*The Chosen,* 2005) describes admissions at Harvard, Yale, and Princeton in the twentieth century. One of the big post-WWII issues was continuing Harvard's admission of a "happy bottom quarter."

393 *Attracting Strong Graduate Students*

People come to graduate schools – at least the strongest students in doctoral programs – because of the quality of the department (not the university) and its ability to place its students in the best jobs. Whatever the National Research Council rankings show, the informed faculty at the strongest schools know more about who's who at U, and who is getting hired. Who are their research competitors? So the schemes for increasing graduate (doctoral) student quality depend surely on having enough money to attract them, but for the very best students you need preeminent faculty. And every faculty member who is not going to be preeminent hurts you. Still, we can make some real improvements with more fellowship money. We might train our students much better than most places – to give better talks, to do more significant research. All of this does not depend on the faculty being preeminent – they just have to be assiduous in training, and have decent taste in research problems. What we keep seeing in our recruiting is how poorly trained are many students from other universities. We can do better.

394   *Market Signaling*

Faculty leaving an institution sends an important message to deans and the provost about its undervaluing some people. I encourage people to look-see other jobs. I never know what the right choice is for each faculty member. (The grass looks greener, the costs of moving are not small, the time in the career is critical.) But a strong university has to step up to the plate often enough to retain and bind its strongest faculty. Surely that makes things a bit unfair to those who are either not in the market or unlikely to get offers from peer or better institutions – but it is then the job of the deans to make things a bit fairer (or not, if they feel that some faculty members do not warrant that), and also to realize that short-term overpayment to bind people to the institution is what you must do. One overpaid faculty member whom you view as desirable and very strong is worth two weaker ones, so the cost/quality is actually lower.

Moreover, for faculty who are not promoted or given step increases or endowed chairs or whatever, outside offers allow the university to rectify its errors and learn how its evaluations systems are defective. Of course, the smart deans anticipate such possibilities and overcompensate the faculty member so that outside offers do not seem so desirable. This may well involve building a group of scholars around a strong faculty member, or maybe just a better office. If the goal is excellence then the choices are not obscure. If the goal is solidarity, then the choices are quite difficult.

395 *You Want a Faculty That's Hard to Keep*

Tenured faculty are the foundation for an institution to become one of the manifestly strong research universities. Why not the best or among the very best?

    1. How to better manage the human capital of our tenured faculty:

        a. clusters with leaders (so energizing lagging faculty);

        b. customized mentoring and guidance
           for the lost – pastoral work;

        c. guidance for full professors on how to up their game.

    2. Hire advanced assistant professors, with a book in press, for example; hire senior faculty, on their way to retirement, for a fixed term. By the way, *did you do a real search,* or is this a setup to hire someone already in mind?

    3. Probationary faculty:

        a. Must do what they are supposed to deliver.
           Nothing else – no book reviews, no encyclopedia
           articles, limited number of conferences: what
           counts is getting the work done and out.

        b. Should encounter no surprises at tenure time if denied: At
           the third-year review, lay out a very clear set of expectations,
           and if they are not met the candidate is unlikely to be
           tenured. Their expectations have to be what we expect.

        c. Should provide a clear understanding of the contribution
           to the field, and an explicit account of their contribution
           to joint work. With multiple authors, one expects
           more work than for singly-authored work.

        d. May have less need to be independent if
           publishing joint work, especially if the
           contribution is outstanding and essential.

        e. Will be prima facie denied tenure if there is no book
           out, if no grants of the right sort have been obtained, if
           the articles are not there. Same for depth of articles. In
           essence, there is nothing for letter-writers to review.

    4. Tenure review:

        a. No excuses, unless they are about family or illness, and
           those should have been dealt with earlier with extensions.

b. Ask, *Is this the best we can get?* Is this among the best there is? Not, does the candidate meet the bar or the hurdle?

c. Letters must come from the right people. And they must be balanced and substantive. Reviews of the CV or gushing praise are useless. Any demurrers need to be investigated – whether they are in letters or in unwillingness to write.

d. Votes that have minority nos in them should also be accounted for. Hence the *no* voters owe the dean an account of why they say so. They may well be the canary in the coal mine.

e. If there is doubt, denial is appropriate. Fairness is not whether this dossier is as strong as the weakest one recently tenured. Fairness is whether the dossier has been properly handled and whether this dossier is as strong as the strong recent dossiers (previous mistakes do not justify new mistakes).

f. Would you buy a used car from a dean given the dean's previous recommendations?

5. Mistakes will be made. Sometimes they are surprising, but most often they are already seen in the promotion dossier. What we learn from those mistakes is what we need to attend to in the future.

6. Fairness concerns cannot trump excellence – as long as we try to be fair. One always hears stories of unfairness, but when examined closely, those stories rarely hold up. Again, if there is doubt, deny tenure. This will produce fewer marginal cases that set you up for fairness comparisons.

7. Underrepresented minorities should be told to do less service rather than more. It's too vulnerable a time.

396   *Ranking Departments*

The most interesting feature of American education is its diversity and variety. Yes, there are top universities, in terms of endowment, research accomplishment of faculty, student statistics. But what is remarkable (and has often been so remarked) is the wide distribution of talent, students, and faculty. In other words, the sorting function is far from perfect – there is no "Paris" to which all aspire. People like to live in different places, salaries and honorifics are widely different within a single university, and so forth.

What you would want, if you are in the rating business, is a multidimensional vector or matrix, which would then be combined with a person's particular preferences, to rank institutions. Chanel has superbly made clothing with fabrics that are fabulous, but many younger women would not wear Chanel, no matter the quality. Also, the deeper question is whether you can adapt an institution to your own particular needs. Of course, if your need is recognizable prestige, a trophy university degree, a single ranking may be most appropriate.

A major contribution is to help students (and faculty) choose the kind of place where they would be most comfortable. There are too many mismatches. Is this the place that would allow you to grow and thrive? If you have family obligations, how can you fulfill them and also do well as a student or a faculty member?

1. Markets and niches: Most institutions have comparatively narrow regional markets, sometimes by law in the case of state universities. I am not sure, but many should have more narrow niches in subareas of their disciplines. Specialization would give them advantages that small size and weak location will not hurt.

2. Sensitivity: I recall when a department moved up one or two rankings in some survey. They made a big deal of such. It would be helpful to have a sense of the sensitivity of the rankings to changes in parameters. What would happen to a ranking if some of the parameters moved 5 percent plus or minus?

3. Population: Fewer doctoral programs or more specialized ones would be better for everyone. If you count up the faculty, even of the strong research universities, there is no way the stronger journals can accommodate their publications.

4. Locality: Most institutions are adequate or good, while few are inadequate or strong. There is a large middle, as we might expect. In the United States, with its decentralized systems, people are proud of "their" university, often a state land-grant university or a local college. What they want to know are the strengths of their university.

397 *Tenure Markets*

As faculty, we need to better signal excellence, and our economist colleagues suggest that to do so we go out into the market and get job offers from distinguished institutions. If you are coming up for tenure or promotion, nothing is so powerful as an offer from a peer or better university. More generally, in addition to your work itself and its being recognized by your community of scholars, such an offer signals your and the university's strength. (For many if not most of us, this is not a realistic strategy. Senior scholars rarely move around, for example. Others of us could not move without much too great disruptions to our families.)

Whether you accept an external offer is a matter for you, your dean, and your family to work out.

And if you find that you are stuck in your research career or feel insufficiently recognized, a good solution is to change institutions. Get an offer from a place that will make better use of your strengths, whether they be in teaching or administrative leadership. A new venue may revitalize your research.

Tenure is, in part, a way of keeping faculty off the market.

398 *The Ones That Got Away*

What happens to the people you do not promote? Or to the articles or books editors decide not to publish? Sometimes they then appear elsewhere.

1. Sometimes it is a matter of fit. They get offers, go off to other places, and perhaps do very well. You can tell yourself you've not made an error, especially if the places or venue is less prestigious. But what if those candidates are then very successful, much more so than the people or articles you have accepted?

2. Sometimes it is a matter of incorrect judgment. Same story, but now you made a mistake.

3. Look at the folks or articles or books you have accepted. Do they look good compared to the ones that got away (for whatever reason)? Now you are asking a cumulative question, about what you have vs. what you could have had. You decide to tenure Joe, and Harvey goes

elsewhere, and twenty years later Joe has gone nowhere in his work and Harvey has a Nobel or a Pulitzer or a Lasker. Similar cases come up in the National Academy of Sciences, where they find they have to make sure X gets in this year, now that X has received the Nobel Prize.

Are you honest enough to admit that you made a mistake, when you could have done better, that your strategic plan for growth led you to comparative mediocrity?

More important, do not assume that unfavored members of your team have no alternatives. They might not, but that's never obvious.

399 Propinquity Learning

In my education, I either read Great Books or was trained to think like a physicist. Of course, there were textbooks in the sciences, but they were always seen as less important than learning to think like a physicist and to solve problems. And in reading the Great Books, and I was not so good at this, what I seem to have learned was an analytic skepticism, figuring out what was going on in these works.

My point here is that what we offer to our students is the chance to watch someone do their work – whether it is thinking, creating, analyzing. We also offer them some ideal of performance, one they can see in practice. And we offer them the chance to play in this arena, safely, with our support and guidance.

Laying on of hands seems best done in person.

400 Showing Up

You've got to do your part to maintain the community that is called the department or the school. You need to show up for faculty meetings, or committee meetings, and you must make an appearance at retreats, parties, and memorials. But you don't have to say anything other than polite greetings.

If you are so booked with external obligations you cannot make many events, you will lose the commitment of your colleagues. If you do not need any favors or goodwill from them, no problem. But if you do need favors or goodwill you want your colleagues to think you have done your part.

If you are an academic supernova, perhaps you can get away with missing most events. But if not, make sure you schedule your trips around such events where *face-time matters,* and rearrange your schedule so that you show up more often. Excuses do not work, and it is best to assume that your absence will be noted by your head or dean, but even more importantly by the people who were there and wished they could get away with what you did. Actually, you got away with nothing, as you will discover in time.

401 *Learning to Think*

University education is rarely if ever about mastering a textbook or a method. Usually, it is learning to think (to think like a lawyer, like a city planner, like an engineer, like a reader of literature, like a scientist). It may be that the instructor does this in class, demonstrating how to think by actually doing it. It may be that you have to figure it out from the more didactic lectures and texts. It may be that you learn it from anecdotes or biographies or your classmates. But, in the end, that is what you need to learn.

Yes, you do need to be able to write clear, coherent prose. Yes, you need to be able to do high school elementary algebra and to do arithmetic on a calculator. And yes, you do need to be able to use basic computer applications and learn new ones. And for some fields you need specialized skills such as foreign languages, calculus, abstract algebra. These are preliminaries. If you do not have them down, you will be too limited in your skills to do real work and real thinking.

It also helps to have judgment, the capacity to criticize your own work, to have good taste in choosing topics, and to be able to balance conflicting sources of information. Often, you learn this through case studies, watching your instructor think, and making mistakes and learning from them.

Most of my college instructors were not particularly good didactic teachers. We learned by watching them think out loud, get lost, correct themselves. Outside of class, there was not only the textbook, but other texts so that we could find out what was going on. Even if I did well in a course, it took perhaps 2–3 years for me to understand what was really going on, and in some fields it took me 20 years. Those years were sometimes spent studying more advanced subjects, while sometimes it was a matter of maturity. What was in the background, always, was my teachers' thinking as examples of how to go about the work. That thinking was the guiding light, even if it took me a long time to appreciate how it was illuminating.

402   *The Resistance of the Entrenched and Preserving the Institution's Heritage*

All units in a university have some degree of variation in the strength of their faculty. If there is a push to make the university stronger, ideally the less strong members of the faculty, often there for longer than average, would welcome the new members and appreciate the strength of the department, and yield judgments of quality and appointment to them. Or, even better, they would be partisans of their new stronger faculty.

There are units and departments that might be characterized as having some senior weaker faculty, some very strong senior faculty (newly hired or not), and a more junior faculty that may or may not be very strong. The problem is to retain the strong senior faculty and those junior faculty who prove to be quite strong – and to grow that strong contingent in time. *The senior weaker faculty may resist this, whether by a claim to democratic governance, or a commitment to traditional values and the institution's heritage and mission, and will approve appointments and tenures that are comparatively weak and resist appointments that will upset those traditions.*

Stronger faculty have the greatest mobility, and so if they do not see their values mirrored in their unit's behavior, they just might leave. One told me he was for the first time thinking about departure from his university (not soon, he tells me), since he felt that his autonomy and capacity to do research were being bureaucratically stifled. The second, having joined his institution in the last two years, had finally bumped into the dominant weak parts of his unit.

The problem is to face up to depreciated assets rather than carry them on the books at original value. Insofar as it does not acknowledge the problem, the institution is likely to suffer, making incorrect allocation decisions. Time will help, the passing of a generation (or two) being crucial. And an incremental growth strategy is sensible.

Losing strong mid-career faculty, such as those above, would be grievous losses for their units and for the university. Of course, an institution will survive. It will get better. But the transformation will go more slowly and with greater difficulty. Maybe that is how it must go.

403 *Surviving and Thriving in the Research University of ~2025*

Given the high cost of research university education, and the competition provided by lower-cost institutions, research universities have to distinguish themselves and enhance their revenues if they are to survive and prosper.

Moreover, as time goes on we will have a less forgiving system, up and down the line. There was, in effect, a promotion and overhead-recovery bubble, and the bubble has burst. So if you must have a certain depth of publications and contribution, that is what it must be. If your manuscript for a book has not been accepted for publication, the delay will not be so readily forgiven. And if the book is not first-rate, a "book" will not count for much. If your plan is to publish articles, have them in the right venues, not second-rate ones. Do not mislead yourself about their quality. What I am saying is simple – *standards have not been raised so much as the ongoing ones are being more deliberately demanded.* For example, if you need a leave for family purposes, they are more available I suspect. And as a consequence, such excuses often made in the past will no longer be probative. *Your colleagues, the dean, and the provost want you to succeed.* They do what they can to help you. But in the end, it has to happen. Do not tell yourself stories.

There will be a slow but steady rise in expectations of faculty performance, so that more of us will be expected to perform at levels comparable to the current top 5–10 percent of the faculty.

So, what does this mean for the rest of us?

It's vital to raise research funds or fellowships for your work, and not in piddling amounts, and not from internal sources (except for startup funds). Raise enough money to buy out courses, to get the equipment you need. For some of us, this is a natural concomitant of our work, but for others it will require a different mindset.

Promised books or articles that are not delivered do not become more valued. Rather, they become seen as lead weights around your neck. You have to deliver.

National prominence, in the strongest venues, is part of your mission.

Well-defined contributions (rather than *N* articles that do not add up) are crucial.

Your doctoral students need to get jobs at the strongest institutions.

Do not tell yourself stories about the value of your teaching or unusual university service or community service unless it is nationally recognized as a contribution. Writing up your articles in a private notebook is no more valuable.

In the next ten years, *if you do not perform at the top levels you will find that the university has left you behind.* If you do so perform, you will find yourself part of a more powerful institution. For *the strongest people at research universities are world-class leaders.*

The institution depends on us to move it forward, and we have to do that. Of course, if you are a more junior faculty member, your job is to tend to your own garden. But the strongest junior faculty come up for tenure with job offers from peer or much better institutions waiting in the wings. We might become a university the football team could be proud of.

404   *Standards and Thriving*

It is best to keep in mind that you are evaluated for promotion at the university level in a context of other candidates from other schools and departments. The strong cases are really spectacular, and they are people who have had the same level of time and obligation that you have. When they come up in book publishing fields, they have a book out that has won awards, or two such for associate professors, and a new one on the way. If articles are the requirement, they appear in the prime journals of the field and they are more than sufficient in quantity. If substantial grants are needed, they are there. And in every case the contribution is well defined and significant and widely recognized. Sometimes, they have offers from peer or better institutions.

The letter-writers, mostly from peer or better schools, take up the accomplishment substantively (and even if they disagree with the work, their respect for it is evident). And the comparisons with others in the cohort are specific and illuminating. The school reports are balanced, and they take up deficiencies and consider them. The amount of hyperbole from the dean is small compared to the considered evaluation.

Those spectacular cases are the people that the university counts on for its future. Yes, it requires focus and hard work, but genius is never the issue. Don't tell yourself that you are the exception for some reason. (Always *compare yourself to the strongest scholars you know, at your university or elsewhere.*)

What I say here applies to the football team, too.

Again, I know that what I write is rarely comforting. But I hope it is realistic and encourages you. If you have not been doing what you should, now is the time to start.

405   *Late Bloomers*

I published one book (and lots of articles, some influential and one a home run) before 40 (15 years after my PhD), and eight books afterward. I was tenured about twenty years after my doctorate. I am lucky to have survived, very, having been offered a second chance. Do not do what I did.

406   *Why I Should Not Attend Most Seminars*

I was brought up to think of the research talk or seminar as the occasion for inquiry. People would ask incisive questions, and the speaker would do the best they could. Everyone is a grown-up, and respect is shown by how seriously you take someone's work, how you find its problems and opportunities.

But in most seminars the premium is on being nice. If someone is telling you nonsense, you are not supposed to press on that. People give talks where patent nonsense is presented (statistical nonsense, or assumptions that are patently false), or where they present work as new that in fact is old hat, and one is supposed to entertain the talk as if it had any content.

The clinical psychologist Paul Meehl wrote (in *Psychodiagnosis*, 1973) why he did not attend case conferences, pointing out the obvious flaws in much of the discourse. Real scholarship and science matter, and it is doing no one a favor to be nice if the work is not good. Of course, you want to be polite and gracious, but there's no reason to let someone get away with intellectual murder. At least no more than you would allow a used car salesman to get away with making a lemon smell like a rose.

407   *Awarding Chairs and Honorary Professorships*

I note the following practices of awarding honorary chairs or professorships.
Good:
  · Retaining or attracting a strong faculty member.
  · Adjusting the focus of a chair to suit the candidate the
    school wants to retain or attract. Often this adjustment
    is substantial, but it avoids the "Someone who fits"
    problem below. Consultation with donor is essential.
  · Ensuring that most faculty have chairs.
  · Acknowledging an associate professor who fits the chair
    handsomely, but is not ready to be promoted to full. So it is a
    chaired associate professor, eventually to be promoted to full.
  · Instituting career chairs (given to junior people for fixed
    terms, which gives them more time to do their research).
  · Awarding a chair for a long, distinguished career.
  · Chairs that go with roles – dean, provost, president, institute head.
Less good, since they indicate that a chair/professorship is not really about distinguished excellence:
  · Booby prize. Candidate was not made dean/provost,
    or has retired from such a role. Sometimes it is given
    to an advisor to dean/provost, as a reward.
  · Someone who fits. You have a chair in Psychological
    Dentistry (no, this is not real), and the person
    who fits is in fact not very strong.

· Solving a budgetary problem. You award the chairs so that
the flow of funds will help you solve a budget problem.
· Payoffs. By giving chairs to X and to Y, both factions of
a department are happy. Probably the right solution is to
recruit from outside in an entirely different direction.

408   What Do Deans Do?

The dean's job is to make decisions, maybe 500–600 decisions a year. If
500 are right, then things are great; if only 400, the dean is in trouble.

409   FICO Scores for Deans/ Departments: Trust in Practice

In effect, the university is making a long-term loan of a few millions to a
school when it makes an appointment with tenure. Will the school pay
it back?

One might study the school's past experience. We might examine
the evidence presented in the appointment/promotion dossiers. If we
do, we might counsel deans and schools:

Be consistent: Treat similar cases similarly, or at least make clear
just how they are not similar; as the dossier builds up deal with issues
presented at earlier levels; arguments made in one dossier in one school
should not be contradicted by arguments made in another dossier from
that school.

Deal with problems up front.

Letters should be evidentiary.

The crucial point is: Insofar as you produce credible dossiers, your
FICO score goes up. (A FICO score, from the Fair Isaac Corporation,
measures one's credit worthiness, and here I use it by analogy.) Deans
should keep in mind that the university promotion committee has a long
memory among its members. A poor dossier lowers your FICO score for
several years.

If your FICO score is high, and you want to appoint Fido (a German
Shepherd) to a chair, the provost will at least take you seriously.

410 *When a University Gets Stronger*

Strong faculty provide a comparison group for others at the university – when those others come up for promotion and tenure, and more generally. The standards have not changed, but the cohort for comparison has changed due to the efforts of the deans and the faculties.

What distinguishes these strong faculty is the focus and intensity of their work, its wider impact and influence, the regard in which it is held by the strongest scholars at other institutions, and the external support they earn for their work. They are good teachers, and they are well recognized by awards and positions of influence in national bodies. They do it all.

The university becomes a more desirable scholarly institution, and we are fortunate to be here. Our obligation is now to enhance that strength. Our new colleagues encourage us to publish more widely and prestigiously, to make our contributions to scholarship more deep and more widely known, to have our work recognized by the leaders in our fields and allied fields, and to add an extra zero onto the amounts of the grants we raise. This requires careful consideration of what we are now doing, perhaps saying *no* to distracting paths, and raising the expectations we have of ourselves. *I do not believe this is a matter of having sufficient brains; rather it is about discipline, notions of one's personal best, and an honest assessment of where one is located in the scholarly arena.*

We'll know that we have a stronger department and university: when doctoral students choose us over our competitors, and later they get better jobs; more of our publications appear in stronger venues; when we have a reputation for having a deep bench in some areas, and we choose to develop in areas that are not overcrowded but are quite promising (don't worry about being number one, but focus on depth and innovation, on selective excellence or *compelling excellence*); when we hire stars who aim to make their colleagues stronger and want to teach at all levels. Moreover, I observe that the strongest faculty in all fields have internalized their norms of behavior, and conventional incentives will not change what they do. Typically, they do it all: teach well, research productively, serve in many institutions. Moreover, they do not whine or complain; rather, they solve problems.

411   *Family Friendliness*

The best thing about a university is that they do not get in your way. My colleagues have been supportive; the scheduling of classes suits my family needs; my son has attended more faculty meetings and other events than many faculty. We have had some serious demands on us, and I have been able to do my work and attend to him (giving him priority). People have been terrific.

In this time, I have published books and received my share of fellowships and grants. I had to be focused and directed, and that served my son as well as my work. I gave up breakfast meetings or those after 3 PM and most out-of-town meetings or talks. If I was needed later on in the day, I could make it (often with my son in tow). My major service has been at flexible times.

You might have asked whether things were impossible when he was an infant, and the answer is no. I had someone come five days a week during the day, and my son was a good sleeper, so I worked when he slept or napped. It was much more demanding when we had a crisis of sorts, but fortunately I had fellowships and grants and a sabbatical at that time. It also helps that I am self-motivated and I was willing to give up a social life of the more conventional sort.

I did not bear my son, and so women who have their own children are in a different position, and the demands placed on them are different. And I did all of this fairly late in life.

Now, we might ask if the desire to make us "a university the football team would be proud of" would affect family-friendliness. Could we have each person who plays a faculty position play at "an extremely high level" and the university be family-friendly? Family-friendliness is the road to such excellence. Being responsive to your family (and its needs) focuses the mind wonderfully, in my experience. And I believe that *playing at an extremely high level academically is a matter of focus, discipline, and ambition.*

412   *Campus Life*

Helen Lefkowitz Horowitz's *Campus Life* (1987) is a history of campus life in American universities. There are three cultures: college (fraternities, student government, band), rebel (artsy, political activist), and outsider (nerds, poor kids trying to get into medical school). They have always been present, albeit in varying ratios that depend in part on the institution, in part on the times. Not only students but faculty belong to these cultures, often choosing one to "major" in. Hence, faculty may be part of college life, part of rebellion, or part of outsider culture (flying to meetings and grant panels). Perhaps no more than a third of the faculty is outsider, often less, and even then many of them may be into consulting and moneymaking. My favorite of late is Lionel Gift, a character in *Moo* by Jane Smiley.

413   *Do You Wear Knife-Proof Undergarments?*
Academic Contest and Dialectic

There is a firm that makes Kevlar-based clothing, including knife-proof undershorts, much appreciated by prison wardens.

Our business is both polite and highly competitive. The idea is not only to be right but to prove it to others, and that may involve throwing sand in their eyes, or going below the belt rhetorically. Hence the Kevlar. The knife-proof undershorts are doing a superb job in your research and writing when you are thinking defensively: *What will they ask about this research that will show it up?* Why would they not believe what I say here? (If you write a novel, the problem becomes, will they just close the book and not read further?)

If you go to a Berkeley or an MIT or a Columbia or a Chicago you will find they are much less polite in seminars, much more aggressive. They have nothing against you other than that you exist and your work might take up space they occupy. They want to be sure that your argument is a valid one. Of course, you could go much lower on the prestige pole, but my experience is that you'll need your shorts everywhere. Some places are polite but then talk behind your back in ways that make the Berkeleys seem generous.

It's not that we live in a dog-eat-dog world. Rather, we are part of a dialectical tradition, very well honed, which believes that in such argument and attack there lies both truth and fortune. (See Walter Ong on rhetoric and dialectic.)

B. A DIFFERENT UNIVERSITY

414   A Low-Cost, Low-Overhead University

A university could provide a first-rate education at lower total cost than it does nowadays. (I use total cost because tuition at non-profit universities typically covers a fraction of the cost of education – whether at private or state-supported institutions. The rest is made up by gifts, endowment, overhead recovery from research. In no conventional sense are you "buying" your education, and that you pay a lot is payment for the chance to be subsidized.) You could cut out all the ancillary services, so that the whole university is in a high rise or rents space by the hour, with no student health, no buildings and grounds, no bookstore, no student activities, no exercise center, no library, no computer help or networking. And you could have a first-rate research-oriented faculty.

Now, you could have little research and scholarship on the part of the faculty, and so get more teaching hours, perhaps renting the faculty by the hour, too. That may not provide the kind of exemplary teaching of how to think. The lowest-cost producers have not captured the market for prestige, scholarly contribution, and excellence, even if they are good at didactic instruction and their graduates do reasonably well.

Some people want the full-facility research university or small liberal arts college, and of course they would like it at the low cost – but as far as I can tell this is not possible. Intermediate models, ones that provide services à la carte or reduce emphasis on research and scholarship, usually have intermediate prestige. A great invention would be a high-prestige à la carte provider, with limited facilities and first-rate faculty – a no-frills Harvard or Berkeley. I suspect that online recorded lectures and courses are not what we need.

This analysis applies to hotels or clothing or proprietary private universities, but again in those cases the providers have to make sure you pay the full cost since they have no other sources of income.

The attack on the cost of university education is fueled by scandal. Every month or so, there is one more revelation of e-mail. While it is tempting to flame, or to be cute, in general you have to assume that your e-mail might well become public. Similarly, your contributions to public web discussions tell people more about you than what you happen to say. *You want to be sure that the "bread crumbs" you leave behind serve you well.* Google will find them.

415   Authority

Saul Bellow, the Nobel Prize–winning novelist, apropos of criticism:

> "Now, do not get sensitive with me. . . . I am your teacher."
> He [SB] reminded many people of their incompleteness, perhaps because he knew of his own. There was a rawness to him, almost like a wound, underneath the genteel polish and fiendish wit . . . about his teaching. It allowed no excuses. We are here, in this fallen state, riven by contradictions, given to understand some things, but never others, faltering in our wills, flawed in our abilities, uncertain in our actions. But that is where we must begin and there is no excuse for not taking the task seriously. (Interview with E. Rothstein, a former student, *New York Times*, 9 April 2005)

I was brought up in a world where authority was unavoidable, and where the honor was to be able to follow in its footsteps, albeit haltingly. If you could understand the authorities, that was itself a very great achievement. To equal them was Pride itself. Some of my books are an attempt to understand work that is more profound and difficult than I would ever imagine myself being able to do. If I could make sense of that work, it would be sufficient. S. S. Schweber describes his studies of the work of Richard Feynman and Freeman Dyson and Hans Bethe and the like as studies of "off-scale" scientists, beyond any conventional measure.

The greatest humility is to have a sense of your own authority, where it is warranted and where not. In a university, while a whole bunch of people are professors, some are much more authoritative than are others.

C. MENTORING

416   *Mentoring and Dementoring*

"I like bench work. When people become principal investigators, [often] they leave that to graduate students. And yet, the experiment you do yourself is much better than the one you tell a student to do. You can see all the little details. . . . If your mentor is not good, leave him. . . . For scientific research, you have to learn how to do it from a good researcher." – Avram Hershko, Nobel Laureate in Chemistry, 2004, *New York Times*, 19 June 2012, p. B2

No one makes it on their own. Someone is guiding them, telling them the unwritten rules, preventing them from making grievous errors, supporting them at uncertain times, teaching them. Correspondingly, you would not want the professor of surgery to promote a candidate who is not first-rate as a surgeon; you would not want a university department to promote a candidate who is not first-rate as a scholar. Would you trust your own children or spouse to this person's care and tuition?

The coach as mentor in athletics is a good model for a university. Now, coaches "own" their mentees, by the nature of sport. (Students in your lab or work-study students may also be "owned.") They speak of athletes as being "coachable."

417   *Faculty Mentoring Faculty*

People succeed as academics and scholars when they have received good guidance from their more senior colleagues (and they have taken the advice). They learn how to teach better, how to publish more successfully, how to promote their own ideas and their careers, and how to be good colleagues. They need explicit guidance, early on. The probationary period is just long enough for most academics to build up fine records, get their work known to the community in their field, publish more than adequately. It requires focus, no excuses, and a desire to do what needs to be done.

If there is an extraordinary path, the dean and the department and the faculty member must put it all in writing early on, indicate how it is to be measured, and support the candidate down the line if the candidate delivers.

Candidates who have had difficulty often have been poorly advised, or did not take the good advice they received. They did not focus. They did not present their work at meetings. They somehow got caught in committee work, or in running a program, or in teaching too many new courses without anyone making provision for their extraordinary contribution. They thought they did not have to publish in the main journals, or get a book manuscript done and published and reviewed, or make clear their contribution and make clear to others that they had made a contribution. Their personal statements were unhelpful in making their own case, their CVs mixed in strengths with irrelevancies. And they did not plan their next steps in research and teaching.

Rather: What have you done lately? How is your work a contribution? Where do you plan to go in the next five years?

418   *Coaching Professors*

- We need benign but firm critics, showing us how to do better, telling us we can do better.
- We need models, so that several strong faculty, by their example, will encourage stronger work from their colleagues.
- We need to understand that "no excuses" means that we cannot deceive ourselves. There are real reasons – illness, for example, but even those excuses may eventually get in the way of doing work that allows you to recover.
- The coach of a team seeks the interventions that bring out the best in each player. Who can coach the faculty?
- We need a bit of fear (not too much), so that we realize that there are consequences for not delivering.
- We need cheerleaders, who set forth the larger goals, and indicate we can meet them. Sometimes this is a chair or dean, sometimes a provost or president, sometimes a colleague.

The assistant professor job may be lonely: there are precious few pats on the head or suggestions on what you should do to get yourself going, you make a lot of mistakes, you get a lot of criticism and rejection (which hurts), and you have to be your own cheerleader an awful lot of the time even when you have supportive mentors in the department (and many times you do not when you first get out of graduate school). It often feels like you are on your own, even when you are surrounded by very good colleagues and mentors who do support you. I think this is the case because so much of the battle we are fighting is with ourselves, about what we think and what we want to explore and how to express those ideas to others. Senior faculty feel much the same.

419 *Mentoring*

In general, most successful scholars have been sponsored by their advisor or by someone distinguished, all the way up the ladder and into National Academies. (*Sponsored contest* is the technical term – you represent your patrons, and your success accrues to them.) Almost no one does it on their own.

From a colleague:

- Many junior faculty are unaware that the cost of being a below-average teacher in the classroom will probably be higher than the cost they spend in time to improve their teaching.
- Many junior faculty members are frustrated in going through the process of multiple submissions-rejections for the work they try to land in major journals. It will be very helpful for the junior faculty members if the mentor can help them to read the referee reports and offer suggestions how to revise the manuscripts following the referees' comments before resubmission.
- Presenting/discussing papers in major conferences of your fields is one of the most effective ways for junior faculty members to do networking. Invited seminar presentations to peer institutions are also highly valuable for junior faculty. One may use the invited seminar presentations as an opportunity to get feedback/ideas for some half-baked initial draft, but this is risky and only possible in friendly circumstances. One may present some well-prepared work (even though it has been presented multiple times), especially when such presentation is given at the strongly competitive departments, as someone in

the audience may turn out to be your promotion letter-writer.
On such an occasion, you want to show your best work.
· If there is strong indication that a junior faculty member
will have problems in meeting the tenure criteria at the
current department, the mentor still has the responsibility
to advise and prepare the person to get the next-best job.

420   *Tormentoring*

There is sometimes a distinction between being a dementor and being
a tormentor. *Dementors* give you guidance that is diabolical: impossible
to follow, won't help you in your work or career, cookbook with no sense
of your particular situation, inadvertently about their issues rather than
your own. *Tormentors* are not so much out to guide you as to scare you,
to set you up for anxiety and failure, although sometimes they act as
if all they are doing is being realistic. They may deliberately hurt you.
They exhibit *Schadenfreude*. Both dementors and tormentors will say
something like, "It was good enough for me, it is good enough for you,"
perhaps actually internalizing the aggressor, perhaps believing they are
toughening you up just like they were toughened up (rather than admit-
ting that they suffered).

MARTIN H. KRIEGER is Professor of Planning in the Sol Price School of Public Policy at the University of Southern California and a Fellow of the American Physical Society. He has taught at Berkeley, Minnesota, MIT, and Michigan, and has been a fellow at the National Humanities Center and at the Center for Advanced Study in the Behavioral Sciences. He is author of *Doing Physics* (1992, 2012), *Urban Tomographies* (2011), *Doing Mathematics* (2003), *What's Wrong With Plastic Trees?* (2000), *Constitutions of Matter* (1996), *Entrepreneurial Vocations* (1996), *Marginalism and Discontinuity* (1989), and *Advice and Planning* (1981).